RELIGION, EQUALITY AND EMPLOYMENT IN EUROPE

The management of religious and ideological diversity remains a key challenge of our time—deeply entangled with debates about the nature of liberal democracy, equality, social cohesion, minorities and nationalism, security and foreign policy. This book explores this challenge at the level of the workplace in Europe. People do not surrender their religion of belief at the gates of their workplace, nor should they be required to do so. But what are the limits of accommodating religious belief in the workplace, particularly when it clashes with other fundamental rights and freedoms?

Using a comparative and socio-legal approach that emphasises the practical role of human rights, anti-discrimination law and employment protection, this book argues for an enforceable right to reasonable accommodation on the grounds of religion and belief in the workplace in Europe. In so doing, it draws on the case law of Europe's two supranational courts, three country studies—Belgium, the Netherlands and the UK—as well as developments in the US and Canada. By offering the first book-length treatment of the issue, it will be of significance to academics, students, policy-makers, business leaders and anyone interested in a deeper understanding of the potentials and limits of European and Western inclusion, freedom and equality in a multicultural context.

Note on cover image *Koppen—Herman van Nazareth—1967*

In his form of 'protest art', Van Nazareth uses striking depictions and interpretations of reality to raise a voice against abuse of power and injustice. While the work of Van Nazareth—the pseudonym of Belgian-born painter and sculptor Herman Van Aerden—is embedded in and provides insights into apartheid South Africa, it serves as a metaphor for the various pressures and oppressions targeting the visibility of human individuality and identity. In particular, the 'abstract' portraits depict the 'normative' employee or public servant who—devoid of distinct features, personality and identity—represents but a blurred, dehumanised version of the self.

* This research was supported by the RELIGARE project, which received funding under the European Commission's Seventh Framework Programme (Socio-economic Sciences and Humanities; grant agreement No 244635). The views expressed are those of the author; they should not be taken to reflect the opinion or position of the European Union, its institutions or existing EU policy.

Religion, Equality and Employment in Europe

The Case for Reasonable Accommodation

Katayoun Alidadi

·H A R T·
PUBLISHING
OXFORD AND PORTLAND, OREGON
2017

Hart Publishing
An imprint of Bloomsbury Publishing Plc

Hart Publishing Ltd	Bloomsbury Publishing Plc
Kemp House	50 Bedford Square
Chawley Park	London
Cumnor Hill	WC1B 3DP
Oxford OX2 9PH	UK
UK	

www.hartpub.co.uk
www.bloomsbury.com

Published in North America (US and Canada) by
Hart Publishing
c/o International Specialized Book Services
920 NE 58th Avenue, Suite 300
Portland, OR 97213-3786
USA

www.isbs.com

**HART PUBLISHING, the Hart/Stag logo, BLOOMSBURY and the
Diana logo are trademarks of Bloomsbury Publishing Plc**

First published 2017

© Katayoun Alidadi 2017

Katayoun Alidadi has asserted her right under the Copyright, Designs and Patents Act 1988
to be identified as Author of this work.

British Library Cataloguing-in-Publication Data
A catalogue record for this book is available from the British Library.

ISBN:	HB:	978-1-50991-137-0
	ePDF:	978-1-50991-139-4
	ePub:	978-1-50991-138-7

Library of Congress Cataloging-in-Publication Data

Names: Alidadi, Katayoun, author.

Title: Religion, equality and employment in Europe : the case for reasonable accommodation / Katayoun Alidadi.

Description: Oxford [UK] ; Portland , Oregpon : Hart Publishing, 2017. | Includes
bibliographical references and index.

Identifiers: LCCN 2017003842 (print) | LCCN 2017004791 (ebook) (print) |
LCCN 2017004791 (ebook) | ISBN 9781509911370
(hardback : alk. paper) | ISBN 9781509911387 (Epub)

Subjects: LCSH: Religion in the workplace—Law and legislation—Europe. | Freedom
of religion—Europe. | Discrimination in employment—Law and legislation—Europe. | Religious
minorities—Legal status, laws, etc.—Europe. | Equality before the law—Europe. | European
Court of Human Rights. | Convention for the Protection of Human Rights and Fundamental
Freedoms (1950 November 5)

Classification: LCC KJC2945.R44 A74 2017 (print) | LCC KJC2945.R44 (ebook) | DDC 344.2401/58—dc23

LC record available at https://lccn.loc.gov/2017003842

Typeset by Compuscript Ltd, Shannon

To find out more about our authors and books visit www.hartpublishing.co.uk. Here you will find extracts,
author information, details of forthcoming events and the option to sign up for our newsletters.

FOREWORD

Freedom of religion or belief in the European workplace: towards a resolutely protective approach in an age of religious revival?

MARIE-CLAIRE FOBLETS[*]

Europe today faces the very complex question of how legal techniques can and should contribute towards achieving a vision of society that is at once inclusive and respectful of ethnic, cultural and religious diversity. This complexity is linked in part to the division of powers across various political levels—European, national and regional—as regards the fight against all forms of discrimination.

There can be no doubt that the question has gained urgency. In Europe, a political climate has been developing that seems increasingly unfavourable to signs of diversity, and in particular diversity that is considered to be extraneous, that is, coming from outside Europe. Political decision-makers have therefore been reluctant to show much interest in implementing structural measures that would make it possible to move towards greater inclusion of minorities and new-comers in day-to-day life. One can try to explain this lack of interest (without in any way justifying it). For instance, in the context of the European 'refugee crisis', popular opinion of various persuasions across the continent is concerned about the ineffectiveness of the response of public authorities—administrative, legislative and judicial—to uncontrolled and continuing migration. In such a context of anxiety, the knee-jerk reaction is to turn inward, and a vision of society that seeks to be inclusive and respectful of diversity in its various forms of expression is met with serious resistance. This resistance can be seen in public debates, in electoral results that favour restrictive policies towards immigrants and, more recently, in the use of referenda on the question of whether to maintain solidarity with other European Member States.

In this major work of scholarship, which adds substantial insights to the blossoming field of law and religion at a critical time, Katayoun Alidadi shows undeniable courage in unambiguously advancing the idea that only a radical openness to religious and ideological diversity will enable European societies to ensure a prosperous, sustainable and economically competitive future in an

[*] Director of the Max Planck Institute for Social Anthropology, Halle, Germany. Professor at the Law Faculty, Catholic University of Leuven, Belgium, and Honorary Professor of Law and Anthropology, Martin Luther University Halle-Wittenberg, Germany.

increasingly mobile and globalised world. Alidadi's remarkably rich analysis combines unparalleled depth and scope, and will be of great interest to scholars, policy-makers and the general public not only because it offers explanations for the current anxiety and *Zeitgeist*, but also because it proposes a number of ways forward. To be sure, Alidadi does not, for all that, position herself as an ideologue of diversity; her analysis is firmly embedded in the legal, socio-economic and political realities of today. She has scrupulously studied what one might, in a given time or place, reasonably expect from the implementation of a particular legal technique that was developed to guarantee freedom of religion or belief or to combat certain forms of discrimination. This includes the concept of reasonable accommodation, regarding which this book will no doubt become a work of reference for years to come.

Religion at work

The workplace is a key area in debates on the governance of religious diversity in contemporary society.[1] In practice, employers and other stakeholders such as labour union leaders all too often fail to recognise the right to express one's religion in the workplace, arguing that religion or belief should remain confined to the private lives of individuals. From this point of view, people are free to hold religious beliefs, but should keep them to themselves and not express their religious identity when outside the comfort of their own homes and certainly not at work. What is to be done, then, when there is a conflict between workplace rules and religious obligations, potentially leading to exclusion from the workforce, and thus socio-economic marginalisation, of individuals who not only identify with minority religions but who also wish to practise their religion or belief openly? Should the law give support to people who seek to assert such claims?

As Alidadi explains in detail, in Europe two separate but intertwined legal frameworks permit one to assess the role of religion or belief in the area of employment: the non-discrimination framework and the human rights framework. In the European Union, an important legal instrument for combating discrimination on the grounds of religion and belief in the area of employment was established with the enactment of Council Directive 2000/78/EC (the Employment Equality Directive). This Directive, which aims to put into effect the principle of equal treatment in all EU Member States as regards employment and occupation, prohibits direct discrimination, indirect discrimination, harassment and incitement to discriminate on the grounds of religion or belief, disability, age or sexual orientation.[2] The Directive also protects against victimisation on the basis of the

---

[1] See in particular *Interim report A/69/261 (2014) of the Special UN Rapporteur on freedom of religion or belief* (Part III: 'Tackling religious intolerance and discrimination in the workplace').

[2] Council Directive 2000/78/EC of 27 November 2000 establishing a General Framework for Equal Treatment in Employment and Occupation, [2000] OJ L303, 02/12/2000, 16–22.

same grounds. Freedom of thought, conscience and religion is guaranteed by Article 9 of the European Convention on Human Rights and Article 10 of the EU Charter of Fundamental Rights, as well as national (constitutional) provisions. Neither the Employment Equality Directive nor Article 9 explicitly provides a right for employees to request (or obtain) reasonable accommodation from their employers or labour unions on the basis of religion or belief in the workplace. The concept of reasonable accommodation was introduced into the Employment Equality Directive, but limited to the ground of disability.

The requirements of the two legal frameworks leave ample leeway for different approaches to the protection of religion or belief and allow for divergent reactions that all too often make court decisions unpredictable. National courts interpret the existing protections against religious or belief-related discrimination, including indirect discrimination, very differently. Alidadi's findings, based on a comparative examination of the case law, show that, especially in cases involving indirect discrimination, some courts have hitherto shown limited willingness to provide practical protection for employees in Europe belonging to minority religions or even to the majority religion.

This book engages extensively with available European and national case law in Belgium, the Netherlands and Britain, both before and after the Employment Equality Directive was adopted and implemented in national instruments. However, individuals only very rarely call upon the courts, as Alidadi justifiably reminds the reader. Instead, in a labour market where rules and expectations are not designed with the needs of religious minorities in mind, people experiment with a variety of 'coping mechanisms' to deal with obstacles and exclusion. Litigation is the exception. The case law, which is meticulously examined, thus may not reveal all aspects of the empirical reality (indeed, case law rarely does). Adopting a socio-legal perspective, Alidadi is interested in what occurs on the ground and how the law shapes, but does not determine, the realities of millions of jobseekers, employees and employers, and others. One such consideration involves the under-investigated phenomenon of 'self-exclusion'. Today, a Muslim woman wearing a headscarf is at risk of being excluded from some job opportunities in various parts of Europe. Hence, she may consider it futile to apply for certain jobs if she is not prepared to 'compromise' on her head covering, even if she is highly educated and well qualified for the job. The loss to the woman and her family is clear. But the labour market also loses, in terms of valuable competition and talent. Society fails to realise its equal opportunity and non-discrimination policies. The self-exclusion or self-limitation is due to the interplay of restrictive or failing laws and policies, on the one hand, and minority coping mechanisms on the other. In this regard, Alidadi's findings counter the negative stereotype that members of religious minorities are assertive and demanding; on the contrary, some of the data point to a (problematic) tendency on the part of individuals to develop an attitude of passive acquiescence. Coping mechanisms are manifold. Some may find creative ways to realise their potential, refusing to see themselves as victims. Many will find success despite obstacles and limitations, but others may lack the resilience to overcome our societies' failure to make good on their promises of non-discrimination and equal opportunity.

Reasonable accommodation and neutrality policies

One of the admirable features of *Religion, Equality and Employment in Europe* is the concern for answers and solutions (which often come in the form of considered trade-offs). According to Alidadi, legislators, courts, labour unions, employers and other stakeholders all need to work towards realising genuine religious freedom and combating discrimination, stigmatisation and exclusion, thereby countering engrained propensities to self-exclusion on the part of some minorities. This is all the more true as courts are limited in their scope of action and can only address the disputes that are submitted to them.

Alidadi's in-depth treatment of so-called neutrality policies that are adopted by private companies should spark considerable interest among decision-makers and the wider public, as it is a major cause of concern in certain European countries. Such policies invoke the criterion of 'neutrality' as the grounds for banning all religious, philosophical, and even political expressions in the workplace. However, as Alidadi compellingly argues, this emphasis on neutrality often amounts to direct discrimination on the basis of religion or belief. The widespread exclusionary effect of such policies on, for instance, employees who wear religious attire contradicts the entire rationale underpinning anti-discrimination law, yet courts still too often appear to condone and even approve of such policies.[3]

How can one create the conditions necessary for adopting a more resolutely protective approach when it comes to taking account of religious diversity in matters of employment? Religious diversity in the workplace presents many challenges to the relationship between employees and employers, who need to find ways to get along with one another despite differences, stereotypes and biases. The challenges do not, of course, concern the workplace exclusively. A shared workplace, a shared public space, educational facilities, institutions of deliberative democracy, etc, each in its own way may offer an opportunity to overcome these differences, stereotypes and biases along the path towards a smooth coexistence, but it requires work to achieve such positive outcomes. How do we get there, in particular when it comes to enabling individuals—regardless of their convictions—to participate in the labour market?

---

[3] On 14 March 2017, just before this book was sent to press, the CJEU issued two highly anticipated judgments interpreting the prohibition of religious discrimination under the Employment Equality Directive. The Court rejects the argument that private company neutrality policies constitute direct discrimination, legitimises such policies as justified indirect distinctions under certain conditions (eg consistent and systematic application, limited to employees who come into contact with customers), but also advances a limited form of reasonable accommodation (offering an alternative, back-office positions instead of dismissal). These being the first CJEU judgments on religious discrimination under EU law, but many questions remain (eg the interaction with ECtHR cases) and will have to be worked out in the years to come. See Case C-157/15, *Achbita v G4S Secure Solutions NV*; Case C-188/15, *Bougnaoui v Micropole SA*.

Here the case for reasonable accommodation provides food for serious thought. Arguing for such resolutely minority-protective[4] legislative intervention in the current European climate, where religion—particularly Islam and certain other minority religions—is part of an anxiety-triggering 'religious revival', indeed requires courage and conviction. Alidadi emphasises that accommodations that are *reasonable* should be legally enforceable; such workplace adjustments, however, always have to be balanced against the interests of employers, other employees and customers, and should be able to be refused if a disproportionate burden or cost to any of these other stakeholders can be demonstrated. Her expectation is that a generalised right of job applicants and employees to request reasonable accommodation would entail a shift in the mentality of employers with regard to the role of religion in the workplace and in the lives of the individuals concerned.

Some may argue that European society is not ready to take on board Alidadi's valuable findings or to adopt the proposal with regard to reasonable accommodation. My own experiences as the co-chair of the Belgian Round Tables on Interculturalism in 2010 certainly bear this out.[5] At these roundtables a veritable gulf separated two positions, one that seems almost insurmountable given the opinions that underlie the social debate on the question. The report aptly referred to this gulf in the following terms:

> [S]hould one adopt a more confident, and above all a more open attitude to the increasing diversification of identity claims? And if so, to what extent? For some people, our democratic societies have opted for a secularised law that refuses to allow any religious, philosophical and/or cultural specificities to gain in power. This reality cannot be ignored or relativised. For others, this option does not in any sense present an obstacle to reassessing—substantially, if necessary—certain historical choices made with regard to policies on cultural and religious pluralism. This is a question of justice, in particular toward new communities in our midst.[6]

The recommendation on reasonable accommodation, which was not unanimously accepted by the members of the Round Tables' steering committee, therefore remained cautious: while the committee sought to promote good accommodation practices, it did not advance more than a voluntary 'citizen route' to get there.

---

[4] It must be stated that a duty of reasonable accommodation is a symmetrical right, meaning that it applies to all irrespective of (minority/majority) religion or (non)belief, although in the current context it would be more relevant for minorities.

[5] The Round Tables on Interculturalism were set up by the Belgian federal government to make 'recommendations ... for reinforcing the chances of shaping a society based on diversity, respect for cultural identities, non-discrimination and the affirmation of shared values' (Governmental accord of 8 March 2008). The report focused on particular difficulties experienced by persons and communities belonging to ethnic, cultural and religious minorities, with much of the attention focused on the issue of religious symbols in education and the workplace. See, generally, M-C Foblets and JP Schreiber (eds), *Les Assises de Interculturalité/De Rondetafels van de Interculturaliteit/The Round Tables on Interculturality* (Brussels, Larcier, 2013).

[6] M-C Foblets and C Kulakowski, *Final report Roundtables of Interculturalism (Rondetafels van de Interculturaliteit)* (Brussels, 8 November 2010) 8.

Reasonable accommodation has many opponents, and Alidadi does a formidable job of addressing the oft-heard arguments. Certainly, the right to request accommodation places the primary responsibility not on an external adjudicator but on the parties involved—the employer and the employee. This process encourages them to reach an agreement among themselves regarding the terms of the requested accommodation and in good time, that is, before a conflict arises. The proposed approach does not lend itself to abstract determinations nor does it dictate *a priori* a certain outcome before the actual facts surrounding the request for accommodation have been thoroughly reviewed and evaluated. However, in Alidadi's view, a legal right to reasonable accommodation institutes a shared societal project, and the employee—often the weaker party in the negotiations— is thereby not without remedy if negotiations are rejected outright or fail to lead to a mutually agreeable result. Relying on an enforceable right adopted by the European or national legislatures, courts can then apply the general framework to the specific facts of the case, balancing different interests and interpreting the boundaries of the law.

In his monograph *Law and Religion*, Russell Sandberg identifies three forms of 'juridification of religion' in contemporary societies: (1) the expansion of law to regulate an increasing number of activities within what he calls the 'religious marketplace', a process that, in my view, has in recent years produced mainly punitive, restrictive and eclectic pieces of legislation; (2) a growing tendency for conflicts to be resolved by or with reference to law; and (3) a process of 'legal framing' whereby people increasingly think of themselves and others as legal subjects and holders of rights.[7] The right to request accommodation resonates with the second, and even more so with the third form of 'juridification of religion': pre-empting conflicts by negotiating, very concretely, differences in understanding of religion and belief, equality and human rights. A right to request accommodation is just one illustration of a measure that would make it possible to 'govern' religious diversity outside the realm of the judiciary and adversarial proceedings.

The combination of rich empirical and analytical insights with various forward-looking suggestions on topics including, but not limited to, reasonable accommodation make this book appealing to the widest possible audience. The law is in constant transition when it comes to the historically volatile issue of religious difference and co-existence, and *Religion, Equality and Employment in Europe* offers not a snapshot, but a dynamic reel of contemporary sociolegal developments in the critical area of employment relations. Governance of religious diversity is very likely one of the questions, if not *the* question, that will determine the future of European societies. We need to prepare for a future that has yet to be built and that takes account of the needs of the present situation, in which many members of minority religious groups are in vulnerable economic positions. There is much to be gained from a nuanced, balanced way of

---

[7] R Sandberg, *Law and Religion* (Cambridge, Cambridge University Press, 2011) 193.

handling their requests when it comes to enabling and facilitating the participation of all members of our society in the labour market. Legislators should consider whether it might be appropriate to introduce a right to request reasonable accommodation as a means of increasing the level of participation of members of religious minorities in the workplace. Doing so may well open up a more constructive and inclusive path to a new religious diversity that, come what may, will have to be governed in Europe in the decades to come.

PREFACE

Religion, Equality and Employment in Europe critically assesses and evaluates the legal protections for the religion or belief of employees in private-sector employment within a multi-layered European normative framework. Besides examining relevant case law of Europe's two supranational courts—the European Court of Human Rights and the Court of Justice of the EU—the study engages three European countries that exhibit both striking socio-legal commonalities and differences. Three different Western European legal cultures, namely Belgium, the Netherlands and Britain, serve as in-depth country studies for this thematically focused systematic comparison. Interactions between the applications of national-level and Europe-wide norms are also considered throughout. While showing important realizations and potentials of the anti-discrimination law and human rights frameworks, notable gaps and shortcomings in legal protection are illustrated through case law examples. Building on the analysis, various ways forward are proposed for an inclusive Europe which accepts, respects and—where possible and reasonable—accommodates the religious and philosophical diversity of its citizens and inhabitants. One of these proposals focuses on the legal concept of *reasonable accommodation*, which has been the subject of much debate and controversy.

Going beyond the paradigmatic headscarf cases by investigating a wide array of religious requests and needs which have arisen or are bound to arise in the near future in the European workplace, this book aims to make a constructive contribution to ongoing debates surrounding the sensitive and controversial issue of the accommodation of religion and belief in Europe in the domain of employment, which is interlinked with other important areas of social life such as education, housing and health care. Besides the display of religious dress and symbols in the workplace, the possibility to celebrate religious holidays or days of rest, religiously motivated objections to certain employment-related functions, and a number of issues which concern the workplace as social context (eg, the observance of dietary rules, shaking hands with members of the opposite sex) are investigated. The often varied responses such questions have received in the different countries that are the focus of this study provide food for thought for any stakeholder concerned with the uniform, or at least convergent, understanding of European anti-discrimination and human rights norms.

This study engages deeply with the relevant normative frameworks at both national and EU levels and bridges disciplines by drawing insights from legal theory and empirical disciplines such as the sociology of law, sociology of religion, legal anthropology and socio-legal studies. Because of the topic and the interdisciplinary approach, this book will appeal to a broad range of scholars, practitioners and students, as well as to segments of the larger public seeking to gain insights into issues of religious diversity and accommodation which go beyond media sound bites. Indeed, the discussion on reasonable accommodation may provide a genuine barometer for the perspectives and debates on the ground in Europe regarding religion's undeniable role in society. Such debates are hardly outside the ambit of the EU, considering that the EU has progressed far beyond its humble origins as an economic unit into a more complete political and social model, with issues related to social cohesion and human rights amongst its core concerns. While religion and religious symbols in Europe have drawn increasing attention in the past two decades, it should be clear that the recent influx of millions of refugees from Muslim majority countries—prospective European employees—will anchor the continued topicality of the issue of religion and work as a crucial part of integration policies in Europe. Much stands to be gained by adopting appropriate measures which aim to fight discrimination and exclusion while sending critical messages of inclusivity and togetherness within the management of religious and philosophical diversity in general.

ACKNOWLEDGEMENTS

This monograph builds on the research conducted in the frame of an interdisciplinary EU research project on secularism and religious diversity in Europe, which culminated in my doctoral thesis defended at the Catholic University of Leuven.[1] Within the frame of the RELIGARE project[2] I had the great privilege of collaborating with numerous remarkable legal and social science scholars on an ambitious, open-ended journey exploring and proposing ways forward for a Europe faced with the reality of religious and philosophical diversity. I am indebted to many of these scholars who have since become colleagues and friends. When it comes to the dissertation writing process that accompanied and followed the project, I am grateful to many more individuals for the useful insights and resources, questions and suggestions, and often lively discussions along the way.

First of all, I thank my doctoral supervisor, Prof Marie-Claire Foblets. For the many stimulating exchanges and collaborations, the unconditional support and continuous encouragement, the incessant faith in my abilities and for the freedom to discover and to potentially fathom, I genuinely thank her. My admiration and respect for her tireless intellectual engagement has continued to grow since I was a student taking her class on Migration Law back in 2002 at the Catholic University of Leuven. During that class, she helped open my (and many of my co-students') eyes to the law's ambitions and limitations in addressing pressing social, political and cultural matters, a theme which has hardly lost its appeal since in Europe and elsewhere. Prof. Foblets truly is a one-of-a-kind scholar, role model and mentor and I consider myself extremely privileged to be able to benefit from her wisdom and advice. Her willingness and ability to genuinely consider the positions of the people concerned in a given research project and to empathise with their everyday struggles is a constant reminder that the academic aspiration for objectivity does not imply being passive or insulated, a lesson I took to heart in shaping this monograph.

I also thank the many individuals who took time to read, comment on and discuss the texts which lead to this monograph. This includes in particular the members of my doctoral examining committee: Prof Paul Lemmens, Prof Stefan Sottiaux, Prof Heiner Bielefeldt, and Prof Maleiha Malik. I was fortunate that

[1] *Faith, Identity and Participation in the Workplace. A Comparative Legal Study on the Role of Religion and Belief in Individual Labour Relations and Unemployment Benefits Litigation*, KU Leuven (Faculty of Law) thesis, 850 pp.
[2] RELIGARE—'Religious Diversity and Secular Models in Europe—Innovative Approaches to Law and Policy'—was a three-year project (2010–13) funded by the European Union under the 7th Framework Programme.

scholars of their calibre agreed to take on the task of evaluating an 850-page thesis along with everything else that each of them had going on. This book would not have been the same without the discussions, highly useful comments, and suggestions for improvement. Also, without seeking to be exhaustive, I thank Veit Bader, Prakash Shah, Rik Torfs, Jørgen Nielsen, W Cole Durham Jr, Silvio Ferrari, Adriaan Overbeeke, Floris Vermeulen, Lori Beaman, Lucy Vickers, Jogchum Vrielink, Thalia Kruger, Javier Martínez-Torrón, Jean-François Gaudreault-Desbiens, Eugenia Relaño Pastor, Julie Ringelheim, Louis-Léon Christians and my former colleagues at the Leuven Institute for Human Rights and Critical Studies, in particular Prof Koen Lemmens and Toon Agten, and at the Max Planck Institute for Social Anthropology for the many resourceful exchanges, discussions and suggestions. Special thanks also go out to Dr Brian Donahue, Dr Monica Sandor and the editors at Hart Publishing for the many comments and corrections of earlier versions of the manuscript.

Further, insights into the topic and the data in this research would not have been as complete were it not for the willingness of different institutions and individuals welcoming my curiosity and inquiries and facilitating the collection of data. This includes the former Belgian Centre for Equal Opportunities and Opposition against Racism/Interfederal Centre for Equal Opportunities (now Unia), where I was able to spend several weeks reading through 'religion and workplace' files and picking staff's brains, the Netherlands College voor de Rechten van de Mens, and the British Equality and Human Rights Commission.

Finally, I want to express gratitude to my family. Any book project involves considerable time researching and writing, but this should not be a (good) excuse to hold back on life's many delights and struggles. Time does not stop when we are thinking, rethinking, writing and rewriting (even if the ability to stop time would be my chosen superhero power). Although I never had the feeling of getting a firm grasp on the delicate balance between family and work (both felt like guilty indulgences at times), I am grateful it was always mediated (and often remedied) by my sweet, reassuring husband Sam. Without his time, efforts and sacrifices—which I often took (and take) for granted—I could not have brought this project to good completion. Thank you for all that and more. I am the luckiest woman to have you by my side—an amazing husband and father, and my best friend who at times knows me better than I know myself.

In another place and time, I would not have had the luxury of time or opportunity to devote myself to what I consider a compelling and fascinating topic of law and society. Without my parents' courageous decisions to do what they saw best for their children, their incessant positivity despite the many hardships and sacrifices of embarking upon a new life in unfamiliar and sometimes unreceptive surroundings, I would not be the person I am today. To my parents, Mahmoud Alidadi and Effat Banimostafa Arab, I dedicate this book.

Katayoun Alidadi
Houston, Texas
October 2016

CONTENTS

**PART II. Religion or Belief in the Belgian, Dutch and British Private
Sector Workplace: Between Assimilation Demands
and Reasonable Accommodation**

LIST OF ABBREVIATIONS

ADA	Americans with Disabilities Act (US)
ACLU	American Civil Liberties Union
Bouchard-Taylor Commission (Report)	Consultation Commission on Accommodation Practices Related to Cultural Differences (Québec, Canada)
CEOOR	Centre for Equal Opportunities and Opposition to Racism (Belgium, now 'Unia')
CJEU	Court of Justice of the European Union
EAT	Employment Appeal Tribunal (UK)
EC Treaty	Treaty establishing the European Community
ECHR	European Convention on Human Rights
EComHR	European Commission of Human Rights
ECtHR	European Court of Human Rights
EED	Employment Equality Directive
EEOC	Equal Employment Opportunity Commission (US)
EHRC	Equality and Human Rights Commission (UK)
EIDHR	European Initiative for Democracy and Human Rights
ENAR	European Network Against Racism
ENORB	European Network on Religion or Belief
ET	Employment Tribunal
ETC	Equal Treatment Commission (the Netherlands)
ETUC	European Trade Union Confederation
EU	European Union
GETA	General Equal Treatment Act (the Netherlands)
HALDE	Haute Autorité de Lutte contre les Discriminations et pour l'Egalité (France)
ICCPR	International Covenant on Civil and Political Rights
NGO	Non-Governmental Organisation
NHRI	National Human Rights Institution

RFRA	Religious Freedom Restoration Act (US)
WRFA	Workplace Religious Freedom Act (US)
UDHR	Universal Declaration of Human Rights
Unia	Interfederal Centre for Equal Opportunities (Belgium)

TABLE OF CASES

EUROPEAN COURT OF HUMAN RIGHTS /EUROPEAN COMMISSION ON HUMAN RIGHTS

COURT OF JUSTICE OF THE EUROPEAN UNION

BELGIAN CASES

DUTCH CASES

Equal Treatment Commission/Netherlands Institute for Human Rights

BRITISH CASES

OTHER CASES

US Supreme Court cases

Other US court cases

Canadian cases

French cases

Introduction: Religion and Employment in Europe. Thick Identities Colliding with Muscular Liberalism

I. The Turn Towards Religion and Accommodation

'[M]odernity does not necessarily bring about secularization. What it does bring about, in all likelihood necessarily, is pluralism'.[1]

The period during which religion was expected to progressively fade from public life in the West, especially in Europe, now lies well behind us.[2] Over the last three decades religion has re-established itself as a phenomenon to be reckoned with in the globalised West.[3] Even in Europe, 'the exceptional case'[4] when it comes to the importance of religion in the lives of the (majority) population, previously ignored or neglected issues related to religion in public life have turned into favoured research topics for political, social and legal scholars in a 'relatively new area of reflection'.[5]

Since the end of World War II, the racial and religious make-up of Western Europe has been altered significantly as immigrants, asylum seekers and 'guest workers' have established new homes here. A new-fangled religious diversity, with Islam in Europe at the forefront, has added to religious diversities of predominantly Judeo-Christian nature which have been a fixture of Europe for centuries. It is not merely the (re)surrection of religion as such which raises a variety of

---

[1] P Berger, G Davie and E Fokas, *Religious America, Secular Europe? A Theme and Variations* (Aldershot, Ashgate, 2008) 12–13.

[2] See, eg, WC Durham Jr. and BG Scharffs, *Law and Religion: National, International, and Comparative Perspectives* (Wolters Kluwer, 2010) xxxi ('today we are more likely to make the mistake of seeing religion as everywhere and dangerous, rather than viewing it as nothing and irrelevant').

[3] In the words of Gilles Kepel, God has 'taken revenge'. G Kepel, *La Revanche de Dieu. Chrétiens, juifs et musulmans à la reconquête du monde [The Revenge of God: The Resurgence of Islam, Christianity and Judaism in the Modern World]* (Le Seuil, 1991).

[4] G Davie, *Europe: the Exceptional Case. Parameters of Faith in the Modern World* (Darton, Longman & Todd Ltd, 2002); Berger, Davie and Fokas, *Religious America, Secular Europe? A Theme and Variations*, n 1 above, 9.

[5] Linda Woodhead, *'Religion or belief': Identifying issues and priorities* (London, Equality and Human Rights Commission Research report 48, 2009) iii.

challenges in the twenty-first-century modern Western society but the fact of religious (super)*diversity* which, for some, calls for adopting an accompanying paradigm of *religious pluralism*.[6] From a political, social and legal perspective, vital standing is provided to the perennial *accommodation question*: how can and should religious or philosophical needs, whether rooted in immigration or long-standing diversities, be accommodated within liberal-democratic legal systems?[7] And where do the limits lie of the fundamental right to freedom of religion or belief and to equality irrespective of religion or belief, in particular in cases of tension or head-on clashes with other fundamental rights and freedoms? Indeed, debates on religious freedom, equality and accommodation cannot be divorced from some highly intertwined and important contemporary debates on gender equality, LGBTQ rights and the freedom of speech. These debates must also take into account the larger socio-political context and concerns of multiculturalism, secularism and the role of (state) neutrality.

Employment is one area aptly illustrating the tensions that arise when religion or belief-based claims are formulated in twenty-first-century liberal-democratic Europe. For many individuals, religion and belief (including non-belief) remain a core part of their personal identity,[8] and are not necessarily 'shed' when entering the workplace for the duration of one's professional time.[9] Between the *micro level* of personal and family life and the *macro level* of state policies and international relations, the role and treatment of religion and religionists at the *meso level* of the workplace thus take shape in pluriform ways. Conversely, employment participation is often the gateway to effective societal integration and social mobility. Otherwise stated: exclusion from employment significantly hurts people's opportunities for social integration and their sense of societal acceptance. And while individuals may realise all too well that their religious (or non-religious) affiliation and practices are cause for discrimination and socio-economic disadvantage in

---

[6] While diversity and pluralism are often used synonymously, a useful distinction is drawn by Diana Eck in that 'pluralism is not diversity alone, but the energetic engagement with diversity'. See D Eck, *A New Religious America: How a 'Christian Country' Has Become the World's Most Religiously Diverse Nation* (Harper SanFrancisco, 2001). On 'super-diversity', see S Vertovec, 'Super-diversity and its implications' (2007) 30 *Ethnic and Racial Studies* 1024, 1024–54.

[7] See, generally, V Bader, *Secularism or democracy? Associational governance of religious diversity* (Amsterdam, IMISCOE/Amsterdam University Press 2007); The term accommodation does not itself make clear who does the accommodating. Accommodations by a host society may be more visible, but often substantial accommodations—in the form of coping mechanisms—are continuously taking place on the side of the newcomers or minorities.

[8] See, eg, Declaration on the Elimination of All Forms of Intolerance and of Discrimination Based on Religion or Belief, proclaimed by UN General Assembly resolution 36/55 of 25 November 1981, Preamble ('[R]eligion or belief, for anyone who professes either, is one of the fundamental elements in his conception of life').

[9] L Vickers, *Religious freedom, religious discrimination, and the workplace* (Oxford, Hart Publishing, 2008) 4. While religious practice and religious identity are certainly connected, they do not need to go hand in hand. For instance, amongst Turkish and Moroccan youth in the Netherlands a decline in mosque attendance and prayer was coupled with a 'heightened sense of Muslim identity'. See Johannes A van der Ven, *Human rights or religious rules?* (Brill, 2010) 24.

everyday life, they often particularly cherish this element of belonging as a source of empowerment, strength and pride. In fact, marginalisation of individuals and groups because of religion can even serve to reinforce beliefs, practices and belonging.[10] Restraints on religious practices may thus have counter-productive effects.

This book focuses on responses to religious and non-religious belief and practices that are anchored in law. The law at times and in certain situations offers explicit answers, from mandating or allowing particular accommodations to banning certain practices altogether. But in many instances, abstract general principles of law must be applied (or ignored) to address new or unanticipated challenges. Many situations, thus, still await satisfactory resolution.

More particularly, religious and non-religious beliefs and observance are recognised and protected under human rights law and under equality legislation in Europe. Notwithstanding this, on the ground there remain—at times significant—burdens on entering and thriving in the European workplace, and some employees may face what is called 'existential dilemmas'.[11] A testing 'religion penalty'[12] may be the reality for many devout religionists or 'obdurate believers'[13] who strictly observe rules and practices separating themselves from the norms in their largely secular surroundings. Other employees 'may be happy to ignore the religious traditions in order to accommodate an employer's demands'.[14] But perhaps most workers who hold religion or belief dear in their personal life may find themselves somewhere in the middle: not quite existentially torn between the demands of two different worlds and worldviews, but neither entirely content to downplay or effectively abandon at work the beliefs or practices they consider provide ultimate meaning to their life.

The topic of religion or belief in private sector employment remains by and large underexplored territory, as recently noted by the UN Special Rapporteur on Freedom of Religion or Belief.[15] More attention has been directed to educational settings, the public space or public sector employment in Europe, in particular the dress of Muslim women, including the headscarf/hijab, niqab/burqa and more recently the 'burqini'. The analysis in this book aims to fill part of this gap. Since

---

[10] P Connor, 'Contexts of immigrant receptivity and immigrant religious outcomes: the case of Muslims in Western Europe' (2010) 33 *Ethnic and Racial Studies* 376; JR Kunst et al, 'Coping with Islamophobia: The effects of religious stigma on Muslim minorities' identity formation' (2012) 36 *International Journal of Intercultural Relations* 518.

[11] H Bielefeldt, *Interim report of the UN Special Rapporteur on the Freedom of religion or belief. Tackling religious intolerance and discrimination in the workplace*, no A/69/261 (United Nations, 2014) 17.

[12] J Lindley, 'Race or Religion? The Impact of Religion on the Employment and Earnings of Britain's Ethnic Communities' (2002) 28 *Journal of Ethnic and Migration Studies* 427 (finding there is also 'a pure Islamic penalty').

[13] Vickers, *Religious freedom, religious discrimination, and the workplace*, n 9 above, 4; the term 'obdurate believer' is borrowed from A Bradney, 'Faced by Faith' in D Oliver et al (eds), *Faith in law* (Oxford, Hart Publishing, 2000).

[14] ibid, 4.

[15] See Bielefeldt, *Interim report of the UN Special Rapporteur on the Freedom of religion or belief. Tackling religious intolerance and discrimination in the workplace*, n 11 above, 7.

Max Weber's *The Protestant Ethic and the Spirit of Capitalism* (1905), the relationship between religion and economics has been much debated in sociology of law studies.[16] However, research rooted in secularisation theory has disconnected religion and the workplace, since these were seen to be distinct spheres: 'The former are seen by many as concerned with issues of meaning, value, and ultimate significance with the latter concerned primarily with making money'.[17] More recently the compartmentalisation is being challenged by experiences on the ground. The dilemmas faced by 'modern Antigones', torn between their religious commitments and professional duties, can only fully be appreciated within a framework which recognises that religion can play *a legitimate role* in an employee's life, including during work hours and in the workplace.

Indeed, Vickers frames this pertinent question as follows:

> A preliminary question that arises when considering the interaction of religion and the workplace is why the work relationship, traditionally viewed as a private contractual arrangement between master and servant, should be a forum in which religion has any traction at all. After all, the main aim of employers is the running of efficient and profitable businesses; and employees give up a degree of autonomy when they enter the workplace, in return for a wage. Why then should religious employees expect their religious interests to be accommodated at work at all?[18]

From a legal point of view, one can refer to relevant protections: the right to freedom of thought, conscience and religion (in short: the freedom of religion or belief) is a fundamental human right, with horizontal effect, and the prohibition of discrimination is even more closely tailored towards private, contractual relations. But this evokes the deeper, underlying policy question of *why* to adopt or continue to support such protection, or even to advocate more effective protection under existing or new frameworks that may offer better guarantees that reasonable accommodation takes place on the ground. This is a vital debate and one which defies easy answers. But it is reasonable to assert that companies and businesses—whether large or small—do far much more in society than simply pursue profits for their owners or shareholders; they operate within a certain socio-cultural context, sometimes with considerable power and influence and are important 'distributive agents'[19] with regard to scarce goods (including jobs and positions which have financial and intangible benefits such as respect, confidence, security etc). This power, position and (at times) status justify obligations towards social justice.

---

[16] See A van Hoorn and R Maseland, 'Does a Protestant work ethic exist? Evidence from the well-being effect of unemployment' (2013) 91 *Journal of Economic Behavior and Organization* 1; A Strhan, 'Book Review: *Spirituality, Inc.: religion in the American workplace* by L Lambert III (NY University Press, 2009)' (2014) 11 *Journal of Management, Spirituality & Religion* 91.

[17] Strhan, 'Book Review: *Spirituality, Inc.: religion in the American workplace*', ibid at 91; S Bruce, *God is Dead: Secularization in the West* (Wiley-Blackwell, 2002).

[18] L Vickers, 'Law, religion and the workplace' in Silvio Ferrari (ed), *Routledge handbook of law and religion* (Abingdon, Routledge, 2015) 272.

[19] For a discussion of employers as distributive agents, see Alexander Somek, *Engineering Equality. An Essay on European Anti-Discrimination Law* (Oxford, OUP, 2011).

Conversely, employees do not give up their personal autonomy entirely when they contract out their labour, but their interests and rights may compete with those of other employees, the employer, customers and the larger society. This makes the balancing of interests and rights a justifiable and necessary undertaking in any system which values fundamental rights, and the exercise may point to the potential of *reasonable* accommodation in meeting the needs of particular workers. The emphasis on reasonableness, in the prior sentence and the title, is significant as there are limits; not to the willingness to meet the other halfway (or somewhere there) but to the practical possibility and expediency of doing so in particular cases and circumstances. I will return to this point later.

To be sure, accommodation of religious needs in Europe does not concern only immigrants or Muslims, its implications and applications have never been restricted to certain groups. I argue for reasonable accommodation on the basis of religion *or belief*, thus including non-belief, as a symmetrical right. Yet the issue and the proposed right to reasonable accommodation cannot be divorced from the current socio-economically and culturally precarious status of newcomers in Europe. At the basic level, openness towards accommodation only makes sense when a society rejects an assimilative policy towards newcomers and by extension towards all those who in certain ways derogate from the majority—sometimes seen as 'neutral'—norm. Assimilation is 'one-way integration', 'where the newcomers do little to disturb the society they are settling in and become as much like their new compatriots as possible'.[20] Tariq Modood has written that

> [f]rom the 1960s onwards, beginning in the Anglophone countries and spreading to others, assimilation as a policy has come to be seen as impractical (especially for those who stand out in terms of physical appearance), illiberal (requiring too much State intervention) and inegalitarian (treating indigenous citizens as a norm to which others must approximate).[21]

Johannes Van der Ven similarly concludes that assimilation is 'politically impracticable, judicially objectionable, and morally reprehensible'.[22] With assimilation as a policy discredited, even the attacks on multiculturalism have not been accompanied by explicit calls to bring it back. Also, various scholars 'have begun to focus on the problems that an assimilationist bias and, more concretely, that specific employment demands to assimilate raise for the equality ideal'.[23] This does not take away from the fact that to many politicians in Europe, a 'successful integration' nonetheless approximates to assimilation. For instance, former

---

[20] T Modood, 'Four modes of integration' in MC Foblets and JF Schreiber (eds), *Les Assises de Interculturalité/De Rondetafels van de Interculturaliteit/The Round Tables on Interculturality* (Brussels, Larcier, 2013) 44.

[21] ibid, 44. In 1966, UK Home Secretary Roy Jenkins in a now famous speech argued that integration is 'not a flattening process of assimilation but equal opportunity accompanied by cultural diversity in an atmosphere of mutual tolerance'.

[22] van der Ven, *Human rights or religious rules?*, n 9 above, 231–32.

[23] TK Green, 'Work culture and discrimination' (2005) 93 *California Law Review* 623; see also K Yoshino, 'Covering' (2002) 111 *Yale Law Journal* 769.

French President Nicolas Sarkozy argued the primary responsibility of the person who is to successfully integrate in the following terms:

> C'est de la part de celui qui arrive la volonté de s'inscrire sans brutalité, comme naturellement, dans cette société qu'il va contribuer à transformer, dans cette histoire qu'il va désormais contribuer à écrire. La clé de cet enrichissement mutuel qu'est le métissage des idées, des pensées, des cultures, c'est une *assimilation réussie* (emphasis added).[24]

This may have been a proverbial slip of the tongue, but even when the term 'assimilation' is not used expressly, what is intended in political and popular discourse on integration and participation is 'a flattening process of assimilation', which implies leaving behind 'outlandish' religious beliefs and practices. The risk is that the bar is placed 'so high that newcomers either can't or do not want to jump over it'.[25] Therefore, the case for reasonable accommodation and the rejection of assimilation policy go hand in hand.

II. Scope of Analysis and Overview

An increasingly heterogeneous Europe thus presents politicians, policy-makers, lawyers and judges with a variety of societal challenges, including the setting of appropriate parameters for the fundamental right to freedom of religion and belief and non-discrimination on the basis of religion and belief in the area of employment. Considering the link with multiculturalism, integration, social cohesion concerns, and dire socio-economic inequality of Muslims and other ethno-religious minorities in Europe, the (non) accommodation of religion or belief should be considered a highly volatile, pressing and intractable matter.

Operating within a non-assimilative 'integration by accommodation' framework,[26] this book critically examines and evaluates the legal protections in place for issues of religion or belief arising in the private sector European workplace.[27]

---

[24] N Sarkozy, 'Respecter ceux qui arrivent, respecter ceux qui accueillent', *Le Monde*, 8 December 2009. This view has consequences as far as religious practices are concerned, since former President Nicolas Sarkozy argues that 'Chrétien, juif ou musulman, homme de foi, quelle que soit sa foi, croyant, quelle que soit sa croyance, chacun doit savoir *se garder de toute ostentation et de toute provocation* et, conscient de la chance qu'il a de vivre sur *une terre de liberté*, doit pratiquer son culte avec *l'humble discrétion* qui témoigne non de la tiédeur de ses convictions mais du respect fraternel qu'il éprouve vis-à-vis de celui qui ne pense pas comme lui, avec lequel il veut vivre'.

[25] B Eeckhout, 'Het besef rijpt dat integratie alleen kan werken als iedereen zijn eigen identiteit en cultuur mag ontwikkelen', *De Morgen*, 12 March 2014.

[26] This is the perspective from the state; for the point of view of non-dominant ethnocultural groups and individuals towards the dominant society, see JW Berry et al (eds), *Cross-cultural psychology: research and applications*, 2nd edn (Cambridge University Press, 2002) 354. See also van der Ven, *Human rights or religious rules?*, n 9 above, 21; Y Lamghari, *L'Islam en entreprise: La diversité culturelle en question* (Editions L'Harmattan, 2012) 25–26.

[27] The demarcation between the public sector and the private sector is not always clear-cut. My distinction depends on the identity of the employer (the state or another entity or person).

The *dual and multilayered framework*[28] in place necessitates a multilevel, transnational legal analysis,[29] simultaneously taking into account legal developments at supranational and domestic levels in human rights and equality law.[30] The private sector angle also provides insights into the dynamic of labour relations and illustrates the tensions in the (at least theoretical) absence of *state* neutrality[31] concerns, while revealing at the same time dominant standards in the organisation of labour and working life that form particular barriers to the participation of religious workers.

Religion in the workplace issues, then, can be analysed under two main legal frameworks, which exhibit significant overlaps and interactions.[32] First, the human rights law framework protects all human beings' freedom of thought, conscience and religion and right to non-discriminatory treatment, a protection which is not specific or tailored to the area of employment. In contrast, under EU anti-discrimination law different forms of disadvantaging and discrimination, including based on the grounds of religion and belief, are prohibited specifically in the economic site of employment and occupation.[33] In Europe, these two frameworks largely correspond to the legal tools of the European Convention on Human Rights (ECHR) and EU Directive 2000/78 pertaining to the area of employment, occupation and vocational training (Employment Equality Directive),[34] as implemented in national legislation. The meaning of these two frameworks and their effectiveness for the protection of religious interests and claims are concretised through their application by national as well as supranational courts, prominently

Public sector employment represented more than 29% of the total employment on average between 2008–11 in Belgium (31.5%), the Netherlands (29.5%) and the UK (29.7%), all countries with a 'very large public sector' (Eurostat).

[28] In addition, there may be other relevant laws and provisions, such as a general duty to act in good faith/act as a good employer under general labour laws. However, considering the marginal role of these norms and the prominence of human rights and especially non-discrimination law in religion in the workplace cases, the latter forms the focus.

[29] G Shaffer, 'Transnational Legal Process and State Change' (2012) 37 *Law & Social Inquiry* 229 (defining Transnational Law as 'law in which transnational actors, be they transnational institutions or transnational networks ... play a role in constructing and diffusing legal norms').

[30] Other levels, in particular the international level, are also important but arguably have played less of a role than the ECHR and EU in this area and will therefore only briefly be discussed.

[31] This concern for neutrality in the area of religion and culture may be 'an attempt to grasp an illusion'. SD Smith, *Foreordained Failure: The Quest for a Constitutional Principle of Religious Freedom* (Oxford, Oxford University Press, 1995) 96. Some nonetheless consider it a worthwhile political ideal. A Koppelman, 'The fluidity of neutrality' (2004) 66 *The Review of Politics* 633.

[32] Article 14 ECHR is an auxiliary non-discrimination provision. The protocol establishing a freestanding non-discrimination provision has a limited role considering the lack of wide-spread ratification.

[33] A proposed Directive would extend the area of protection against religious discrimination beyond employment and vocational training into social protection, social advantages, education, and the access to and supply of goods and services available to the public, including housing, see Proposal for a Council Directive on implementing the principle of equal treatment between persons irrespective of religion or belief, disability, age or sexual orientation, COM(2008) 426 final.

[34] Council Directive 2000/78/EC of 27 November 2000 Establishing a General Framework for Equal Treatment in Employment and Occupation, [2000] OJ L303, 02/12/2000, 16–22.

the European Court of Human Rights (ECtHR) and the Court of Justice of the European Union (CJEU).[35]

Recent case law of the ECtHR, for instance the 2013 *Eweida* case,[36] aptly illustrates the fluidity and flexibility of the 'law in practice' and consequently of the relation between the human rights and anti-discrimination law frameworks. The question is not just which is more effective or useful than the other, but rather how the respective frameworks interact and influence each other to define an appropriate level of protection. To what extent (and through which legal mechanisms) are private sector employees' religious or non-religious beliefs and practices (best) protected? Are there particular limitations or shortcomings associated with the respective legal frameworks? The employee-angle implies ample attention for the position and role of *individual employees'* religion and belief in (a wide variety of) private sector employment, which can (but need not) come into tension or conflict with rights and interests of others or with abstract principles.[37]

Understanding and analysing the jurisprudence of the ECtHR and relevant EU law form the first step towards a more contextual analysis of three country studies, namely Belgium, the Netherlands and the United Kingdom.[38] The key reason for the selection of these countries—all sharing the common EU frameworks—was the existence of relevant and developing domestic *law and jurisprudence* as well as important *societal* developments and public debates surrounding law and religion, multiculturalism, and the integration of minorities.[39] The country studies illustrate the achievements and potential, but also the gaps in, limitations of and lack of coordination between current multilevel legal protections. Experiences and insights from other jurisdictions—including the United States and Canada, where

---

[35] There is also interaction between the two supervisory courts (CJEU-ECtHR), sometimes with explicit references in cases. The process of the EU's accession to the ECHR has, however, come to a halt following the CJEU opinion 2/13 of 18 December 2014 on the Accession of the European Union to the ECHR.

[36] *Eweida and Others v United Kingdom*, Application nos 48420/10, 59842/10, 51671/10 and 36516/10 (ECtHR, 15 January 2013).

[37] This book does not include self-employment, public sector employment or employment in religious-ethos companies. However, there are undeniable overlaps and cross-over effects with the situation of public servants, as discussed below.

[38] The United Kingdom consists of Great Britain (England, Wales and Scotland) and Northern Ireland. The focus of the research is on the situation in Britain (England and Wales) which differs both socially and legally from that in Scotland and Northern Ireland. On 23 June 2016, 51.9% of the voting British electorate voted to leave the EU. The withdrawal of the UK from the EU will have widespread effect, including in the area of human rights and non-discrimination law, but I will not engage with this issue here since the research for this book was conducted before the Brexit vote and at the time of finalising the manuscript, neither the timetable nor any concrete terms for withdrawal were yet established.

[39] The three selected countries are 'visionary' to some extent: the state and stakeholders such as equality bodies are actively engaged in developments in the areas of law and policy, and are not merely passive addressees of supranational norms. What goes on on the ground is considered relevant and worthy of debate. Two of the countries may even be called vanguards in the area of anti-discrimination and equality: in the case of the UK and the Netherlands anti-discrimination law developed before and was a driving force in the process leading to the adoption of EU law standards, so that these should be home to various good practices.

a duty of reasonable accommodation on the basis of religion is operative—are also analysed so as to shed light on the current European state of play and possible future developments.

While this book focuses on legal responses and developments, these cannot be divorced from the larger social and political background and *Zeitgeist* in Europe. Legal cases form the proverbial 'tip of the iceberg' when it comes to realities and conflicts on the ground.[40] Employee 'coping mechanisms'[41] often fall short of litigation, which can be seen as the *ultimum remedium* or an option if relations have already gone awry. The legal topography remains a patchy reflection of societies' challenges and successes in dealing with religious diversity in the ground. For instance, the absence of case law on an issue in a given jurisdiction can signify very different conditions: it may mean an issue (say, wearing religious dress at work) is unproblematic in that jurisdiction, but conversely it may be explained by a lack of a minimum level of integration needed for the request to even come up. It may (also) be due to highly problematic trappings, obstacles and exclusions preventing potential claimants[42] from obtaining legal redress.[43] Indeed, a general reason for the existence of sporadic case law on religious affiliation or accommodation discrimination relates to the lack of knowledge about rights and avenues to pursue claims when faced with such discrimination. The Special Eurobarometer 393 relating to discrimination in the EU in 2012 showed that 17 per cent of Europeans and 27 per cent of Europeans self-identifying as part of an ethnic minority have personally experienced discrimination in the past 12 months.[44] Yet, a staggering 37 per cent admit not knowing their rights, and even those who have personally experienced discrimination are not significantly more aware of their rights.[45] Interestingly, the most popular place to turn to when faced with discrimination seems to be the police (34 per cent), which is listed way before equality bodies (16 per cent) and tribunals and trade unions (10 per cent).[46] In addition, one can imagine other barriers and obstacles of time and resources for victims of discrimination. Against

---

[40] On the process of reframing tensions and problems into conflicts, legal conflict, and religious legal conflict, see K Alidadi and MC Foblets, 'Framing multicultural Challenges in Freedom of Religion Terms. Limitations of minimal human rights for managing religious diversity in Europe' (2012) 30 *Netherlands Quarterly of Human Rights* 388, 388–416.

[41] See M Galanter, 'Justice in many rooms: courts, private orderings, and indigenous law' (1981) 19 *Journal of Legal Pluralism* 1 ('avoidance', 'exit', 'lumping it', 'self-help'). In John Berry's terms, these could be regarded as 'acculturation strategies' of non-dominant ethno-cultural groups towards the dominant group. JW Berry, 'Integration and Multiculturalism: Ways towards Social Solidarity' (2011) 20 *Papers on Social Representations* pp 2.1–2.21, 2.5.

[42] The most 'fundamental' religionists may thus not appear as claimants in the cases discussed: they may have long adopted an exit strategy.

[43] eg (FRA) European Union Agency for Fundamental Rights, *Access to Justice in Europe: An Overview of Challenges and Opportunities* (2011).

[44] European Commission. Directorate-General Justice, *Special Eurobarometer 393 'Discrimination in the EU in 2012'* (November 2012), 6–7 of summary report.

[45] ibid, 6–7 of summary report.

[46] ibid, 8 of summary report. Minorities are somewhat less inclined than the average to turn to the police in case of discrimination.

this background, the occurrence of requests, implicit or explicit, and legal claims to wear religious dress at work, to take short breaks to pray or to find alternative job duties for conscientiously objecting employees can be regarded as a positive signal of attempted inclusion and participation.

Cases which reach the courts may be indicative or symptomatic of larger developments taking place on the 'shop-floor of social life' and serve as a gateway to a better understanding of those grassroots developments. It is the *combination* of legal analysis and empirical data, then, which can produce the most insightful results; indeed, social science studies provide much needed data to contextualise case law analysis. At times, such studies can tell of things to come, for instance by revealing issues that have not yet been raised in legal cases. Case law decisions illustrate the 'special effect of the law', ie the application of the law in official enforcement. But anyone interested in the social working of legal measures should look for the 'general effects of the law', that is the use of rules 'outside the context of official application and enforcement'.[47] This points to the (lack of) difference law makes in concrete social situations or its (in)ability to bring about social change.

Law and society cannot be isolated from one another; even if artificially represented as separate, they mutually influence each another. Specific case law decisions can trigger certain developments on the ground, in particular in case of significant radiating effect or societal messaging. For instance, there are strong indications that Belgian case law on the legality of company 'neutrality' policies in the private sector has promoted a mushrooming of such practices—which have exclusionary effects—on the ground. Also, an employer who believes he can legally reject an applicant who wants to wear a headscarf or other religiously distinct dress will feel free to ask certain questions and make certain dress demands. Not only distributive agents like employers (whose understandings of legal rules are the basis for everyday organisational decision-making) are influenced by legal messaging; published and publicised cases can effectively change *employee* behaviour as well. Imagine a young Muslim woman who wears a headscarf in search of an internship or first job; she may reconsider applying for a job at a clothing store if she has heard of a recent judgment of a labour court siding with an employer who fired an employee for 'refusing to dress neutrally'. In anticipation of or as a reaction to experienced restrictions, this woman may decide to focus her efforts on pursuing a back-office job instead, exploring self-employment, or continuing her studies. Her coping mechanism may amount to, what Ghumman and Jackson call, 'self-handicapping' behaviour[48] which can go so far as halting any search for gainful employment.

This book consists of two main parts. Taking on a European and comparative perspective, Part I discusses the legal frameworks in place under Article 9 of the ECHR and the protection against discrimination on the basis of religion under

---

[47] J Griffiths, 'The social working of anti-discrimination law' in MLP Loenen and PR Rodrigues (eds), *Non-Discrimination Law: Comparative Perspectives* (Kluwer, 1999) 319.

[48] S Ghumman and L Jackson, 'The downside of religious attire: the Muslim headscarf and expectations of obtaining employment' (2010) 31 *Journal of Organizational Behavior* 4.

the EU Employment Equality Directive.[49] The ECtHR has emphasised the 'margin of appreciation' of states when it comes to controversial issues such as religious manifestation and religious pluralism where no consensus can be found amongst the Council of Europe Member States.[50] In addition, until the 2013 *Eweida* case, the 'freedom to resign' doctrine prevented adequate consideration for employees' religious interests. Conversely, religion or belief has ascended the equality agenda in the last two decades. The EU's adoption of the Employment Equality Directive in 2000 forms a highlight. This Directive has provided EU Member States with a largely unified language, but interpretations under national anti-discrimination legislation vary considerably. The CJEU has not yet received an opportunity to decide on the scope and extent of protection against religious discrimination in the workplace 16 years after the adoption of the prohibition of discrimination on the basis of religion or belief in EU law, but this is soon set to change as two very relevant cases stand to be decided by the CJEU.[*]

Considering the relatively narrow guidance from the ECtHR and the CJEU, decisions on the proper limits or accommodations of employees' religions essentially remain the purview of Member States and their domestic courts. Part II offers a comparative and contextualised analysis of relevant Belgian, Dutch and British cases involving religious dress and grooming, religion-worktime conflicts, affiliation discrimination and a number of other religion-workplace accommodations matters that pertain to religious employees in the mainstream (private sector) workplace.

Since 'a lot of European countries seem to wrestle with this issue [of religious pluralism and its limits] and are increasingly torn apart over it', Loenen and Goldschmidt regard 'more comparative legal work [as] urgently needed'.[51] Sensitive conflicts involving the role of religion in public life and multiculturalism will necessarily be culturally embedded into broader and evolving societal circumstances. Legislative responses and judicial decision-making reflect strategies and choices best understood within the context of broader societal circumstances that are always in motion. For instance, minority policy in the Netherlands has experienced an important 'shift away from policies of multiculturalism' following a number of public tensions and occurrences.[52] In the UK, the 'race prism' is

---

[49] Another level includes the ILO. This will not be discussed *in extenso* considering the limited role it has played in the area of non-discrimination on the basis of religion or belief.

[50] *Leyla Şahin v Turkey*, Application no 44774/98 (ECtHR, 10 November 2005) para 109 ('where questions concerning the relationship between states and religions are concerned, on which the opinion in democratic society may reasonably differ widely, the role of the national decision-making body must be given special importance').

[*] On 14 March 2017, the CJEU issued two highly anticipated judgments interpreting the prohibition of religious discrimination under the Employment Equality Directive. See Case C-157/15, *Achbita v G4S Secure Solutions NV*; Case C-188/15, *Bougnaoui v Micropole SA*.

[51] MLP Loenen and JE Goldschmidt, 'Religious pluralism and human rights in Europe: reflections for future research' in MLP Loenen and JE Goldschmidt (eds), *Religious Pluralism and Human Rights in Europe: Where to Draw the Line?* (Intersentia, 2007) 319.

[52] BP Vermeulen, 'On Freedom, Equality and Citizenship. Changing Fundamentals of Dutch Minority Policy and Law (Immigration, Integration, Education and Religion)' in MC Foblets, JF Gaudreault-DesBiens and AD Renteln (eds), *Cultural Diversity and the Law State Responses from Around the World* (Bruylant/Éditions Yvon Blais, 2010); The murders of Pim Fortuyn and Theo Van Gogh can be noted as the most marking and shocking recent events in the struggles of the Dutch multicultural society.

slowly but surely being supplemented, but not supplanted, with a religion-based and social class perspective. And in Belgium, a country which teeters between progressivism and conservatism, the success of the Flemish nationalist party (Nieuw-Vlaamse Alliantie (N-VA)) in the 2014 general elections has signified a further shift towards curtailing employment equality policies instead of seeking ways to realise the potential of existing laws (let alone adopting new ambitious ones).[53] In the three countries under review, case law decisions, including some divergent interpretations of similar legal EU law concepts, reflect the role of different legal cultures, historical developments and concerns, as well as policy and prevailing perceptions of religion in society.

In the conclusion, I engage both levels of analysis and summarise a sustained *argument in favour of an explicit duty of reasonable accommodation on grounds of religion and belief in the European labour market.* This duty is to complement and reinforce, rather than to replace, the current legal protections to achieve greater substantive equality and a genuine freedom of religion or belief for the forum internum *and* externum in the mainstream employment setting.

Currently, there is no explicit right to reasonable accommodations for religion or belief under either legal framework. This is in contrast to the situation in the United States and Canada, where employers have a legal obligation to accommodate the religious or non-religious beliefs, practices and observances of workers, albeit to different extents and enforced with different levels of zeal. The question of whether to adopt in Europe a similar right to reasonable accommodation for reasons of religion or belief as in North-America has generated much debate and controversy in a number of Member States. I highlight some of the 'added value' by contrasting a right to reasonable accommodation with the legal tools of human rights law (Article 9 ECHR) and EU non-discrimination law, as interpreted in the case law of the ECtHR, the CJEU and a number of EU Member States, as well as comparing to 'voluntary' accommodation practices on the ground.

Arguing for effective freedom of religion or belief for employees in the current European socio-political context is a perilous task—even apart from any context of economic crisis—considering that the 'first human right' itself is under pressure.[54] Indeed, the basic idea behind a (separate) protection for the freedom of religion in today's multicultural and religiously diverse societies has repeatedly been called

---

[53] Appointing a staunch opponent of any equality legislation to the board of the Interfederal Centre for Equal opportunities, now Unia, is surely a warning sign. J Van Horenbeek, 'N-VA'er aangesteld bij Gelijkekansencentrum: "Discrimineren is een fundamentele vrijheid". Matthias Storme (N-VA): controleur of saboteur?', *De Morgen*, 25 October 2014 (noting that the coalition agreement sets forth a 're-evaluation' of the anti-discrimination act in the future).

[54] See, amongst others, H Bielefeldt, 'Freedom of Religion or Belief—A Human Right under Pressure' (2012) 1 *Oxford Journal of Law and Religion* 1; H Bielefeldt, 'Misperceptions of Freedom of Religion or Belief' (2013) 35 *Human Rights Quarterly* 33.

into question.[55] At the same time, non-discrimination law has known a steady rise, becoming the 'fastest growing part of labour law'[56] but its effectiveness in addressing instances of *religious or philosophical* disadvantage has remained limited. To some, the religion strand under discrimination law is less worthy of protection than other human characteristics such as race/ethnicity, gender, disability, and sexual orientation.[57] Often the argument that religion or belief, as opposed to the other 'immutable' characteristics, involves a 'personal choice' figures strongly in the balance.[58] Such challenges to *the principle* of protection for religious freedom or non-discrimination have real consequences when it comes to the level of *practical application* on the ground and before the courts.

Before turning to the analysis of the relevant supranational and domestic law, the subsequent two sections explore two key overarching themes: the issue of reasonable accommodations (III) and the larger philosophical debate of why religion-workplace clashes are taking place in today's liberal-democratic Western countries (IV).

III. Reasonable Accommodation: Typology, Hard Cases, Substantive Equality and Decommodification

The legal concept of 'reasonable accommodations' originates in the United States[59] and was further developed in Canada.[60] In both countries, the concept was introduced with regard to religious employment discrimination and later extended to disability (in the United States) and other grounds (Canada). It is now firmly established as a right for persons with disabilities under both international and EU law.[61] Yet, what in effect are religious accommodations cases, ie adjustments of work rules or practices that remove or alleviate conflicts between work obligations

---

[55] Even while Western governments have taken it upon themselves to proclaim this fundamental right abroad; see USCIRF, Canada agency for freedom of religion abroad; see also EU Guidelines for the Protection and Promotion of Freedom of Religion or Belief.

[56] M De Vos, 'Worden Europese arbeidsrelaties Amerikaans? Kritische rechtsvergelijkende perspectieven bij de discriminatieverboden in het arbeidsrecht' in D Cuypers (ed), *Gelijkheid in arbeidsrecht: gelijkheid zonder grenzen?* (Intersentia, 2003) 243.

[57] A McColgan, 'Class wars? Religion and (in)equality in the workplace' (2009) 38 *Industrial Law Journal* 1.

[58] ibid.

[59] Title VII of the US Civil Rights Act of 1964 (42 US Code Chapter 21) prohibits employers from discriminating against individuals because of their religion in hiring, firing, and other terms and conditions of employment. Title VII was amended in 1972 to include a legal mandate on employers with 15 or more employees to accommodate the religious practices and observances of their employees or prospective employees, unless to do so would create an 'undue hardship' on the employer.

[60] *O'Malley v Simpsons-Sears* [1985] 2 SCR 536.

[61] See the UN Convention on the Rights of Persons with Disabilities of 2006; Art 5 Employment Equality Directive.

and religious obligations of the employee,[62] have been occurring for some time in Europe as well. In 1969, after a heated conflict between the UK's Wolverhampton Transport Committee and several of its Sikh conductors and drivers, a ban on turbans and beards was retracted. A Sikh group leader, Sohan Singh Jolly, regarding the ban as a 'direct attack' on his religion, had even 'threatened to burn himself to death in protest'.[63] The matter was laid to rest, and was never introduced in court. While luckily not all cases get so heated, legal cases involving religious dress and other issues have become more frequent in recent years, in part because of the growing religious diversity and assertiveness of minorities in EU Member States as well as because of facilitating legal developments.

A. Towards a Typology of Reasonable Accommodation

Over the years, religious individuals have requested time off to fulfil religious duties, observation of special days of rest or the celebration of festivals, permission to wear religious garb (eg Islamic headscarves) or symbols (eg necklace with crucifix) on the job, and exemptions of general labour laws or workplace policies in most—if not all—European Member States[64] and at the European level.[65]

Besides 'employment accommodation cases', which often involve dilemmas like that in play in Antigone's tragedy (ie a hard choice between 'the law' and the tenets of one's faith), there are also cases which can be categorised as religious discrimination cases *sensu strictu*.[66] In such cases, workers are discriminated, excluded, harassed or victimised simply on account of their (perceived) (non)adherence to a particular religion.

Surprisingly perhaps, court cases involving such egregious patterns are far rarer; cases typically raise some element—practice, appearance, manifestation—apart from non-manifested belief or affiliation. This may lead to a—mistaken—impression

---

[62] This typology, relating to secular workplaces, was developed within the frame of the European RELIGARE project. See MC Foblets and K Alidadi, 'The RELIGARE Report: religion in the context of the European Union: engaging the interplay between religious diversity and secular models' in MC Foblets et al (eds), *Belief, Law and Politics What Future for a Secular Europe?* (Aldershot, Ashgate, 2014). For an extensive list of illustrations from across 9 European Member States and Turkey, see K Alidadi, 'Reasonable Accommodations for Religion and Belief: Adding Value to Article 9 ECHR and the European Union's Anti-Discrimination Approach to Employment?' (2012) 37 *European Law Review* 693.

[63] X, 'Sikh busmen win turban fight', *BBC News*, 9 April 1969. While not all of the then estimated 130,000 British Sikhs approved of this move, 14 workers 'had vowed to follow suit and set fire to themselves if their request was not granted'. After the resolution, Mr Jolly said 'I am a moderate and religious man and would never have taken the extreme step of threatening my life if they had not refused to listen to reason'.

[64] Vickers, *Religious freedom, religious discrimination, and the workplace*; D McGoldrick, *Human Rights and Religion: The Islamic Headscarf Debate in Europe* (Oxford, Hart Publishing, 2006).

[65] See, eg, *Dahlab v Switzerland*, Application no 42393/98 (ECtHR, 15 February 2001).

[66] This can be access discrimination preventing a person from obtaining gainful employment or treatment discrimination once a person is on the job.

that this is not an important issue on the ground.[67] One reason behind the dearth of such cases may be that in the case of ethno-religious minorities, such cases are framed as ethnic discrimination as opposed to religious discrimination as the two forms of discrimination coincide and the former is subject to a stronger legal regime.[68] For instance, in March 2014 a job applicant named Ahmed received an email from a Belgian construction company he had applied to telling him his application was rejected because they had bad experiences with foreigners such as calling in sick too frequently.[69] With the overlap between ethnic/racial origin and religious discrimination in such cases involving Muslims of an ethnic minority background, such as Moroccan Muslims in Belgium, the potential discrimination claim based on (presumed) religious affiliation can disappear in the background, 'absorbed' as it were by a more solid ethnic discrimination framing.

One may consider all relevant cases—accommodation cases and discrimination cases *strictu sensu*—under the banner of 'discrimination', and certainly if one wants to apply equality or non-discrimination law,[70] this appears an imperative. But for analytical reasons, it makes sense to distinguish the two since in the latter instance there is no 'request', 'demand' or even unexpressed 'wish' for some form of work accommodation.[71] The issue simply never arises because the individual is excluded a priori from employment opportunity or promotion, possibly but not necessarily because of certain assumptions about the need for accommodation.

While in practice a number of religious manifestations have come up regularly as issues in the workplace, the scope of requested accommodations is potentially endless and it is impossible to be exhaustive considering the wide variety of new and old religions or beliefs and workplace practices in Europe. As far as requests

---

[67] See, eg, *Ivanova v Bulgaria*, Application no 52435/99 (ECtHR, 12 April 2007).

[68] L Waddington and M Bell, 'More equal than others: Distinguishing European Union equality directives' (2001) 38 *Common Market Law Review* 587 (arguing protection of racial and ethnic discrimination is at the top of the equality hierarchy in the EU).

[69] X, 'Geen job voor Ahmed door "vreemde naam"', *De Standaard*, 7 March 2014.

[70] I use the terms *equality law* and *non-discrimination law* as equivalents throughout this analysis. Some commentators do see a difference in emphasis in that equality law is broader and represents a further (more audacious) stage in the development of this area of law. eg B Hepple, *Equality: The New Legal Framework* (Oxford, Hart Publishing, 2011) 1, noting the 'shift of focus from negative duties not to discriminate, harass or victimise, to positive duties to advance equality, justify the re-invention of this branch of law as equality law, of which discrimination law is an essential but not exclusive part'. In this sense, reasonable accommodation represents a fitting approach under equality law.

[71] How cases and controversies are described and framed is of crucial importance: 'the employee's demand was not taken into account' versus 'the employee requested a certain exception' versus 'the employee refused to accommodate the employee'. These different ways of saying the same thing may conjure up very different images of the parties involved and the process of negotiation between them. As far as possible, I use 'demand' and 'request' as synonyms, without intended difference. Indeed, it has been said that a central issue in the debate on cultural diversity remains the 'search for the right vocabulary to talk about difference and citizenship'. See Monique Nuijten, 'Legal Responses to Cultural Diversity: Multi-Ethnicity, the State, and the Law in Latin America' in M-C Foblets, Jean-François Gaudreault-DesBiens and Alison Dundes Renteln (eds), *Cultural Diversity and the Law: State Responses from Around the World* (Bruylant/Éditions Yvon Blais, 2010) 237.

for accommodations by employees are concerned, the following proposed typology has guided the analysis throughout:

— first, some requests are due to tension or conflict between dress code mandates derived from religious and workplace codes or practices, both for front-office and back-office positions;[72]
— second, requests may be motivated by a need to reconcile conflict or tension between working time obligations and religious time demands;[73]
— third, requests may seek to take away conflict or tension related to certain job duties, including conscientious objections; and
— finally, there may be particular tensions or conflict related to workplace socialising expectations, demands or work conditions which may raise difficulties and objections for workers with certain religious beliefs or practices.[74]

As said, the question of whether to extend a similar right to accommodation for reasons of religion or belief has generated much debate and controversy. A number of scholars who support the protection against religious or belief discrimination have nonetheless spoken out against adopting an explicit duty, questioning the appropriateness and feasibility of strengthening religious rights in the European context given that tensions between religious freedom and other values and rights (including non-discrimination of other vulnerable persons) are hard to deny and that (some forms of) religious expressions in the public sphere generate anxiety and restrictive legislation. In this debate, the concept is sometimes misinterpreted as an unrestricted right to workplace adaptations and a complete exemption from carrying any personal burden for one's religious commitments. Properly understood though, claims for reasonable accommodation are claims for inclusion through the facilitation of a substantive form of equality and there are good reasons why we should principally accept the approach when requests are based on religion or belief in the European workplace setting.

Some instances (but certainly not all) involve sensitive 'hard cases' which necessitate a delicate and difficult balancing act between conflicting interests, values and rights, including those of employers, co-workers, and the employee involved.[75] 'Soft cases', where accommodations harm no compelling interests and are (nearly)

---

[72] This most often relates to the headscarf. On the front-office/back-office distinction and the role it plays when it comes to the accepting of religiously distinct dress, see K Alidadi, 'From Front-Office to Back-Office: Religious Dress Crossing the Public–Private Divide in the Workplace' in S Ferrari and S Pastorelli (eds), *Religion in Public Spaces* (Aldershot, Ashgate, 2012) 159–190.

[73] See, eg, requests for time off to observe a day of rest/Sabbath, a religious holiday, an extended bereavement period, or daily and weekly prayers.

[74] The line between the last two categories is somewhat fuzzy when the debate revolves around what is an actual job duty and what is not.

[75] L Vickers, *Religion and Belief Discrimination in Employment—The EU law* (Brussels, European Network of Legal Experts in the Non-Discrimination Field, 2006) 5 ('One disadvantage of such a fact-sensitive approach is that predicting the outcome in any particular case becomes difficult as so many interests are being weighed in the balance. However, the advantage of such an approach is that it can provide consistency in terms of clear procedural safeguards, to ensure that restrictions on religious

cost-free, can also be identified. Contrary to what one may think, even these 'soft cases' have not been unequivocally successful in courts across Europe. What's more, frequently cases do not even receive adequate consideration. Various modes of arguments have prevented due consideration of the (religious) employee; these include arguments that the employee is free to resign and look for alternative employment, an adherence to formal equality standards or (certain conceptions of) 'neutrality'.

B. Substantive Equality and Decommodification

Indeed, in this area, choices have to be made between (mere) formal equality[76] and laws and policy initiatives that aim for a more audacious substantive equality. Reasonable accommodations are, as Sandra Fredman argues in the disability rights context, a 'challenge to the existing anti-discrimination paradigm'.[77] While 'non-discrimination law is traditionally underpinned by the idea that the protected characteristic, such as race or gender, is rarely relevant to the employment decision ... [and] the protected characteristic should therefore be ignored', the idea behind reasonable accommodations is that 'ignoring, by failing to accommodate, the characteristic can result in denying an individual equal employment opportunities'.[78] Reasonable accommodation can indeed promote social inclusion, by allowing for (and at times mandating) the recognition and appropriate facilitation of relevant differences in a given social context. The concept of equality undergirding accommodation, then, is one that not only allows but at times 'requires adaptation and change'.[79]

The issue of the underpinning notion of equality is not merely of theoretical interest. A focus on equal or consistent treatment (under formal equality's

freedom, and exceptions to the non-discrimination principle are only imposed after proper consideration of the varied interests at stake, in the cultural and political context of the particular Member State').

[76] While formal equality is of utmost importance, there are shortcomings in the approach *solely* based on this concept of equality. Anatole France captured the disingenuous effects of laws that apply equally to everyone in a famous quote: 'In its majestic equality, the law forbids the rich as well as the poor to sleep under bridges, to beg in the streets, and to steal loaves of bread': Anatole France, *The Red Lily* (1894), chapter 7.

[77] S Fredman, 'Disability Equality: A Challenge to the Existing Anti-Discrimination Paradigm?' in Anna Lawson and Caroline Gooding (eds), *Disability Rights in Europe. From Theory to Practice* (Oxford, Hart Publishing, 2005) 199.

[78] L Waddington, 'Chapter six: reasonable accommodation' in D Schiek, L Waddington and M Bell (eds), *Cases, materials and text on national, supranational and international non-discrimination law* (Oxford, Hart Publishing, 2007) 632. This leaves many questions open; eg which differences are to be taken into account (since surely it is unfeasible to take every individual characteristic into account)? Which form of (different) treatment is called for and how far should that difference or need be accommodated?

[79] Fredman, 'Disability Equality: A Challenge to the Existing Anti-Discrimination Paradigm?' in *Disability Rights in Europe*, n 77 above, 203.

mandate to 'to treat like cases alike') can have a vastly different outcome than under a substantive conception mandating unalike treatment of inherently unalike situations. For instance, requests by an employee seeking a dress code alteration or a work schedule amendment may be rejected by reference to formal equality, ie the employee is being treated identically to their colleagues. However, this is a needs-blind position without regard for the identity and starting position of groups and individuals. A more substantive conceptionalisation that looks to participation and inclusion as an overarching goal offers backing for certain adjustments; this is based on an acknowledgement that genuine equality calls for such accommodations, in particular for workers who want to participate in work contexts that were largely shaped without taking into account their religious or cultural beliefs and practices.

In his former position as UN Special Rapporteur on the freedom of religion or belief, Heiner Bielefeldt wrote that

> [a]gainst a widespread misunderstanding, the purpose of reasonable accommodation is not to 'privilege' members of religious minorities at the expense of the principle of equality. In fact, the opposite is true. What reasonable accommodation encourages is the implementation of substantive equality.[80]

The challenge is to broaden the *legal* concept of equality to include a substantive approach in various areas of law.[81] In light of the limits of existing primary legal instruments aiming to protect and include employees from increasingly diverse religious backgrounds in the European workplace, the concept of reasonable accommodations has its merits as part of a substantive equality approach with an eye for the *effects* of measures (or of the status quo) on the equality *in practice* of different groups.

The progression of non-discrimination law in the EU has coincided with a noticeable decline in social policies, with much weight put on the principle of equality and equal opportunities to realise solidarity.[82] Anti-discrimination law is less objectionable to neo-liberals since it can be framed as seeking to correct

[80] Bielefeldt, *Interim report of the UN Special Rapporteur on the Freedom of religion or belief. Tackling religious intolerance and discrimination in the workplace*, n 11 above, 16.
[81] ibid, 56–57. Similarly, De Vos sees three main weaknesses in formal equality, many of which are remedied by *adding* substantive equality (but certainly not by deserting formal equality altogether): 'it requires comparison with a comparator in order to establish discrimination, it is essentially passive and static and does not assure any particular outcome, and it disregards the inherent collective dimensions of inequality such as group membership, entrenched inequality or societal realities': M De Vos, *Beyond Formal Equality. Positive Action under Directives 2000/43/EC and 2000/78/EC* (Brussels, European Network of Legal Experts in the Non-Discrimination Field, 2007) 10. See also K Wentholt, 'Formal and Substantive Equal Treatment: the Limitations and the Potential of the Legal concept of Equality' in MLP Loenen and PR Rodrigues (eds), *Non-Discrimination Law: Comparative Perspectives* (Kluwer, 1999) 53 ('A broad concept of equality encloses both the formal and the substantive component').
[82] The difference lies in that non-discrimination law can be seen as a 'neo-liberal mechanism', which fully operates within and embraces the market paradigm while having some redistributive goals, while social policies aiming at decommodification go further in trying to lessen the 'relentless grasp of the market' on individual's lives.

market failures such as irrational prejudice and exclusion and reinstates market rationality and efficiency.[83] Somek, offering a leftist critique of EU law, has argued that non-discrimination law alone cannot and should not carry the day, and that the visibility of equality law should not stand in the way of other measures in the area of social policy.[84] Somek sees equality law, despite its main utility in fighting stereotypes and disadvantage, as 'normatively deficient': '[r]ather than stating what it takes to realise equality, anti-discrimination norms merely exclude single acts or cumulative practices that impact unequally on members of different groups'. Also, equality law 'tries to accomplish redistributive objectives by deontological means',[85] meaning it relies on correcting the actions and intentions of actors such as employers. Yet, Somek also rightly recognises that non-discrimination law is not merely about redistribution. Indeed, properly applied equality law 'spills over into the pursuit of decommodification'.[86]

Progressive interpretations of anti-discrimination law notions have the potential to approach such decommodification by rejecting the idea of the employee as an impersonal, standardised ideal-type mold which is deprived and denuded of particularity and individuality. In particular, under a reasonable accommodation approach this is so, since the focus is not only on the context which has excluding effects but also on the particular individual(s) raising the issue or making a request. The employee is not just a member of the labour force, bartering time and labour for a salary, but a real live individual with human dignity and individual identity traits which deserve respect and, if needed, accommodation. By making the workplace more 'humane' and thus necessarily diverse, the law has the potential to outreach automatic market thinking which renders labour just another commodity and the worker as a seller of his/her skills, abilities and time. The cover image to this book, the work of artist Herman Van Nazareth, offers a striking visual depiction of the risks of erasing personal characteristics. The blurred images of the 'neutral worker' devoid of personality, identity and a reflective sense of self can act as a metaphor for the dehumanising effect of conformist pressures and demands targeting the visibility of human individuality. Various developments in Europe, like the mushrooming of 'neutrality policies' in the private sector, operate in that very direction. Reasonable accommodation can be an antidote, in particular if accompanied by effective human rights and non-discrimination enforcement as well as proactive policies and company practices working towards employment inclusion and workplace diversity.

---

[83] See the economic justifications of the Employment Equality Directive in recitals 7, 11, 17, and 37.
[84] Somek, *Engineering Equality*, n 19 above, 141.
[85] Somek, ibid, 93. With employers and other gatekeepers as important 'distributive agents'.
[86] Somek, ibid, 136. A commodity being 'that which is produced in order to be sold on a market ... Labour ... is a fictitious commodity ... not produced for sale but for entirely different reasons, nor can this activity be detached from the rest of life, be stored or mobilized', at 94 fn 6. See also S Choudhry, 'Distribution vs. Recognition: The Case of Anti-Discrimination Laws' (2000) 9 *George Mason Law Review* 145; IM Young, *Justice and the politics of difference* (Princeton NJ, Princeton University Press, 1990).

IV. Liberalism, Thick Identities and Coping Mechanisms

The treatment of deeply-held beliefs and practices of individuals in the secular workplace is an illustration of the more general issue prevalent in political philosophy, namely of how liberalism treats religion and religionists, and more specifically how (political) liberalism treats those with 'thick' identities.[87] These are 'identities thick with affiliations, beliefs and moral positions'[88] and religious identity is a prime example. The conflict and dangers of extending the ideology beyond the political are aptly noted as such:

> A particular liberal ideal is that of the 'self prior to its ends.' On this view, the self can be detached from its beliefs, tastes or preferences: ends are not intrinsic to the self but separate. The extension of this philosophical view into the social realm might be an expectation that, when people emerge into public space, they leave behind their 'thick' identities (and the symbols that go with them) and bring only their 'pure' 'unencumbered' self.

> The danger is that this reasoning may be applied far beyond the political, to mean that expression of 'core doctrines' or fundamental philosophical or moral beliefs should not be carried beyond the private realm, so that they are never to be made visible to others. One might think that liberalism involves a great plurality of identities, symbols and forms of expression in public space. But it's also possible for liberalism to be distorted, requiring that these cultural markers be left behind, so that the public space remains 'neutral'—bland and unproblematic.[89]

What lies behind this is the functional differentiation and separation of 'spheres'—such as 'public' and 'private'—and the isolation of social settings such as 'work' and 'family' with each their own codes, symbols, norms, standards and expectations.[90] Transgressing those norms may hold consequences and be frowned upon, as any parent who, through circumstances, is forced one day to bring his or her child to work can attest.

Michael Walzer calls liberalism 'a world of walls' and sees the erection of these walls as creating new liberty.[91] But this way of framing the world, and expecting people to rigidly live by it, is also an estrangement from the reality many people live in and, by extension, also separates, or requires individuals to separate out, the different aspects of their individual identity: indeed, 'such an understanding

---

[87] On identity, see van der Ven, *Human rights or religious rules?*, n 9 above, 53 et seq: 'Identity and difference are interrelated, which makes it a relational concept as in classical ontology. Identity may be defined as continuous awareness that individuals, groups, and communities, despite all discontinuity, remain 'the same', remain 'themselves' over time'.

[88] See B Coleridge, 'Religious expression in the public sphere', *EuropInfos (Christian perspectives on the EU) #158*, March 2013.

[89] ibid.

[90] On functional differentiation, see van der Ven, *Human rights or religious rules?*, n 9 above, 53–54; Also A Seligman, 'Socio-Historical Perspectives on the Public and the Private Spheres' in S Ferrari and S Pastorelli (eds), *Religion in Public Spaces* (Aldershot, Ashgate, 2012).

[91] M Walzer, 'Liberalism and the Art of Separation' (1984) 12 *Political Theory* 315–30.

avoids the essential unity of a person's life: it not only separates various dimensions of society, but also different dimensions of the person'.[92]

Religious identity does not only function in the 'religious sphere', but 'also functions in areas pertaining to primary relations and the life world (social identity), careers (professional life)'.[93] In fact, many of the world religions emphasise the importance or even sanctity of work, awarding it ethical value. In addition, some employees (religious or not) may regard work as an extension of family and do not differentiate strongly between these different settings. When 'there is a hybrid combination of diverse identities without any optimal harmony between them [taking more or less pathological forms like the dissociation, levelling and elimination of areas of identity, as well as a double bind when two or more areas conflict]', various coping mechanisms are possible. Following Albert Hirschman, three prototypical possible 'ways out' can be reconstructed.[94] First, an employee who faces conflicting demands may decide to quit his or her job, or find alternative ways to eliminate the conflict (exit or 'voting with one's feet'). Secondly, he or she may attempt to negotiate, to raise a voice, to 'critically champion changes' (voice). Finally, there is the option of 'loyalty', ie one accepts various cognitive discords in order not to have to give up any of the identities. Various case law analyses can attest to the fact that the availability and prospect of various coping mechanisms are influenced by the law and its messaging.

'Strongly held faith', argues American literary and constitutional critic Stanley Fish, are 'exhibits in liberalism's museum'[95] and simply cannot be 'taken seriously' because they go against the prime value of liberalism, namely 'Reason'.[96] Rawls' distinction between 'political liberalism', which is value-neutral with regard to various worldviews, and 'comprehensive doctrines', of which religious systems are one form, has been heavily attacked. In this regard, James Hitchcock speaks of 'comprehensive liberals'.[97] As secularism becomes more muscular, and thus takes more clear and assertive stances similarly to comprehensive doctrines on moral matters, it would seem that more extensive and generous accommodation becomes

---

[92] Coleridge, 'Religious expression in the public sphere', n 88 above. However, certain positions, which can also be considered 'liberal' would allow for the visibility of thick identities in public spheres. Coleridge considers Charles Taylor's politics of recognition as such a position.

[93] van der Ven, *Human Rights or Religious Rules?*, n 9 above, 57.

[94] A Hirschman, *Exit, Voice, and Loyalty: Responses to Decline in Firms, Organizations, and States* (Cambridge MA, Harvard University Press, 1970).

[95] S Fish, 'Our Faith in Letting It All Hang Out (op-ed)', *New York Times*, 12 February 2006 (Following the Danish Cartoon affair in 2006, American constitutionalist Stanley Fish discussed the double-sided defence of Flemming Rose, the culture editor of the Danish *Jyllands-Posten* newspaper; 'Mr. Rose may think of himself, as most journalists do, as being neutral with respect to religion—he is not speaking as a Jew or a Christian or an atheist—but in fact he is an adherent of the religion of letting it all hang out, the religion we call liberalism').

[96] S Fish, *There's no such thing as free speech: and it's a good thing, too* (Oxford University Press, 1994) viii (noting that 'reason' is an ideologically charged construction, as are terms such as 'neutrality' and 'tolerance').

[97] J Hitchcock, 'The Enemies of Religious Liberty' (February 2004) *First Things: A Monthly Journal of Religion & Public Life* 26.

necessary if the state is to robustly guarantee freedom to live according to one's own conscience. For one, Fish denotes liberalism itself as an ideology,[98] and even a 'religion' or 'faith' itself, with the 'first tenet of the liberal religion' being that:

> [E]verything (at least in the realm of expression and ideas) is to be permitted, but nothing is to be taken seriously. This is managed by the familiar distinction—implied in the First Amendment's religion clause—between the public and private spheres. It is in the private sphere—the personal spaces of the heart, the home and the house of worship—that one's religious views are allowed full sway and dictate behavior ... But in the public sphere, the argument goes, one's religious views must be put forward with diffidence and circumspection. You can still have them and express them—that's what separates us from theocracies and tyrannies—but they *should be worn lightly* (emphasis added).[99]

'Religion worn lightly' implies that religious views, and arguably symbols and appearances as well, 'should not be urged on others in ways that make them uncomfortable'.[100] In liberalism, religions are to be accorded 'respect; nothing less, nothing more', respect may not 'cost you anything' but its generosity remains barely skin-deep and is in fact a form of condescension: 'I respect you; now don't bother me'. Accordingly, Fish sees liberalism (and liberals) as being condescending to those with strong beliefs. Strongly held faiths do not fare well in liberal states, and as Fish sees it this is not only the case in secularist Europe, as he also refers to examples of this approach in the United States, where religion is of enduringly significance for large segments of the population and is much more openly utilised in public and political discourse. In various cases the demands made by liberalism, in some eyes 'modest' demands to enable liberty for all, may be impossible to follow for those whose actions are informed by their 'thick identities' and 'moral compass' and for whom exemptions to neutral rules may be necessary to guarantee freedom and equality.[101]

Jürgen Habermas, with Western Europe in mind, has argued that we are transitioning from a secular to a 'post-secular society' in which 'secular citizens' have to award a previously denied respect for 'religious citizens'. The latter should even be encouraged to draw from their religious convictions to offer criticism of

---

[98] Fish, *There's no such thing as free speech*, n 96 above.

[99] Fish, 'Our Faith in Letting It All Hang Out': 'in the same vein, we can speak of 'faith in moderation': see J Schwedler, *Faith in Moderation: Islamist Parties in Jordan and Yemen* (2006); J Spinner-halev, 'Liberalism and Religion: Against Congruence' (2008) 9 *Theoretical Inquiries in Law* 553 ('Rawls worries that advocates of comprehensive views of religion will want to impose their views on others, but in fact it is his comprehensive view of justice that is in danger of imposing itself on religion. Liberal views of justice are much more imperialistic than most religions. Most religions (with some exceptions) realise that they cannot impose their views on others. In Western liberal democracies, many religious people want to be able to live by their own practices. They are less interested in imposing their views on outsiders (though some are), and are more interested in being able to adhere to their own rules', at 554). In the same vein, Oldenhuis calls this '*dempen*' ('toning down'), which in particular for public functions he considers justified: see FT Oldenhuis (ed), *Religie op de werkvloer* (Protestantse Pers, 2013) 9.

[100] Fish, ibid. See also the concept of 'covering' as a form of assimilation demand. E Goffman, *Stigma: notes on the management of spoiled identity* (Touchstone, 1963); Yoshino, 'Covering', n 23 above.

[101] See, eg, US Supreme Court, *Yoder v Wisconsin*, 406 US 205 (1972).

established contemporary solutions.[102] But it is also argued that two characteristic developments of modern, Western society, namely functional differentiation and globalisation, have produced a 'religious identity crisis' linked to the pluralist condition:

> [o]ngoing contact with members, groups, and duties of other religions not only puts one's own religion's claims to uniqueness, universality, and absoluteness at risk, but also raises questions about what religious truth and authority still mean in a religiously pluralistic context.[103]

Consequently, when it comes to questions of religion and belief in the secular labour market, Europe is facing a real 'test of faith'. When an employee raises an issue of accommodation or even makes an explicit request, there has already been a level of (self) negotiation of religious beliefs, practices and principles. A level of 'accommodation' has already taken place behind the the scenes. The accommodation exercise may have led to the decision not to pursue employment at all and to search for alternative modes of meaning. After all, perhaps the coping strategy which allows for the most undisturbed religious fervour may be pulling out of the workplace or even the labour market as a whole. This coping mechanism is one to take into account when assessing accommodation requests: the issue transcends the employee-employer relationship and touches on issues of societal fairness and inclusion with the labour market playing a mediating role. Not engaging in such a balancing exercise, and merely viewing the matter from the point of view of business discretion or business prerogatives, risks creating unintended counterproductive effects in society. Excluding minorities and those with perceived (too) thick identities from employment opportunities may block out some problems in the mainstream labour market but it will channel problems elsewhere. Clearly, many responses are possible: employees may re-assess and amend their religious practices or may search for alternative ways of leading productive lives, but negative experiences may make some into credulous receptors of intolerant and violent messages.

---

[102] J Habermas, 'Religion in the Public Sphere' (2006) 14 *European Journal of Philosophy* 1.
[103] van der Ven, *Human rights or religious rules?*, n 9 above, 54.

PART I

Freedom of Religion out of its Comfort Zone. Religion in the Workplace and Europe's Two Supranational Courts

Manoeuvring a Multi-layered Fundamental Rights Architecture

This Part addresses the legal protection for religion or belief in the European workplace under the dual frameworks of human rights and non-discrimination law. Claimants (and their counsel) can utilise one or both instruments to argue their case and also have some choice with regard to legal forums to turn to.[1] The first supranational framework which will be analysed is the human rights framework under the highly influential regional human rights instrument which is the ECHR and the Strasbourg Court's *evolutive interpretation of this living instrument.*[2] A brief discussion of early developments of international human right law precedes this and offers a wider socio-legal context for subsequent European developments. Secondly, I turn to the role of the European Union, an organisation which has more recently taken the lead in formulating non-discrimination standards under a series of directives, overseen by the CJEU.

While the ECHR was adopted in 1950, the history of EU equality law is a more recent one. Article 13 of the EC Treaty (now Article 19 TFEU), which provides the legal basis for the Employment Equality Directive, was adopted through a Treaty of Amsterdam amendment in 1997 and came into effect in 1999.[3] Yet the EU has triggered and promoted a 'new equality era',[4] which has quickly caught up with the protections provided by the ECtHR under Article 9 ECHR. Indeed, the 'freedom to resign' or the 'choice principle' had been the cornerstone of the interpretation of Article 9 in the area of employment until recently.[5] The Strasbourg institutions

---

[1] See, eg, the discussion of why the *Eweida v United Kingdom* case (and the related British cases) were taken to the ECtHR and not to the EU even when a main issue was the interpretation of group disadvantage required under the EU Treaty prohibition of indirect discrimination.

[2] Carolyn Evans notes that the ECHR is considered to be the most effective treaty for the protection of Human Rights. C Evans, *Freedom of religion under the European Convention on Human Rights* (Oxford, Oxford University Press, 2001) 2. This is despite the fact that at times treaty bodies have approached the protection of freedom or religion and belief 'in an incoherent and inconsistent manner' and 'have generally been favourable to States and have little consideration to the importance of freedom or religion and belief'.

[3] R Allen, 'Article 13 EC, evolution and current contexts' in H Meenan (ed), *Equality law in an enlarged European Union: Understanding the article 13 Directives* (Cambridge, Cambridge University Press, 2007) 38.

[4] H Meenan (ed), *Equality law in an enlarged European Union: Understanding the article 13 Directives* (Cambridge, Cambridge University Press, 2007) preface, viii.

[5] See, eg, P Cumper, 'The Accommodation of 'Uncontroversial' Religious Practices' in MLP Loenen and JE Goldschmidt (eds), *Religious Pluralism and Human Rights in Europe: Where to Draw the Line?* (Intersentia, 2007) 208—noting that this 'free to resign and find another job approach' was not the approach

repeatedly found 'no interference' with the manifestation of religion or belief when the employee had entered into a work relationship voluntarily, thereby consenting to certain limits on his or her exercise of religion within that context and role. This jurisprudence was rightly criticised for its formalism and hollowing effect.[6] After all, the protection of religion or belief is thereby rendered largely meaningless in contexts where in fact there might not be easy options for the religious adherent to move on to another job of similar worth without considerable hardship. This doctrine, effectively blocking Article 9 claims, is now overruled, but its effect and reasoning have left enduring scars on the domestic protection provided to religious employees.

As said, legal instruments protecting religion or belief in employment have been eagerly adopted at EU level. However, jurisprudential developments remain largely lacking. Sixteen years after the adoption of the Employment Equality Directive, the CJEU has not yet issued a decision interpreting the concept and content of the legal protection against religion or belief discrimination. However, this is only a matter of time.[7] With two references for preliminary rulings currently pending before the CJEU—one submitted by the Belgian Cour de cassation and another by the French Cour de cassation—regarding the headscarf in the Belgian and French workplace, the prospect of the CJEU (re)shaping the law on religious discrimination in employment is not far away.[8] Two Advocate General opinions, the first delivered on 31 May 2016 by AG Juliane Kokott in the Belgian *Achbita* case and the second delivered on 13 July 2016 by AG Eleanor Sharpston in the very similar French headscarf-discrimination *Bougnaoui* case, present the court with starkly divergent approaches to the protection against religious discrimination in the EU, with reasonable accommodation caught in the middle.[9]

the ECtHR took in an employment dispute involving sexual orientation in *Smith and Grady v United Kingdom*, Application nos 33985/96 and 33986/96 (ECtHR, 27 September 1999) (under Art 8 ECHR).

[6] Vickers, *Religious freedom, religious discrimination, and the workplace* (Oxford, Hart Publishing, 2008) 87; see the British case of *Copsey v WWB Devon Clays Ltd* [2005] EWCA Civ 932, where all three judges of the Court of Appeal criticised the decisions in *Ahmed v United Kingdom* (1982) 4 EHRR 126, *Konttinen v Finland*, Application No 24949/94 and *Stedman v United Kingdom*, Application No 29107/95, finding them to be logically unsatisfactory, excessively harsh and limiting of the right to religious freedom.

[7] See MLP Loenen, 'Accommodation of Religion and Sex Equality in the Workplace under the EU Equality Directives: a Double Bind for the European Court of Justice' in K Alidadi, MC Foblets and J Vrielink (eds), *A Test of Faith? Religious Diversity and Accommodation in the European Workplace* (Aldershot, Ashgate, 2012).

[8] See (BE) Cour de cassation, 9 March 2015, AR S.12.0062.N; (FR) Cour de cassation (social chamber), n° 630, 9 April 2015 (13-19.855). Both relate to the question of the wearing of a Muslim headscarf in the workplace and whether a refusal to accommodate constitutes direct discrimination on the basis of religion or belief. The CJEU issued its first judgments on 14 March 2017. It rejected the argument that neutrality policies constitute direct discrimination, but set certain conditions and held that 'the desire to display, in relations with both public and private sector customers, a policy of political, philosophical or religious neutrality must be considered legitimate'. See Para 37, Case C-157/15, *Achbita v G4S Secure Solutions NV*; Case C-188/15, *Bougnaoui v Micropole SA*.

[9] Case C-157/15, *Samira Achbita and Centrum voor gelijkheid van kansen en voor racismebestrijding v G4S Secure Solutions NV*, Opinion of Advocate General J Kokott, 31 May 2016; Case C-188/15, *Asma Bougnaoui and Association de défense des droits de l'homme (ADDH) v Micropole SA*, Opinion of Advocate General E Sharpston, 13 July 2016.

Since the entry into force of the Lisbon Treaty on 1 December 2009, the EU has a legally binding Charter of Fundamental Rights. The Lisbon Treaty anticipated the EU's accession to the ECHR, which was seen as 'a major step forward towards a stronger and more coherent system of fundamental rights protection'.[10] However, it would appear that in the foreseeable future[11] such an institutional link will remain lacking at the supranational level, since the CJEU, in a contentious December 2014 opinion, found the draft accession agreement to be incompatible with EU law and its primacy on various grounds.[12] This effectively makes fundamental rights protection 'a matter for two courts'.[13] Whether the emergence of two sets of fundamental rights standards in Europe is something to applaud or regret is an open question; certainly one can imagine a dynamic competition between two 'fundamental rights courts' which becomes conducive to effective human rights protection. Indeed, under both of these supranational frameworks there have been recent developments relevant to the issue of religion in the workplace and these developments, as well as the complex and reciprocal interaction between the two frameworks, is the subject of this Part. But this is hardly a given.[14]

From a conceptual point of view, arguments on the basis of the fundamental right to freedom of thought, conscience and religion and those on the basis of anti-discrimination standards may contradict one another in specific cases, such as when a religious-ethos employer draws on its (collective) freedom of religion to legitimise a hiring practice which excludes employees on the basis of, for instance, their (lack of) religion or sexual orientation. However, in cases concerning religious employees in secular workplaces, both modes of arguments often complement each other,[15] allowing a claimant to invoke the protection against religious or belief-based discrimination under anti-discrimination law as well as the freedom of religion or belief. For instance, a Muslim saleswoman dismissed from a grocery store for donning a headscarf on the job can argue that her dismissal was

---

[10] See Art 6(2) TEU; J Polakiewicz, 'The EU's Accession to the European Convention on Human Rights—A Matter of Coherence and Consistency' in S Morano-Foadi and L Vickers (eds), *Fundamental Rights in the EU: A Matter of Two Courts* (Oxford, Hart Publishing, 2015).

[11] Steve Peers identified 10 issues which would have to be renegotiated in the accession agreement to meet the CJEU's objections. See S Peers, 'The CJEU and the EU's accession to the ECHR: a clear and present danger to human rights protection', 18 December 2014, available at: eulawanalysis.blogspot.com.

[12] Opinion 2/13 of the CJEU (Full Court) on 18 December 2014 on the Accession of the European Union to the ECHR, [2014] ECLI 2454; Steve Peers called the judgment an 'unmitigated disaster' from the point of view of human rights advocates.

[13] S Morano-Foadi and L Vickers (eds), *Fundamental Rights in the EU. A Matter for Two Courts* (Oxford, Hart Publishing, 2015).

[14] L Vickers, 'Freedom of Religion and Belief, Article 9 and the EU Equality Directive: living together in perfect harmony?' in F Dorssemont, K Lörcher and I Schömann (eds), *The European Convention and the Employment Relation* (Oxford, Hart Publishing, 2013) 1–25, noting that the workings of the two frameworks is sometimes complementary in their operation, sometimes in clear tension.

[15] Vickers, *Religious freedom, religious discrimination, and the workplace*, n 6 above; Vickers, 'Freedom of Religion and Belief, Article 9 and the EU Equality Directive: living together in perfect harmony?', n 14 above.

unlawful as it constituted, first, discrimination based on her religion (Islam) *and*, secondly, her fundamental human right to manifest her religion in practice and observance. The same goes for a factory worker who because of religious beliefs wishes to greet a superior of the opposite sex without engaging in physical contact. This worker can complain that a dismissal or demotion due to the request not to have such physical contact constitutes a violation of her/his human right to religious freedom *and* a (direct or indirect) discrimination on the basis of her/ his religion. In both of these cases, those opposing accommodation of employees may invoke the principle of gender equality and argue that the behaviour singled out for judicial protection itself discriminates against members of the opposite sex and should not be accepted. While I do not agree with this conclusion, or with other modes of argument that outright reject reasonable accommodation of religious employees by superimposing a trumping principle—gender equality, equal rights for sexual minorities, etc—I do underscore the limits of accommodation on the basis of religion or belief in the workplace setting; but these limits are derived from an interplay of the specific circumstances in a given case with mandates of equality, fairness and justice rather than from an implied hierarchy of rights and interests.

1

Religion or Belief in the Workplace under the Human Rights Framework

I. Human Rights, Religious Freedom and Diversity

A. Introduction

> It is not the diversity of opinions (which cannot be avoided), but the refusal of tolera-
> tion to those that are of different opinions (which might have been granted), that has
> produced all the bustles and wars that have been in the Christian world upon account
> of religion.[1]

Human rights have emerged as the moral language of our time, replacing to a
certain extent the role of religion in earlier days. As one prominent legal technique to deal with the multiplicity of norms, values and practices in everyday life,
including issues of religious diversity,[2] much emphasis and reliance has come to be
placed on the framework and discourse of human rights over the last three decades,
both when it comes to longstanding struggles and new societal challenges. Specifically, a variety of 'multicultural issues' are being argued and thus 'framed' in terms
of human rights, in general, and the freedom of religion or belief, in particular.[3]

The fundamental right to freedom of thought, conscience or religion is a classic
'first generation'[4] human right recognised and protected under international and
supranational conventions, and national constitutions and laws. Yet today in multicultural societies it is also challenged as being redundant, irrelevant and even
dangerous. While the freedom of religion is not conceptually limited to religious

---

[1] J Locke, *A Letter concerning Toleration (1689)* (Merchant Books, 2011) 57.
[2] K Alidadi and M-C Foblets, 'Framing multicultural Challenges in Freedom of Religion Terms. Limitations of minimal human rights for managing religious diversity in Europe' (2012) 30 *Netherlands
Quarterly of Human Rights* 388.
[3] ibid.
[4] While human rights are said to be 'indivisible, interdependent and interrelated', this is contested.
See Daniel Whelan, *Indivisible Human Rights. A History* (Philadelphia, University of Pennsylvania
Press, 2010) 1. Generally, three generation of rights are distinguished: first generation or 'blue rights' of
a political and civil nature; second generation or 'red rights' of an economic, social and cultural nature;
and third generation rights or 'green rights' which often are only established in soft law.

minorities, in the European context it is highly minority-relevant.[5] The very perception that it serves most prominently the causes of a Muslim religious minority, with an ethno-cultural identity diverging from the white majority, plays an important role in debates on freedom of religion or belief in Europe. This is in contrast to what has been the case in the United States, where denominational diversity is also a core feature of a vital Christianity. In fact, Europe's multicultural condition has given new vitality to the tool of human rights, in particular by shedding new light on the debate on the meaning and limits of fundamental rights such as the freedom of religion or belief, the freedom of expression and the right to non-discriminatory treatment. The frequent mobilisation of the tool of human rights to address the new societal reality of Europe's increasing religious heterogeneity will, in the long run, no doubt transform our understanding of the human rights system itself. In the more short term, the question is what type of diversity our current understandings and conceptions of human rights and, in particular, the freedom of religion allow for: a truly 'deep diversity'[6] where minorities or 'non-conformists' are allowed space to live out their lives on their own terms according to own norms and aspirations; or rather a more limited diversity which restricts practices and ways of life that are considered beyond the acceptable confines surrounding dominant/majority-biased (even if implicit) Western standards. Whether a minimal or rather a maximal perspective is the appropriate scope of human rights protection relates to this issue.[7]

B. From Toleration of Minorities to Religious Freedom for All?

As said, freedom of religion or belief is seen as 'the first human right', of which the historical developments can be traced 'from oppression via passive tolerance to active tolerance, and, eventually, religious freedom'.[8] It is argued that since the

---

[5] See, eg, Justice, *Special Eurobarometer 393 'Discrimination in the EU in 2012'*, 6–7 of summary report (Europeans who are members of religious—or other—minorities are also much more likely to have personally experienced discrimination than Europeans on average).

[6] 'Deep diversity' refers to an open-ended engagement with the *already-there* factual heterogeneity in beliefs, practices and values on the ground in Europe, which is not a priori limited by conceptions and categories motivated by more common or majoritarian values in society. Under such an approach, individual interests (of minorities) are 'taken seriously' (R Dworkin, *Taking Rights Seriously* (Cambridge MA, Harvard University Press, 1978)) and not easily trumped by considerations derived from 'social cohesion' or 'common values', which are the marks of a more 'utilitarian' approach. This concern for 'deep diversity' shows some affiliation with the 'deep equality' advocated in the Canadian context and discussed below. See Alidadi and Foblets, 'Framing multicultural Challenges in Freedom of Religion Terms. Limitations of minimal human rights for managing religious diversity in Europe', n 17 above.

[7] E Brems, 'Human Rights: Minimum and Maximum Perspectives' (2009) 9 *Human Rights Law Review* 349, 349–72.

[8] Johannes A van der Ven, *Human rights or religious rules?* (Brill, 2010) 11.

pre-modern and early modern times, the focus in Western society has moved from religious tolerance to religious freedom. Yet the question remains:

> Has the politics of tolerating other religious groups, and the concomitant striving for the religious superiority and power of one's own faith, been totally superseded by respect for and recognition of all religious groups, including their right to unrestricted practice of their religion? Has asymmetrical tolerance made way for symmetrical religious freedom?[9]

Liberal philosophers such as John Locke and John Milton considered the religious relationship as 'the core of conscience, for that was where the individual account[s] to God—and to God alone—for her life'.[10] For that reason tolerance was not extended to atheists and Unitarians, since they were considered to lack a moral compass. In contrast, since the start of the modern human rights movement, non-religious thought, conscience and belief were put on par with religious thought, conscience and belief;[11] religious liberty refers to the freedom of all, including non-believers.[12] Limitation towards certain religions or towards non-believers would certainly today appear anachronistic, and indeed is rare,[13] but one may question arguments and decisions which in essence limit the freedom of minority religions and their believers through various legal techniques and interpretations.[14] Also, it would be wrong to proclaim that religious freedom has entirely replaced the more limited toleration framework, particularly in the broader cultural sphere,[15] even if the international legal framework has moved away from the remnants of the age of toleration towards the concept of religious and philosophical freedom.

The freedom of religion or belief is also a symmetrical human right, meaning it applies to all and is not reserved for (religious) minorities. Indeed, the Universal Declaration and the UN International Covenant on Civil and Political Rights (1966) signified a rupture from the route taken in the League of Nations (1919):

> One issue in the debates on the League was whether religious freedom should be specified in the treaty, and whether it should include minority rights. Both questions were

[9] ibid, 265–266.

[10] ibid, 277.

[11] See J Ringelheim, 'Athéisme et liberté de conscience en droit international des droits de l'homme' (2011) XIX *Quaderni di Diritto e Politica Ecclesiastica* 33.

[12] van der Ven, *Human rights or religious rules?*, n 23 above, 280. Van der Ven considers for this reason that religious freedom is 'indicative of a more advanced civilization'.

[13] The treatment of Scientology is a case in point; while Scientology is recognised as a religion (with some tax-exempt benefits) in the United States or EU countries like Italy and Spain, Germany refuses to consider it a religion but rather as a business. The argument is thus that freedom of religion applies to all religions, and Scientology is simply not a religion, but this in essence comes down to limiting the freedom of religion or belief to less controversial (religious) movements.

[14] The same could be said about those who advocate abandoning the freedom of religion at a time when new minority religions in Europe desperately need protection against public and private interference and can benefit from meaningful accommodation.

[15] When issues of religious freedom are discussed in the popular press, the idea and (much more limiting) discourse on 'tolerance' is never far away: eg T Dernstädt, 'Religious Tradition or Political Symbol? Muslim headscarves Test the Limits of German Tolerance', *Spiegel Online*, 20 June 2008.

answered negatively because of their interrelationship. Religious freedom was considered an issue for minorities—the majority's religion required no such safeguard—and granting this right along with others was seen as incurring the risk of national and international conflict. Instead a system of separate treaties was instituted between Allies and a number of East European countries, including Poland with its large Jewish minority. However, the inconsistency and uneven application lead to mounting protests, and in 1934 Poland abandoned the system, precipitating its collapse.[16]

At the inception of the United Nations, this communitarian and minority rights approach to religious freedom made way for an individual rights interpretation anchored in Article 18 of the Universal Declaration of Human Rights (1948).[17] Again, in the conception of the 1966 International Covenant on Civil and Political Rights (ICCPR), minority rights are derivative of individual rights in various areas such as language, culture and religion.[18]

Despite the textual clarity as to the existence of a universal right to freedom of religion or belief and other human rights, one cannot deny that human rights remain predominantly relevant for minorities, since in general '[t]he majority can take care of itself, and does so in legislation, administration and jurisprudence'.[19]

A similar discussion can be had about a right to reasonable accommodation on the basis of religion or belief. Is such accommodation a universal, symmetrical (human) right or is it rather a right reserved for religious minorities?

Reasonable accommodation will be most relevant for religious minorities across Europe. However, this need not always be the case, as various high-profile legal cases involving Christians seeking accommodation (and often pinpointing more favourable treatment of Muslims and Sikhs) illustrate.[20] Also, the minority status is multi-faceted, relative and continuously shifting. In a recent UK case a woman was fired after taking All Hallows' Eve (Hallowe'en) off work to attend a Wiccan ceremony.[21] Interestingly, her employers, who allegedly ridiculed her way of life,[22]

---

[16] van der Ven, *Human rights or religious rules?*, n 23 above, 229, 244–45. Historically 'Religious freedom was the freedom of minorities, evidenced by the following examples: ... Peace of Augsburg (1555) and the Peace of Westphalia (1648); the Union of Utrecht (*Unie van Utrecht* 1589) and the Declaration of Independence (*Plakkaat van Verlatinghe* 1591) ... Edict of Nantes (1598) ... lastly, the French Constitution of 1791, which granted religious freedom not only to Protestant but also to Jewish, Islamic, and Chinese minorities ... religious freedom was not needed for the majority but for the minority group or minorities'. See also Malcolm D Evans, *Religious liberty and international law in Europe* (Cambridge University Press, 1997) 83–171

[17] See J Morsink, *The Universal Declaration of Human Rights* (Philadelphia, University of Pennsylvania Press, 1999) 241–52; see also M Evans, *Religious Liberty and International Law in Europe* (Cambridge University Press, 1997) 177–83.

[18] P Weller, *The rights of minorities in Europe* (Oxford University Press, 2005) 77–96. The appeal of minority rights really took hold after the fall of the Berlin wall, after the collapse of the Soviet bloc and the various conflicts in the Balkans.

[19] van der Ven, *Human rights or religious rules?*, n 23 above, 7.

[20] eg *Eweida* case, below.

[21] P Bentley, 'Witch sacked for taking Halloween off work to attend Wiccan ceremony wins £15,000 after claiming religious discrimination', *Daily Mail*, 13 December 2013 (case of Karen Holland).

[22] They allegedly asked her if modern day witches could fly on broom sticks. The employers denied this and argued the dismissal was due to her stealing a magazine and lottery ticket.

were Sikhs, so that it becomes clear that religious minorities are not only beneficiaries of legal tools (here, non-discrimination law) but should also be considered addressees who may at some point be called on to accommodate employees. Even today in certain employment settings with a high concentration of Muslim or other workers of particular religions, Christians or non-believers who otherwise would not be considered a minority at a national level, may find themselves in a situation calling for reasonable accommodation. Therefore, to consider reasonable accommodation a general, symmetrical right which can benefit any employee— Christian, non-believer, Muslim, Sikh, Jew, or otherwise—is vital.

Accommodation can be conceptualised within the human rights framework, as being mandated by the fundamental right to freedom or religion or belief. However, before intrinsically linking the two one must take into account the fact that this framework and the place of religious freedom is itself not uncontroversial.[23] In other words: (what) does reasonable accommodation stand to gain by an absorption into the human rights framework? One overarching— but rarely addressed—issue is whether, and to what extent, the population at large in the West still subscribes to the religious freedom.[24] Even if the actual abolition of this internationally enshrined right may not be nascent, one can expect dwindling political and public support to translate itself into waning and weakening protection for religious 'special rights' on the ground. Indeed, human rights are not isolated from the spirit of the age, and the human right to freedom of religion seems to find itself in the eye of the storm: 'When the spirit of the age is secularized, so is religious freedom. Against this background, advocating religious minority rights resembles the pursuit of an illusory utopia'.[25]

It is notable that in all three countries which I have reviewed, various scholars and opinion-makers have argued that the right to freedom of religion as it now stands needs to be abolished and absorbed into the more 'general' freedom of expression.[26] Some are able to admit that would actually entail some loss, but see no good justification for the (continued) special treatment of religion. Others may not go as far as to ask that religious freedom should be struck out altogether,

[23] Human rights 'are said to be products of Western individualism, centering on self-concern and personal profit, with little regard for social relations or commitment to the community': van der Ven, *Human rights or religious rules?*, n 23 above, 3.
[24] See ibid, 11 et seq (presenting results from empirical data amongs three groups of youths in the Netherlands). B Vermeulen, 'Waarom de vrijheid van godsdienst in de Grondwet moet blijven' (2008) 65 *Socialisme en democratie: Maandblad van de Wiardi Beckman Stichting* 17, speaks of 'dominant forces in the Dutch society that are of the opinion that religion as such is outdated and in a modern society should be relegated to and contained in the private sphere' (own translation).
[25] van der Ven, *Human rights or religious rules?*, n 23 above, 243.
[26] Some examples include Patrick Loobuyck (Belgium); Paul Cliteur; Paul de Beer (the Netherlands). The same discussion has taken place in the US, see Christopher L Eisgruber and Lawrence G Sager, *Religious Freedom and the Constitution* (Cambridge MA, Harvard University Press, 2010); WC Durham Jr, 'Against Free Exercise Reductionism', *ICLARS Religious Freedom Discussion Series*, 20 March 2013 (offering counterarguments for such argued redundancy at both national and international levels which are a testimony to the 'paradigm shift from freedom to equality norms as the deep structure of human rights').

but by specific proposals for measures, do promote dilution of the protection for the freedom of religion. For instance, in the Netherlands, the Dutch People's Party for Freedom and Democracy (*Volkspartij voor Vrijheid en Democratie* (VVD)) proposed that 'in cases of collision between religious freedom and the prohibition of discrimination, the latter merits preference if the relevant interpersonal differences arise from factors beyond the person's control because they are of physical nature'.[27] This means that gender and sexual orientation merit elevated protection and, in all circumstances, will override freedom of religion or belief notwithstanding any specifically compelling factors in given cases. The resolute rejection of any balancing exercise when religion, amongst other issues, is at stake is an evocative signal of the interpretation of human rights that seems to resonate with the times when anxieties over religious home-grown and imported religious fundamentalism and terrorism are at a boiling point. But this mode of argumentation is misguided and can be counter-productive, as it works against inclusion and participation and breeds resentment amongst minorities that feel targeted. Thus, from the point of view of accommodation proponents, there are at least two concerns with regard to human rights to take note of: first, the public legitimacy of freedom of religion and, secondly, the protective potential of the freedom of religion in practice. When these factors are not particularly strong, eg relevant jurisprudence is so watered down that mere lip-service is paid to its role, it may not help the accommodation cause to anchor it (solely) in human rights or freedom of religion terms. This concern is pressing in the debate on clashing fundamental rights where the freedom of religion often plays an important role.

C. Early Developments under International Law to Horizontalisation of Human Rights

In *The Last Utopia*, Harvard historian Samuel Moyn argues that the success of the contemporary human rights movement is due to the failure of other great ideologies such as communism and nationalism.[28] He takes issue with scholars who have traced the roots and foundations of human rights to the distant past, creating imaginary precursors. Indeed, others have noted the link and overlap between religion and human rights or see the roots of human rights in religious convictions.[29] Moyn maintains that human rights are a relatively recent invention,

---

[27] VVD, *Om de vrijheid, partijprogramma*, 2005; VVD, *Voor een samenleving met ambitie*, 2006.

[28] S Moyn, *The Last Utopia: Human Rights in History* (Belknap Harvard, 2012) 4–5.

[29] eg van der Ven, *Human rights or religious rules?*, n 23 above, 136 et seq (describing the development of human rights starting from premodernity (the work of Thomas Van Aquino in the 13th century and the British Magna Carta of 1215), to early modernity (the Unie van Utrecht 1579) to modernity (the Virginia Bill of Rights of 1776 and the United States Bill of Rights of 1789) to the Universal Declaration of Human Rights of 1948); M De Blois, 'Two Cities in Conflict' in MLP Loenen and JE Goldschmidt (eds), *Religious Pluralism and Human Rights in Europe: Where to Draw the Line?* (Intersentia, 2007) 170–71.

gaining traction only since the 1970s. However one may regard the foundation of human rights, early on in the development of international law the link between religion and human rights was consciously blurred. This started with the 1948 Universal Declaration of Human Rights (UDHR); the Commission headed by US first lady Eleanor Roosevelt prepared a text that, whilst open to any foundation, lacked any reference to religious or worldview-related foundations.[30] The Universal Declaration follows the well-known 'four freedoms' structure (two freedoms *of* and two freedoms *from*) in US President Roosevelt's 1941 historic State of the Union address to Congress; that is, the freedom of speech and *of belief*, and the freedom from fear and from want.[31] The second freedom was formulated as the 'freedom of every person to worship God in his own way—everywhere in the world'.[32] Thus, the freedom of religion (as freedom *of belief*) was seen as a 'freedom of' and not as a 'freedom from'. The preamble to the UDHR refers not to 'freedom to worship God', but instead to the 'freedom of belief'. Also, religious thought, conscience, and belief were put on par with non-religious thought, conscience and belief in Article 18 of the UDHR.

Julie Ringelheim, discussing the origin of the protection of atheism as 'belief' under international law, notes that various human rights declarations adopted at the end of the eighteenth century—including the United States First Amendment—only speak of the freedom of religion, and not of conscience in general 'as in the contemporary sense of protecting both religious and non-religious convictions'.[33] The idea of freedom of conscience, separated from any religious foundations but rather based on moral capacities and reason, was only developed in the nineteenth century in (French) political thought, with 'the freedom of atheists and the indifferent becoming a major theme in their reflection'.[34] This led to the French Act of 9 December 1905 related to the separation of church and state, declaring the 'freedom of conscience' more generally and the free exercise

[30] J Morsink, *the Universal Declaration of Human Rights: Origins, Drafting and Intent* (Philadelphia PA, University of Pennsylvania Press, 1999); van der Ven, *Human rights or religious rules?*, n 23 above, 161; The Declaration is thus a 'foundation-open' (*begründungsoffen*) text which does not mean it is value-free.

[31] van der Ven, *Human rights or religious rules?*, n 23 above, 147. ('The Declaration spells out the four freedoms in 30 articles, each dealing with one or more human rights, without any further classification, although they are frequently grouped into categories, also known as generations').

[32] See www.archives.gov/exhibits/powers_of_persuasion/four_freedoms/four_freedoms.html: ('At a time when Western Europe lay under Nazi domination, Roosevelt presented a vision in which the American ideals of individual liberties were extended throughout the world. Alerting Congress and the nation to the necessity of war, Roosevelt articulated the ideological aims of the conflict').

[33] Ringelheim, 'Athéisme et liberté de conscience en droit international des droits de l'homme', n 26 above, 2; the Belgian constitution of 1831 only speaks of the freedom to worship in Art 19 ('La liberté des cultes, celle de leur exercice public ... sont guaranties'), and the more general freedom of belief is not explicitly mentioned since it was so obvious it was not felt necessary to be explicitly mentioned. It may also have been the influence of the ninetheenth-century French Constitutions, in particular Art 26 of the French Constitution of 1852 which, as Ringelheim notes also referred to 'liberté de culte'.

[34] Ringelheim, ibid, 3.

of religion as a particular instance of that.[35] From then onward, in contemporary human rights instruments since the twentieth century, freedom of religion is conceived as part of a broader freedom of conscience and thought.[36] What also played an undeniable role in highlighting the need for protection of non-religious, and even anti-religious, beliefs and practices was the presence of the Soviet Union at the table.[37]

At UN level, there is no separate international treaty devoted to the protection of freedom of religion and belief, but the first international legal instrument devoted fully to the freedom of religion was the Declaration on the Elimination of all Forms of Intolerance and Discrimination Based on Religion or Belief of 1981.[38] Despite issues regarding its foundation, the role and significance of human rights has undoubtedly grown considerably, not in the least in the Western world.

The 'horizontalisation' of human rights has played a crucial role in this regard.[39] Human rights were initially seen as necessary protections against the power of the state, which stands in a vertical relationship with citizens.[40] Non-state actors were not the addressees of human rights norms. Of course, countries can (and do) give protection to 'civil and political rights in the private sphere through ordinary law like torts, contracts, property law etc. based on common law or civil law codes or statutory provisions'.[41] Non-discrimination law or labour law is a case in point. But in addition to such tools targeting non-state actors, through various techniques human rights law was expanded towards horizontal relations between private (non-state) actors, including between private employers and their employees:

> While traditionally it has been understood that citizens require legal protection against state excesses, today it is being widely recognized that citizens also need protection against abuses of power by private bodies. In this globalised world, multinational corporations have emerged as powerful entities ... Moreover, in this era public-private partnerships for the delivery of services like housing, education and health, identified as a shift from government to governance are very common. This makes the traditional

---

[35] 'Le République assure la liberté de conscience. Elle garantit le libre exercise des cultes' (Art 1 French Act of 9 December 1905 related to the separation of Church and State).

[36] Article 18 of the Declaration states in part that (in French) 'Toute personne a droit à la liberté de pensée, de conscience et de religion; ce droit implique la liberté de changer de religion ou de conviction ainsi que la liberté de manifester sa religion ou sa *conviction*'. Ringelheim notes the role that the French delegate, René Cassin, played in having the more neutral term 'convictions' adopted instead of 'croyance'. Ringelheim, 'Athéisme et liberté de conscience en droit international des droits de l'homme', n 26 above, 4–5. However, Cassin's proposal to leave out religion as this was already covered under thought and conscience was not adopted.

[37] For belief cases at the ECtHR level, see *Lautsi v Italy*, Application no 30814/06 (ECtHR, 18 March 2011) and *Arrowsmith v United Kingdom*, Application no 7050/75 (EComHR, 12 October 1978).

[38] UN Doc A/36/51 (1982).

[39] R Goswami, 'Human rights and the private sphere: a comparative analysis' (2008) 1 *National University of Juridical Sciences Law Review* 185.

[40] J Krzeminska-Vamvaka, 'Horizontal effect of fundamental rights and freedoms–much ado about nothing? German, Polish and EU theories compared after Viking Line' (Jean Monnet Working Paper 2009), available at: centers.law.nyu.edu.

[41] Goswami, 'Human rights and the private sphere: a comparative analysis', n 54 above, 187.

distinctions between state and non-state bodies problematic. In such a context human rights protection of citizens against such powerful entities becomes an imperative.[42]

Under the ECHR, only state parties can be brought before the ECtHR. But through the construction of positive state treaty obligations, actions by private parties, such as employers, can be brought *against the state*. This may be regarded as an indirect and cumbersome way of addressing the real issue at hand, but at times it can work. For instance, in the joint case of *Obst and Schüth v Germany*,[43] Mr Obst—the director of the Public Relations Department of the Mormon Church in Europe— argued that his (faith-based) employer violated his right to respect for private life (Article 8 ECHR) by dismissing him for committing adultery in his private life, which was in breach of a term in his employment contract requiring marital fidelity. The Court addressed the issue of applicability of Convention rights as towards non-state, private parties via the positive obligations of the state under treaty provisions:

> [T]he applicant has not complained of an action by the State but of a failure on its part to protect his private sphere against interference by his employer [the Mormon Church, which does not exercise public authority of any kind in Germany] … although the object of Article 8 is essentially that of *protecting the individual against arbitrary interference by the public authorities*, it does not merely compel the State to abstain from such interference: in addition to this primarily negative undertaking, *there may be positive obligations inherent in an effective respect for private life.* These obligations may involve the adoption of measures designed to secure respect for private life even in the sphere of the relations of individuals between themselves. *The boundaries between the State's positive and negative obligations under Article 8 do not lend themselves to precise definition,* but the *applicable principles are nonetheless similar* (emphasis added).[44]

When 'putting in place both a system of employment tribunals and a constitutional court having jurisdiction to review their decisions' the state 'in theory complied with its positive obligations towards citizens in the area of employment law', and the ECtHR evaluates whether or not the conclusions drawn by the employment tribunals were unreasonable.[45] In the case at hand, the German state was not considered to have violated the margin of appreciation; taking into account the important position Mr Obst occupied in the Church, which justified a heightened duty of loyalty, the employment tribunal had struck a fair balance between various

---

[42] ibid, 185.

[43] *Obst and Schüth v Germany*, Applications nos 1620/03 and 425/03 (ECtHR, 23 September 2010); In the *Schüth* case of the same date the applicant, an organist and choirmaster at a Catholic church, was successful in his claim. Both cases involve Churches as employers, thus fall outside the scope of this analysis, but they are discussed as illustrative of the approach of the ECtHR when the applicant is bringing the case against the State for a violation by a non-state employer.

[44] *Obst and Schüth v Germany*, Application nos 1620/03 and 425/03 (ECtHR, 23 September 2010), paras 40–41, 43.

[45] *Obst and Schüth v Germany*, Application nos 1620/03 and 425/03 (ECtHR, 23 September 2010), para 45 and para 50 (held that the conclusions drawn by the German employment tribunal, holding in favour of the employer the Mormon Church, was not unreasonable).

competing interests.[46] Thus, the Court has developed an extensive reasoning assessing the positive duty of the state under Article 8 in the case of a non-public labour law dispute, and did not reject the case merely because there was, at first sight, no talk of a state action.

Similarly, when the dispute centres on the role of religion in the secular workplace the positive obligations of the state are assessed.

> Where ... the acts complained of were carried out by private companies and were not therefore directly attributable to the respondent State, the Court must consider the issues in terms of the positive obligation on the State authorities to secure the rights under Article 9 to those within their jurisdiction.[47]

The Court is essentially called upon to decide '*to what extent ... the Government [should] impose a reasonable policy to accommodate different religious beliefs, convictions and practices in the workplace*' (emphasis added).[48] In order to fall within the margin of appreciation, domestic courts must have conducted a thorough balancing of the various interests concerned, including giving due weight to the fundamental rights of the employee.[49]

II. The European Convention on Human Rights and the ECtHR

A. Article 9 ECHR and Religion or Belief in the Workplace: Overview

Echoing the UDHR and the ICCPR, Article 9 ECHR states:

> 1. Everyone has the right to freedom of thought, conscience and religion; this right includes freedom to change his religion or belief and freedom, either alone or in community with others and in public or private, to manifest his religion or belief, in worship, teaching, practice and observance.
>
> 2. Freedom to manifest one's religion or beliefs shall be subject only to such limitations as are prescribed by law and are necessary in a democratic society in the interests of public safety, for the protection of public order, health or morals, or for the protection of the rights and freedoms of others.

---

[46] *Obst and Schüth v Germany*, Application nos 1620/03 and 425/03 (ECtHR, 23 September 2010), para 52.

[47] *Eweida and Others v United Kingdom* (ECtHR 13 January 2013), para 84.

[48] Council of Europe, *Overview of the Court's case-law on Freedom of Religion* (CoE Research Division, updated October 2013) 22.

[49] See, eg, *Siebenhaar v Germany*, Application no 18136/02 (ECtHR, 3 February 2011). In this case the dismissal of a Catholic child-care provider working for a Protestant parish for reason of belonging to another church was considered necessary to preserve the Church's credibility.

Under Article 14 of the Convention, the prohibition of discrimination—including on the basis of religion or belief—is limited to the areas of enjoyment of other rights provided by the Convention.[50]

Article 9 ECHR protects the freedom of thought, conscience and religion in its two core facets, the *forum internum* and the *forum externum*. The *forum internum* refers to the right to have inner thoughts and beliefs and as this is absolute, the state cannot intervene with it. The *forum externum*, on the other hand, refers to expressions[51] or manifestations of inner convictions in public and private spheres. There is significance in this duality, which some see as a product of Christian theology, where the focus is on orthodoxy rather than orthopraxy.[52] Further, Article 9 ECHR not only *distinguishes* between beliefs and practices/manifestations, but it also *prioritises* the *forum internum* over the *forum externum*. In *Kokkinakis v Greece*, the Court, while emphasising the holistic understanding of the freedom of religion or belief, implied this hierarchy by noting that '[w]hile religious freedom is *primarily* a matter of individual conscience, it also implies, inter alia, freedom to "manifest [one's] religion". Bearing witness in words and deeds is bound up with the existence of religious convictions'.[53] This ordering, however, may feel very unnatural and counter-intuitive to practitioners of certain minority religions that have now made their way into Europe. As Lucy Vickers has noted:

> In religious traditions with a focus on orthopraxy, codes of conduct related to attire, diet and prayer are more common and have much greater significance as ways to practice and observe the religion. In many cases it is these practices which then lead to conflict with the secular world.[54]

While the protection for inner thoughts and beliefs is 'absolute' and no interference is accepted,[55] acts of 'worship, teaching, practice and observance' which bring

---

[50] Protocol No 12 to the Convention for the Protection of Human Rights and Fundamental Freedoms (ETS No 177), adopted on 4 November 2000, in contrast entails a freestanding discrimination provision. The Protocol is in force in only 17 Council of Europe countries, including the Netherlands (since 2005) but has not been ratified by Belgium or the UK.

[51] In light of the general protection for freedom of expression in Art10 ECHR, Art 9 ECHR can be considered *lex specialis*; Malcolm Evans, 'From Cartoons to Crucifixes: Current Controversies Concerning the Freedom of Religion and the Freedom of Expression before the European Court of Human Rights' (2011) 26 *Journal of Law and Religion* 345, 368 (noting that religious manifestations as forms of expressions require additional protection to be meaningful).

[52] L Vickers, 'The relationship between religious diversity and secular models: an equality-based perspective' in MC Foblets et al (eds), *Belief, Law and Politics What Future for a Secular Europe?* (Aldershot, Ashgate, 2014) 2. J Spinner-halev, 'Liberalism and Religion: Against Congruence' (2008) 9 *Theoretical Inquiries in Law* 563, referring to Gavin Flood, *An Introduction to Hinduism* (1996) ('Hinduism is a religion centered around practice much more than belief and morality',)

[53] See *Kokkinakis v Greece*, Application no 14307/88 (ECtHR, 25 May 1993), para 31. See also *Metropolitan Church of Bessarabia and Others v Moldova*, Application no 45701/99 (ECtHR, 13 December 2001), para 114.

[54] Vickers, 'The relationship between religious diversity and secular models: an equality-based perspective', n 67 above, 2.

[55] 'No one can be subject to coercion which would impair his or her freedom to have or to adopt a religion or belief of his or her choice'. See Council of Europe, 'Overview of the Court's case law on freedom of religion', n 63 above, 4.

those beliefs to expression can be limited in accordance with Article 9(2) as long as they are 'prescribed by law' and 'necessary in a democratic society in the interest of public safety, for the protection of public order, health or morals, or for the protection of the rights and freedoms of others'.[56] *'Necessary in a democratic society'* means that there must be a *pressing social need*:[57] 'thus, the notion "necessary" does not have the flexibility of such expressions as "useful" or "desirable".'[58] In the employment relations context, the 'rights of others' includes the right of employers, colleagues and customers who value the negative aspect of religious freedom, ie the right to be free from religion and to work or have services delivered in a 'neutral' or non-religious setting.[59] However, drawing this out could essentially negate the freedom of religion of the employee in circumstances where it is most needed. Furthermore, any interference with the basic freedom must be proportionate to the legitimate aim pursued.

Accordingly, even apart from applications in particular cases, limitations to the enjoyment the freedom of religion (and (most) other human rights) are ingrained in the human rights system,[60] the formulation of Article 9(2) ECHR itself being such that it offers potential justification for the limitation of religious liberties.[61] 'Article 9 of the Convention protects a person's private sphere of conscience but not necessarily any public conduct inspired by that conscience'.[62] In particular, limitations can be the effect of tensions or clashes between various (or the same) human rights ('freedoms of others'), eg the right to equal treatment on the basis of gender, sexual orientation or religion/belief versus the freedom of religion, or the freedom of religion of X (collective dimension) versus the freedom of religion of Y (individual).[63] In such cases, where 'the State is required to strike a balance

---

[56] Article 9.2 of the ECHR; Emmanuel Bribosia, Isabelle Chopin and Isabelle Rorive, *Rapport de synthèse relatif aux signes d'appartenance religieuse dans quinze pays de l'Union européenne* (2004) 24 (noting that while secularism is not included in this list, it de facto sweeps in).

[57] See, *Kokkinakis v Greece*, Application no 14307/88 (ECtHR, 25 May 1993) (no such pressing social need to convict a member of Jehovah's Witness for proselytism).

[58] See Council of Europe, 'Overview of the Court's case law on freedom of religion', n 63 above, p 19, referring to *Svyato-Mykhaylivska Parafiya v Ukraine*, Application no 77703/01, 14 June, § 116.

[59] Vickers, *Religious freedom, religious discrimination, and the workplace*, n 6 above, 102.

[60] FM Gedicks, 'The Permissible Scope of Legal Limitations on the Freedom of Religion or Belief in the United States' (2005) 19 *Emory International Law Review* 1187–275 (noting that the 'permissible scope' of 'legal limitations' on freedom of religion is the European 'syntax', and 'The American law of limitations on freedom of religion is not easily stated in this grammar, because freedom of religion in the United States is less a liberty right than an equality right').

[61] Article 9(2) ECHR states that the *freedom to manifest one's religion or beliefs* is subject to such limitations 'as are prescribed by law and are necessary in a democratic society in the interests of public safety, for the protection of public order, health or morals, or the protection of the rights and freedoms of others'.

[62] Council of Europe Europe, 'Overview of the Court's case law on freedom of religion', n 63 above, 8.

[63] Emmanuel Bribosia and Isabelle Rorive, *In search of a balance between the right to equality and other fundamental rights* (European Network of Legal Experts in the non-discrimination field, 2010).

between competing private and public interests or different Convention rights', there is a wide margin of appreciation.[64]

The ECtHR has developed its case law on freedom of religion or belief through-out the years in a non-linear fashion. Through the Court's case law, freedom of religion was first indirectly and then more directly 'elevated' to the level of a substantive right under the Convention. In *Moscow Branch of the Salvation Army v Russia* (2006), the Court stressed both the importance of the rights protected by Article 9 and the limits to the state's right to interfere:

> Article 9, the freedom of thought, conscience and religion is one of the foundations of a 'democratic society' within the meaning of the Convention. It is, in its religious dimen-sion, one of the most vital elements that go to make up the identity of believers and their conception of life, but it is also a precious asset for atheists, agnostics, sceptics and the unconcerned. The pluralism indissociable from a democratic society, which has been dearly won over the centuries, depends on it.[65]

The European Court has talismanically repeated this paragraph.[66] But it has also stressed that in diverse democratic societies restrictions on the freedom to mani-fest one's religion or belief may be necessary to reconcile the interests of various groups.[67] In the last decade, due to the increasing role of religion in the socio-political sphere noted in the introduction, Article 9 cases have been on the rise and challenges are thus taking shape in case law.

For a long time, the significance of Article 9 ECHR, whether or not in combina-tion with Article 14 ECHR,[68] remained insignificant when it came to accommo-dation issues in the 'voluntary setting' of the mainstream workplace. As noted by Lord Bingham in an important UK House of Lords case concerning the regulation of religious dress (the jilbab) in public schools:

> The Strasbourg institutions have not been at all ready to find an interference with the right to manifest a religious belief in practice or observance where a person has volun-tarily accepted an employment or role which does not accommodate that practice or observance.[69]

---

[64] See *Obst and Schüth v Germany*, Application no 1620/03 and 425/03 (ECtHR, 23 September 2010) para 42.

[65] *Moscow Branch of the Salvation Army v Russia*, Application no 72881/01 (ECtHR, 5 October 2006) para 57 (references omitted). The court explained its view of pluralism at para 61: 'pluralism is also built on the genuine recognition of, and respect for, diversity and the dynamics of cultural traditions, ethnic and cultural identities, religious beliefs, artistic, literary and socio-economic ideas and concepts. The harmonious interaction of persons and groups with varied identities is essential for achieving social cohesion'.

[66] *Kokkinakis v Greece*, Application no 14307/88 (ECtHR, 25 May 1993) para 31.

[67] *Kokkinakis v Greece*, Application no 14307/88 (ECtHR, 25 May 1993) para 31 and *Leyla Şahin v Turkey*, Application no 44774/98 (ECtHR, 10 November 2005) para 106.

[68] Article 14 ECHR is broad since it contains an open-ended list of discrimination grounds, but its scope is limited since it only prohibits discrimination with respect to rights under the Convention. It states 'The enjoyment of the rights and freedoms set forth in this Convention shall be secured without discrimination on any ground such as sex, race, colour, language, religion, political or other opinion, national or social origin, association with a national minority, property, birth or other status'.

[69] *R (SB) v Governors of Denbigh High School* [2006] UKHL 15, (2006) 23 BHRC 276, para 2. Inter-estingly in the *Eweida* decision the ECtHR considers (and re-evaluates) this statement explicitly.

Certainly, in a number of cases the ECtHR found a violation of the right to religious liberty and/or discrimination in employment settings. In particular, in the pivotal *Thlimmenos v Greece*,[70] the Court found a violation of Article 14 ECHR taken in conjunction with Article 9 ECHR. The applicant was a member of the Jehovah's Witnesses and was refused appointment to a post of chartered accountant because of his criminal conviction for conscientiously objecting to military service at a time of general mobilisation without exemption for conscientious objectors. The ECtHR considered that he was treated differently from other applicants for the post:

> The Court considers that such difference of treatment does not generally come within the scope of Article 14 in so far as it relates to access to a particular profession, the right to freedom of profession not being guaranteed by the Convention.

> However, the applicant does not complain of the distinction that the rules governing access to the profession make between convicted persons and others. His complaint rather concerns the fact that in the application of the relevant law no distinction is made between persons convicted of offences committed exclusively because of their religious beliefs and persons convicted of other offence … *Seen in this perspective, the Court accepts* that the 'set of facts' complained of by the applicant … 'falls within the ambit of a Convention provision' (emphasis added).[71]

In other words, it was the particular *framing* in an occupational setting (but not a traditional employment relationship) that was successful for applicant. *Thlimmenos* is sometimes credited with having introduced to the case law of the ECtHR the notion of 'indirect discrimination'[72] and even of reasonable accommodation by stressing a positive state duty under Article 9 ECHR. However, those terms were never utilised by the Court. The Greek government had argued that the law in question, disqualifying the claimant from civil posts on account of his criminal conviction, was 'neutral' and 'served the public interest', but the Court held that there can be circumstances which call for differential treatment and this was one of those situations. Announcing the innovating element in the case, the Court explained:

> The Court has so far considered that the right under Article 14 not to be discriminated against in the enjoyment of the rights guaranteed under the Convention is violated when States treat differently persons in analogous situations without providing an objective and reasonable justification … However, the Court considers that *this is not the only facet of the prohibition of discrimination in Article 14.* The right not to be discriminated against in the enjoyment of the rights guaranteed under the Convention is *also violated when*

---

[70] *Thlimmenos v Greece*, Application no 34369/97 (ECtHR, 6 April 2000).

[71] *Thlimmenos v Greece*, Application no 34369/97 (ECtHR, 6 April 2000) paras 41–42.

[72] See K Henrard, 'A Critical Appraisal of the Margin of Appreciation Left to States Pertaining to "Church-State Relations" under the Jurisprudence of the European Court of Human Rights' in K Alidadi, MC Foblets and J Vrielink (eds), *A Test of Faith? Religious Diversity and Accommodation in the European Workplace* (Aldershot, Ashgate, 2012) 81.

States without an objective and reasonable justification fail to treat differently persons whose situations are significantly different (emphasis added).[73]

Following Aristotle's formulae, formal equality mandates that equals are to be treated equally, but also implies that differential treatment is called for in cases where there can be no talk of equals/equal situations.[74] The difficulty is knowing when the situation of persons is *significantly different* to justify or mandate differential treatment because in reality there are no absolute equals; not even twins are identical in every aspect. *Thlimmenos* offers one example where the religious motivation behind an action justifies differential treatment. In this sense, it comes very close to the concepts of indirect discrimination and reasonable accommodation,[75] which are associated with a substantive equality approach, but the formulation used agrees very well with a formal conception of equality as well.[76] After all, the second limb of the Aristotelian equality concept prohibits unalike cases from being treated similarly, and the 'group-based disparate impact analysis', which is the typical corollary of an indirect discrimination analysis, played no role in *Thlimmenos*.[77]

In any case, the *Thlimmenos* approach has not been extended to cases of religious accommodation in the workplace. This is not to say Article 9 ECHR was entirely meaningless in the employment context: on occasion a violation was found in straightforward religious (affiliation) discrimination cases. In *Ivanova*,[78] Article 9 was held breached after a claimant was fired from her position as a swimming pool manager at a public school after *refusing to resign or renounce her faith under pressure*. Ms Ivanova was a member of a Christian Evangelical Group known as 'Word of Life', which was refused legal recognition by the Bulgarian State and which—as the Court noted—was subject to a 'policy of intolerance on the part of the authorities'. Here the Court saw that 'at the heart of the applicant's case was whether her employment had been terminated solely ... because of her religious beliefs' (emphasis added).[79]

---

[73] *Thlimmenos v Greece*, Application no 34369/97 (ECtHR, 6 April 2000) para 44.

[74] In fact, Aristotle is to have said that inequality arises 'when either equals are awarded unequal shares or unequals, equal shares'.

[75] L Waddington, 'Chapter six: reasonable accommodation' in D Schiek, L Waddington and M Bell (eds), *Cases, materials and text on national, supranational and international non-discrimination law* (Oxford, Hart Publishing, 2007) 747 ('the reasonable accommodation requirement of the law recognises that, where people's impairments or relevant characteristics result in them being differently situated regarding employment opportunities, identical treatment may be a source of discrimination, and different treatment may be required to eliminate it. Recognition of this need for real, not merely formal equality is the basis of the obligation to make individualized adjustments to permit particular individuals to participate in particular employment-related activities').

[76] See also discussion of the *Thlimmenos* case by M Bell, 'Chapter two: direct discrimination' in D Schiek, L Waddington and M Bell (eds), *Cases, materials and text on national, supranational and international non-discrimination law* (Oxford, Hart Publishing, 2007) 189–90.

[77] ibid, 190. It should be noted that the concept of indirect discrimination is developed in other ECtHR cases, in particular, *DH and Others v Czech Republic*, Application no 57235/00 (ECtHR, 7 February 2006).

[78] *Ivanova v Bulgaria*, Application no 52435/99 (ECtHR, 12 April 2007).

[79] *Ivanova v Bulgaria*, Application no 52435/99 (ECtHR, 12 April 2007) para 81.

On the other hand, the Court (following the former Commission) rather easily dismisses religious *accommodation* cases, where requests involve time off to observe religious duties or holidays or the right to wear religious dress, even if those requests were for very modest adaptations having negligible costs at most. Either no interference was found with Article 9, often with the filter of 'freedom to resign'[80] blocking successful claims, or when a case did pass the admissibility test, a broad margin of appreciation or a very meek justification test deferred to the state restricting religious manifestations.[81]

B. Facing the Restraints of Time: Religious Time Claims before the ECtHR

The 'freedom to resign' filter, blocking claims, was repeatedly utilised in a line of religious time cases, such as *X v United Kingdom*, *Konttinen v Finland* and *Stedman v United Kingdom*.[82] In each of these cases, the former European Commission on Human Rights held that the refusal by employers to alter employees' working hours to accommodate religious practices did not interfere with Article 9. The employees were considered 'free to resign' and find an alternative post (eg work part-time) which would not conflict with their religious commitments. Taylor noted that

[e]ven when it is claimed that restrictions conflict with religious observance, the European Commission has been unsympathetic towards applicants who have voluntarily accepted obligations that compromise their observance (*Stedman v United Kingdom*), and has shown its reluctance to accept the applicant's characterisation of such conflict (*Valsamis v Greece*).[83]

---

[80] This doctrine was first used in cases involving personnel of state Churches, such as *X v Denmark* (1976) and *Knudson v Norway* (1985). See Evans, *Freedom of religion under the European Convention on Human Rights*, n 2 above, 84–85.

[81] See S Knights, 'Approaches to Diversity in the Domestic Courts: Article 9 of the European Convention on Human Rights' in R Grillo, R Ballard, A Ferrari, A Hoekema, M Maussen and P Shah (eds), *Legal Practice and Cultural Diversity* (Aldershot, Ashgate, 2009) 283–98; S Ouald Chaib, 'Religious Accommodation in the Workplace: Improving the Legal Reasoning of the European Court of Human Rights' in K Alidadi, MC Foblets and J Vrielink (eds), *A Test of Faith? Religious Diversity and Accommodation in the European Workplace* (Aldershot, Ashgate, 2012) 33–58. On the basis of an extensive case law review of cases between 2000–2010, Ouald Chaib shows this for the two most frequent types of cases, namely those involving requests for time off or alternative scheduling and requests involving religious dress codes, and notes the differences between the two kinds.

[82] *X/Ahmad v United Kingdom*, Application No 8160 /78 (EComHR, 12 March 1981), *Konttinen v Finland*, Application no 24949/94 (EComHR, 3 December 1996) and *Stedman v United Kingdom*, Application no 29107/95 (EComHR, 9 April 1997).

[83] PM Taylor, *Freedom of religion: UN and European human rights law and practice* (Cambridge University Press, 2005) 281–82. In the last case (*Valsamis v Greece* (1997) 24 EHRR 294, Application no 21787/94), the case before the Commission concerned the suspension from school of a Jehovah's Witness student for failure to take part in a school parade on ground of religious beliefs of the pupil and her parents.

The protection for days of rest or holidays was thus insubstantial. What's more, the Strasbourg case law took for granted a public calendar solely based on the majority's holidays, observing as matter of fact in *X/Ahmad v United Kingdom* that

> in respect of the general question of religious and public holidays ... in most countries, only the religious holidays of the majority of the population are celebrated as public holidays. Thus Protestant holidays are not always public holidays in Catholic countries and vice versa.[84]

A holiday schedule coinciding with the religion or cultural practices of the majority is not necessarily a problem,[85] so long as certain accommodations are provided for minorities to observe their days of rest or religious holidays. But, in stark contrast with the approach of the Canadian Supreme Court in *O'Malley v Simpsons-Sears*,[86] which mandated reasonable accommodation for the Saturday Sabbath observers, such accommodation was not considered imperative.

The former Commission's decision in *X v United Kingdom*[87] is illustrative of the formalistic, inflexible approach: a school teacher of Islamic faith working for the Inner London Education Authority (ILEA) sought a (modest) time accommodation to be able to attend collective Friday prayers at the local mosque. The Commission dismissed his claim as inadmissible based on the reasoning that the employer could rely on the terms of the contract the employee had signed and committed to. It also underlined the employee's freedom of choice: he was free to resign if he found his teaching obligations conflicting with his religious duties.[88] Thus, there was little sympathy for the dilemmas faced by the full-time teacher of Muslim faith in a context where work was organised to fit the needs and schedule of the majority only. The teacher had 'of his own free will, accepted teaching obligations under his contract' but his choice was effectively between a rock and a hard place; either follow the regular work schedule which preventing him from fulfilling his religious duty, or quit his job and face the financial and other consequences. In a setting where 'the Christian tradition has had an irreversible effect on the shaping of time and space',[89] the range of options for a practising adherent of a minority religion seemed very limited, making the 'freedom to resign' doctrine—amongst others—ignorant of the larger socio-economic consequences of such a policy.

Similarly, in *Konttinen*,[90] the former Commission found the religious time accommodation claim 'manifestly ill-founded' and thus inadmissible for reason

---

[84] *X/Ahmad v United Kingdom*, Application No 8160 /78 (EComHR, 12 March 1981) at 38.

[85] In fact, this would appear to make practically very good sense. See Art 2(5) European Social Charter (contracting parties to provide a weekly day of rest which as far as possible coincides with the day of rest recognised 'by tradition or custom' in the country or region concerned).

[86] *O'Malley v Simpsons-Sears* [1985] 2 SCR 536.

[87] *X v United Kingdom*, Application no 8160/78 (ECtHR, 12 March 1981), para 13.

[88] ibid, at para 15.

[89] G Davie, 'Is Europe an exceptional case?' (Spring & Summer 2006) *The Hedgehog Review* 24.

[90] *Konttinen v Finland*, Application no 24949/94 (EComHR, 3 December 1996). See also *Stedman v United Kingdom*, Application no 29107/95 (EComHR, 9 April 1997) (involving a Christian who refused to sign a new employment agreement requiring regular work on Sundays).

of lack of interference with claimants' freedom of religion. The claim concerned a member of the Seventh-day Adventist Church who sought to have his work schedule altered so that he need not work on his Sabbath starting from sunset Friday afternoon (which would be the case during working hours on, at the most, five Fridays a year). Again, the Commission noted the contractual commitment the employee was under:

> The applicant was not dismissed because of his religious convictions *but for having refused to respect his working hours*. This refusal, even if motivated by his religious convictions, cannot as such be considered protected by Article 9 ... Nor has the applicant shown that he was pressured to change his religious views or prevented from manifesting his religion or belief ... having found his working hours to conflict with his religious convictions, *the applicant was free to relinquish his post. The Commission regards this as the ultimate guarantee of his right to freedom of religion.*[91]

This line of jurisprudence was—rightly—criticised as too formalistic, with too little appreciation for good faith efforts to reconcile work and religious commitments.[92] It in effect places contractual obligations on a higher footing than the fundamental right to religious freedom. Direct pressure or force to change or abandon one's religion is recognised as a violation of the freedom of religion or belief,[93] but what is ignored are the various pressures *to conform* (which may or may not be as subtle) or forfeit religious practices in the workplace when employees object to a downgrading of their socio-economic situation. These decisions fail to recognise that religious commitments place an employee in a situation that is significantly different than those without such commitment, thus mandating a differential treatment. Some academics expressed hope that Article 9 case law emphasising positive duties in areas other than employment[94] could be applied by the Court in the employment context once a suitable case came along. In 2012, the Court's internal division over the issue of reasonable accommodations for religion or belief became glaringly clear in *Francesco Sessa v Italy*.[95] The applicant was a Jewish attorney representing a civil party in a large criminal case. In the proceedings, he was faced with a hearing date set on one of the most important Jewish holidays (Yom Kippur). Even though there was a legislative basis[96] to rely on for religious time accommodation and the applicant had raised the issue four months before

[91] *Konttinen v Finland* App no 24949/94 (EComHR, 3 December 1996) 9.

[92] Ouald Chaib, 'Religious Accommodation in the Workplace: Improving the Legal Reasoning of the European Court of Human Rights', n 96 above, 33–58.

[93] See also *Ivanova v Bulgaria*, Application no 52435/99 (ECtHR, 12 April 2007).

[94] See, eg, *Jacóbski v Poland*, Application no 18429/06 (ECtHR, 7 December 2010) (prison context); *Konstantin Markin v Russia* Application no 30078/06 (ECtHR, 22 March 2012) (parental leave, military).

[95] *Francesco Sessa v Italy*, Application no 28790/08 (ECtHR, 3 April 2012). Note by Adriaan Overbeeke, (2012) 7 EHRC 1645–56; see also S Ouald Chaib, 'Francesco Sessa v Italy: A Dilemma Majority Religion Members Will Probably Not Face', *Strasbourg observers*, 5 April 2012.

[96] Italian Law nr 101 of 1989 gives Jewish people the right to observe the Sabbath and 15 important religious holidays including Yom Kippur and Sukkoth.

the initial hearing was set, the requests for adjournment were repeatedly rejected by the Italian courts. The European Court found that Article 9 had not been breached; there was no interference and, even if there was, it was proportionate on grounds of the protection of the rights and freedoms of others—in particular the public's right to the proper administration of justice—and the principle that cases be heard within a reasonable time. But what makes a closer look at this case worthwhile is the interesting dissenting opinion. The majority's decision of inadmissibility referred to *Konttinen* and *Stedman* as precedents, but the dissent written by three judges—Tulkens,[97] Popović and Keller—explicitly argued for incorporating a reasonable accommodation duty under Article 9, stressing that that the 'inconvenience' that may have resulted was simply the price that must be paid in a multicultural society that values religious pluralism. The dissent rebuts the majority reasoning quite convincingly: there clearly was an interference with the freedom of religion and, where several alternatives are imaginable to achieve the pursued legitimate aim, the proportionality test requires the authorities to resort to 'the least restrictive means'. *Reasonable accommodation* is seen as such a means in the given circumstances:

> Nous pensons que les conditions étaient réunies pour tenter d'arriver à un aménagement et un aménagement raisonnable—c'est-à-dire qui n'entraîne pas pour les autorités judiciaires une charge disproportionnée—de la situation. Avec quelques concessions, celui-ci aurait permis d'éviter une ingérence dans la liberté religieuse du requérant, sans pour autant compromettre la réalisation du but légitime que constitue de toute évidence la bonne administration de la justice' …
>
> Certes, le report demandé de l'audience pouvait entraîner certains inconvénients administratifs, comme par exemple la nécessité de renouveler la notification de la date d'audience aux parties impliquées. *Mais ceux-ci nous paraissent minimes et constituent peut-être le modique prix à payer pour le respect de la liberté de religion dans une société multiculturelle* (emphasis added).[98]

Ouald Chaib, who considered the case an apt candidate for referral to the Grand Chamber, supports the dissenting opinion:

> Indeed, the question at stake is how far we can go in a multicultural society in accommodating religious minorities. The majority, instead, focuses on how a member of a religious minority should adapt to a societal system based on the majority religion, thus placing the burden of accommodation entirely on the applicant. By not finding interference with the applicant's freedom of religion and by not acknowledging that he is *de facto* treated differently compared to adherents of majority religions, the Court shows little understanding of religious minorities' concerns.[99]

---

[97] In September 2012, Paul Lemmens became the new Belgian judge at the ECtHR as the successor to Françoise Tulkens. See P Lemmens, 'A Grand Lady Leaves the Court', September 2012, Strasbourg Observers' blog.

[98] *Francesco Sessa v Italy*, Application no 28790/08 (ECtHR, 3 April 2012) paras 10 and 13 of dissent.

[99] Ouald Chaib, 'Francesco Sessa v. Italy: A Dilemma Majority Religion Members Will Probably Not Face', *Strasbourg observers*, 5 April 2012.

Not much later, in *Eweida and others v UK*, the Court steered its case law in a more encouraging direction. The 'freedom to resign' doctrine can be considered overruled following *Eweida*, even if the new approach—which takes the consent of the employer into account as one element in the balance between various interests—has not yet been applied in a religious time accommodation case. It will be interesting to see how cases similar to *X/Ahmad v UK* or *Stedman v UK* will be decided in the future. Perhaps, it would go a bit like the *García Mateos* case,[100] which involved a conflict between professional and family life and the question of how a caretaker of a young child was to combine the two. Mrs García Mateos, a supermarket employee, asked for a reduction in her worktime because she had to look after her son, who was then under six years old. This was denied, but the Court found a violation of the principle of non-discrimination on grounds of sex.

C. Religious Dress before the ECtHR: Surrender of the 'Clashing Headscarves' Debate to Member States

While the 'freedom to resign' reasoning effectively gridlocked claims in religion-worktime cases before the Strasbourg institutions, the state's wide 'margin of appreciation' in addressing working conditions restricting the exercise of individuals' religious freedom has been the main obstacle in religious dress cases.[101] The issue of religious dress in private sector employment was only first presented to the ECtHR with the *Eweida* case. Earlier religious dress decisions in education and public employment, however, were indicative of weak protection for religious manifestations through dress under Article 9 ECHR, whether or not in conjunction with Article 14 ECHR.[102] Dress has also been explicitly recognised as a way of manifesting religious beliefs,[103] but the 'rights of others' limitation ground was found to be strengthened by the particular circumstances, and the (former) employee's interests have received limited attention.[104] Concerns about gender equality have also played an important role in these previous dress cases where applicants have predominantly been female, in contrast to religious time cases (where the applicants have typically been male). Moreover, the Court has

---

[100] *García Mateos v Spain*, Application no 38285/09 (ECtHR, 19 February 2013).

[101] Dress can be an element of freedom of expression under Article 8 ECHR, but it has received limited weight under the proportionality test and easily trumped by other rights and principles; see *Kara v United Kingdom*, Application no 36528/97 (EComHR, 22 October 1998) (claim of a cross-dressing man was manifestly ill-founded since it was not considered disproportionate to interfere with expressional rights to protect the right of the employer to carry out a particular image).

[102] For example, *Dahlab v Switzerland*, Application no 42393/98 (ECtHR, 15 February 2001) (public education), *Kurtulmuş v Turkey*, Application no 65500/01 (ECtHR, 24 January 2006) (university professor) and *Kavakçi v Turkey*, Application no 71907/01 (ECtHR, 5 April 2007) (parliament).

[103] *Leyla Şahin v Turkey*, Application no 44774/98 (ECtHR, 10 November 2005); *Ahmet Arslan and Others v Turkey*, Application no 41135/98 (ECtHR, 23 February 2010).

[104] See, eg, *Dahlab v Switzerland*, Application no 42393/98 (ECtHR, 15 February 2001) (noting the influence of a veiled teacher over the emotional and intellectual development of young children).

expressed a number of (highly criticised) opinions on the meaning of the Islamic headscarf and the position of women in Islam.

Two important ECtHR decisions with regard to the headscarf involve a public educational setting. In both cases, the interference could be attributed directly to the state. Interestingly, the Court has not yet ruled on a headscarf issue in favour of the applicant.[105] First, in *Dahlab v Switzerland*[106] the Court found the claims based on Articles 9 and 14 ECHR made by a Swiss public school teacher, who had been dismissed for wearing a headscarf on the job, 'manifestly ill-founded' and thus inadmissible. Taking into account the specific circumstances, particularly the fact that the applicant's pupils were at a 'tender age' between four and eight, the Court found that it 'cannot be denied outright that the wearing of a headscarf might have some kind of proselytising effect'. Taking this concern into account in its balancing of the respective rights and freedoms—the freedom of the teacher to manifest her religion and the need to protect pupils by preserving religious harmony—the Court concluded that the measure taken by the Geneva authorities (dismissal of the teacher because of her headscarf) had not been unreasonable. The dismissal was considered 'necessary in a democratic society' so the state was not considered to have exceeded the margin of appreciation. Secondly, the landmark case of *Şahin v Turkey*[107] concerned a ban on headscarves for university students at Turkish state universities, where the situation has since altered considerably. The applicant, Ms Leyla Şahin, came from a traditional Islam practising family and saw it as her religious duty to wear a headscarf. She was at the time a medical student at Istanbul University, where she was not allowed to don the headscarf during class or during exam sessions. Here the European Court, in an oft-criticised decision, held that the then-existing ban on headscarves in Turkish public universities fell within the margin of appreciation of the secular Turkish state; the interference could be considered as 'necessary in a democratic society' for the purpose of Article 9(2) and there was thus no violation of Article 9 ECHR. Gwyneth Pitt, bridging this education case with the line of employment cases like *X/Ahmad v UK* and *Stedman v UK*, argued that

> in reality, if all higher education institutions in the country impose this rule, the 'choice' of complying, foregoing higher education or going abroad to study is not really

---

[105] See also *Dogru v France* Application no 27058/054 (ECtHR, December 2008), and *Kervanci v France* Application no 31645/04 (ECtHR, December 2008) (no infringement of the right to religion found in the case of 12-year-old Muslim girls expelled in 1999 from French elementary school for covering their head during physical education class).

[106] *Dahlab v Switzerland*, Application no 42393/98 (ECtHR, 15 February 2001).

[107] *Leyla Şahin v Turkey*, Application no 44774/98 (ECtHR, 10 November 2005); see also *Dogru v France*, Application no 27058/05 and *Kervanci v France*, Application no 31645/04 (ECtHR, 4 December 2008) (no Art 9 violation for ban on wearing of a veil in sports classes); *Aktas v France*, Application no 43563/08, *Bayrak v France*, Application no 14308/08, *Gamaleddyn v France*, Application no 18527/08, *Ghazal v France*, Application no 29134/08, *J. Singh v France*, Application no 25463/08 and *R. Singh v France*, Application no 27561/08 (ECtHR, 30 June 2009) (various claims by Muslims and Sikhs against the French 2005 Act banning conspicuous religious symbols in public schools found inadmissible; interference with the pupils' freedom to manifest their religion was prescribed by law and pursued the legitimate aim of protecting the 'rights and freedoms of others' and of 'public order').

meaningful, any more than it is meaningful for an employee to choose between a job on the employer's terms and unemployment.[108]

The Court in the *Şahin* and *Dahlab* cases referred to the Islamic headscarf as 'a powerful external symbol' and endorsed the notion that the headscarf is a symbol of women's inferiority and 'hard to square with the principle of gender equality'.[109] This sweeping generalisation about the meaning of the headscarf has been rightly contested.[110] Research shows that there are complex and multidimensional reasons why Muslim women choose to wear or not to wear the headscarf.[111] For some young educated Muslim women in the West it can be a source of empowerment to be able to show that they hold on to their Islamic identity in the face of adversity.[112]

Since there are so many different and varying veiling (and non-veiling) practices amongst Muslim women, the question often comes up whether the *headscarf* is a religious *obligation* under Islamic doctrine. The European Court has held that Article 9 ECHR 'excludes any discretion on the part of the state to determine whether religious beliefs ... are legitimate'.[113] Indeed, the freedom to interpret one's own doctrine itself is a core part of religious freedom. With such stance, the Court gives deference to the subjective understanding of the person concerned,[114] without however unquestioningly accepting an applicant's characterisation of an act or behaviour as a religious manifestation.[115] However, the practical effect of this seemingly generous stance is limited since, under Article 9.2 of the ECHR, wide restrictions on the manifestation of a religious belief or practice have been accepted.

In a religious case not involving the hijab, it was held that the *criminal* conviction of 127 members of the religious order known as *Aczimendi tarikatÿ* for wearing

---

[108] G Pitt, 'Religion or belief: aiming at the right target?' in H Meenan (ed), *Equality law in an enlarged European Union: Understanding the article 13 directives* (Cambridge University Press, 2007) 218. Interestingly, the applicant eventually left Turkey and continued her studies in Austria, but clearly not all students may have this option.

[109] See, eg, *Dahlab v Switzerland*, Application no 42393/98 (ECtHR, 15 February 2001); *Leyla Şahin v Turkey*, Application no 44774/98 (ECtHR, 10 November 2005) para 111.

[110] See, eg, I Rorive, 'Religious Symbols in The Public Space: In search of a European Answer' (2009) 30 *Cordozo Law Review* 2669, 2669, 2680 and 2683; MLP Loenen, 'Botsing tussen de vrijheid van godsdienst en gelijke behandeling ongeacht geslacht of seksuele oriëntatie' in A Nieuwenhuis and C Zoethout (eds), *Rechtsstaat en religie* (Wolf Legal Publishers, 2009).

[111] Eg C Joppke, *Veil: Mirror of Identity* (Polity, 2009) 3–5 ('it has become commonplace to stress the modernity of the headscarf ... as a self-chosen sign of female emancipation').

[112] C Killian, 'The Other Side of the Veil: North African Women in France Respond to the Headscarf Affair' (2003) 17 *Gender & Society* 567, 567–90; F El Guindi, *Veil: Modesty, Privacy And Resistance* (Berg, 1999) (for the position that contemporary veiling tends to be about resistance).

[113] *Metropolitan Church of Bessarabia and Others v Moldova*, Application no 45701/99 (ECtHR, 13 December 2001).

[114] See, eg, *Moscow Branch of the Salvation Army v Russia*, Application no 72881/01 (ECtHR, 5 October 2006).

[115] *Kosteski v Former Yugoslav Republic of Macedonia*, Application no 55170/00 (ECtHR, 13 April 2006).

their distinctive religious clothing—reminiscent of the Prophet Mohammad's dress—while touring the streets of Ankara following a religious ceremony and during a judicial proceeding, violated Article 9 ECHR.[116] The members of the religious order had been convicted in Turkey for a breach of the law on the wearing of headgear and the wearing of religious garments in public other than for religious ceremonies. According to the ECtHR, the Turkish ruling was not based on legitimate aims of protection of public safety and protection of the rights and freedoms of others but solely upon a reference to legal provisions. While this case may have pointed to real limits in regulating and restricting dress practices, the criminal punishment and public sphere contexts set it apart from the educational cases as well as cases involving contractual employment relations.

It can also be noted that, in 2013, the European Court dismissed the claim of Shirley Chaplin, a public hospital nurse in the UK, to wear a cross-necklace while working in a geriatric ward.[117] The Court did not consider itself well-placed to second-guess the health and safety risk assessment made by the hospital and the lower British courts, and found the balance struck to be within the state's margin of appreciation under Article 9 ECHR. Thus, in case of legitimately regarded aims, such as health and safety concerns, as well as in the case of (perceived) conflicts between fundamental rights, the margin of appreciation is bound to continue to play a (deferential) role, justifying potentially far-reaching limitations on religious dress in the employment context.

D. Other Religious Practices before the ECtHR

Besides religion-worktime and religious dress cases, a range of other religious practices or beliefs can come up in the workplace setting. These includes issues such as prayer (space), dietary accommodations, religious objections[118] to job duties, social customs or socialisation standards (eg shaking hands controversies). Until now though, the European Court has largely been spared such matters in the private employment context cases. In this sense, ECtHR cases are hardly representative of the array of issues which arise on the ground.[119] In non-employment

---

[116] *Ahmet Arslan and Others v Turkey*, Application no 41135/98 (ECtHR, 23 February 2010).

[117] See *Eweida and others v United Kingdom*, Application nos 48420/10, 59842/10, 51671/10 and 36516/10 (ECtHR, 15 January 2013).

[118] The case law of the ECtHR on conscientious objections to military service is extensive and has known several developments, see: *N v Sweden*, Application no 10410/83 (EComHR, 11 October 1984); *Ülke v Turkey*, Application no 39437/98 (ECtHR, 24 January 2006); *Thlimmenos v Greece* Application no 34369/97 (ECtHR, 6 April 2000); *Bayatyan v Armenia*, Application no 23459/03 (ECtHR, 7 July 2011); *Grandrath v Germany* Application no 2299/64 (EComHR, 12 December 1966); *Erçep v Turkey* Application no 43965/04 (ECtHR, 22 November 2011); *Savda v Turkey*, Application no 42730/05 (ECtHR, 12 June 2012); see also M Yildirim, 'Conscientious Objection to Military Service: International Human Rights Law and the Case of Turkey' (2010) 5 *Religion & Human Rights* 65.

[119] See, eg, in Lamghari, some religious accommodation issues discussed as relevant in the transportation company where field research was conducted (MIVB-STIB), such as prayers, dietary restrictions,

settings, the issue of religious diets has come up. In *Jacóbski v Poland*, Article 9 ECHR was held to have been violated because the prison had refused to provide 'simple meat-free meals' to a Buddhist prisoner.[120]

Cases where discrimination or restriction on freedom of religion or belief is justified merely on the basis of religious affiliation, as said, are rare.[121] Generally, such cases are difficult to prove, as employers seem sophisticated enough to wrap direct bias in less straightforward terms. Such cases of belief or affiliation discrimination may at times also coincide with ethnic or racial discrimination.[122]

Cases involving objections to particular job duties have come up across Europe, and may reach the European Court sometime in the future. Since different domestic courts faced with such issues have on a number of occasions come up with very different approaches and decisions, the ECtHR guidance would be welcomed. For instance, the French Cour de cassation[123] in 1998 held, in the case of a supermarket employee of Muslim faith who refused to handle pork and asked to be transferred from the butchery to another department, that religious convictions of workers are not protected by the employment contract absent any express contractual clause. Hence, the employer had done nothing more than to ask the employee to execute the tasks for which he was hired. In other words, the employer is free to ignore religious requests by employees without having to provide any justification, so that contractual obligations easily override the right to religious freedom. German courts have adopted a different approach, rejecting such formalistic standards. For instance, the Higher Labour Court of Hamm[124] held that an employee 'does not resign his constitutional right to religious freedom' by signing an employment contract which is in conflict with religious duties. Here, it was held that an employee can be excused from work to pray unless it would cause business disruptions violating the employer's relevant constitutional rights. This approach to conflicting rights under German Constitutional law, termed *praktischen Konkordanz* ('practical concordance'), aims to find a 'compromise with minimal restrictions of both rights'.[125] This may be a promising approach to reasonable accommodation involving clashing rights.[126] In contrast, the French approach essentially ignores

---

shaking hands, have not come up in any legal cases in Belgium. In addition, the issue of Muslim men wearing beards and pantacourts (shortened pants), an important element explaining various social tensions at MIVB-STIB has also not come up in Belgian case law.

[120] *Jacóbski v Poland*, Application no 18429/06 (ECtHR, 7 December 2010). See K Alidadi, 'Gevangene heeft recht op religieus aangepast gevangenisdieet [Prisoner Entitled to Religiously Appropriate Prison Diet]', *De Juristenkrant*, 22 December 2010, 6–7.

[121] eg *Ivanova v Bulgaria*, Application no 52435/99 (ECtHR, 12 April 2007), discussed above.

[122] See, eg, Case C-54/07, *Centrum voor gelijkheid van kansen en voor racismebestrijding v NV Feryn* [2008] ECR I-5187.

[123] French Cour de cassation of 24 March 1998, no 95-44738.

[124] Higher Labour Court of Hamm, 18 January 2002, 5 Sa 1782/01.

[125] E Brems, *Conflicts between fundamental rights* (Antwerp, Intersentia, 2008) 3.

[126] However, even if the result may be the same, this case perhaps need not be framed as a 'clashing rights' case: under reasonable accommodations, the question would be whether a religious accommodation would be reasonable and not impose a disproportionate burden.*

the reality of power asymmetries in the labour relations context: when employees have no legally enforceable right to reasonable accommodation, it makes no strategic sense to jobseekers to request accommodations right off the bat (in fact even if such a right were to exist, strategically it might be more advisable to hold off on making certain requests until things are more settled). In addition, religious commitments do not necessarily remain static over time. Employees can change religions, or alter their interpretation, or the intensity of their commitments and practices. The rigid 'contract supremacy' ignores this possibility.

With regard to job duty objections, the Court's own case law with regard to practices associated with religion will be pertinent. The reasoning of cases such as *Buscarini*[127] may not be considered entirely applicable in the case an employee refuses to, for instance, perform 'secular duties' which violate his/her religious beliefs such as handling pork or alcohol but it can be an inspiration. *Buscarini* concerned a number of San Marino parliamentarians who were required to swear an oath on the Bible before and in order to take up their duties. The Court found a violation of Article 9 ECHR because mandating such oath was

> tantamount to obliging them to swear allegiance to a particular religion. Likewise, in accordance with the principle of free choice, a person cannot be obliged to take part against their will in the activities of a religious community when they do not belong to that community.[128]

Similarly, in *Alexandridis*[129] the freedom of an Athens lawyer to not have to manifest religious beliefs was violated when he was obliged to reveal that he was not an Orthodox Christian, in order to be exempt from a particular form of swearing oath as a precondition to practising law. The state has thus limited scope to impose religious practices and oblige people to divulge information about their religion or beliefs.[130]

When it comes to proselytising religion in the workplace, ECtHR case law shows that employees have some rights, but that there are boundaries that should not be crossed. In *Larissis*[131] three applicants—air force officers who were members of a Pentecostal Church—had been convicted in Greece for trying to convert a number of people, including airmen who were their subordinates while on duty. While the ECtHR agreed the measures taken against the officers were justified for the attempts to convert subordinates, since the state had a duty to protect

---

[127] See *Buscarini and Others v San Marino*, Application no 24645/94 (ECtHR, 18 February 1999).

[128] In constrast see *Lautsi v Italy*, Application no 30814/06 (ECtHR, 18 March 2011).

[129] *Alexandridis v Greece*, Application no 19516/06 (ECtHR, 21 February 2008).

[130] See also *Dimitras and Others v Greece*, Application nos 42837/06, 3237/07, 3269/07, 35793/07 and 6099/08 (ECtHR, 3 June 2010). Violation of Art 9 was established because as witnesses in judicial proceedings, applicants had to disclose their religious convictions in order to avoid having to take an oath on the Bible.

[131] *Larissis and Others v Greece*, Application nos 23372/94, 26377/94 and 26378/94 (ECtHR, 24 February 1998). See also *Kokkinakis v Greece*, Application no 14307/88 (ECtHR, 25 May 1993) (Art 9 violation for the criminal conviction for proselytism after a member of the Jehovah's Witnesses engaged the wife of a cantor at a local Orthodox church in a conversation about religion).

subordinates from undue pressure from senior staff, it did find an Article 9 violation for the measures against the air officers imposed because they had tried to
convert civilians (who were not subject to similar pressures as the airmen, considering the lack of authority over them). This involved a special (public) workplace
setting (the army), but translated to the general secular workplace; there would
seem to be thus some room to proselytise and certainly to *discuss* matters of religion at the workplace without this justifiably leading to disciplinary measures by
the employer. This should be a warning for employers who, in the spirit of shun-
ning possible conflict, ban any talk of religion at work. In fact, ECtHR case law
clarifies that the *desire to prevent tensions* is also not a justification for depriving
employees of their freedoms or their jobs. A particularly interesting case in this
regard was *Redfearn v UK*.[132] The applicant—a driver transporting disabled pas-
sengers from mainly Asian backgrounds—had been dismissed because he was a
member of the British National Party (BNP).[133] The European Court found that
the dismissal, motivated by such fear of conflict, violated the freedom of association (under Article 11 ECHR) of the employee.

E. Human Rights in the Workplace in Flux: *Eweida* and its Ramifications

Before *Eweida*, the likelihood that Article 9 ECHR would become a basis for introducing a right to reasonable accommodation for religious dress in the European
workplace seemed slim, whereas the anti-discrimination framework appeared the
more promising avenue to that end.[134] Since under EU law and the Employment
Equality Directive, fundamental rights must be interpreted in line with the principles developed under the ECHR, ECtHR case law parameters under Article 9 and/
or Article 14 ECHR would remain of considerable *indirect* use.[135] However, *Eweida*
brought much change to the landscape, necessitating new analyses and assessment
of the relative strengths of the two respective supranational layers.

Before this landmark case which pertained to religion in the private sector
workplace, the European Court had started chipping away at the 'freedom to

---

[132] *Redfearn v United Kingdom*, Application no 47335/06 (ECtHR, 6 December 2012).

[133] The membership of the British National Party only being open to white nationals at the time.

[134] eg Loenen, 'Accommodation of Religion and Sex Equality in the Workplace under the EU Equality Directives: a Double Bind for the European Court of Justice', n 7 above (arguing that religious dress
claims may be more successful before the CJEU since the margin of appreciation did not apply and the
Court had a track record of strict reviews in gender discrimination cases). However, some commentators had argued that support can be found in other areas of ECtHR's jurisprudence for the notion that
dismissals or other work-related detriments can amount to interference with Convention rights. See
Vickers, *Religious freedom, religious discrimination, and the workplace*, n 6 above, 87; see also Ouald
Chaib, 'Religious Accommodation in the Workplace: Improving the Legal Reasoning of the European
Court of Human Rights', n 96 above, favouring this cross-fertilisation approach.

[135] See Art 6(2) of the EU Treaty and Recital 1 of the Employment Equality Directive; see Vickers,
Religious freedom, religious discrimination, and the workplace, n 6 above, 119.

resign' jurisprudence that had resulted in too narrow protection for freedom of religion in the workplace. In *Konstantin Markin*, the ECtHR rejected the 'free to resign' argument advanced by the Russian Government in the context of paid parental leave for military personnel, but here the Court pointed to the 'unique nature of the armed forces and, consequently, the difficulty in directly transferring essentially military qualifications and experience to civilian life' as compromising that freedom to resign.[136]

Then, in 2013, the European Court found that Article 9 ECHR was violated in the case of Ms Nadia Eweida.[137] The case had made headlines across the UK and Europe before even reaching the ECtHR. Ms Eweida, a check-in assistant for British Airways at Heathrow airport, had been prohibited from visibly wearing a modest cross on a necklace while at work. British Airways had eventually amended its dress code to allow the visible wearing of such religious symbols but the dispute concerned the situation in the months when she had been sanctioned. The European Court engaged in a thorough balancing exercise and found that the balance struck between the business interest of British Airways towards a certain image or brand, while legitimate, should not have trumped the fundamental right of an employee to manifest her religion by way of a discrete religious symbol which—it noted—could have little impact on the employer's image. In other words, it held that contractual obligations cannot simply outdo the freedom of religion or belief in the absence of special circumstances (eg safety and security requirements).

In the same decision, the religious freedom and discrimination claims of three other British Christians—two women and one man—were dismissed as it was considered that the restrictions in those cases fell within the UK's margin of appreciation: two cases involved a conflict between Convention rights (ie freedom of religion versus equal treatment irrespective of sexual orientation in the cases of Liliane Ladele and Gary McFarlane).

The main ramification of the *Eweida* case is that domestic courts must now consider more seriously the employment claims of religious employees under the ECHR, at times necessitating substantial changes in domestic jurisprudence. I argue that the ECtHR decision in particular affects the legitimacy of company 'neutrality policies' which are currently mushrooming on the ground, having been accepted too readily in Belgian case law, and which form formidable obstacles for Muslim women wearing a hijab and other visible religious minorities. This merits a closer discussion of *Eweida et al v United Kingdom*.

---

[136] *Konstantin Markin v Russia*, Application no 30078/06 (ECtHR, 7 October 2010), para 58: In addition, it was considered that servicemen who choose to resign from military service to be able to take care of their new-born children, would encounter particular difficulties in obtaining interesting civilian posts.

[137] For a discussion of the *Eweida* decisions before the domestic British courts, see, amongst others, L Vickers, 'Indirect Discrimination and Individual Belief: Eweida v British Airways plc' (2009) 11 *Ecclesiastical Law Journal* 197.

Ms Eweida, a Coptic Christian, started working for British Airways (BA) in 1999. In 2004, BA changed its staff uniforms and a new detailed uniform code specified that religious accessories and dress should—if at all—be worn *under* the uniform. When this was impossible to do (eg with headscarves or turbans), an approval would have to be obtained. Such approvals were, amongst others, routinely given to Muslim employees who wished to wear a headscarf in BA colours. Ms Eweida initially did not wear a cross at work, but in 2006 she started to wear it on a necklace as a sign of her Christian faith. She was repeatedly asked to conceal the cross, and at first did so hesitantly. But then one day she refused and was sent home until she would be willing to abide by the uniform code. BA offered her a back-office position, which did not require the wearing of a uniform and would allow her to wear a cross openly, but she rejected this offer.

At this time, the dispute had reached the British and international media. Ms Eweida argued that BA's policy was discriminatory: Muslim employees were allowed to wear a headscarf but she was unable to wear a discrete cross 'the size of a five-cent penny'. In the media, BA's double standards were criticised,[138] and this led to the eventual amendment of the dress code and Ms Eweida's return to the workplace.[139] The dispute, however, continued regarding the four and a half months prior to the amendment of the uniform code, during which Ms Eweida had remained at home without pay.[140] Her attorneys presented claims on the basis of equality law—direct and, principally, indirect discrimination—and also argue a violation of Article 9 ECHR. Thus, they fully utilised the dual framework available to them. However, these arguments failed to convince the UK employment courts (tribunal and appeal) and the UK Court of Appeal.[141] The wearing of a cross was seen by the Court of Appeal as the applicant's *personal choice*, not as a religious obligation. Thus, the Court considered the requirement of a *group disadvantage* to be lacking. Therefore, it held there could not be talk of indirect discrimination since that implies discrimination against a defined *group*, not only disadvantage to the individual claimant. Here, a difference from a duty of reasonable accommodation can be noted; since under a duty of reasonable accommodation the focus is on the individual case at hand, and the existence of a group disadvantage is not required, the fact that a case would be unique to an idiosyncratic claimant is no reason to dispel the duty to accommodate. The existence of an explicit duty of reasonable accommodation would thus have had tangible result at the Court of Appeal level in the *Eweida* case.

The Court of Appeal also argued that the dress code, even if it were to be indirectly discriminatory towards a certain religious group, was in fact justified since

---

[138] Even Tony Blair weighed in on the matter; BBC News, Blair advises BA to end cross row, 27 November 2006, news.bbc.co.uk/2/hi/uk_news/politics/6188606.stm.

[139] BBC news, Woman to sue BA in necklace row, 15 October 2006, news.bbc.co.uk/2/hi/uk_news/england/london/6052608.stm.

[140] Ms Eweida was sent home from 20 September 2006 until 3 February 2007.

[141] *Eweida v British Airways plc*, UK Employment Tribunal and *Eweida v British Airways PLC*, UK Employment Appeal Tribunal, 20 November 2008; *Eweida v British Airways plc* [2010] EWCA Civ 80.

it pursued a legitimate aim (establishing a professional image) and the ban on religious symbols was proportionate to that aim.[142]

While the argument based on Article 9 ECHR was presented, the Court of Appeal devoted minimal attention to it; it held that the provision was of little assistance to Ms Eweida's case and found no interference. The Court, referring to the above quote by Lord Bingham in the jilbab Denbigh school case, noted the *Stedman v UK* case where the 'freedom to resign' argument had been 'fatal' to the claim. Thus, by analogy the UK Court of Appeal expected the 'freedom to resign' doctrine to act as an effective bar to Ms Eweida's potential ECHR claim.

When Ms Eweida's legal team took the case to Strasbourg (a criticised move), the UK government's main defence relied on the application of the established doctrine. However, in a long-awaited yet startling exchange, the European Court moved explicitly away from this formalistic line of reasoning:

> Given the importance in a democratic society of freedom of religion, the Court considers that, where an individual complains of a restriction on freedom of religion in the work-place, *rather than* holding that the *possibility of changing job would negate any interference with the right, the better approach would be to weigh that possibility in the overall balance when considering whether or not the restriction was proportionate* (emphasis added).[143]

The European Court then proceeded to examine whether 'Ms Eweida's right freely to manifest her religion was sufficiently secured within the domestic legal order and whether a fair balance was struck between her rights and those of others'.[144] It held that such balance was not reached, and pointed to the importance of the better approach to both the individual applicant and a diverse society as a whole:

> [A] fair balance was not struck. On one side of the scales was Ms Eweida's desire to manifest her religious belief. As previously noted, this is a fundamental right: *because a healthy democratic society needs to tolerate and sustain pluralism and diversity*; but also because of the value to an individual who has made religion a central tenet of his or her life to be able to communicate that belief to others. On the other side of the scales was the employer's wish to project a certain corporate image. The Court considers that, while this aim was undoubtedly legitimate, the domestic courts accorded it too much weight. Ms Eweida's *cross was discrete* and cannot have detracted from her professional appearance. There was *no evidence that the wearing of other, previously authorised, items of religious clothing, such as turbans and hijabs, by other employees, had any negative impact on British Airways' brand or image* (emphasis added).[145]

Thus, not merely is an important interest of the employee involved, but a more overarching consideration points to the socio-political need to 'tolerate and *sustain* pluralism and diversity' including in its religious aspect in the workplace setting.

---

[142] *Eweida v British Airways plc* [2010] EWCA Civ 80.

[143] *Eweida v United Kingdom* (ECtHR, 15 January 2013), [2013] ECHR 37, para 83.

[144] ibid, para 91.

[145] ibid, para 94. Since BA was a private employer, the Court also emphasised the positive duties of the State under Art 9: 'domestic authorities failed sufficiently to protect the first applicant's right to manifest her religion, in breach of the positive obligation under Article 9' (para 95).

While the European Court considers the aim of the employer to establish and reflect a certain corporate image as legitimate, the balancing shows that its weight cannot easily crush fundamental rights of an employee and societal interests. This implies that employer interests, even if set out in the employment contract or other documents, cannot trump the fundamental freedom of religion or belief of an employee, who may then not need to disconnect from a religious practice or belief when entering the workplace.

In *Eweida*, the European Court did not consider it essential that the state have specific legal provisions 'regulating the wearing of religious clothing and symbols in the workplace'. While Member States may not have *general* dress regulations relating to 'the workplace', various regulations and practices have an effect on the (non-)accommodation of religious dress in private workplaces. First, restrictions on civil servants' dress could have spill-over effect on the private sector, obstructing the sort of fair balance the Court advocated in *Eweida*. Secondly, company neutrality policies more directly block any balancing of interests in religious dress cases, diluting the employee side of the scales and allowing the employer's wish to establish a 'neutral image'[146] total priority. Enforcing such general policies thus amounts to denial of the fair balance exercise in all cases. Conversely, one could see an explicit duty of reasonable accommodation as a good practice under *Eweida*; one which seeks to give additional guidance to the level of balance that needs to be struck in religious dress (and other) cases.

The *Eweida* decision introduces a new, better approach to religion in the workplace cases which aims to safeguard a fair balance between the fundamental right of an employee, and rights and interests of an employer as well as those of democratic pluralist societies. With the holding, the European Court asserted the Convention's re-found relevance in this emerging area where law has an important role to play. The decision no doubt has great importance for religious minorities such as Muslims and Sikhs in Europe, even if it did involve the cross, a symbol of Christian faith, which was said to have been discriminated against. The decision embedded in the human rights framework also lays bare the weakness and ramifications of requiring 'group' disadvantage under the concept of indirect discrimination in EU law. Indeed,

> the exercise of trying to find a disadvantaged 'group' should be unnecessary if what law is really seeking to do is fulfill a basic principle that those with religious beliefs should be able to manifest them *reasonably* in the workplace.[147]

---

[146] Whereas the corporate image aim was generally regarded as legitimate in *Eweida*, the legitimacy of general neutrality policies is another matter. Neutrality may justify religious dress restrictions in particular cases, but a general policy cannot be considered legitimate and is in any case overbroad. Such policies may be pretext for discrimination and exclusion of religious minorities and part of an 'avoidance strategy' to the realities of an integrated, diverse workplace.

[147] J Davies and T Heys, 'Reinventing indirect discrimination', 26 September 2012, at: www. lewissilkin.com/Journal/2012/September/Reinventing-indirect-discrimination.aspx#. U2MHn9FOUdU ('If indirect discrimination is not 'fit for purpose' in such cases, a new approach [reasonable accommodations for religion or belief] is needed').

Indeed, the European Court may have opened the door for the protection of more individualistic manifestations of religion. This may approximate employee rights under a duty of reasonable accommodation, as opposed to indirect discrimination which requires group disadvantage and a showing that 'persons', other than the applicant, would be put at particular disadvantage by the measure in question. This is because the Court held that:

> In order to count as a 'manifestation' within the meaning of Article 9, the act in question must be intimately linked to the religion or belief. An example would be an act of worship or devotion which forms *part of the practice of a religion or belief in a generally recognised form*. However, the manifestation of religion or belief is *not limited to such acts*; the existence of a sufficiently close and direct nexus between the act and the underlying belief must be determined on the facts of each case. In particular, there is *no requirement on the applicant to establish that he or she acted in fulfilment of a duty mandated by the religion in question* (emphasis added).[148]

In sum, the *Eweida* decision has important and potentially far-reaching consequences for (some) domestic courts, when they are called to resolve religious accommodation cases. Since it requires that there be adequate consideration for the employee's fundamental religious freedom, one can argue that this implies a degree of reasonable accommodation under Article 9 ECHR, even if the Court did not utilise this concept in its framing of the issues. If so, this signifies a potent revitalisation of freedom of religion or belief in the employment context with Article 9 playing a much more prominent role in multi-layered analyses of religion in the workplace cases. However, many questions remain: does the *Eweida* holding ring true for all forms of religious practice or does it only apply to religious dress and symbols? Are the standards different for private and public workplaces? How strictly will the proportionality test be scrutinised/what margin does there remain? What about all-encompassing company neutrality policies which a priori signal the denial of all, or categories of, religious dress accommodation? Clearly, arguments can be made based on the judgment but debates, and divergent Member State practices, will no doubt continue as to the meaning and ramifications of ECtHR jurisprudence until more guidance comes forth. Now that the possibility for an employee to find alternative employment no longer bars the finding of an interference with a Convention right but rather forms *a factor* in the justification and proportionality assessment, an interference with a right can be more readily found and the Court can proceed to verify whether a fair balance was made between the varying rights and interests (employee, employer, others, society as a whole). While the balancing in *Eweida* was specific to the facts of the case (the cross example), and the Court explicitly regards this as a 'discrete' symbol of faith, it also included other religious dress and symbols—the Islamic headscarf and the Sikh turban—in its consideration. But does the same apply to religion-worktime cases? What about objections to certain job duties violating religious beliefs? It

---

[148] *Eweida v UK*, [2013] ECHR 37, para 82.

may be years before such a case comes to the European Court, until which the analysis above forms part of the European Convention's guidance in existing and emerging 'religion in the workplace' disputes.

F. Clashing Rights and Religious Accommodations: Calling for the Wisdom of Solomon?

While Ms Eweida prevailed before the ECtHR, the claims of three other Christian employees were rejected. The first of these cases involved a Christian who also wanted to visibly wear a cross at work. Shirley Chaplin, a nurse who worked in a public hospital, lost her case before the ECtHR. Unlike in the case of Ms Eweida, where no health and safety concern was presented, it was argued against Ms Chaplin that wearing the necklace presented a health and safety risk; elderly patients could grab and pull on it. The European Court did not consider itself well-placed to second-guess the health and safety assessment performed at the hospital and the domestic court level, and deferred to these as being within the margin of appreciation. This means an employer who can demonstrate convincingly that the wearing of certain items involves a health and safety risk can also justify restrictions on religious symbols and dress. What is not clear is how definite or conceivable the concern should be and how much leeway to allow so that health and safety does not become pretext for the violation of freedom of religion at work.

The last two cases of the quartet involved two Christian applicants who had objected to certain job tasks because of their conservative religious views and beliefs on marriage and homosexual relationships. Both Liliane Ladele, a marriage registrar, and Gary McFarlane, a relationship consultant, had sought a work accommodation for reasons of their religious beliefs. Ms Ladele, who was a marriage registrar long before same-sex partnerships were allowed in the UK, objected to performing same-sex partnership ceremonies while Mr McFarlane was not comfortable with providing psycho-sexual relationship therapy to homosexual couples. In their cases, the European Court deferred to the domestic British courts' rejection of the applicants' claims and held that the resolution of their cases fell within the state's margin of appreciation. When there is a conflict between Convention rights, in this case the freedom of religion versus equal treatment irrespective of sexual orientation, a broader margin of appreciation is given to states. While giving states a margin is certainly justified, the European Court could have taken up the opportunity to provide some guidelines, both with regard to factors that can play a role when balancing various rights and interests and with regard to the outer limits of the state's discretion.

It is noteworthy that the *Eweida* decision was taken 5–2, with a dissenting opinion by judges Nicolas Bratza (UK) and David Thór Björgvinsson (Iceland). There was also a dissenting opinion by judges Nebojša Vučinić (Montenegro) and Vincent De Gaetano (Malta), arguing why in their view Article 9 (in particular the freedom of conscience) had in fact been violated in the case of Ms Ladele.

The Civil Partnership Act 2004 which had been adopted years after Ms Ladele became a marriage registrar foresaw accommodations for employees who were unwilling to officiate at same-sex partnerships, and switches between colleagues had taken place for some time before the conflict arose. However, according to the two dissenting judges, it was: 'a combination of back-stabbing by her colleagues and the blinkered political correctness of the Borough of Islington (which clearly favoured "gay rights" over fundamental human rights) [which] eventually led to her dismissal'.[149] Further, while accommodation 'could have been achieved without detriment to the overall services provided' this did not happen:

> Instead of practising the tolerance and the 'dignity for all' it preached, the Borough of Islington pursued the doctrinaire line, the road of obsessive political correctness. It effectively sought to force the applicant to act against her conscience or face the extreme penalty of dismissal—something which, even assuming that the limitations of Article 9 § 2 apply to prescriptions of conscience [sic], cannot be deemed necessary in a democratic society. Ms Ladele did not fail in her duty of discretion: she did not publicly express her beliefs to service users. Her beliefs had no impact on the content of her job, but only on its extent.

This indignant-toned dissenting opinion laments the fact that an initial reasonable accommodation for the conscientiously objecting civil servant was not safeguarded despite it being feasible and in line with the principles of the Borough's own equality and inclusion agenda. Such a reconciliatory approach, which rejects the forsaking of concrete rights in the name of abstract principles and laudable words of inclusion, should be supported as a principle at the supranational level. Indeed, there is no compelling reason why in the case of clashing Convention rights reasonable attempts should not be made to promote inclusion of minorities. Accommodation could still be feasible, in particular when the core of the rights of others are not at stake.

'Clashing fundamental rights' cases, especially with religion-based claims on one side, have emerged as a major theme in human rights and non-discrimination (case) law and literature.[150] Since such—real or perceived—clashes are pertinent in various religion in the workplace cases (although by no means in all), the issue merits closer attention. Eva Brems has noted that clashing rights situations raise a fundamental challenge for human rights jurisprudence since '[f]undamental rights normally function as "trumps" … in cases of a conflict between fundamental rights, the "trump" aspect is no longer relevant, and any solution of the conflict risks being perceived as arbitrary'.[151] Brems lists two main reasons why clashing rights situations are becoming 'increasingly frequent'. First, the list of fundamental

---

[149] *Eweida v UK*, Joint (dissenting) opinion of Judges Vucinic and De Gaetano, para 5.
[150] Brems, *Conflicts between fundamental rights*, n 140 above; Bielefeldt, 'Misperceptions of Freedom of Religion or Belief' (2013) 35 *Human Rights Quarterly* 33 (discussing three examples where freedom of religion has been pitted against: 1. freedom of expression, 2. gender equality, and 3. LGBT rights).
[151] Brems, *Conflicts between fundamental rights*, n 140 above, 2.

rights is continuously expanding, through adoption of new treaties but mainly through interpretation of provisions in existing treaties like the ECHR. Secondly, the inflation in clashing rights situations is also due to the horizontal effect of fundamental rights, ie the application of fundamental rights with respect to various non-state actors.[152]

What is a fair, non-arbitrary, but potentially politically non-correct, approach to such continuously sprouting conflicts cases? Some favour a hierarchical approach, which may place religious freedom in the losing corner.[153] For others, this amounts to 'occluding one horn of the dilemma'.[154]

The first endeavour should be to reduce the issue to its appropriate proportions, rather than to see conflict cases all around. Zucca and Bader, amongst others, have also called for distinguishing between 'genuine conflicts' (Zucca: 'constitutional dilemmas'—Bader: 'hard cases') and other cases (Zucca: '*sensu lato* conflicts'— Bader: 'softer or symbolic cases').[155] The borders between the two categories will necessarily remain fuzzy; 'softer cases often turn out to be hard in various liberal-democratic states',[156] and, conversely, conflicts between fundamental rights are 'frequently not recognised as such'.[157] Susanne Baer warns against a temptation to reduce such situations to their abstract antagonistic clash-dimension and pleads for appreciating political agendas, including the culturalisation of religion and the 'othering' of sex equality.[158] Heiner Bielefeldt has similarly advocated a 'maximum reconciliary' approach. Bielefeldt, the current UN Special Rapporteur on Freedom

---

[152] ibid, 2; O De Schutter and F Tulkens, 'Rights in Conflict: The European Court of Human rights as a Pragmatic Institution' in E Brems (ed), *Conflicts between fundamental rights* (Antwerp, Intersentia 2008) 171 et seq.

[153] M Malik, *Religious Freedom in The 21st Century (Westminster Faith Debates)* (2012) 4 ('there should be no accommodation for the religious where the exemption is from a key constitutional or human right such as the right to equality'; Norrie, 'Conscience and public service' (14 April 2008) *The Journal of the Law Society of Scotland* ('where public duties are involved, there should be no place for invoking rights of conscience at the expense of those in civil partnerships'). See also CR Feldblum, 'Moral Conflict and Liberty: Gay Rights and Religion' (2006) 72 *Brooklyn Law Review* 61.

[154] A Koppelman, 'You can't hurry love: why antidiscrimination protections for gay people should have religious exemptions' (2006) 72 *Brooklyn Law Review* 125, 125.

[155] Lorenzo Zucca, 'Conflicts of Fundamental Rights as Constitutional Dilemmas' in E Brems (ed), *Conflicts between fundamental rights* (Antwerp, Intersentia 2008) 20; V Bader, *Secularism or democracy? Associational governance of religious diversity* (IMISCOE/Amsterdam University Press, 2007) 129, 153.

[156] V Bader, *Secularism or democracy? Associational governance of religious diversity*, n 170 above, 154 ('dominant ethnicity, religion and ruling versions of the history of a polity are inevitably inscribed in its national political identity ... due to the influx of migrants with different ethno-religious cultures, this also became visible ... This explains why more or less purely symbolic issues such as wearing hijabs, turbans, crosses and the architectural styles of mosques are so hotly contested and why resistance to symbolic accommodation is so fierce, although in principle accommodation of dress codes and pluralization of how public cultures and symbols should be fairly easy because no conflict with liberal-democratic morality is involved and also no costly redistribution is required ... The softer cases often turn out to be hard in various liberal-democratic states as well').

[157] Brems, *Conflicts between fundamental rights*, n 140 above, 4.

[158] S Baer, 'A closer look at law: human rights as multi-level sites of struggles over multi-dimensional equality' (2010) 6 *Utrecht Law Review* 56, 68.

of Religion or Belief, has observed how the rhetoric of fundamental rights clashes affects and diminishes the protection of freedom of religion or belief.[159]

Indeed, *seeing* hard cases may as such be a construct, the result of a *framing* exercise.[160] Such conflict framing should be resisted lest important aspects of the human right to freedom of religion or belief (or other freedoms or rights) are forfeited. When the gender equality argument can be countered by focusing on minority women's agency and empowerment as defined by themselves (rather than by those self-perceived liberal-minded commentators determined to liberate them from their alleged oppression),[161] these instances elude the 'hard cases' pile. This opens the way for reasonable accommodation of religious minority women. Other clashing rights cases can also be 'unpacked', by showing falsity or superficiality in the argued conflict of interests, for instance between freedom to religion and freedom from religion or by showing that the other right or 'value' in the equation (routinely: the freedom of expression, certain interpretations of gender equality, secularism or neutrality, LGBT rights) is being used as a cover to justify discrimination and exclusion.[162]

The enduring, genuine conflicts cases, then, call for principally contextualised approaches, not 'hard and fast' rubrics detailing which particular right prevails in any given scenario. Bader argues against adopting a '*context-independent hierarchy* and foundational strategies [to] reproduce conflicts only on a deep "meta level"' but reassures that this does not mean 'we are condemned to "anything goes" or drowned in the abyss of relativism'.[163]

Perhaps clashes betwee–n the freedom of religion and equality for sexual minorities, which Bielefeldt calls 'perhaps the most difficult challenge to the indivisibility of human rights',[164] is the most contentious contemporary issue that also relates to the workplace context. In a close second position comes religion, in particular Islam, versus gender equality patterns. In popular discourse, sexual heteronormativity, intolerance towards sexual minorities and rejection of women's rights is often associated (solely) with religious minorities and in particular Muslims,

---

[159] Bielefeldt, 'Misperceptions of Freedom of Religion or Belief', n 165 above, 60.

[160] W Van Rossum, 'Introduction to Framing Multicultural Issues in terms of Human Rights: Solution or Problem?' (2012) 30 *Netherlands Quarterly of Human Rights* 382.

[161] E McCarron, 'Veiled racism: the manipulation of gender equality to oppress Muslim women', *enargywebzine*, 20 November 2102 ('Concern for the rights of Muslim women has thus provided a veneer of respectability to Islamophobic discourses. Muslim women suffer from … a complacent European belief that we have achieved and monopolised gender equality'). Also B Ceuppens, '"De mijne is van de Filippijne": Racisme en seksisme in het hoofddoekendebat' (2005) 12 *Samenleving en Politiek*.

[162] European Network Against Racism, *Shadow Report 2012–2013 on Racism and Discrimination in Employment in Europe* (ENAR, March 2013).

[163] V Bader, 'Constitutionalizing secularism, alternative secularisms or liberal-democratic constitutionalism? A critical reading of some Turkish, ECtHR and Indian Supreme Court cases on "secularism"' (2010) 6 *Utrecht Law Review* 8, 11–12.

[164] Bielefeldt, 'Misperceptions of Freedom of Religion or Belief', n 165 above, 65.

but considering the diversity of opinions and developments within Europe[165] this may be an instance of false 'abstract antagonism'. Clearly intolerance towards and stigmatising of sexual minorities is not limited to religious groups,[166] although it would be hard to deny the exclusion and stigmatisation of sexual minorities under certain religious interpretations.[167] Guaranteeing equality and fair treatment of women and sexual minorities remains a challenge in the mainstream society as well, and the effect of the 'othering' of intolerance against sexual minorities and women should not veil this fact. Certainly, religious minorities must be both object and subject of tolerance and fair treatment, but it is important that new inclusions do not perpetuate other exclusions or contribute to new ones. In fact, some of the concerns with regard to LGBT rights and the frames used to address their socio-cultural problems, eg the pressures of 'covering' and 'passing' on LGBT persons and the negative psychological effects of being closeted, are highly relevant to the debates on the visibility of religious minorities in the European context.[168] That being said, real conflicts may arise and need to be addressed openly and genuinely.

Turning this discussion more concrete and linking it with reasonable accommodation, a closer look at the *Ladele* case is useful. The case involved a government sector employment situation, but the same debate can occur in a variety of private sector situations where the conservative, non-conformist beliefs of a worker collide with new equality projects. Indeed, once same-sex couples are married (or when they want to wed),[169] they may seek various private sector services previously reserved for heterosexual couples, and service providers and/or their employees may seek to object to providing some services on the basis of religion or belief.[170] The US example shows this is an area of emergent legal disputes.

Could reasonable accommodation be the contextualised framework which saves us from 'the abyss of relativism' yet offers much guidance for reasoning in hard conflict cases? Not everyone would agree; for Maleiha Malik, cases such as *Ladele*, show the excessiveness of a right to reasonable accommodation on the basis of religion.[171] However, one could argue that the *Ladele* case offers an apt illustration of the very aptitude of the reasonable accommodation framework to address

---

[165] eg ILGA Europe's tracking of LGBT rights developments and the 'rainbow map'.

[166] See, eg, the perilous state of LGBT rights in Russia, in the news extensively around the time of the 2014 Winter Olympics in Sochi. Jeff Sharlet, 'Inside the Iron Closet: What it's like to be Gay in Putin's Russia', *GQ magazine*, 4 February 2015.

[167] The same can be said about the status of women; certainly various religions have been detrimental to women's interests and equal status (eg reserving certain positions of authority for men), but this too is not the monopoly of religions by any means.

[168] K Yoshino, 'Covering' (2002) 111 *Yale Law Journal* 769.

[169] See, eg, the New Mexico gay wedding photographer case in the US. Other cases have involved a florist in Washington, a baker in Colorado and a T-shirt printer in Kentucky refusing to serve gay customers.

[170] See, eg, marriage counselling: *McFarlane* case discussed below. Even at the time of the wedding (preparations), same-sex couples could be faced with recalcitrant service-providers such as wedding photographers and florists.

[171] Malik, *Religious Freedom in The 21st Century (Westminster Faith Debates)*, n 168 above, 3.

such conflict situations. While Ms Ladele's conscientious objection would receive a serious consideration, her wish would not *necessarily* be accommodated. Under reasonable accommodation, religious requests would not systematically override equality norms or other rights. The right to *reasonable* accommodation—under any adopted standard—has bounds: the specific outcome in a given case would depend on the surrounding factual circumstances. The question would often turn on the issue of feasibility and proportionality, negotiated by parties willing to engage in conversation and to search for accommodation that does not force the employee into seclusion. For instance, if Ms Ladele is the only registrar in a given jurisdiction, the accommodation would be unreasonable, as same-sex couples would not be able to access a service on the same basis as other couples. On the other hand, if Ms Ladele is part of a large enough team of registrars, and her work can be scheduled such that she does not have to officiate over same-sex partnership ceremonies or marriages but can deferentially leave that to her colleagues, it would be possible to allow her to carry on her job without compromising her deeply-held beliefs about marriage. This would also be a triumph for societal inclusion and deep pluralism. The 'principle' of sexual minority equality should not foreclose this outcome in concrete circumstances.

Focusing on the feasibility of accommodations is an important way in which the framework negotiates or evades potential contentiousness. But 'dignitary factors'-that is, the argument that a certain solutions would violate the personal dignity of certain individuals or groups—will have to be accounted for as well; only, such dignitary arguments can come from both sides and can cause gridlocked situations. Here another added value of reasonable accommodation is that it allows players to move away from the discrimination rhetoric. Indeed, the characterisation of certain beliefs and practices as discriminatory is a hard pill to swallow for those who base their lives on those values, and it also constitutes unfair characterisation. Religious people will dispute that their beliefs on traditional institutions as marriage and divorce amount to 'discrimination' or even 'bigotry'. A good illustration is the statement by the former Archbishop of Canterbury, Lord Carey of Clifton, in the *McFarlane* case:

> The description of religious faith in relation to sexual ethics as 'discriminatory' is crude; and illuminates a lack of sensitivity to religious belief. The Christian message of 'love' does not demean or disparage any individual (regardless of sexual orientation) …

> The comparison of a Christian, in effect, with a 'bigot' (i.e. a person with an irrational dislike to homosexuals) begs further questions. It is further evidence of a disparaging attitude to the Christian faith and its values.[172]

In response Laws LJ called the observations 'misplaced': 'the proposition that if conduct is accepted as discriminatory it therefore falls to be condemned as disreputable or bigoted is a non sequitur; but it is the premise of Lord Carey's position'.

---

[172] *McFarlane v Relate Avon Limited* [2010] EWCA Civ 880, [2010] IRLR 872, para 18.

However, the inherently negative (and disparaging) connotation of discrimination cannot be denied, whether it be towards religious persons or employers. Thus,
dignitary or disparaging sentiment—on the side of religious groups or on the side
of sexual minorities—may be crippling the debate at times. The pejorative connotation of discrimination pleads in favour of framing such issues in terms of
'reasonable accommodation'.

Some may accept accommodation for conscientiously objecting civil servants
like Ms Ladele as long as the fact of accommodation stays behind the scenes and
is not made public; same-sex couples or others need not even be confronted with
internal schedule arrangements. This would meet the feasibility concern. However, others would critique the need for 'back-office' arrangements for religionists or non-conformists, considering the inherent value of explicit recognition of
people's moral conscience in a pluralist and inclusive context. On the other end,
others may object even to such 'back-office' arrangements on emotional grounds:

> Could Ms Ladele argue that Islington Council should find another registrar willing to
> perform the same sex civil ceremony? But there are problems with this approach even if
> a gay or lesbian couple, living in Islington, seeking a same sex civil partnership, received
> exactly the same service. It would be a significant step backward … we [need to] also use
> our 'inner eyes'. Imagine how it would feel if you were that couple. How would you feel
> if a public official was not willing to offer you a key symbolic public service because you
> were gay or lesbian? … Ultimately, allowing an exemption would also undermine the
> wider public culture of safeguarding our constitutional values, and especially equality
> and dignity for gays, lesbians and same sex couples.[173]

But this amounts to a selective inclusion. One could point to the same feelings of exclusion and attacks on personal dignity by objecting religious people,
whose rights are also protected by constitutional and international law. Andrew
Koppelman argued for recognising 'similarities between the felt situation of
both sides'.[174] Feldblum considers that 'gay people—of all individuals—should
recognise the injustice of forcing a person to disaggregate belief or identity from
practice'.[175] Further, it must also be noted that dismissing religious claims cat-
egorically by reference to often relatively recent and still largely unfulfilled, 'core
values of a society' (such as gender equality and sexual orientation equality) goes
against the grain of political neutrality. This is a challenge for the interaction of
human rights and anti-discrimination law. The rise of anti-discrimination law in
various strands has affected how courts and equal treatment commissions address
conflicts between rights, leaving some religious groups 'intensely concerned that

---

[173] Malik, *Religious Freedom in The 21st Century (Westminster Faith Debates)* (2012), 3–4. See also
M Malik, *'From conflict to cohesion': competing interests in equality law and policy*, Equality and Diversity Forum, 2008, at 8.

[174] Koppelman, 'You can't hurry love: why antidiscrimination protections for gay people should
have religious exemptions', n 169 above, 125.

[175] CR Feldblum, 'Moral Conflict and Liberty. Gay Rights and Religion' (2006) 72 *Brooklyn Law
Review* 61, 103.

equality law has become the primary vehicle by which [they are] marginalised'.[176] In his *Political Liberalism*, Rawls asks 'How is it possible for there to exist over time a just and stable society of free and equal citizens, who remain profoundly divided by reasonable religious, philosophical, and moral doctrines?'[177] Reasonable accommodations could be an antidote/counterbalance to hierarchical solutions to conflicts cases, instead allowing for more balanced and tailored approaches that fit within fairness standards of our time. Certainly, the framework is set up to secure adequate attention for the religion- or belief-based claim made by an employee, but there is ample room under the reasonableness angle to appreciate competing fundamental rights interests, including the right to equal treatment for sexual or other minorities. While the legislator (or a regulator) by adopting such duty can signal the importance of religious freedom in a multicultural society (recognition function) and give certain guidance as to the desirability of individualised measures, deciding whether accommodations are reasonable and do not constitute a disproportionate burden/undue hardship requires taking stock of fact-specific circumstances.

In that sense, reasonable accommodation offers a framework which is 'facilitative' rather than necessarily outcome-determining. Indeed, '[s]ome law is explicitly facilitative; it is intended to give opportunities for private negotiation rather than to achieve specific outcomes'.[178] It is the purview of the judiciary to review what goes on case-by-case on the ground. It is the flexibility of the tool in the hands of judges that allows it to play a useful role in diverse situations involving a variety of beliefs and practices in diverse organisations (private sector/public sectors; small, medium, large companies, etc) in the changing societal context (minorities climbing the corporate ladder; faith-based organisations adopting more inclusive hiring policies, etc). That flexibility, in the hands of the judiciary called upon to 'balance' claims in a non-arbitrary fashion with an eye for an individual analysis and a tailored individual solution, reviewing what went on between the employer and employee in case of an ensuing dispute, forms the core and strength of reasonable accommodations.

---

[176] A Donald, *Religion or belief, equality and human rights in England and Wales* (London, EHRC 2012) xii: with regard to 'some strands of Christian opinion'. Within interviews conducted in the RELIGARE project similar sentiments were expressed by Jewish and Muslim representatives, who also pointed to specific cases of freedom of religion claims losing out from non-discrimination, see Floris Vermeulen, *Socio-legal research on accommodation of religious diversity in family and labour law, in public space and state funding of religions in the Netherlands* (RELIGARE project, 2012) 66 et seq.

[177] J Rawls, *Political Liberalism* (New York, Columbia University Press, 1993) 4.

[178] D Nelken, 'Towards a Sociology of Legal Adaptation' in D Nelken and J Feest (eds), *Adapting Legal Cultures* (Oxford, Hart Publishing, 2001) 46.

2

The EU and Religion or Belief in the Workplace: From the Rapid Rise of EU Non-Discrimination Law to the Limits of Market-Rationalised Equality Law

I. Introduction: The EU 'Fundamental Rights Revolution'

A. The Story of Equality Law as a Metaphor for the EU project

The second supranational layer of legal protection with regard to religion or belief in the workplace is the non-discrimination framework developed by the European Union (EU).[1] This chapter analyses the specific *EU dimension* of the topic at hand, focusing on the Employment Equality Directive and the role of the Court of Justice of the European Union (CJEU). The implementation of this Directive in domestic law and subsequent application by the domestic courts of Belgium, the Netherlands and the UK in cases involving religion or belief in employment are the subject of Part II.

The EU has evolved from a regional economic project of the 'Inner Six' to a more complete socio-political union of 28 Member States[2] which sees the protection of

---

[1] The EU is founded on two main treaties: the Treaty on European Union (TEC) and the Treaty on the Functioning of the European Union (TFEU), with each having the same legal value. See Art 1 TEU and Art 1.2. TFEU. Articles refer to the version consolidated after the Lisbon treaty of 2007 and in effect since 2009.

[2] This is the number of Member States after Croatia joined the EU in 2013. In 2004 the enlargement added 10 Member States to the EU. This impending enlargement is often cited as having been one impetus for the adoption of the Article 13 Directives. Helen Meenan, 'Introduction' in Helen Meenan (ed), *Equality law in an enlarged European Union: understanding the article 13 directives* (Cambridge, Cambridge University Press, 2007) 4.

fundamental rights as its 'core business'.[3] One might say that crisis has been a constant reminder of the inherent frailty of such a novel project, and efforts to find acceptable solutions to the issues of the day have been the EU's modus operandi all along, as the goal of the harmonisation exercise expanded from the economic sphere to include the political, legal, monetary, and social. The EU is said to have engaged in 'an experiment in making human rights real in the market context'.[4] From its 'humble origins', EU non-discrimination or equality law has grown into the 'jewel in the crown of the European Social Model and the darling subject of the "progressive"'.[5] The development and expansion of EU non-discrimination law itself can serve as an apt metaphor for the transformation of the EU as an economic, market-integration focused institution into a more comprehensive union which puts much emphasis on the protection of fundamental rights in its internal and external policies.[6]

The 'humble origin' of EU anti-discrimination law lies in the equal pay provision,[7] which was included in the original 1957 EC Treaty at the behest of France because of concerns that French equal pay protection would result in a competitive disadvantage in the new common market.[8] Thus, the reason behind the equal pay provision was mainly economic, a far cry from the 'moral and social justifications which have since dominated academic discourse' on anti-discrimination.[9] Fast-forward to some decades later when the EU starts to pursue an active human rights and democratisation policy in its *external policies* as well, for instance since the 1990s insisting on a 'human rights clause' in bilateral trade and co-operation agreements and through its European Initiative for Democracy

---

[3] *cf* Herman Van Rompuy (then President of the European Council): 'Freedom and human rights … now belong to our core business', RELIGARE final conference, University of Leuven, 4 December 2012; Treaty Provisions emphasising the importance of fundamental rights in the EU include: Arts 2 and 6 TEU; Arts 9 and 10 TFEU. In 2007, the European Union Agency for Fundamental Rights was established to provide independent, evidence-based advice on fundamental rights in line with the EU Charter of Fundamental Rights. See Council Regulation (EC) No 168/2007, establishing the European Union Agency for Fundamental Rights.

[4] C McCrudden and H Kountouros, 'Human Rights and European equality law' in H Meenan (ed), *Equality law in an enlarged European Union: Understanding the article 13 Directives* (Cambridge, Cambridge University Press, 2007) 116.

[5] A Ludlow, 'Book review of *Engineering Equality: An Essay on European Anti-discrimination Law* (by Alexander Somek)' (2012) 50 *Journal of Common Market Studies* 534.

[6] In the eyes of the Nobel Peace Prize Committee, this project has been highly successful. In 2012, the EU received the Nobel Peace Prize 'for over six decades contribut[ing] to the advancement of peace and reconciliation, democracy and *human rights* in Europe' see: www.nobelprize.org/nobel_prizes/peace/laureates/2012/eu-facts.html.

[7] Currently Art 157 TFEU ('1. Each Member State shall ensure that the principle of equal pay for male and female workers for equal work or work of equal value is applied').

[8] Meenan, 'Introduction', n 2 above, 11–12. By contrast, nationality discrimination has been prohibited throughout the entire Treaty scope (originally on the basis of Art 7 TEC Treaty) Despite the fact that Art 13 TEC (now Art 19 TFEU) is closer in many respects to former Art 7 TEC considering the parallelism in scope, the sex discrimination *acquis communautaire* converged much more with the new Art 13 grounds while nationality discrimination has remained somewhat of a separate issue, and 'currently stalled as an equality and non-discrimination issue, by comparison'.

[9] Ludlow, 'Book review of *Engineering Equality: An Essay on European Anti-discrimination Law* (by Alexander Somek)', n 5 above.

and Human Rights (EIDHR), which seeks to promote human rights, including equality, in third countries.[10] With its own human rights agenda, the EU thus is not only a 'consumer' or recipient of international law; it also contributes to its development in various ways.[11] Still, the progressive incorporation of fundamental rights in the Treaties and the adoption of the Charter are of recent date, with the first 'hard law' reference to human rights in a Treaty coming as late as 1992 with the Treaty of Maastricht.[12]

Following the Amsterdam Treaty's incorporation of (then) Article 13 EC Treaty (now Article 19 TFEU),[13] three directives were adopted: the Racial Equality Directive 2000/43/EC, the Employment Equality Directive 2000/78/EC, and the Equal Treatment Directive between men and women in access to and supply of goods and services 2004/113/EC. These directives significantly elevated the level of protection throughout the EU; only a handful of countries—including the Netherlands, Ireland and the UK—had previously developed anti-discrimination legislation, while most Member States had only 'a patchy and ineffective legal framework' in place.[14] The geographical expansion of the EU since adoption of these directives renders the decision-making process[15] considerably more challenging, and to some extent can account for the stalling of further developments in non-discrimination law.[16]

The Charter of Fundamental Rights of the European Union (Charter)[17] solidifies the fundamental rights revolution in the EU, and is in itself a major

---

[10] McCrudden and Kountouros, 'Human Rights and European equality law', n 4 above, 83.

[11] eg by actively participating in the drafting process of treaties, such as the UN Convention on the Rights of Persons with Disabilities.

[12] Article 6 TEU. Prior to that, the CJEU applied fundamental rights by way of 'general principles of Community law', derived from Member States' constitutional traditions and international law, including the ECHR.

[13] Although the EU competency in the area of anti-discrimination was 'debatable' before then, the EU did introduce a number of noteworthy initiatives (eg European Council Resolutions on the fight against racism and xenophobia of 29 May 1990). See Isabelle Chopin, 'The Starting Line Group: A Harmonised Approach to Fight Racism and to promote Equal Treatment' (1999) 1 *European Journal of Migration and Law* 111–129.

[14] ie the 1994 Equal Treatment Act in the Netherlands, the 1998 Employment Equality Act in Ireland, and the Race Relations Act 1976 in the United Kingdom; Isabelle Chopin and Thien Uyen Do, *Developing Anti-Discrimination law in Europe. The 27 Member States, Croatia, Former Yugoslav Republic of Macedonia and Turkey compared.* (comparative analysis of country reports) (Brussels, European Network of Legal Experts in the Non-discrimination Field, 2010) 16. In addition, all Member States were bound by article 14 ECHR, but few had ratified Protocol No 12 (general prohibition of discrimination) to the ECHR.

[15] Article 19.1 TFEU requires that the Council act unanimously in accordance with a special legislative procedure and after obtaining the *consent* of the European Parliament when taking action to combat discrimination based on sex, racial or ethnic origin, religion or belief, disability, age or sexual orientation. In fact, there has been tightening of requirements, since the original Art 13 only required the *consultation* of the European Parliament.

[16] The 'Horizontal Directive' proposed by the European Commission (COM(2008) 425, Brussels, 2 July 2008) that aims to extend the scope of anti-discrimination to fields beyond the labour market is still pending but arguably has long lost momentum. Germany has been a vocal objector.

[17] The Charter was adopted on 7 December 2000 but was only made binding when the Lisbon Treaty entered into force in 2009.

development in symbolic[18] and real terms. The Charter draws on Member States' constitutional traditions, international legal instruments, particularly the ECHR, and the case law of the ECtHR and the CJEU, and is to be applied by EU institutions and the CJEU[19] as well by the Member States 'when they are implementing EU law'.[20] McCrudden and Kountouros argue the Charter is to be seen as a 'work in progress' rather than the 'apex of the achievement of human rights in the EU'.[21] Charter provisions 'shall not extend in any way the competences of the Union as defined in the Treaties'.[22] The Charter's specific scope of application makes clear that the Charter is not meant to replace the ECHR (which also applies beyond the EU).

The Charter divides human rights into six, as opposed to the original two, groups, under the headings 'dignity', 'freedoms', 'equality', 'solidarity', 'citizens' rights', and 'justice'. Article 10 protects the freedom of thought, conscience and religion;[23] equality before the law and non-discrimination including on the basis of religion or belief are protected under Articles 20 and 21.[24] Article 17 TFEU concerns the status of and the dialogue with churches, and religious and philosophical organisations.[25]

The protections provided by the Charter can exceed those under the ECHR.[26] Accession of the EU to the ECHR is expressly foreseen in the Treaty[27] following a 1996 CJEU opinion holding that the EU did not have the competence to accede to the Convention.[28] Accession to the ECHR and adoption of the Charter were once seen as interlinked, and expected to contribute to a more effective protection of human rights in the EU. However, as noted, following extended negotiations

---

[18] See Preamble 'it is necessary to strengthen the protection of fundamental rights in the light of changes in society, social progress and scientific and technological developments by making those rights *more visible* in a Charter' (emphasis added).

[19] See, eg, Cases C-293/12 and C-594/12, *Digital Rights Ireland Ltd v Minister for Communications, Marine and Natural resources and Others* and *Kärntner Landesregierung M Seitlinger and Others* [2014] ECLI 238 (invalidating the Data Retention Directive 2006/24/EC for violating fundamental rights under the Charter, ie the right to respect for private life and right to the protection of personal data).

[20] Article 51.1 of the Charter.

[21] McCrudden and Kountouros, 'Human Rights and European equality law', n 4 above, 101.

[22] See Art 6.1 TEU; Art 51.2 of the Charter.

[23] Art 10.1 of the Charter is similar to Art 9.1 of the ECHR. The limitation clause similar to Art 9.2 is included in Art 52.1 of the Charter (a general limitation clause) Art 10.2 specifically recognises 'the right to conscientious objection ... in accordance with the national laws governing the exercise of this right'.

[24] The open-ended list diverges from Art 14 ECHR, revealing its 'modern' status by including grounds such as genetic features, language, membership of a national minority, property, birth, disability, age and—particularly—sexual orientation.

[25] See C Joppke, 'Religion in the European Union: Comments on the RELIGARE Project' in MC Foblets et al (eds), *Belief, Law and Politics What Future for a Secular Europe?* (Aldershot, Ashgate, 2014).

[26] Article 52.3 and Art 53 of the Charter. As far as the relationship of the Charter's provision towards the constitutional protection is concerned, the situation is vaguer: Charter rights shall be 'interpreted in harmony with those traditions'. Art 52.4 of the Charter.

[27] Article 6.2 TEU.

[28] Opinion 2/94 of the CJEU of 28 March 1996 regarding the Accession by the Community to the ECHR [1996] ECR I-1759.

between EU and Council of Europe officials reaching to a draft accession agreement, the CJEU in its December 2014 Opinion 2/13 held that accession would not be compatible with the supremacy of EU law, so that accession at this time is indefinitely stalled.[29]

B. From Market Efficiency to Decommodification?

The advancement of the principle of equality is part and parcel of the EU 'fundamental rights revolution'. Since the 1990s, EU anti-discrimination law has expanded exponentially in reach, depth and importance, meriting the label of 'the most growing part of labour law'.[30] De Vos considers this growth as 'essentially a step-by-step organic development through an ever expanding array of case-law and secondary legislation without an overarching conceptual framework'.[31] Meenan similarly describes it as 'unpredictable, lacking in uniformity, sometimes timid and at other times daring'.[32] In particular, it is unclear which conception of equality—formal equality, substantive, equality of opportunities, equality of outcomes—EU law adopts.[33] De Vos argues that the 'primary emphasis of EC equality law lies on *formal equality*',[34] but that is not always the case, so that it is apt to say that the equality approach depends on the specific terrain of EU equality law.[35]

In addition, many areas of EU non-discrimination law remain rooted in, and at the same time limited by, an economic market-orientation; the goal being 'to ensure the establishment and proper functioning of the common market.[36] Indeed, the 'business case for equality' remains highly relevant as a convincing discourse in the EU, in particular in the aftermath of an economic crisis.[37] 'The right to equal treatment was gradually emancipated from the need to be formally legitimated by economic justifications',[38] but the status of equality as an 'autonomous principle' of human rights (ie having value independent of any economic or social benefits) remains a challenge. McCrudden and Kountouros have warned against turning back from this (still incomplete) advancement towards an autonomous

---

[29] Opinion 2/13 of the CJEU (Full Court) on 18 December 2014 on the Accession of the European Union to the ECHR, [2014] ECLI 2454.

[30] M De Vos, *Beyond Formal Equality. Positive Action under Directives 2000/43/EC and 2000/78/EC* (Brussels, European Network of Legal Experts in the Non-Discrimination Field, 2007).

[31] ibid, 10.

[32] Meenan, 'Introduction', n 2 above, 11.

[33] De Vos, *Beyond Formal Equality. Positive Action under Directives 2000/43/EC and 2000/78/EC*, n 30 above, 10.

[34] ibid, 10.

[35] Eg Art 141. 4 EC (now Art 157.4 TFEU) is drafted in substantive law terms with reference to the aim of 'ensuring full equality in practice between men and women in working life'. See also Daniela Caruso: 'the uncertain boundaries of equality in the EU', 22–24 (The EU has adhered to a 'traditional version of the equality paradigm, based on individual rights and identity-neutral justice').

[36] McCrudden and Kountouros, 'Human Rights and European equality law', n 4 above, 112.

[37] cf EU Equality Summit, 22–23 November 2012, Nicosia, Cyprus. The title of this Summit was 'Equality for growth' and much debate centered around the 'business case' for equality.

[38] McCrudden and Kountouros, 'Human Rights and European equality law', n 4 above, 112.

equality principle,[39] seeing equality as an object in itself instead of as a proxy to promote other—economic/efficiency—objectives.

The CJEU has recorded the organic shifts in the goal of this principle—from market integration to human rights—in a number of landmark cases, starting with *Defrenne v Sabena* in 1978,[40] where it was held that the equal pay provision in the EC Treaty has a 'double aim, which is at once economic and social' and recognising early on the right not to be discriminated against on grounds of sex as a fundamental personal human right and a general principle of European law.[41] But arguably equality had not yet reached a completely autonomous status in the EU, and the limitation of the Employment Equality Directive (2000) to employment and occupation illustrated such for the grounds of age, religion or belief, sexual orientation, disability.[42]

C. The Employment Equality Directive: Convergence of Terminology, Divergence of Understanding?

The Employment Equality Directive is the starting point for the analysis since it lays down the general framework for combating discrimination, including on the ground of religion or belief, in employment, occupation and vocational training. Member States were to implement the provisions in their domestic laws and have by now done so; the transposition was hardly unproblematic, but that chapter is now closed off. This means the European Commission's focus can shift to the effective application of the non-discrimination norms across the EU.[43] Still, it is noteworthy that infringement proceedings due to non-conformity under Article 258 TFEU were initiated by the European Commission against 25 Member States, mostly between 2005 and 2007.[44] According to the European Commission,

---

[39] ibid, 112–13. See also More, 'The principle of Equal Treatment: From Market Unifier to Fundamental Right?', 547.

[40] Case C-149/77, *Defrenne v Société anonyme belge de navigation aérienne Sabena (No 3)* [1978] ECR I-1365.

[41] Meenan, 'Introduction', n 2 above, 11–12.

[42] L Waddington, *The Expanding Role of the Equality Principle in European Union Law* (European University Institute, Robert Schuman Centre for Advanced Studies, 2003) 29.

[43] Press release European Commission 'Equality: EU rules to tackle discrimination now in place in all 28 EU Member States'—IP/14/27, 17/01/2014. ('further efforts are needed to apply them in practice ... Key challenges include a lack of public awareness of rights and underreporting of discrimination cases').

[44] European Commission, *Joint Report on the application of Council Directive 2000/43/EC of 29 June 2000 implementing the principle of equal treatment between persons irrespective of racial or ethnic origin ('Racial Equality Directive') and of Council Directive 2000/78/EC of 27 November 2000 establishing a general framework for equal treatment in employment and occupation ('Employment Equality Directive') from the Commission to the European Parliament and the Council, Brussels, 17.1.2014,* COM(2014) 2 final (17 January 2014) 3. In one case infringement proceedings led to a decision by the CJEU finding a breach of the obligation to properly implement Directive 2000/78//EC (in relation to reasonable accommodation for disabled persons in employment); Case C-312/11, *European Commission v Italian Republic* [2013] ECLI 446.

'the novelty of the two Directives at the time' explains the multiple problems with transposition.[45] With regard to religion or belief in the Directive, the main implementation issue concerned the derogation in Article 4(2) of the Directive for religious-ethos companies, which appeared as a problem for six Member States, including the Netherlands and the UK.[46] The religious-ethos exemption proved to be intricate and adding to the complexity was the fact that at the same time a number of Member States were adopting or expanding rights for same-sex couples to marry or register for partnerships.[47]

The stated aims of the Directive, as apparent from the recitals, fall under three different headings: fundamental rights (recitals 1, 4, 5, 6), economic justifications (recitals 7, 11, 17, 37) and social integration/inclusion (recitals 8, 9, 27), without elaborating on the relations between these different goals, or stating any particular hierarchy.[48] The issue of overarching justification for EU equality law can be significant in the application and interpretation of the specific protections provided, since for instance the economic efficiency argument would seem to limit the extent of discrimination protection and accommodations much more than in a fundamental rights or social inclusion discourse mode.[49] More recently, a return to the economic roots of anti-discrimination law has in fact taken place,[50] despite the fact that some commentators have argued that 'the human rights rationale of the Employment Directive [was] a dominant rationale of that instrument' and that 'these principles are no longer merely related to market integration'.[51]

The Employment Equality Directive prohibits direct and indirect discrimination as well as harassment and instruction to discriminate on the basis of religion or belief, disability, age and sexual orientation.[52] 'Direct discrimination' occurs when one person is treated less favourably than another on the basis of one of the protected characteristics, while 'indirect discrimination' means 'an apparently neutral provision, criterion or practice' which places persons having such a protected characteristic at a particular disadvantage compared with other persons.[53]

---

[45] ibid, 3 ('Typical problems concerned the definitions of direct and indirect discrimination, harassment, victimisation, legal standing of interested organisations, limitations to the scope and too extensive interpretation of the derogations which are permitted under the Directives').

[46] See Chopin and Uyen Do, *Developing Anti-Discrimination law in Europe. The 27 Member States, Croatia, Former Yugoslav Republic of Macedonia and Turkey compared*, n 14 above, 32.

[47] ibid, 87.

[48] Some commentators have argued that 'the human rights rationale of the Employment Directive [was] a dominant rationale', see Meenan, 'Introduction', n 2 above.

[49] Recital 17, restating the 'merit principle' in employment arguably limits the fundamental rights/ social inclusion aims, not limited to the case of persons with disability. For revealing this merit principle as a myth, see IM Young, *Justice and the politics of difference* (Princeton NJ, Princeton University Press, 1990), 200 et seq ('The myth of merit').

[50] See C O'Brien, 'Equality's false summits: new varieties of disability discrimination, "excessive" equal treatment and economically constricted horizons' (2011) 36 *European Law Review* 26. See also the holding back of the Horizontal Anti-discrimination Directive, which goes beyond employment and occupation.

[51] Meenan, 'Introduction', n 2 above.

[52] Article 1 Employment Equality Directive.

[53] Article 2.2(a) and (b) of the Employment Equality Directive.

Differences in treatment based *directly* on religion or belief cannot be justified unless conditions for a 'genuine and determining occupational requirement' are met and provided also that 'the objective is legitimate and the requirement is proportionate'.[54] When the link to religion or belief under a difference of treatment is *indirect*, however, there is an open justification regime, ie the apparently neutral 'provision, criterion or practice' can be justified by showing that 'there is a legitimate goal and the means of achieving this goal are appropriate and necessary'.[55]

The concept of direct discrimination was included in the original EC Treaty in respect to the forerunner grounds of sex and nationality. Under Article 2(a) of the Directive it is defined as 'where one person is treated less favourably than another person'. However, EU law has long recognised that treating differently situated persons in the same way may also constitute discrimination.[56] Despite being a 'relatively straightforward legal concept', the application of direct discrimination and its proof raises various challenges, such as the presence of causation, the (ir)relevance of a motive and whether there is a need for a comparator.[57] In the Member States, the issue of discrimination comparator is handled differently, with eg such 'emphasis on identifying an appropriate comparator [being the] strongest in the UK'.[58]

The more intricate concept of indirect discrimination was developed through ECJ/CJEU case law in the 1960s and 1970s with regard to sex and nationality discrimination. In *Defrenne v Sabena (No 2)* the Court made a distinction, between 'direct and overt discrimination' and 'indirect and disguised discrimination', which was maintain for a few years only.[59] The 'real birth' of the concept was *Jenkins v Kingsgate*.[60] *Bilka-Kaufhaus* then set out the test for justifying indirect sex discrimination, ie the requirement to show a 'real need on the part of the

---

[54] Article 4.1 of the Employment Equality Directive: a difference in treatment based on religion or belief may be justifiable under the Directive; Art 4.2 refers to the particular regime for so-called religious ethos companies.

[55] Article 2.2(b)(i) of the Employment Equality Directive.

[56] Meenan, 'Introduction', n 2 above, 21; Case C-279/93, *Finanzamt Köln-Altstadt v Schumacker* [1995] ECR I-225 ('discrimination can arise only arise through the application of different rules to comparable situations or the application of the same rule to different situations'. para 30).

[57] Bell, 'Chapter two: direct discrimination', in D Schiek, L Waddington and M Bell (eds), *Cases, materials and text on national, supranational and international non-discrimination law* (Oxford, Hart Publishing, 2007) 185; with regard to the comparator question, some commentators have argued direct discrimination claims are impossible to deal with without going over the issue of a comparator, while others argue discrimination as a social practice does not depend on comparisons; direct discrimination may be 'self-evident without the need for a comparator'. ibid, 206.

[58] ibid, 208 (discussing who the appropriate comparator to a man who is undergoing gender reassignment: a man who is not undergoing such procedure, or rather a woman who is also undergoing gender reassignment?) In the case of religion discrimination, one can imagine the question on the relevant comparator being between a secular employee or rather an employee of the same religion but which does not practise to the same extent as the employee allegedly discriminated.

[59] Case 43/75, *Defrenne v Sabena (No 2)* [1976] ECR 455. The CJEU later acknowledged that direct discrimination can also be disguised. Case C-69/80, *Worringham v Lloyds Bank Ltd* [1981] ECR I-767.

[60] Case C-96/80, *Jenkins v Kingsgate (Clothing Productions) Ltd* [1981] ECR I-911; Meenan, 'Introduction', n 2 above, 19.

undertaking' which is 'appropriate' and 'necessary' to achieve the set-out objectives.[61] The language of objective justification for indirect discrimination under Article 2(b)i of the Directive differs only slightly, in that a 'real need' was replaced by a 'legitimate aim'.

In 2014, the European Commission explicitly acknowledged the difficulties surrounding this concept in both the implementation as well as in the application case, saying:

> The concept of indirect discrimination is complex and many Member States had initial difficulties in transposing it correctly. It is now enshrined in law, but its application in practice remains a challenge. To illustrate the problem, some Member States report that concerns have been expressed about the lack of clarity or lack of understanding of the concept of indirect discrimination in national courts. Other Member States point out that they do not yet have any case-law providing interpretation of indirect discrimination.[62]

Harassment, a concept with roots in sex discrimination law, is defined under Article 2(3) of the Directive as 'unwanted conduct related to any of the grounds referred to in Article 1 [which] takes place with the purpose or effect of violating the dignity of a person *and* of creating an intimidating, hostile, degrading, humiliating or offensive environment'.[63] The Directive extends this to the ground of religion or belief. Some leeway is provided to Member States in the definition of this concept which is reflected in the textual divergences in Member State anti-discrimination laws, some requiring a violation of dignity *and* a certain environment, while under other national anti-discrimination codes *either* of the two elements— violation of human dignity or the existence of the negative environment—can constitute harassment.[64] The Directive does not give additional guidance on how to determine whether conduct is such as to violate a person's dignity or to create a negative environment.[65] Harassment does not require less favourable treatment in comparison with other workers; there are no foreseen justifications once harassment is established. Also, an employer is responsible not only for his own conduct

---

[61] Case 170/84, *Bilka-Kaufhaus GmbH v Weber von Hartz* [1986] IRLR 317, para 36.

[62] Commission, *Joint Report on the application of Council Directive 2000/43/EC of 29 June 2000 implementing the principle of equal treatment between persons irrespective of racial or ethnic origin ('Racial Equality Directive') and of Council Directive 2000/78/EC of 27 November 2000 establishing a general framework for equal treatment in employment and occupation ('Employment Equality Directive') from the Commission to the European Parliament and the Council, Brussels, 17.1.2014, COM(2014) 2 final*, 8.

[63] See Art. 2 (3) of the Employment Equality Directive (emphasis added); however, 'the concept of harassment may be defined in accordance with the national laws and practice of the Member States'.

[64] One could argue that creating such an undesirable work environment violates employees' dignity, but such interpretation would run counter to the textual strategy in listing both circumstances under harassment. Under UK law, either element is sufficient while under Belgian and Dutch law both must be shown. For the UK, see G Pitt, 'Religion or belief: aiming at the right target?' in H Meenan (ed), *Equality law in an enlarged European Union: Understanding the article 13 directives* (Cambridge, CUP 2007) 220. Compare Art 4.10 of the Belgian Anti-discrimination Law ('*intimidatie*'); Art 1.a.2 of the Dutch Equal Treatment Act harassment ('*intimidatie*').

[65] Chopin and Uyen Do, *Developing Anti-Discrimination law in Europe. The 27 Member States, Croatia, Former Yugoslav Republic of Macedonia and Turkey compared.*, n 14 above, 8.

but also for the conduct of co-workers and customers.[66] There is a recurring question of whether offence should be subjectively or objectively grounded, but with the lack of case law this issue remains rather theoretical: in practice, ethno-religious employees, even when they feel they are justified to feel offended, often seem to choose to carry on or dismiss the issue in favour of a highly reconciliatory and accepting strategy.[67]

The harassment concept may offer interesting perspectives for addressing discriminatory work cultures[68] and mediating the proper scope of (discussed) religion in the workplace. As of yet, there is not much experience under EU or domestic law when it comes to addressing religious harassment in the workplace.[69] Concerns involve the chilling effects on free speech in the work setting, particularly if sensibilities run high.[70] Indeed, co-workers may feel 'inhibited from saying something if they fear that a person may perceive it is a violation of their dignity or is creating an offensive environment'.[71] Banning religious discrimination in the workplace may have 'an inevitable interference with individual freedom of speech; members of staff are not free to speak to colleagues as they might otherwise wish, where that speech would cause offence or create a hostile environment'.[72] On the other hand, if the right to free speech is seen to justify 'the right to offend religious minorities',[73] there is also a danger that antagonistic 'critical' attitudes towards

---

[66] J Łopatowska, 'Discrimination based on religion or belief in the EU legal framework' in *Derecho y Religión. Vol IV: Religion in the European Law* (Delta Publicaciones, 2009) 79; Chopin and Uyen Do, *Developing Anti-Discrimination law in Europe. The 27 Member States, Croatia, Former Yugoslav Republic of Macedonia and Turkey compared.*, n 14 above, 66 ('Another area left open by the Directives is the responsibility of the employer for acts of harassment by other workers or by third parties such as customers. In many states, employers can be held liable for the actions of their workers to varying degrees. Some Member States have chosen to place a specific duty on employers to take action to prevent and redress harassment in the workplace ... In Belgium, further to the dismissal of a trade union representative charged with harassment in November 2010, the Belgian association of employers called for the development of a general code of practice on harassment with trade unions').

[67] ENAR *Shadow Report 2012–2013 on Racism and Discrimination in Employment in Europe* (Netherlands. March 2013), 26.

[68] TK Green, 'Work culture and discrimination' (2005) 93 *California Law Review* 623.

[69] L Vickers, *Religion and Belief Discrimination in Employment—the EU law* (Brussels, European Network of Legal Experts in the Non-Discrimination Field, 2006) 15–16; Łopatowska, 'Discrimination based on religion or belief in the EU legal framework', n 66 above, 79–80.

[70] Vickers, *Religion and Belief Discrimination in Employment—the EU law*, n 69 above, 16 (speaking of 'particular problems with regard to religious harassment, as not only are the terms religion and belief undefined, but there may a relative lack of shared understanding of the likely effects of certain behaviour on religious people. Members of the same religion will not all agree on what might cause offence ... too subjective a test of offence could have a chilling effect on freedom of speech'); Łopatowska, 'Discrimination based on religion or belief in the EU legal framework', n 66 above, 80 ('using the same rules for religious harassment and other grounds of harassment might be problematic. Unless harassment provisions are very carefully drafted they can punish or inhibit the free expression of opinion').

[71] Łopatowska, 'Discrimination based on religion or belief in the EU legal framework', n 66 above, 80.

[72] Vickers, *Religion and Belief Discrimination in Employment-the EU law*, n 69 above, 40.

[73] In the case of the Netherlands: see Netherlands ENAR Shadow report, n 67 above, 3 ('the freedoms of thought and speech have increasingly been interpreted as the freedom to insult').

minority religions, in particular Islam, are taken too far in the workplace.[74] For instance, what happens if a group of workers assert that 'all Muslims are terrorists' and a Muslim co-worker overhears this or is the main recipient of the comment? How far can such 'discussions' reach before a person starts to feel uncomfortable, stigmatised, or harassed?

A workplace clearly becomes a negative environment for employees of particular religions or beliefs in the case of physical abuses or unmediated and repeated derogatory comments and critique of one's religion. But can the imposition of a strict ban on *discussing* religion be indicative of a workplace hostile to religion? At times,

> an employer might end up in the unenviable position of either trying to justify a ban on discussing certain kinds of 'sensitive' subjects in the workplace, which could potentially be indirect discrimination on the basis of religion or belief, or else facing claims of harassment from harassed employees on grounds of a hostile environment.[75]

This will be an emerging area of case law in the years to come.[76]

Here, ECtHR case law will be relevant, especially considering that EU fundamental rights protection can exceed but not limit ECHR protections.[77] A number of ECtHR cases have addressed the issue of when proselytism, as part of the freedom to manifest religion,[78] becomes 'improper'.[79] In *Larissis v Greece*,[80] a case which concerned the military context, some limits on proselytism in the workplace were set. In particular, the ECtHR held that 'attempts by a manager to influence the religion or belief of his or her subordinates could be regarded as harassment

---

[74] See Netherlands ENAR shadow report, n 67 above, 26 regarding racial/ethnic hostile workplaces ('Recipients of these remarks may also fail to recognise their racist content. Also, managers and supervisors frequently fail to recognise or acknowledge the discriminatory aspects of employees' remarks. Such expressions are often brushed off as a joke, not to be taken seriously. In this way, employees from ethnic minorities need to accept often extremely inappropriate and even racist 'jokes'. In these situations, the responsibility to 'choose not to be offended' is with the minority ... the discriminatory nature of these remarks is, due to lack of evidence, extremely difficult to prove ... complaints they receive in this regard can often not be followed up for this reason').

[75] Pitt, 'Religion or belief: aiming at the right target?', n 64 above, 221.

[76] See Netherlands ENAR shadow report, n 67 above, 26 ('While there is no statistical evidence, interviewees reported that most minorities at times will experience negative references about their—visible—ethnic or religious background or affiliation in the workplace. Minorities are often perceived as 'ambassador' of their religion or ethnicity, and thus are rebuked for actions of another individual of that ethnic or religious community ... true for Jewish people who are sometimes held accountable for the situation in Israel') With regard to comments made towards Jewish employees in the Belgian workplace, see Efrat Tzadik, 'Jewish Women in the Belgian Workplace: An Anthropological Perspective' in K Alidadi, M-C Foblets and J Vrielink (eds), *A Test of Faith? Religious Diversity and Accommodation in the European Workplace* (Aldershot, Ashgate, 2012) 237.

[77] Article 52.3 and Art 53 of the Charter.

[78] See *Kokkinakis v Greece*, Application no 14307/88 (ECtHR, 25 May 1993).

[79] Similarly, under ECHR law: see, eg, partially, in *Larissis v Greece* that had been the case: 'what in the civilian world would be seen as an innocuous exchange of ideas which the recipient is free to accept or reject, may within the confines of military life, be viewed as a form of harassment or the application of undue pressure in abuse of power').

[80] *Larissis and Others v Greece*, Application nos 23372/94, 26377/94 and 26378/94 (ECtHR, 24 February 1998).

on the grounds of religion or belief through interfering with the employees' own beliefs'.[81] However, the case also indicates important workplace freedoms to discuss and even promote religion. In some cases attempts to convert co-employees may also be seen as offensive, but the mere discussing of religious topics should not fall within such threshold as this is protected under Article 9 and Article 10 of the ECHR.

Instruction to discriminate based on religion or belief[82] and victimisation[83] are also covered under the Directive, and similarly to the case of racial/ethnic instruction to discriminate, may be highly relevant in case of religion or belief. For instance, in the case of employers seeking employees through interim/ employment agencies, the issue comes up. Here as well, the jurisprudential developments regarding the discrimination ground of religion or belief have been slow.

Under Article 7(1) of the Directive, positive action with regard to religion or belief (giving advantages to adherents of particular religions or beliefs in order to prevent disadvantage or to compensate for past disadvantage) is possible, but 'no Member State has indicated any intention to legislate along these lines in relation to religion or belief'.[84] Also, as is apparent from the European Commission's 2014 joint report on the Employment Equality Directive and the Racial Equality Directive,[85] this is a largely dormant option.

D. On 'Religion or Belief' Discrimination under EU Equality Law

Various taxonomies of the protected EU discrimination grounds can be proposed. First, there is a 'hierarchical approach' with the best protected ground on top (race equality, then sex discrimination, with religion or belief further down the line). Another taxonomy is based on the nature of the protected ground (grounds related to ascribed differences, actual and unalterable biological differences, differences

---

[81] Pitt, 'Religion or belief: aiming at the right target?', n 64 above, 221. However, one should bear in mind that ordinary employment relations are less confining than the military so that freedoms can be broader.

[82] Article 2.4 Employment Equality Directive.

[83] Article 11 Employment Equality Directive. Victimisation which 'aims to protect employees against dismissal or other adverse treatment by the employer as a reaction to a complaint within the undertaking or to any legal proceedings aimed at enforcing compliance with the principle of equal treatment'

[84] Pitt, 'Religion or belief: aiming at the right target?', n 64 above, 223, referring to country reports on the implementation of the Anti-discrimination directives in 2004–2005. With the notable exception of the situation in Northern Ireland, see Art 15 Employment Equality Directive regarding police and teachers. See also Chopin and Uyen Do, n 14 above, 91, only referring to the UK with the positive duty to promote/give due regard to equality objectives, including when it concerns religion or belief. 'most positive actions relate to disability in the various Member States, and a handful for race and ethnicity or Roma'.

[85] Brussels, 17.1.2014, COM(2014) 2 final.

viewed as immutable or rather as the product of choice).[86] Interestingly, in her discussion of this issue, Dagmar Schiek places both religion/belief as well as sexual orientation at the bottom of her list, as these are considered to be a result of personal choice. Pitt criticises the allocation of the ground of sexual orientation under the choice category since many people would argue their sexuality is not due to a lifestyle choice and 'the same is arguably true of religious adherence'.[87] Also, Schiek places age and disability under the category of actual biological differences, while Pitt remarks that lifestyle choice, such as smoking, can affect disability as well as someone's perceived age.[88] Instead, Pitt argues that religion or belief, in its three meanings of belief, identity, and way of life, is a ground which 'cuts across [the three] categories'. For instance, Muslims as perceived 'others' in Europe are sometimes discriminated against because of their group identity, irrespective of their actual beliefs. They are then discriminated against based on an 'associated socially constructed difference' rather than because of some personal choice.

Religion or belief is unique compared with the other grounds protected by Article 13, since it is the only one which also appears as a positive freedom under the ECHR.[89] Religion or belief is exceptional for yet another reason amongst the various other discrimination grounds:

> Anti-discrimination provisions for the other protected grounds express a consensus about particular values of equality and the irrelevance of certain characteristics which are relatively straightforward to understand and uncontroversial ... However, a blanket protection for religion or belief potentially provides protection for the holders of completely abhorrent, or irrational, or bigoted beliefs, including those which would certainly not accord equal rights to others if they were to prevail.[90]

The Employment Equality Directive merely refers to 'religion or belief', without defining it (similarly to other international instruments, including the ECHR). Also, '[n]o Member State has attempted to provide a comprehensive definition of "religion or belief" within anti-discrimination legislation'.[91] In the UK, there is some guidance on the terms 'religion or belief' in the anti-discrimination

---

[86] D Schiek, 'A new framework on equal treatment of persons in EC law?' (2002) 8 *European Law Journal* 290, 309–12, discussed in G Pitt, 'Religion or belief: aiming at the right target?' n 64 above, 224–25.

[87] Pitt, 'Religion or belief: aiming at the right target?', n 64 above, 225.

[88] ibid, 226.

[89] 'Religion' is also listed under Art 14 ECHR's open-ended non-discrimination list, as are: sex, race, colour, language, political or other opinion, national or social origin, association with a national minority, property, birth or other status. Disability, age and sexual orientation are not ad nominem included, but can be considered to fall under 'other status'. eg *Salgueiro da Silva Mouta v Portugal*, Application no 33290/96 (ECtHR, 21 December 1999).

[90] Pitt, 'Religion or belief: aiming at the right target?', n 64 above, 213, giving the example of someone with Nazi sympathies who could also not be treated unfavourably. Nazism has been accepted as a belief in *X v Austria*, Application no 1747/62 (EComHR, 13 December 1963).

[91] J Cormack and M Bell, *Developing Anti-Discrimination law in Europe: The 25 EU Member States Compared* (European Network of Independent Experts in the non-discrimination field, September 2005).

legislation. Under the 2010 UK Equality Act, section 10, 'Religion means any religion and a reference to religion includes a reference to a lack of religion' and 'Belief means any religious or philosophical belief and a reference to belief includes a reference to a lack of belief'.[92] Under the Employment Equality (Religion or Belief) Regulations 2003, the Explanatory Notes required 'a certain level of cogency, seriousness, cohesion and importance, provided that the beliefs are worthy of respect in a democratic society and are not incompatible with human dignity'. Pitt noted that '[c]uriously, the guidance given to the UK legislation by the Advisory, Conciliation and Arbitration Service (Acas) was different in a way that "may be unduly restrictive, reflecting a Western Christian, Ethnocentricity and discriminating against newer religions"'.[93] Now, Acas guidance prescribes 'For the purposes of the Equality Act 2010 a religion must have a clear structure and belief system', but then turns to the Equality Act guidance that it summarises.

There is also no distinction as to the different aspects of religion or belief in social life, whereas sociologists of law include at least three meanings of religion: one, religion as belief; second, religion as identity (group membership); and third, religion as a way of life.[94] Some of the meanings bear a striking overlap with race/ethnicity, and thus could be captured under the notion of 'ethnicity-plus'. But this is certainly not the case for all the aspects of religion, justifying its separate adoption as a protected ground.

Taking the different meanings of religion into account, Pitt asks whether the same level of protection should be awarded in all cases where religion—irrespective of whether in the sense of belief, group identity or way of life—is concerned. She argues that a uniform level of protection is not justified, favouring instead a system where 'religion as ascribed characteristic' (the identity component) would be absorbed under the notion of race and ethnic origin. Other aspects of religion—'belief' and 'way of life' manifestations—should then stay at the current lower level of protection since they are the 'product of free choice'.[95] This argument, however, disregards that the various meanings of religion overlap and are closely intertwined: identity is not only something ascribed to an individual or group by

---

[92] The Explanatory Notes on Section 10 offer further guidance, including a list of religions ('The Baha'i faith, Buddhism, Christianity, Hinduism, Islam, Jainism, Judaism, Rastafarianism, Sikhism and Zoroastrianism are all religions for the purposes of this provision') and beliefs ('Beliefs such as humanism and atheism would be beliefs for the purposes of this provision but adherence to a particular football team would not be').

[93] Pitt, 'Religion or belief: aiming at the right target?', n 64 above, 211 (according to Acas, courts would take into account 'factors such as collective worship, a clear belief system and a profound belief affecting the way of life or view of the world').

[94] See JT Gunn, 'The Complexity of Religion and the Definition of 'Religion' in International Law' (2003) 16 *Harvard Human Rights Journal* 189.

[95] Pitt, 'Religion or belief: aiming at the right target?', n 64 above, 226–27. See also at 205 wondering 'whether the classification of religion alongside belief in the scheme of EU equality law is appropriate or whether the problem of exclusion would be better addressed through an expanded notion of race and ethnicity, whether, in fact, Art. 13 [19] and the Framework Employment Directive are aiming at the right target in relation to this protected ground'.

others; it is a social construction which is to some extent influenced by an individual's beliefs and certainly by outward manifestations of those beliefs. People engage in religious manifestations to feel closer/connected to their group identity and—vice versa—the feeling of identity can influence way of life, including dress and observance of religious time commitments. I would argue that religion may be like ethnicity in its aspect of belonging, but not in its performative component (the component of practice) nor in its belief-aspect, so that aiming to include religion in a larger notion of ethnicity fails to include all the relevant aspects while diluting religion to belonging. If the aim is to protect religion and belief in their various facets, it should not be forced into an 'ethnicity-plus' approach. Either way, the textual argument would point to the holistic notion of 'religion or belief' when it comes to legal protection against discrimination.

Another question regarding definition is whether the same definitional tests can be used across different legal contexts, eg human rights and non-discrimination law, asylum law, charity and tax law, etc. Indeed,

> different contexts may quite properly entail different factors being given different weight ... when what is at issue is whether or not an organisation should receive financial privileges or whether members of a sect alleged to engage in harmful practices should be allowed to enter a country, it may be appropriate to focus on the formal structure ... In the case of someone seeking exemption from military service, the person's sincerity, as measured in part by the coherence of his beliefs and the consistency of his behaviour can properly be regarded as the most important factors.[96]

Here, Pitt argues that 'different considerations apply to a positive freedom compared with a negative protection from adverse treatment'. Thus, different definitional tests or approaches may be appropriate when considering different sorts of claims. This could heighten the complexity of religion or belief protection even further. In contrast, Hepple and Choudhury favour a liberal approach to the definition of religion or belief on the grounds that 'anti-discrimination legislation is aimed at protecting individuals from arbitrary treatment on the basis of beliefs which they are believed to hold (whether rightly or wrongly)—thus the validity of the belief itself should not be a major issue'.[97]

---

[96] ibid, 210.

[97] Home Office Research Study 221 (2001), 31; cited by Pitt, ibid, 215 while only partially agreeing since 'if this approach is correct, it has the result that an employer could be liable for discrimination if he or she rejects a job applicant because that person professes belief in a theory of racial superiority ... Is that a satisfactory state of affairs?' To reply to Pitt, it would be different if an employer rejects a person based on the manifestation of their beliefs (including racial or sex superiority, or against homosexual conduct) rather than merely rejects applicants because of their beliefs. The latter would indeed constitute direct discrimination and would only be allowed if a genuine and determining occupational job requirement could be pointed to, eg to work in an equal rights non-profit organisation the person who believes in racial superiority would be out (under human rights law though forum internum is absolute). However, manifestations could lead to problems with other workers, or create a hostile work environment, and could be restricted for those reasons (reasonable accommodations should also not be given if they would create a hostile work environment or otherwise lead to harassment charges.

There is another reason that some argue the definitional test under human rights cannot be adopted when it comes to anti-discrimination law. The 'over-lap confusion' is one important discussion when it comes to the relation between Article 9—which distinguishes between the *forum internum* and the *forum externum*—and anti-discrimination law—which protects against discrimination on the ground of religion or belief without specifying whether this concerns only (religious) belief or also manifestations of it. On the one hand, the ECHR institutions are said to be quite generous with accepting the existence of a religion worthy of protection under the treaty.[98] However, this may be due to the approach of the Commission (until 1998) and the Court to

> move straight to a consideration of whether or not the respondent country has a defence under Art. 9 (2) without first examining closely whether the religion or belief qualifies as a protected 'religion or belief'.[99]

Evans similarly addresses this generous definitional-restrictive coverage strategy as follows:

> [T]he Commission and Court have moved from a very liberal definition of 'religion or belief' to a very restrictive view of what freedom of religion and belief entail … they have in fact developed a conservative conception of these notions that belies the expansive approach taken at the definitional stage.[100]

On the other hand, under EU equality law the protection of 'religion or belief' does not address the *forum internum/forum externum* distinction. It may be stated that, in the more common case of indirect religion or belief discrimination, there will be an opportunity to justify restrictions under an open objective justification test, and that that phase may dominate the judicial reasoning in discrimination cases, just as the considerations with regard to Article 9(2) dominate cases framed under freedom of religion or belief. In the case of direct discrimination, however, some questions arise: if one is discriminated for holding certain beliefs (*forum internum*) a justification of genuine occupational requirement would seem to provide less protection than Article 9(1) ECHR. Still, in case of direct discrimination for certain manifestations of religion or belief (eg dress) the same closed justification regime seems to offer a higher level of protection than under Article 9(2) where restrictions on the *forum externum* can be justified under an open justification regime.

This is significant; 'if manifestation is not included in the concept, then discrimination on grounds of the worker's manifestation of his or her religion or belief would be actionable only if it constitutes indirect discrimination or

---

[98] PM Taylor, *Freedom of religion: UN and European human rights law and practice* (Cambridge, Cambridge University Press, 2005) 208. (eg cases cited with regard to the Church of Scientology, the Moon Sect, the Divine Light Zentrum, Druidism); C Evans, *Freedom of religion under the European Convention on Human Rights* (Oxford, Oxford University Press, 2001) 66.

[99] Pitt, 'Religion or belief: aiming at the right target?', n 64 above, 211.

[100] Evans, *Freedom of religion under the European Convention on Human Rights*, n 98 above, 66.

harassment'.[101] The examples of dress codes and religious time observances can illustrate this. In the case of a Sikh job applicant who wears a turban and was rejected for this very reason, this might make all the difference: it could be considered direct discrimination, or it could be seen as indirect discrimination leading the court to consider objective justification. For Pitt, '[o]ne reason for preferring the indirect discrimination approach is that it gives greater discretion to the adjudicator to weigh the competing interests of the employer and the worker'; she favours a restrictive approach:

> Unlike ECHR Article 9, the Directive makes no overt reference to *manifestations* of religion or belief. It could be argued that 'on the grounds of religion or belief' must include manifesting that belief at least to some extent, but given that ECHR Article 9 specifically differentiates between having a belief and manifesting it, there may be doubt as to whether such an argument would be successful.[102]

But this approach is diluting the protection against religion and belief discrimination unduly, and rendering direct discrimination meaningless. In fact, the argument could not be too far from advocating that all discrimination cases should have open justification (eg like the system in Canada). This approach unduly restricts the reach of anti-discrimination law (particularly, rendering almost meaningless the protection against direct religious discrimination). It can, however, be argued that what was to be protected was not just people's inner beliefs, but people's practices and way of life (as well) when it could relate to the workplace. For instance, the 2010 Equality Act, under the Explanatory Notes, Section 10 on Religion or Belief states:

> This section defines the protected characteristic of religion or religious or philosophical belief, which is stated to include for this purpose a lack of religion or belief. *It is a broad definition in line with the freedom of thought, conscience and religion guaranteed by Article 9 of the European Convention on Human Rights.* The main limitation for the purposes of Article 9 is that the religion must have a clear structure and belief system. Denominations or sects within a religion can be considered to be a religion or belief, such as Protestants and Catholics within Christianity (emphasis added).

Thus, manifestations would seem to fall under 'religion' under the UK guidelines. In fact, in the Netherlands when it comes to dress codes some cases are considered under the direct discrimination angle, others under the indirect discrimination angle, depending on the way the employer framed his restrictive policy: was an applicant rejected for wearing a headscarf or because she was considered to be unable to respect the dress code. The distinguishing factor is not whether a manifestation or merely a belief is at stake (the two are effectively intertwined, and it is difficult to see how discrimination on the basis of non-manifested inner beliefs would lead to discrimination other than in the very rare case), but rather the framing of the demand by the employer: did the demand or policy target the

---

[101] Pitt, 'Religion or belief: aiming at the right target?', n 64 above, 216.
[102] ibid, 216.

The EU and Religion in the Workplace

religion (or certain aspects of it) of the employee directly or rather did it involve an apparently neutral provision, criterion or practice' with repercussions for the freedom of religion or belief? This would prevent the crudest cases of dress code or religious time discrimination from falling under a broad judicial discretion and an open justification regime, and for that reason already is preferable.

Advocate Generals Kokott and Sharpston, in their opinions of 31 May 2016 and 13 July 2016 respectively, weighed in on this debate regarding the relationship between justification for direct/indirect discrimination and justification for freedom of religion restrictions under Article 9(2) ECHR.[103] in the case of *Asma Bougnaoui v Micropole SA*, AG Sharpston considered the dismissal of the Muslim design engineer for wearing a headscarf when dealing with the employer's customers (who complained because her wearing of a veil had 'embarrassed a number of its employees') to constitute direct discrimination based on religion.[104] She writes: 'Does the prohibition laid down by Directive 2000/78 extend not only to the religion or belief of an employee but also to manifestations of that religion or belief? In my view, it does'.[105]

Sharpston reasoned that the protection given by EU law against direct discrimination is stronger that under the ECHR, which does not know the direct-indirect discrimination dichotomy.[106] In contrast, Advocate General Kokott acknowledges that the term 'religion or belief' under the EU Directive 2000/78 is to be interpreted broadly,[107] meaning including both the *forum internum* and *forum externum*,[108] but she nonetheless proceeds to argue that dismissal because of following certain religious practices (here: wearing a headscarf) should not be given the same protection as religious status discrimination because the employee has a freedom/ choice to alter religious practices. Employment exclusion based on religious dress (the headscarf) could thus not amount to *direct discrimination*, according to AG Kokott who writes:

> [I]n its previous case-law concerning various EU-law prohibitions on discrimination, the Court has generally adopted a broad understanding of the concept of direct discrimination, and has, it is true, always assumed such discrimination to be present where a measure was inseparably linked to the relevant reason for the difference of treatment.

> However, all of those cases were without exception concerned with individuals' immutable physical features or personal characteristics—such as gender, age or sexual

---

[103] Case C-188/15, *Asma Bougnaoui and Association de défense des droits de l'homme (ADDH) v Micropole SA*, Opinion of Advocate General E Sharpston, 13 July 2016; Case C-157/15, *Samira Achbita and Centrum voor gelijkheid van kansen en voor racismebestrijding v G4S Secure Solutions NV*, Opinion of Advocate General J Kokott, 31 May 2016.

[104] See para 88.

[105] Paragraphs 85–86.

[106] Paragraph 63.

[107] See para 35: 'The term "religion" used in Article 1 of Directive 2000/78 must be understood in a broad sense. It includes not only the faith of an individual as such (*forum internum*) but also the practice and manifestation of that religion, including in public spaces (*forum externum*) ... The overarching objective of that directive is to create a working environment that is free from discrimination ... If this objective is to be achieved to best effect, the scope of that directive cannot be defined restrictively'.

[108] AG Sharpston addresses this question (and comes to a different conclusion) at paras 85–86.

orientation—rather than with modes of conduct based on a subjective decision or conviction, such as the wearing or not of a head covering at issue here.[109]

This then leads to the argument that the company neutrality policy adopted by the employer in the case, G4S, subsequent[110] to the employee headscarf dispute 'cannot properly be classified as constituting direct discrimination'.[111] The answer the CJEU gives to this issue—whether following the Sharpston or rather the Kokott approach—will shape the law in this area and substantially affect the effective protection against religious discrimination in Europe.

Of course, if in principle negative treatment on the basis of religious manifestations could only amount to an indirect form of discrimination, the relative strictness of the open justification test becomes crucial. Pitt saw the objective justification test under indirect discrimination as a relatively strict one:

> The stipulation that the employer should have to show that the practice having an adverse effect is objectively justified as an appropriate and necessary means of achieving a legitimate aim suggests that a fairly high standard of objective justification will be required. This further implies that national courts and the CJEU should not follow Convention case law in this particular context [referring to *Ahmed v UK* and *Stedman v UK*].[112]

Pitt however considers that '[i]t is inconceivable that the same approach could be taken under the [Employment Equality] Directive'.[113] So, she sees that despite a more restrictive definitional stage under the Directive, the protection provided under EU equality law would nonetheless exceed that under the ECHR. With the UK situation in mind but discussing the situation under the Directive in general, Pitt writes that

> [t]he limitations of the protection against indirect discrimination should not be overlooked. When an employer, for example, imposes a dress code or uniform requirement which conflicts with a Muslim woman's desire to wear a headscarf or to keep her legs covered, there will no doubt be a prima facie case of indirect discrimination, and in practice, it is hard to imagine situations where this could be justified by an employer today.[114]

Pitt clearly did not anticipate Belgian and other Member States' domestic case law under the Employment Equality Directive, which illustrates that there is no guarantee that courts will adhere to such suggested high standard for justification, while being additionally restrictive in the definitional stage, and rather giving important leeway to employers to adopt the policies they see fit in their workplaces including when it comes to banning religiously distinct dress.

---

[109] Paragraphs 44–45, references omitted.

[110] It is argued that prior to this explicit policy, there was an 'unwritten rule' banning religious symbols. AG Kokott (too) readily accept this argument.

[111] AG Kokott goes (much) further when she argues such ban constitutes 'a genuine and determining occupational requirement', see para 84. On 14 March 2017, n its *Achbita* judgment, the CJEU partially followed AG Kokott's advice in this regard, holding that the prohibition on employees wearing any visible signs of their political, philosophical or religious beliefs in the workplace did not give rise to direct discrimination as long as certain conditions were met.

[112] Pitt, 'Religion or belief: aiming at the right target?', n 64 above, 217. *Ahmed v UK* (1982) 4 EHRR 126; *Stedman v UK*, Application No 29107/95 (EComHR, 9 April 1997).

[113] ibid, 217.

[114] ibid, 218.

Moving on to another issue, the Directive lists 'belief' on par with 'religion', and often this seems to go largely unnoticed. Some have questioned whether 'belief' merits being placed on par with 'religion' under EU non-discrimination law and in fact in the initial proposals to include religion as a protected ground in amendments of the EC Treaty in the early 1990s, 'belief' was not mentioned alongside religion.[115]

It may be felt that earlier EU communications on the subject referred to 'religion' only as a sort of shorthand, and that it would always have been intended that non-religious beliefs would receive similar protection. However, it is submitted that the focus on religion (only) in the discussion leading up to Article 13 is actually indicative of the fact that it was the problem of discrimination against members of particular religious groups in many areas of social life, including employment, which was seen by the EU as the major issue to be addressed, rather than the problem which could be conceptualised as one of employers discriminating against people on grounds of their personal belief systems.[116]

While not much legislative discussion was recorded on this, it seems reasonable that the inclusion of 'belief' in the final version of Article 13 of the EC Treaty and the Framework Employment Directive was to clarify that non-religious beliefs, including atheism, were covered. One advantage is that EU anti-discrimination law aligns with international human rights law,[117] making even the right to fair treatment free from discrimination somewhat 'symmetrical'. However, as under ECHR jurisprudence, more will be required than an isolated belief on a particular (employment) issue; 'a worker seeking protection under the Directive for non-religious beliefs will have to demonstrate some sort of belief system'.[118]

E. Direct–Indirect Discrimination Dichotomy and the Duty of Reasonable Accommodation

One of the mainstays of EU equality law is the dichotomy of direct–indirect discrimination.[119] The Supreme Court of Canada, in rejecting the 'bifurcated'

[115] ibid, 205. Eg European Commission, *European Social Policy—a way forward for the Union*, White Paper, COM(1994) 333 final (noting that a number of contributions to its Green Paper had urged the Commission 'to take further concrete action to combat discrimination on the ground of race, religion, age and disability', para 27).
[116] ibid, 207–8, recognising that it may appear logical to protect (certain) non-religious beliefs alongside religion, but that this may cause problems of interpretation.
[117] ibid, 206.
[118] ibid, 212, referring to the *Pretty v UK*, Application no 2346/02 (ECtHR, 29 April 2002) para 31. (the applicant wanted immunity from prosecution for her husband who would help her in her assisted suicide; the Court held that the potential sincere and profound belief in the virtue of assisted suicide 'cannot found a requirement that her husband should be absolved from the consequences of conduct which, although it would be consistent with her belief, is proscribed by the criminal law. And if she were able to establish an infringement of her right, the justification shown by the State in relation to Art. 8 would still defeat it'). However, Art 9 played a very minor role in the case.
[119] S Fredman, *Comparative study of anti-discrimination and equality laws of the US, Canada, South Africa and India* (European Network of Legal Experts in the non-discrimination field, 2012) 80

approach, has famously criticised the distinction between direct and indirect dis-crimination as being malleable, indeed 'chimerical'.[120] Because of this 'an adjudica-tor may unconsciously tend to classify the impugned standard in a way that fits the remedy he or she is contemplating ... so that form triumphs over substance'.[121] In addition, setting boundaries as such may be unrealistic and improve the chances of savvy employers if they play their cards well, thus incentivising 'creative' ways to create exclusionary effects:

> [A] modern employer with a discriminatory intention would rarely frame the rule in directly discriminatory terms when the same effect—or an even broader effect—could be easily realized by couching it in neutral language ... this more subtle type of discrimi-nation, which rises in the aggregate to the level of systemic discrimination, is now much more prevalent than the cruder brand of openly direct discrimination ... The bifurcated analysis gives employers with a discriminatory intention and the forethought to draft the rule in neutral language an undeserved cloak of legitimacy.[122]

Pondering the 'ongoing relevance and utility of direct discrimination within more mature systems of anti-discrimination law', Mark Bell writes:

> If direct discrimination is equated with the most overt forms of discrimination, then these can be expected to diminish in frequency as the law becomes more established. Providing that the sanctions for breach of the law are reasonably effective, most employers ... will seek to conceal discriminatory actions in order to protect themselves against litigation.[123]

The challenge of EU equality law as it expands is *also* how to affectively deal with subtler and more entrenched forms of discrimination, disadvantage and stereotyp-ing and situations that do not fit in easily with the current anti-discrimination law framework, including intersectional and multiple discrimination.[124] The question is whether the dichotomy serves that purpose or, rather, jeopardises the delivery of 'substantive and transformative equality' on the ground by advancing the 'lawyer's law' in a way that leaves the door open to creative backdoor constructions.

('EU law has preferred a relatively rigid distinction between direct and indirect discrimination ... At a statutory level, the Canadian Supreme Court has expressly rejected such a distinction, preferring a single test for justification which is sensitive to the severity of the impact, the availability of alternatives, the possibility of accommodation, and the burden on the respondent').

[120] Canada Supreme Court, *British Columbia (Public Service Employee Relations Commission) v BCGSEU*, [1999] 3 SCR 3, at para 28.

[121] ibid, para 28.

[122] ibid, para 29.

[123] Bell, 'Chapter two: direct discrimination', in Schiek, Waddington and Bell (eds), *Cases, materials and text on national, supranational and international non-discrimination law*, n 57 above, 186.

[124] This includes instances of: see the landmark piece by K Crenshaw, 'Demarginalizing the Intersec-tion of Race and Sex: A Black Feminist Critique of Antidiscrimination Doctrine, Feminist Theory, and Antiracist Politics', 1989 *University of Chicago Legal Forum* 139; (self-reported) discriminations based on multiple grounds are on a rise, as documented by the United Nations International Labour Organi-zation (ILO) *Global Report on Equality at Work 2011: The Continuing Challenge*, available at: www.ilo. org/wcmsp5/groups/public/@ed_norm/@relconf/documents/meetingdocument/wcms_154779.pdf.

The concern is that a 'cloak of legitimacy' arises in indirect discrimination fashioned cases because, even if direct discrimination does not equal intentional discrimination, there remains 'a holdover sense that direct discrimination is more loathsome, morally more repugnant, because the perpetrator intends to discriminate or has discriminated knowingly. By contrast, adverse effect discrimination is viewed as "innocent", unwitting, accidental, and consequently not morally repugnant'.[125]

If discrimination based on religious manifestations can only constitute indirect discrimination, then this 'cloak of legitimacy' attaches to wide-ranging corporate 'neutrality policies'. This (unintentional) effect of the dichotomy thus risks defeating the purposes of equality law by legitimising systemic discrimination. Despite some of these concerns expressed by the Canadian Supreme Court being universal,[126] the dichotomy remains a staple of EU equality law and indirect discrimination—as 'arguably the first major milestone in European anti-discrimination law'[127]—and by some is treasured 'as an important tool for dismantling systemic discrimination and credited with attempting to achieve substantial equality'.[128] In addition, the overemphasis on the dichotomy and the (over)reliance on the concept of indirect discrimination under EU law may have (unintended) consequences as other valuable mechanisms which could contribute to substantive equality and social inclusion, such as positive action and reasonable accommodation, are crowded-out.

A duty of reasonable accommodation on the ground of disability was explicitly introduced under Article 5 of the Directive, which applies in employment and occupation settings. This article states:

> In order to guarantee compliance with the principle of equal treatment in relation to persons with disabilities, reasonable accommodation shall be provided. This means that employers shall take *appropriate measures*, where needed in a particular case, to enable a person with a disability to have access to, participate in, or advance in employment, or to undergo training, unless such measures would impose a *disproportionate burden on the employer*. This burden shall not be disproportionate when it is sufficiently remedied by measures existing within the framework of the disability policy of the Member State concerned (emphasis added).[129]

---

[125] S Day and G Brodsky, 'The Duty to Accommodate: Who Will Benefit?' (1996) 75 *La Revue du Barreau Canadien* 433, 457.

[126] In the Canadian case, different remedies applied to direct or indirect discrimination (the first would be stricken out, while the latter would remain and the Court would look at whether accommodation would be possible), and the Supreme Court found this particularly troubling: ibid, para 30. In contrast, under EU equality law the remedies are set at the national level; they can be different, but often the same sanctions apply irrespective of the kind of discrimination established (although one can be justified more easily than the other, with the adjudicator having important leeway to 'choose' the mode of analysis).

[127] Meenan, 'Introduction', n 2 above, 18.

[128] K Wentholt, 'Formal and Substantive Equal Treatment: the Limitations and the Potential of the Legal concept of Equality' in MLP Loenen and PR Rodrigues (eds), *Non-Discrimination Law: Comparative Perspectives* (Kluwer, 1999) 53.

[129] Article 5 Employment Equality Directive.

Recital 21 of the Directive adds some guidance, specifying that:

> To determine whether the measures in question give rise to a disproportionate burden, account should be taken in particular of the financial and other costs entailed, the scale and financial resources of the organisation or undertaking and the possibility of obtaining public funding or any other assistance.

Article 5 has been criticised for its 'poor drafting' as 'the defence for failing to make a reasonable accommodation (disproportionate burden) is included within the definition of the obligation to make such an accommodation'.[130] Thus, it merges what should be a two-stage test.[131] Also, because of the focus on 'the financial cost of the accommodation as the primary factor in determining whether a "disproportionate burden" exists', it disregards that 'the potential benefits that could accrue to employers from adapting their workplace is to facilitate the employment of disabled people'.[132] The concept of 'disproportionate burden' which is favoured in the EU context finds its functional equivalent in the term 'undue hardship' that is utilised in both the US and Canada. Both of these terms fail to recognise potential benefits and externalities of accommodations for parties other than the accommodated worker, and the divergent standards in the US (ie de minimis) and Canada (ie purposive) illustrate that the latter term is vague enough to allow for more or less generous standards. It seems that terminology is embedded in the legal culture and is not constitutive for developments of a standard in the practice of courts or employers.

The Directive anticipates this duty to play 'an important role in combating discrimination on grounds of disability' (recital 16). Importantly, the Directive, in recital 17, seems to acknowledge that thanks to accommodations, persons with disabilities could be turned into employees competent and capable to perform essential functions of a post: 'This Directive does not require the recruitment, promotion, maintenance in employment or training of an individual who is not competent, capable and available to perform the essential functions of the post concerned or to undergo the relevant training'). Otherwise stated: lack of accommodation can be at the root of why disabled persons are regarded as incompetent or incapable of essentially performing a particular job. If reasonable accommodation can have such game-changing significance, it's a question why it should be prima facie limited to benefitting persons with disabilities when the Directive also seeks to address discrimination against persons on the basis of age, sexual orientation and religion or belief.

---

[130] Waddington, 'Chapter six: reasonable accommodation', in D Schiek, L Waddington and M Bell (eds), *Cases, materials and text on national, supranational and international non-discrimination law* (Oxford, Hart Publishing, 2007) 665–66; Art 5 EU Directive: … (a) the employer must take 'appropriate measures'; (b) unless this would result in a disproportionate burden. At 666: 'It is submitted that this reflects poor drafting, as the defence for failing to make a reasonable accommodation (disproportionate burden) is included within the definition of the obligation to make such accommodation'.

[131] ibid.

[132] Waddington, 'Chapter six: reasonable accommodation', n 130 above, 725.

The relationship between indirect discrimination and reasonable accommodations is not elaborated on in the Directive, and both forms of discrimination seem to exist in parallel for the ground of disability. Some commentators have argued that the duty of reasonable accommodation as framed in the Directive, where a burden would become disproportionate because of cost considerations, in fact constitutes a *limitation* or attenuation of the right to treatment free of indirect disability-related discrimination. This understanding would mean that disability is in fact *less protected* than the other Directive grounds where indirect discrimination is not limited by cost considerations.[133]

However, most scholars would agree that disability is one of the more strongly protected grounds under the Employment Equality Directive. The explicit reserving of the duty of reasonable accommodation is a testament to the considerable 'strand hierarchy' within EU law.[134] The hierarchy also exhibits itself in the practice of the domestic courts, with some grounds receiving better and more generous protection than others. In particular, some have wondered why 'cases brought under religious equality law have, to date, a lower success rate than cases brought under the other equality "strands".'[135]

But even when it comes to the same grounds and very similar cases, different Member States have developed divergent approaches and outcomes. An analysis of the country studies in Part II will illustrate this for the most recurrent religion in the workplace cases. The different treatment of the basic 'headscarf conflict' scenario in the various jurisdictions demonstrates vividly that a common framework does not ensure *harmonisation* of protection throughout the EU.[136] Thus, though the Employment Equality Directive has arguably introduced a converging (not identical) terminology and framework, it has not produced uniformity or even convergence in anti-discrimination practice across Europe.[137] One of the reasons for the lack of genuine harmonisation has been the modest role of the CJEU so far with regard to the interpretation of the Directive.[138] The lack of case law has

[133] M De Vos, 'De bouwstenen van het discriminatierecht in de arbeidsverhoudingen' in M De Vos and E Brems (eds), *De Wet Bestrijding Discriminatie in de praktijk* (Antwerp, Intersentia, 2004) 81 (arguing that requirements under indirect discrimination are more stringent than under reasonable accommodations, related to the ground of disability but also in a general conceptual way).

[134] Another illustration is Art 6 with regard to (direct) discrimination on the basis of age which is subject to an open justification system ('objectively and reasonably justified by a legitimate aim').

[135] (UK) Woodhead, *'Religion or belief': Identifying issues and priorities* (London, Equality and Human Rights Commission Research report 48, 2009).

[136] McGoldrick, *Human Rights and Religion: The Islamic Headscarf Debate in Europe* (Oxford, Hart Publishing, 2006).; See also K Alidadi, *Discussion Paper. Religious Dress in the Workplace* (in Belgium, Bulgaria, Denmark, France, Germany, Italy, the Netherlands, Spain, Turkey, the United Kingdom) June 2010 (29 pp).

[137] See, eg, K Alidadi, 'Muslim Women Made Redundant: Unintended Signals in Belgian and Dutch Case Law on Religious Dress in Private Sector Employment and Unemployment' in K Alidadi, MC Foblets and J Vrielink (eds), *A Test of Faith? Religious Diversity and Accommodation in the European Workplace* (Aldershot, Ashgate, 2012).

[138] See Waddington, *The Expanding Role of the Equality Principle in European Union Law*, n 42 above, 22 (contrasting this limited role to the CJEU's role with regard to the development of EU sex discrimination).

exacerbated the situation, allowing the erosion of the protection against discrimination on the basis of religion or belief in some EU Member States.

F. Indirect Discrimination and Reasonable Accommodations: Different Sides of the Same Coin?

The concepts of indirect discrimination and the duty to reasonably accommodate can play a role towards facilitating an equality standard which challenges the prevailing formal anti-discrimination model, which emphasises the much less controversial 'sameness of treatment' and is justifiable under an economic rationality model.[139] Instead of considering irrelevant a certain personal characteristic, the duty of reasonable accommodation raises the awareness that 'ignoring, by failing to accommodate, the characteristic can result in denying an individual equal employment opportunities'.[140] The notion of indirect discrimination likewise appears promising in addressing structural inequalities that form de facto barriers for religious employees, similarly to a duty to make reasonable accommodation for workers, even if much will depend on the justification and proportionality test applied.[141]

Do the two affiliated concepts constitute different sides of the same coin? Or are there significant differences, leaving a potential added value and distinct role for each? Considering some limitations to indirect discrimination, one could ask which interpretation of the concept of indirect discrimination could confront structural inequalities in the access to employment as well as where reasonable accommodation could come in to contribute to the aim of promoting inclusivity in employment opportunities. In looking at this latter concept, one also needs to address some caveats as it would be applied at the shop floor level.

I argue that the concepts of reasonable accommodations and indirect discrimination are related, and may even be seen as functional equivalents in certain contexts, but the differences are not to be overlooked.[142] On the one hand, the concept of indirect discrimination could be regarded as more encompassing and implying a much higher burden/duty on employers in comparison with a duty to reasonably accommodate.[143] When a measure or situation is considered to disadvantage

---

[139] See O'Brien, 'Equality's false summits: new varieties of disability discrimination, "excessive" equal treatment and economically constricted horizons', n 50 above.

[140] Waddington, 'Chapter six: reasonable accommodation', n 130 above, 632.

[141] Vickers, *Religion and Belief Discrimination in Employment—the EU law*, n 69 above, 4.

[142] On the relation between the two concepts, see Vickers, ibid; K Henrard, 'De Verhouding tussen de concepten redelijke aanpassing, indirect discriminatie en proportionaliteit' in C Bayart, S Sottiaux and S Van Drooghenbroeck (eds), *Les Nouvelles Lois luttant contre la discrimination/De Nieuwe Federale Antidiscriminatiewetten* (Bruges, Die Keure/La Charte, 2008) 257–95.

[143] De Vos, 'De bouwstenen van het discriminatierecht in de arbeidsverhoudingen', n 133 above, 81 (arguing that requirements under indirect discrimination are conceptually more stringent than under reasonable accommodations).

a certain group by its very design (but not purpose), it should be corrected so that it does not hurt potential and future employees. A simple accommodation for a current/individual employee would not seem to suffice.[144] Also, if there is talk of discrimination, economic cost arguments seem unlikely to succeed under the justification test: 'The defense to a complaint of indirect discrimination is that the challenged measure was objectively justified, and issues of cost are less likely to be regarded as meeting this test'.[145]

In this sense, depending on the standard adopted for assessing reasonable accommodations, indirect discrimination could be considered a stronger tool for employees.[146] Reasonable accommodations could also be seen as *limiting* a duty not to indirectly discriminate if the employer can use it as a shield to show he met his obligations under anti-discrimination law.[147]

On the other hand, indirect—as well as direct—discrimination requires a group disadvantage and a comparison exercise. Indeed, the claimant must show that a requirement would put *persons of a particular religion or belief at a particular disadvantage compared with others.* Thus, although a successful claim of indirect discrimination does not require an *actual* comparator (a hypothetical comparator is accepted), a *group* disadvantage is still required. Because of this legal-technical requirement, certain claims have been blocked from receiving appropriate consideration under the equality framework. In contrast, assessing a claim for reasonable accommodations requires no such showing of *group* disadvantage, since the concept aims for tailored measures that meet individual needs and situations. This is significant because:

> [D]isadvantage is not necessarily experienced by all or most members of a particular group, but is ... experienced on the individual level depending on both individual and environmental factors. Such individual forms of disadvantage can only rarely be revealed by making of group comparison, which is characteristic for both direct and indirect discrimination standards. Reasonable accommodation discrimination therefore requires a different approach to do justice to the particularities of an individual in a given situation.[148]

In its individual-personalising effect, the reasonable accommodations approach can be said to form an antidote to generalisation about 'the Muslim employee', 'the Hindu employee' or indeed the 'standard/ideal employee', thus forming a barrier

---

[144] De Vos, ibid, 81.

[145] Waddington, 'Chapter six: reasonable accommodation', n 130 above, 644.

[146] For the United States: R Corrada, 'The Supreme Court and title VII' (January–February 2003) *Liberty Magazine* (describing a case involving an air traffic controller (Don Reed) winning $2.25 million damages in a Denver district court): 'but he won because the jury found disparate treatment, that Reed's employer had treated him differently because of his religion ... If Reed had been left to argue only that his employer refused a reasonable accommodation, Reed might not have prevailed'). In the US, 'disparate impact' is widely used instead of 'indirect discrimination'.

[147] Day and Brodsky, 'The Duty to Accommodate: Who Will Benefit?', n 125 above (criticising the Canadian reasonable accommodations jurisprudence).

[148] Waddington, 'Chapter six: reasonable accommodation', n 130 above, 745.

against commodification of employees. Conceptually, reasonable accommodation calls for stakeholders to engage in an interactive dialogue with due regard for the person to be accommodated, his/her particular needs, struggles and potentials. But the concept requires more than mere procedural justice even if that is a significant part of the exercise; the outcome must also meet certain requirements. The fact that requesting or providing accommodation does not necessitate or imply group disadvantage opens up space for individualised responses; as a symmetrical instrument it not only aims to address minority positions but can also benefit members that belong to the majority religion or have no religious belonging or beliefs. This was illustrated by the series of cases in the UK involving Christian employees. The *Eweida* case[149] illustrates how the *group* disadvantage requirement[150] under the prohibition of indirect discrimination can be paralysing for (true or alleged) 'sole believers', notwithstanding that it could be argued the Court of Appeal erred[151] in qualifying the request to visibly wear a crucifix as an idiosyncratic wish of the employee.

A second reason, besides the group requirement, why 'the same coin' is appealing but inaccurate is that by formulation indirect discrimination intends to tackle discriminatory *'provisions, criterions or practices'*. In this sense, Pitt considers 'it would be stretching the meaning of "provision, criterion or practice"[152] too far to include in it a one-off decision' such as refusing an employee a day off to celebrate a religious holiday or observe a religious obligation.[153] Reasonable accommodations, in contrast, are tailored towards one-off decisions.

> If this view is correct, it does demonstrate an unfortunate gap in protection for workers, contrasting unfavourably with the position in the US and some Canadian provinces where employers have a legal obligation to reasonably accommodate the religious needs of their employees.[154]

---

[149] *Eweida v British Airways* [2010] EWCA Civ 80.

[150] M Bell, *Anti-discrimination law and the European Union* (Oxford, Oxford University Press, 2002) 190 (speaking of statistical evidence and 'the group-based disparate impact analysis' as 'typical within indirect discrimination'); D Schiek, 'Indirect discrimination (Chapter three)' in D Schiek, L Waddington and M Bell (eds), *Cases, materials and text on national, supranational and international non-discrimination law* (Oxford, Hart Publishing, 2007) 330: 'group disadvantage is the starting point of indirect discrimination ... [But] just establishing group disadvantage is not enough to establish a claim for indirect discrimination'. See also C Barnard and B Hepple, 'Substantive Equality' (2000) 59 *Cambridge Law Journal* 562 referred to in Schiek, ibid, 331 with regard to the EU Racial Equality Directive: 'This [individual-oriented] interpretation would conflate the concepts of direct and indirect discrimination'.

[151] Arguably this is not a correct reading of either the belief of the claimant or the indirect discrimination concept, so that this problem is not inherent to the tool of indirect discrimination: Yet this is a standard that is derived from the concept of indirect discrimination as formulated in the Directive, different from a duty of reasonable accommodation which in its formulation (eg Art 5 Employment Equality Directive) recognises the individual nature of measures so that no such requirement could be read in the Reasonable Accommodation duty.

[152] In Dutch (both under the Belgian and the Dutch antidiscrimination law) this is: *'ogenschijnlijk neutrale bepaling, maatstaf of handelwijze'*; *handelswijze* could be seen as way of handling a matter, in which case a one-off decision could without much stretching be seen as falling under this.

[153] Pitt, 'Religion or belief: aiming at the right target?', above n 64, 219.

[154] Pitt, ibid, 219 (references omitted).

Pitt sees reasonable accommodations thus as a step further than indirect discrimination, and does not agree that protection under indirect discrimination comes down to a duty of reasonable accommodation; even if the boundaries are far from clear: 'the express inclusion of reasonable accommodations for disability implies that it was not intended to be covered by the general concept of indirect discrimination in the Directive'.[155]

A subtle yet important difference between discrimination and accommodation lies in the more intuitive nature of accommodation versus the more complex legal concept of indirect discrimination. The concept of indirect discrimination can be quite difficult to grasp, even for legally trained people. Schiek raises the pertinent question: '[w]hy would a legislator introduce a concept as complicated as indirect discrimination?'[156] Some reasons include the need to 'prevent circumvention of specific prohibitions to discriminate',[157] as well as the 'social engineering rationale' of aiding 'the attainment of the wider goals of discrimination law in social reality', ie the aim of discrimination law to change socio-economic reality. Be that as it may, the 'indirectness' or opacity, of the concept of indirect discrimination detracts from its significance and use in everyday life. Considering the complexity of the notion there is a need, on a continuous basis, to demystify the importance of (and the idea behind) indirect discrimination, eg through information campaigns or other resources directed at employers and employees.[158] In contrast, the language and framing of issues in terms of accommodations is much more intuitive and straightforward,[159] even if applying the various elements (reasonable, disproportionate/hardship) raises particular legal issues and even if misunderstandings are by no means precluded either.

Griffiths, whose social working approach strongly nuances the effect of anti-discrimination law, points toward certain 'regulatory strategies that offer some hope of substantially influencing behaviour on the shop floor'. Under the so-called 'individual rights' approach, he argues that despite the fact that many victims would opt out of pursuing claims in court because of various serious obstacles they will face or expect to face on their way, a number of arrangements can improve the effectiveness of anti-discrimination in practice:

> Rules creating individual legal rights (e.g. to equal or preferential treatment) should be designed primarily with their *general* effects in mind, that is, their influence on behaviour in cases in which official institutions are not mobilized. To be effective in social life, such rules must be used by actors in their everyday interactions without the intervention of

[155] ibid, 220.

[156] Schiek, 'Indirect discrimination (Chapter three)', n 150 above, 324.

[157] ibid, 325 (noting that this is the case because of the close list of grounds under EU law; in case of an open list, 'prohibiting indirect discrimination becomes superfluous from this perspective')

[158] See K Alidadi, *RELIGARE project: A comparative legal study addressing religious or belief discrimination in employment and reasonable accommodations for employees' religious or philosophical beliefs or practice*, RELIGARE policy brief (European Commission, 2012) 8 (recommending to 'Demystify the concept of indirect discrimination using information campaigns and informational resources directed at employers and employees).

[159] Waddington, 'Chapter six: reasonable accommodation', n 130 above, 670.

legal officials since, as we have seen, official implementation is rare. Use on the shop floor depends on a number of factors which we have examined above, only some of which lend themselves to legislative manipulation. At a minimum the rules must be known to the relevant non-official actors. This means they must be clear and simple, even if this involves a considerable sacrifice of regulatory refinement. Equal pay rules that depend on highly sophisticated functional classifications, for example, whatever their moral virtue, are unlikely to be used on the shop floor.[160]

Thus, the reasonable accommodations route seems to achieve in a more direct and therefore more effective fashion what indirect discrimination aims to achieve indirectly by way of a legal fiction. 'Directness' of the language of reasonable accommodations refers to the fact that the specific goal is to advance solutions in terms of accommodations that meet individual needs in a given context. More 'indirect' 'lawyer's law' provisions appear less reliable at securing this type of thinking. In this respect, language, as an important element pleading in favour of reasonable accommodations, cannot be overlooked. Language is a key element in debates on discrimination and equality: foreigner, outsider, stranger, newcomer, immigrant, alien, other, minority, etc are all terms that can be used to denote certain outside groups but some terms have (acquired) more stigmatising connotations than others.[161] Language is also key in law and its application. From the perspective of the sociology of law, when the addressees of a legal rule (mainly employees and employers under the current EU non-discrimination law; a much larger target group under the proposed horizontal directive) do not *understand* a rule, that rule is bound to be ineffective *in practice*.

In addition, the 'reasonableness rhetoric' resonates better in a conciliation mode of resolution than in the conflict-based discrimination framework and could produce better results in practice by avoiding the litigation route.[162] Being approached for failing to reasonably *accommodate*[163] or *discriminating against* an employee may mean the same thing in legal parlance but can be perceived very differently by an employer. The first may trigger a far less defensive response that

---

[160] J Griffiths, 'The social working of anti-discrimination law' in MLP Loenen and PR Rodrigues (eds), *Non-Discrimination Law: Comparative Perspectives* (Kluwer, 1999) 319, 327. See also at 330 ('a less than perfect rule that works is better than a perfect one that does not').

[161] In Belgium recently a debate on the term '*allochtoon*' erupted when a leading newspaper, *De Morgen*, announced it would ban the term from its reporting: W Verschelden, 'Waarom wij, De Morgen, "allochtoon" niet meer gebruiken (opinie)', *De Morgen*, 20 September 2012.

[162] For an example of such defensive response by the employer hit by a discrimination claim, see F Vermeulen, *Socio-legal research on accommodation of religious diversity in family and labour law, in public space and state funding of religions in the Netherlands* (RELIGARE project, 2012) 44 (citing a commissioner commenting on ETC opinion nr 2006-215, 27 October 2006 (headscarf/call centre): 'the employer was extremely offended that he was accused of discriminating against people because he was very conscious about providing people with equal opportunities ... And to add insult to injury, an anti-discrimination agency got involved ... Because of all the anger, the people in question weren't able to think creatively for themselves').

[163] Even though the failure to provide accommodations can fall under the definition of discrimination, the term does not necessarily acquire a pejorative connotation by association.

conserves space for negotiation.[164] It is arguable that a discrimination allegation could have a more disparaging effect on employment relations as it carries an undeniably pejorative implication. As noted by Marie-Claire Foblets, 'labels ... exert extraordinary influence'[165] and this applies to the qualification of 'discrimination' as well. Once a *legal* claim has been presented though, this subtle difference in connotations can be considered absolved, but even while negotiations are pending it may be significant to the course of events. The fact that the reasonable accommodations terminology allows a potential conflict situation to be framed in *positive, constructive* language makes it a potentially powerful instrument for employees. One effect may be that this could potentially redress the tricky problem of 'self-excluding' behaviour on the part of employees, who anticipate and avoid conflicts by strongly limiting their own options.[166] For Somek:

> [R]ecognizing the role of accommodation marks a shift from the distributive towards the decommodifying dimension of anti-discrimination law ... Anti-discrimination law protects, where inequality arises, the most fundamental interest of people to stay who they are within society, even if that society is strongly inclined to force them into self-denial or send them away.[167]

Recognising reasonable accommodations signals that employees need not altogether desert their religious identity and commitment when entering the workplace when there are no compelling reasons justifying restrictions.

II. The CJEU and Religious Accommodations in the Workplace

A. Towards the First Two CJEU Religious Discrimination Decisions

In contrast to its invaluable role in expanding the principle of non-discrimination in relation to sex[168] and other grounds, the CJEU has not been the driving force

---

[164] This pejorative connotation of the term 'discrimination' is a reason why the Dutch Equal Treatment Act avoids the term and uses 'distinction' ('onderscheid') instead. This has been the subject of dispute between the European Commission and the Netherlands, the former arguing repeatedly that the Netherlands failed to correctly transpose the terminology used in the equality directives.

[165] MC Foblets, 'Perspective 1: legal anthropology in Imperative Inheritance Law in the Late-Modern Society' in C Castelein, R Foqué and A Verbeke (eds), *Imperative Inheritance Law in a Late-Modern Society: Five Perspectives* (Intersentia, 2009) 43.

[166] S Ghumman and L Jackson, 'The downside of religious attire: the Muslim headscarf and expectations of obtaining employment' (2010) 31 *Journal of Organizational Behavior* 4–23.

[167] A Somek, *Engineering Equality. An Essay on European Anti-Discrimination Law* (Oxford, OUP, 2011) 185.

[168] McCrudden and Kountouros, 'Human Rights and European equality law', n 4 above, 83 (stating that EU sex equality law is 'probably the most advanced of any jurisdiction in the world').

behind the development for the legal protection for the Article 13 discrimination grounds.[169] This does not take away the fact that the existing rich body of sex and nationality discrimination law forms 'an important context within which the Art. 13 Directives where adopted and continue to operate'.[170]

The disparity in CJEU case law depending on the type of discrimination is substantial. Most CJEU case law addressing the Employment Equality Directive has concerned discrimination on the ground of age.[171] When it comes to discrimination on the grounds of sexual orientation, disability and racial or ethnic origin, CJEU case law is much less developed and thus offers minimal guidance to the Member States. At the time of writing, the CJEU is expected to issue its first two decisions regarding religion or belief discrimination under EU law, 16 years since the adoption of the Directive. Its decisions in the Belgian *Achbita v G4S* and the French *Bougnaoui v Micropole SA* cases will be its first on religious discrimination under the Employment Equality Directive.[172]

The underlying reason for the lack of CJEU case law is the refusal of lower domestic courts to refer questions to the CJEU for a preliminary ruling.[173] The Belgian equal treatment body Unia (formerly called CEOOR/Interfederal Centre for Equal Opportunities) has on a number of occasions requested that Belgian labour tribunals pose a series of questions to the CJEU on the issue of religious discrimination, but the courts have found this to be unnecessary in order to resolve the case at hand:[174] local courts can thus form a barrier which prevents pan-European questions that implicate different interpretations of Directives from reaching the CJEU.[175] Under Article 267 of the TFEU only a court of final resort is under an obligation to refer a question for a preliminary ruling to the CJEU when a party requests it.

---

[169] See Waddington, *The Expanding Role of the Equality Principle in European Union Law*, n 42 above, 22.

[170] Meenan, 'Introduction', n 2 above, 10.

[171] Commission, *Joint Report on the application of Council Directive 2000/43/EC of 29 June 2000 implementing the principle of equal treatment between persons irrespective of racial or ethnic origin ('Racial Equality Directive') and of Council Directive 2000/78/EC of 27 November 2000 establishing a general framework for equal treatment in employment and occupation ('Employment Equality Directive') from the Commission to the European Parliament and the Council*, Brussels, 17.1.2014, COM(2014) 2 final, 7, and in particular Art 6(1) under which an open justification regime is in place in case of differences of treatment based on age.

[172] Case C-157/15, *Samira Achbita and Centrum voor gelijkheid van kansen en voor racismebestrijding v G4S Secure Solutions NV*; Case C-188/15, *Asma Bougnaoui and Association de défense des droits de l'homme (ADDH) v Micropole SA*. These CJEU judgments were issued on 14 March 2017.

[173] Lower domestic courts need refer such questions to the CEU for preliminary rulings only if the court considers it 'necessary to enable it to give judgment'. This is different for 'a court of tribunal of a member State against whose decisions there is not judicial remedy under national law'; those courts 'shall bring the matter' before the CJEU. See Art 267 TFEU.

[174] Including in the *HEMA case*, see Tongeren Labour Court, 2 January 2013, AR 11/2142/A.

[175] On this issue see *Ullens de Schooten and Rezabek v Belgium*, Application nos 3989/07 and 38353/07 (ECtHR, 20 September 2011) (refusal to refer questions relating to the interpretation of EU law to the CJEU did not constitute a violation of the applicants' right to a fair hearing under Art 6 ECHR).

The outcome of two references for preliminary rulings by the Belgian and the French Cour de cassation, courts of final resort, to the CJEU are eagerly anticipated.[176] A sign of the need for more guidance regarding the issue of religious dress, both references relate to the question of the wearing of a Muslim headscarf in the workplace and ask the Court essentially whether a refusal to accommodate constitutes direct discrimination on the basis of religion. In particular, the Belgian Cour de cassation posed the question as such:

> Can article 2.2.a [of the Employment Equality Directive] be interpreted to mean that the prohibition for a Muslim to wear the headscarf at work does not imply any direct discrimination when the rule forbids all workers to wear any visible symbol expressing their political, philosophical or religious beliefs?'

The question formulated by the French Cour de cassation is even more focused on the issue of a genuine and determining occupational requirement as it asks whether:

> Article 4 §1 of the Directive 2000/78 needs to be interpreted to mean that banning the headscarf because of the wish of a customer of an IT company to not have services performed by a staff member, with an engineering diploma, does not constitute a genuine and determining occupational requirement.

Advocate General opinions have been issued: for AG Kokott the answer to whether there is direct discrimination in the Belgian case is a clear 'no'; for AG Sharpston there is direct discrimination in the very similar French case.[177] In AG Kokott's opinion, company neutrality policies, such as the one adopted by Belgian employer G4S subsequent[178] to the employee headscarf dispute 'cannot properly be classified as constituting direct discrimination'; 'There is nothing in the present case to indicate that an individual was "treated less favourably".'[179] This is despite the fact that the employee, Samira Achbita, was dismissed for seeking to adhere to a religious practice, which falls under the *forum externum* (which AG Kokott recognised was covered under 'religion or belief'. What's more, AG Kokott goes (much) further when she argues such ban constitutes 'a genuine and determining occupational requirement'.[180] It is because of the essentialist characterisation of religion

---

[176] See (BE) Cass, 9 March 2015, AR S.12.0062.N; (FR) Cass (social chamber), n° 630 of 9 April 2015 (13–19.855), SO00630.

[177] For a more elaborate analysis of these opinions, see K Alidadi, 'Cultural Diversity in the Workplace: Personal Autonomy as a Pillar for the Accommodation of Employee Religious Practices?' in MC Foblets, AD Renteln and M Graziadei (eds), *The Paradoxes of Personal Autonomy* (Abingdon, Routledge, 2017 forthcoming).

[178] It is argued that prior to this explicit policy, there was an 'unwritten rule' banning religious symbols. AG Kokott (too) readily accept this argument.

[179] Para 47-48.

[180] Paragraph 84. See para 94: 'In such a case, a policy of neutrality is absolutely crucial, not only because of the variety of customers served by G4S, but also because of the special nature of the work which G4S employees do in providing those services, which is characterised by constant face-to-face contact with external individuals and has a defining impact not only on the image of G4S itself but also and primarily on the public image of its customers'. However, AG Kokott also does not support the back-rooming of employees, thus accepting very widespread employment exclusion for Muslim

as 'choice', and the separation of the religion or belief ground from other discrimination grounds, that such significant erosion of anti-discrimination protection for religious employees is advocated.[181] Indeed, in her opinion AG Kokott writes

> in its previous case-law concerning various EU-law prohibitions on discrimination, the Court has generally adopted a broad understanding of the concept of direct discrimination, and has, it is true, always assumed such discrimination to be present where a measure was inseparably linked to the relevant reason for the difference of treatment.

However, all of those cases were without exception concerned with individuals' immutable physical features or personal characteristics—such as gender, age or sexual orientation—rather than with modes of conduct based on a subjective decision or conviction, such as the wearing or not of a head covering at issue here.[182]

Under such interpretation, EU law does not protect against religion or belief discrimination, but merely against religious status discrimination. Since the expectation is a religion-free workplace, the pressures on religious employees not to cross lines can hardly be considered to amount to a 'working environment that is free from discrimination', the stated overarching goal of the EU Directive. The 'passing' and 'covering' demands that this justifies and promotes—as Yoshino's convincingly has argued in the case of sexual minorities—are not benign, but in fact tantamount to conversion demands[183] in a context where socially and legally sanctioned 'covering' (eg in the form of laws and practices requiring the *unveiling* of Muslim women) is becoming the contemporary form of (religious and other) discrimination.[184] More importantly, such characterisation of belief or religion as choice is open to challenge on various grounds. Peter Jones states that

> We cannot simply choose or decide what to believe in the way that we might choose to take a holiday in Spain …We can believe only what seems to us to be the case. If I have good reason to believe that Barcelona is in Spain … I cannot choose to believe otherwise. Beliefs therefore would seem to be (in a suitable sense) imposed upon us by the world.[185]

However, if we value the notion of personal autonomy, there is an argument that the choice factor can be considered a bolstering argument, ie *a pillar*, for promoting effective protection against discrimination as well as reasonable

---

women wearing a headscarf and other religiously visible employees. See generally on this issue: K Alidadi, 'From Front-Office to Back-Office: Religious Dress Crossing the Public-Private Divide in the Workplace' in S Ferrari and S Pastorelli (eds), *Religion and The Public-Private Divide* (Aldershot, Ashgate, 2012).

[181] Unsurprisingly then, AG Kokott argues against the extension of a de facto duty to reasonably accommodate on the basis of religion or belief.

[182] Paras 44–45, references omitted.

[183] Yoshino, 'Covering' (2001) *Yale Law Journal* 111, 769.

[184] The term 'status performativity' is used to argue that protecting certain identities may require protecting some practices or characteristics which are constitutive for those identities.

[185] P Jones, 'Belief, autonomy and responsibility. The case of indirect religious discrimination,' in G Levey (ed), *Authenticity, Autonomy and Multiculturalism* 70–71. However, he recognises that there are differences since belief is 'non-fully evidentiary' and 'affords people a domain of epistemological discretion that they do not have in relation to simple factual matters'.

accommodation on the ground of religion or belief. Notably, human autonomy forms such a pillar for the accommodation of the mutable characteristic of religion or belief more than it does for discrimination grounds involving immutable characteristics, such as disability, and to a large degree, gender, age and sexual orientation.[186] Certainly, autonomy arguments are often presented by accommodation protagonists, for instance by those arguing in favour of allowing Muslim female employees to wear a headscarf or other religious dress in the workplace. One may argue in favour of accommodating the religious dress worn by various minorities because it allows these individuals the freedom to choose how they wish to live out their faith and shape their identity in a visible way. Allowing Muslim women to wear a headscarf, a full-face veil or other religious dress is to be preferred over a paternalistic 'knows best' approach as it allows these women the freedom to choose for themselves, ie to act as autonomous agents. It is important to note that contradicting arguments can draw on the discourse of personal autonomy. On this point and others, the Advocate General's respective reasoning and the effective level of discrimination protection they advocate in the case of adverse treatment on the basis of religious manifestation through dress show that the CJEU will need to consider the issues deeply and in parallel in order to avoid contradictory decisions.

In the cases related to other grounds under the Directive, the CJEU has dealt with questions including discrimination by declaration (*Feryn*),[187] the definition of disability and the extent of the duty to accommodate for disability (*Chacón Navas*;[188] *HK Danmark (Ring and Skouboe Werge)*;[189] *Coleman*)[190] and the

---

[186] On mutable versus immutable characteristics, see D Schiek, 'A new framework on equal treatment of persons in EC law?' (2002) 8 *European Law Journal* 290, 309–12, see also A Lester and P Uccellari, 'Extending the Equality Duty to Religion, Conscience, and Belief: Proceed With Caution' (2008) 5 *European Human Rights Law Review* 567–73 ('[u]nlike the other characteristics which are protected under … anti-discrimination legislation, religion is not an essential, immutable element of the individual's birthright and identity').

[187] Case C-54/07, *Centrum voor gelijkheid van kansen en voor racismebestrijding v Firma Feryn NV* [2008] ECR I-5187.

[188] Case C-13/05, *Chacón Navas v Eurest Colectividades SA* [2006] ECR I-6467. The CJEU held that sickness, which did not amount to disability, was not covered by the Employment Equality Directive. The term 'disability' was defined as a physical, mental or psychological impairment which lasts for a long period of time and hinders the participation of the person concerned in professional life. The CJEU thus adopted a strict/medical rather than a social/conceptualised conception, which was critiqued by disability academics, but it has been said that this case played a role in the adoption of a more social concept of disability in the UN Convention on the Rights of Persons with Disabilities (CRPD) 2006. Subsequent to the entry in force of this Convention, the CJEU broadened the definition in *HK Danmark*.

[189] Cases C-335/11 and C-337/11, *HK Danmark v Dansk almennyttigt Boligselskab, and HK Danmark v Dansk Arbejdsgiverforening* [2013] ECLI 222 (The CJEU moved away from the critiqued restrictive definition in *Chacón Navas* in light of the entry into force of the CRPD, holding that 'disability' is to be seen interpreted as a 'long-term physical, mental, intellectual or sensory impairments which in interaction with various barriers may hinder the full and effective participation of the person concerned in professional life'; reduction in working hours is one form of apt reasonable accommodation for disability, but national courts are to assess if there is a disproportionate burden on the employer).

[190] Case C-303/06 *S. Coleman v Attridge Law* [2008] IRLR 88 (Directive protects not only the disabled themselves, but also an employee who is treated less favourably by reason of the disability of a child they care for, but the duty of reasonable accommodation is restricted to the person with disabilities).

exclusion of same-sex partners from employment benefits (*Frédéric Hay*).[191] Some of these decisions are highly relevant for religion or belief issues as well.

In particular, the seminal *Feryn* case[192] involved discrimination on the basis of race or ethnicity but has notable importance for religion or belief discrimination cases. The defendant in that case, NV Firma Feryn, was a Belgian company specialising in the sale and installation of garage gates, which had vacancies for employees to install such gates in customers' houses. During an interview with a Flemish newspaper (entitled 'Customers don't want Moroccans'),[193] the CEO explained that these vacancies were not being filled since he would not recruit persons of Moroccan origin. He confirmed on Belgian national television that he needed to take into account his customers' attitudes: people who wanted such secured gates installed did not want to have Moroccans looking into their houses. According to the Belgian equality body Unia who took up the case, NV Firma Feryn had clearly discriminated against an ethnic group even if there was no specific victim; by stating that 'Moroccans would not be hired', it was guaranteed that Moroccan job applicants (amongst others) would not apply for the open posts. The CJEU, responding to a number of prejudicial questions from the Belgian labour tribunal agreed with this stance, thereby confirming the concept of 'discrimination by declaration' under Directive 2000/43. The CJEU thus recognised that employers can *directly* discriminate by declaration and held that (real or implied) discriminatory preferences of customers are no justification for discriminating (future) employees. Indeed,

> the Court pointed out that the fact that an employer declares publicly that it will not recruit employees of a certain ethnic or racial origin constitutes of itself *direct discrimination* in respect of recruitment, since such statements are likely to strongly dissuade certain candidates from submitting their candidature and, accordingly, to hinder their access to the labour market (emphasis added).[194]

When it comes to the question of legitimacy of religious dress restrictions adopted by employers, the CJEU's guidance would be highly desirable in creating a more harmonised protective approach on a number of questions that have arisen in the practice of the national courts.[195] Questions include: the scope of the term

---

[191] Case C-267/12, *Frédéric Hay v Crédit agricole mutuel de Charente-Maritime et des Deux-Sèvres* [2013] ECLI 823 (where civil partnership is the highest form of union available to same-sex couples, the same employment benefits must be provided as for married couples; at the time France had not yet legalised same-sex marriage)

[192] Case C-54/07, *Centrum voor gelijkheid van kansen en voor racismebestrijding v Firma Feryn NV* [2008] ECR I-5187.

[193] G Fransen, 'Klanten hoeven geen Marokkanen. Firma Feryn vindt geen valabele werknemers', *De Standaard*, 28 April 2005.

[194] European Commission Legal Service, Case summary: C-54/07, *Centrum voor gelijkheid van kansen en voor racismebestrijding v Firma Feryn NV* [2008] ECR I-5187.

[195] Loenen, 'Accommodation of Religion and Sex Equality in the Workplace under the EU Equality Directives: a Double Bind for the European Court of Justice' in K Alidadi, M-C Foblets and J Vrielink (eds), *A Test of Faith? Religious Diversity and Accommodation in the European Workplace* (Aldershot, Ashgate, 2012) 104.

'religion or belief'; the circumstances in which dress restrictions or other restrictions on religious manifestations should be considered direct or rather indirect discrimination; the level of scrutiny for the proportionality test under the prohibition of indirect discrimination (in particular whether the least restrictive means is to be chosen, approaching a duty of reasonable accommodation for employers to offer reasonable adjustments), and the legitimacy of private company neutrality policies.[196] But conflicts between religious and professional time also raise substantial questions. The remainder of this section addresses these two issues.

B. Religious Dress: Direct Discrimination versus Indirect Discrimination, and the Duty to Accommodate

Workplace dress code conflicts can arise in a multitude of ways. It could be that a company has a dress code policy – possibly a uniform policy – that is challenged by a job applicant or an employee because it contradicts religious dress mandates the employee wants to adhere to. It could also be that no such explicit policy is in place but an applicant is rejected (or an employee is dismissed) for wearing religious dress or head covering, with the employer pointing to health and safety or image concerns.

As said, considering the different justification regimes involved, a central question will be whether the rejection of an applicant or the dismissal of an employee because of wearing religious dress or symbols should be considered as *direct* religious discrimination or rather as *indirect* discrimination on the ground of religion.[197] According to the Dutch Equal Treatment Commission (ETC), the Dutch equality body that issues non-binding opinions in concrete disputes and requests for opinions, there is a direct discrimination[198] on the basis of religion when the employer directly refers to the headscarf.[199] However, when the prohibition is based on a broader dress code it concerns an indirect discrimination, which

---

[196] When it comes to the exemption for religious-ethos companies under Art 4.2 of the Directive, two basic approaches are possible and have been adopted in different Member States: on the one hand, a functional approach where religious requirements/discrimination are limited to certain employees because of their role or functions, and on the other hand, an organic approach where these requirements are in place for all employees of the organisation. This is also an issue for the CJEU to decide, and its answer will have effect on the question of legitimacy of company 'neutrality' policies (for non-religious-ethos companies).

[197] Bribosia, Chopin and Rorive, *Rapport de synthèse relatif aux signes d'appartenance religieuse dans quinze pays de l'Union européenne* (Migration Policy Group, 2004) 13.

[198] The Dutch Equal Treatment Act is drafted in terms of 'distinction' ('onderscheid') and does not use the term 'discrimination', while in the case law of the European Court of Justice the two terms are used interchangeably, as is done in this chapter. R Holtmaat, 'Discriminatie of onderscheid: het kleine verschil met grote gevolgen of het grote verschil met kleine gevolgen?' in MLM Hertogh and PJJ Zoontjens (eds), *Gelijke behandeling, principes en praktijken. Evaluatieonderzoek Algemene Wet Gelijke Behandeling* (Wolf Legal Publishers, 2006) 3-113.

[199] Equal Treatment Commission opinion (hereafter ETC) nr 1995-31 (cleaning staff); ETC nr 1999-103 (intern in a school); ETC nr 1999-18 (intern in a school); ETC nr 1997-14.

can be justified.[200] A similar distinction was proposed by Bribosia, Chopin and Rorive, who argue that in a hypothetical case of a department store prohibiting the wearing of head coverings by all personnel, it is probably the indirect discrimination regime (with the possibility of justification) that is applicable.[201] After all, there is a seemingly neutral provision that applies to all staff but results in a particular disadvantage for adherents of certain religions such as Islam (women), Orthodox Jewish religion (men) and Sikhism (both men and women). It would be up to the employer to show a legitimate pursued aim and the fact that the measure (the dress code) is reasonable and necessary (proportionate). Such a legitimate aim could certainly be health and safety,[202] but the issue is more controversial when it is the desire to create a religion-free space or to hold on to a 'neutral' image without any particular specific need therefor (eg a book store selling a wide range of books).

In contrast, when there is no such dress code policy and an applicant is refused a position (or an employee is dismissed) because of wearing a headscarf, turban or *kippa*, that person would be a victim of direct discrimination according to Bribosia, Chopin and Rorive.[203] However, even in the latter scenario courts have accepted company arguments that a pre-existing 'practice', or 'unwritten company dress code' was in existence.[204]

For justification under either form of discrimination, the court is called upon to assess whether the restriction on an individual's religious freedom, eg through a company dress code, is proportionate to this aim. This proportionality exercise in search for a proper balance between conflicting rights will thus determine the scope of the protection for religious 'non-conformist dress', and consequently the look of tomorrow's workforce. The proportionality tool's 'multi-purposive' nature is at the same time its biggest limitation. On the one hand, the proportionality concept is poly-interpretable in that it allows for the taking into account of various factors that could be seen as relevant in particular contexts (and are thus not established a priori). This does not mean that 'anything goes' and that *any* kind of argument can be taken into account: clearly certain arguments can be considered unreasonable or simply not to the point. Nonetheless, on the other hand, the resulting factual and cultural specificity of the balancing method does not promote the development of clear precedent and legal certainty in the

---

[200] ETC 2001-53 (clerk); ETC 1996-85 (packaging); ETC nr 1996-16 (doctor's assistant); ETC nr 2002-125; ETC nr 2002-123.

[201] Bribosia, Chopin and Rorive, *Rapport de synthèse relatif aux signes d'appartenance religieuse dans quinze pays de l'Union européenne* (2004) 13.

[202] However, health and safety concerns should not be able to automatically trump other concerns. When it comes to disability accommodations, for instance, restaurant health and safety standards have not barred accommodations for blind persons who would be allowed to bring in their seeing eye dog unlike other customers. There, health and safety is taken into account, but it does not trump accommodations for people with disabilities. See *Roche v Alabaster*, Equality Tribunal Ireland, 1 August 2002.

[203] Above n 201 at 32.

[204] See Antwerp Labour Tribunal, 27 April 2010.

non-discrimination area on a national level, let alone on a European scale. This is one reason that CJEU guidance would be highly useful.

Some 200 national employment cases collected within the framework of the RELIGARE project from nine European Member State countries demonstrate the divergent approaches within Member States when it comes to the meaning of 'indirect discrimination' on the basis of religion or belief (and to what extent the prohibition of discrimination requires employers to offer reasonable adjustments).[205] In Dutch cases, the efforts of employers to look for alternative solutions to keep the employee on the job are evaluated. For instance, when the job application of a Muslim woman was refused by a call centre because the employer was of the opinion that the sound transition over the headset would be of lesser quality when worn over a headscarf (thus lowering the quality of the communication between phone operator and customers), a (cost-free) alternative that would satisfy both employer and employee was available. Namely, the headset could be worn *under* the headscarf (ETC nr 2006-215, 27 October 2006). In contrast, in an employment dispute between a private employer and a saleswoman who sought to wear a headscarf on the job, a Belgian judge found it pointless to look into whether the parties had considered a possible transfer to a 'back office position' since 'there exists no duty of reasonable accommodation'.[206] The Belgian approach not only leads to the channelling of the religious employee into the unemployment line, but also fails to recognise that offering an existing employee some accommodation can also be to the employer's advantage (eg someone familiar with and already trained in the company can remain a valued employee in an alternative position within the firm).

This is also where the link with European Union human rights protection comes in. In the assessment of the proportionality of exceptions to the non-discrimination principle, limitations that have been accepted in the scope of the duty to respect the freedom of religion can be considered.[207] The role the CJEU will play in the enforcement and harmonisation of the Employment Equality Directive is not entirely clear. While the CJEU to a large extent follows the jurisprudence of the ECtHR in interpreting human rights,[208] it must be noted that the role of the CJEU as a supranational court differs from that of the ECtHR. The fact that EU Directives are binding as to the result to be achieved[209] would seem to justify a much protective case law from the CJEU in the area of religious employment discrimination. Arguments based on the free movement of workers in the private

---

[205] These cases are collected in an online case law database, available at: religaredatabase.cnrs.fr.

[206] Labour Court of Appeal (4th ch) nr 48.695, 15 January 2008.

[207] Vickers, *Religion and Belief Discrimination in Employment—the EU law*, n 69 above, 39.

[208] See, eg, Case C-94/00, *Roquette Frères v SA v Directeur général de la concurrence* [2002] ECR I-9011, 29.

[209] Article 288, para 3 of the Treaty on the Functioning of the European Union ('A directive shall be binding, as to the result to be achieved, upon each Member State to which it is addressed, but shall leave to the national authorities the choice of form and methods').

sector, an important objective of the EU, could strengthen the case for clarity of guidance and require a level of uniformity across Member States.[210]

C. Reconciling Work and Religious Time under EU Equality Law: Remembering *Vivien Prais*

Regarding the issue of religious time accommodations there is an older ECJ case, not under the Directive and regarding education, which the Court may draw upon if and when it is presented with such case in the future. The 1976 *Vivien Prais*[211] judgment concerned a British national of Jewish faith who had signed up for the open competition for recruitment of a linguistic expert at the EU. When she was notified of the test date (16 May 1975), she promptly notified the Council that that day was the first day of Shavuot (Pentecost) during which she could not travel or write, so that she was unable to sit for the examination and she asked for an alternative day. The Council refused to set another day for her and, since other people were already notified, refused to change the test date. Prais' complaint was dismissed by the Council. Before the ECJ, Prais argued that the setting of the date on a religiously significant date violated Article 27 of the Staff Regulations which prohibited discrimination on the basis of race, 'creed' or sex and on the basis of Articles 9 and 14 of the ECHR. She, however, did not prevail in her claim because the Court held that the appointing authority had *no duty to set a date which avoids conflicting with a religious holiday* of which it had not been notified in advance (that is, before setting an exam date), although it stated obiter dicta that it 'is desirable that an appointing authority informs itself in a general way' of dates which may be unsuitable for religious reasons'.[212] Since Prais had 'only' notified the Council about the conflict after the test date had been set, it was within the Council's discretion to award her an alternative date (which it never did).[213] Thus, when *designing* rules, the aim should be to include as many interests as possible and choose avenues that accommodate all, or at least restrict and disadvantage vulnerable minority groups as little as possible. There will be occasions where it is

---

[210] See consideration 11 of the Employment Equality Directive; art 45 (ex-39) of the Treaty on the Functioning of the EU (not applicable on employment in the public service) and Art 15.2 of the EU Charter of Fundamental Rights of the European Union.

[211] Case C-130/75, *Vivien Prais v Council of the European Communities* [1976] ECR I-1589.

[212] It can be noted that in another context, European elections, the EU does take into account the religious calendar, albeit of the majority population in Europe. The European Parliament elections of 2014 were initially planned for 5–8 June, but MEPs voted to have the date be moved to 22–25 May, in part seeking to avoid that it would fall on the Pentecost weekend (50 days after Easter) which could lead to lower voter turnout. See: www.hln.be/hln/nl/957/Binnenland/article/detail/1637141/2013/05/21/Europa-bekrachtigt-25-mei-als-Belgische-verkiezingsdatum.dhtml (another reason being that this would give more time for the election of the new president of the European Commission in July).

[213] In this 1976 case, there is some debate whether Art 9/14 ECHR applies to the access to the public services and actions of the EU, and even the applicant is not convinced of the applicability but tries to argue around it.

possible to choose concrete ways to avoid having to deal with reasonable accommodations ex post if the (foreseeable) interests have been taken into account when setting up the initiative.

The holding of *Vivien Prais* indicates that while the CJEU may regard some level of religious time accommodation as desirable (a 'good practice'), it would likely not go so far as considering it a legal duty under EU law for an employer to accommodate the religious needs of its employees. The recent CJEU decision, *HK Danmark (Ring and Skouboe Werge)*,[214] which holds that a reduction in working time can be an appropriate reasonable accommodation for persons with disabilities as long as there is no disproportionate burden, would not seem to have much influence on the CJEU's prospects of ruling the same in the case of religion or belief, considering the lack of an explicit duty of reasonable accommodation for religion or belief under the Directive. The Court's decision in *Coleman*,[215] a British disability case, would add support to this argument; that is that the CJEU will strictly guard this right as benefiting only individuals with disabilities. *Coleman* involved the question of whether the caregiver (in this case the mother) of a disabled child was also protected from discrimination and harassment on the basis of disability when she was treated less favourably at work by reason of close association with (having to care for) a disabled person. The CJEU held that the principle of equal treatment enshrined in the Employment Equality Directive should not be interpreted strictly, so that a carer is covered by the provisions on direct and indirect discrimination and harassment. However, it denied a right to reasonable accommodation under the Directive to the carer:

> [I]t must be noted in that regard that the provisions ... *relate specifically to disabled persons either because they are provisions concerning positive discrimination measures in favour of disabled persons themselves or because they are specific measures which would be rendered meaningless or could prove to be disproportionate if they were not limited to disabled persons only.* Thus, as recitals 16 and 20 in the preamble to Directive 2000/78 indicate, the measures in question are intended to *accommodate the needs of disabled people at the workplace and to adapt the workplace to their disability. Such measures are therefore designed specifically to facilitate and promote the integration of disabled people* into the working environment and, for that reason, *can only relate to disabled people* and to the obligations incumbent on their employers and, where appropriate, on the Member States with regard to disabled people (emphasis added).[216]

Thus, in *Coleman*, an instrumental case when it concerns the concept of discrimination by association, the CJEU may have forecast a conservative line of jurisprudence when it comes to reasonable accommodation beyond disability.

---

[214] Joined Cases C-335/11 and C-337/11, *HK Danmark v Dansk almennyttigt Boligselskab, and HK Danmark v Dansk Arbejdsgiverforening* [2013] ECLI 222.

[215] Case C-303/06 *S Coleman v Attridge* Law [2008] IRLR 88.

[216] Case C-303/06 *S Coleman v Attridge* Law [2008] IRLR 88, para 42. In para 43, the Court however saw this as not preventing a more encompassing approach when it comes to the principle of equal treatment enshrined in the Directive.

Somek, who finds the reservation of reasonable accommodations to one category indefensible, argues that the *Coleman* decision shows that the protection from discrimination for the carer without an accompanying right to accommodation is 'nugatory'.[217] O'Brien discusses the *Coleman* case and other CJEU cases as instances which 'reveal the inherent conceptual and practical constraints that the market-based origins of European Union anti-discrimination law place upon the European Union's equality agenda'. While O'Brien criticises the CJEU for rejecting substantive equality measures which could counter labour market exclusions—such as 'persisting tolerance of forms of indirect discrimination, and reluctance to describe a "right" to differential treatment'[218] —for reasons that they would be economically irrational, she does not dismiss such approach off-hand but argues a broader, alternative approach to economic rationality which would facilitate substantive equality becoming set firmer in EU equality law. Offering such an alternative answer, she writes:

> The anti-substantive equality framework could undermine the impact of future Union legislation, creating labour market exclusion ... It is suggested that we are not faced with as stark a choice as these different equality models would suggest, between a human rights based individualism, or an economically rooted utilitarianism in which equal treatment is a superficial factor. It is possible to conceive of equal treatment as part of the greater good in itself. In other words, utilitarian economics may well be legitimate, but we must be prepared to ask 'what utility?' and to confront short-sighted 'economic rationality', and to recognise that the protection of minorities is a concern for the majority to avoid creating sub-citizenship.[219]

In sum, with regard to the duty of reasonable accommodation, this is a good indication that the CJEU would see an employer accommodation mandate to be a step beyond protection against (indirect) discrimination, and would strictly guard this right as benefiting only individuals with disability and refuse to extend it to other grounds besides disability. As does Pitt, the CJEU may consider that even if the boundaries between the two concepts are far from clear: 'the express inclusion of reasonable accommodations for disability implies that it was not intended to be covered by the general concept of indirect discrimination in the Directive'.[220]

When it comes to conflicts with religious time, EU working time legislation could offer solutions. The current Working Time Directive (the third)—currently under revision—does not include any provisions related to the religious needs of some employees.[221] While the goal of working time used to relate to health and

---

[217] Somek, *Engineering Equality. An Essay on European Anti-Discrimination Law*, n 167 above, 182.
[218] O'Brien, 'Equality's false summits: new varieties of disability discrimination, "excessive" equal treatment and economically constricted horizons', n 50 above, 30 ('Measures that promote the 'sameness' of treatment are less controversial and perceived as more economically viable'; 'Sameness is politically far less challenging, as it accords with an approach of 'minimum interventionism', suggesting a politics of individualism and state passivity, and ultimately serving ... to reinforce the status quo and 'protect dominant interests').
[219] O'Brien, ibid, 30.
[220] Pitt, 'Religion or belief: aiming at the right target?', n 64 above, 220.
[221] See: ec.europa.eu/social/main.jsp?catId=706&langId=en&intPageId=205.

safety, more recently the debate has broadened and other objectives have come to be included, such as improving productivity, enhancing competitiveness, supporting work-life balance, and confronting the growing diversity of preferences and working patterns.[222] Some religious accommodation issues relate to health and safety, for instance the needs of employees fasting for religious reasons; and other issues relate broadly to work-life balance and diversity, so that religious accommodation seems fit for inclusion and regulation in the Working Time Directive. Nonetheless, the European Commission, perhaps unsurprisingly, has indicated a lack of enthusiasm for handling this potentially sensitive matter:

> The question of whether weekly rest should normally be taken on a Sunday, rather than on another day of the week, is very complex, raising issues about the effect on health and safety and work-life balance, as well as issues of a social, religious and educational nature. However, it does not necessarily follow that this is an appropriate matter for legislation at EU level: in view of the other issues which arise, the principle of subsidiarity appears applicable.[223]

---

[222] Communication from the Commission to the European Parliament, the Council, the European Economic and Social Committee, and the Committee of the Regions, Reviewing the Working Time Directive, Brussels, 24.3.2010, COM(2010) 106 final, 5.

[223] Communication from the Commission to The European Parliament, The Council, The European Economic and Social Committee and the Committee of the Regions, Reviewing the Working Time Directive, Brussels, 21.12.2010, COM(2010) 801 final, 11.

Concluding Remarks on Part I

The interactions between ECHR and EU law are complex, including when it comes to issues of religion or belief in the workplace. Under EU law, fundamental rights guaranteed under ECHR (and domestic constitutions) 'constitute general principles of the Union's law'.[224] One could see the ECHR protections as the baseline, with EU fundamental rights protection adding another layer to the protection of religion or belief in the workplace. But is this an accurate depiction of the situation?

When it comes to Article 9 ECHR protections it was expected that protections under the Charter would go further. For instance, Gwyneth Pitt in 2007 (thus before the *Eweida* judgment) argued that

> [a]s many commentators regard the ECtHR as having taken an unduly narrow view of the protection offered by Art. 9 in relation to claims by employees,[225] if a similar approach is taken to the legal interpretation of the [Employment Equality] Directive, the Directive may be found to have a disappointingly limited impact.[226]

One reason is that the role of the CJEU as a supranational court differs from that of the ECtHR.

Also, the fact that EU Directives are binding as to the result achieved[227] justifies a much more guided case law from the CJEU in the area of religious employment discrimination. Arguments based on the free movement of workers in the private sector, an important objective of the EU, could strengthen the case for clarity of guidance and require a level of uniformity across Member States.[228]

Finally, even if the issue is addressed through the angle of religious freedom, it is not excluded that the human rights protection offered under the EU Charter of

---

[224] Article 6. 3 TEU. Art 6.2 TEU states that 'The Union shall accede to the European Convention for the Protection of Human Rights and Fundamental Freedoms'.

[225] referring amongst others to Evans, *Freedom of religion under the European Convention on Human Rights*, n 98 above, 127–32.

[226] Pitt, 'Religion or belief: aiming at the right target?' n 64 above, 209.

[227] Article 288, para 3 of the Treaty on the Functioning of the European Union ('A directive shall be binding, as to the result to be achieved, upon each Member State to which it is addressed, but shall leave to the national authorities the choice of form and methods').

[228] See consideration 11 of the Employment Equality Directive; art 45 (ex-39) of the Treaty on the Functioning of the EU (not applicable on employment in the public service) and Art 15.2 of the EU Charter of Fundamental Rights of the European Union. In addition, one can note that private transactions can be referred to the CJEU, even in first instance, while only States can be the defending party in cases before the ECtHR.

Fundamental Rights exceeds that under the ECHR.[229] Discussing the *Şahin* case and *Dahlab* case, Pitt thus argued that 'this line of cases would need to be reconsidered when the issue arises under the Framework Employment Directive'.[230]

Part I illustrated that the human rights framework, in addition to the non-discrimination law framework, holds potential for requiring private employers to take the religious needs of their employees seriously into account. Despite the remarkable coming of age of EU equality law and the recent developments at the level of the ECtHR, notably with the *Eweida* judgment which calls for a thorough balancing between rights and interests (including that of the religious employee), it can be argued that the supranational guidance to Member States such as Belgium, the Netherlands and the UK in this area remains limited.

On the vexed question of the proper limits of the fundamental right to freedom of religion and right to non-discrimination as it arises in religious workplace accommodation cases in Europe, it seems the domestic courts hold much leeway. This is because of the lack or dearth of cases addressing the various issues that have come up at the domestic level (or could come up if certain barriers were removed). But it also is inherent to the open justification systems under EU law and Article 9 ECHR which allows for (widely) divergent decisions/outcomes in very similar cases, within the same legal system but particularly across different Member States with divergent legal cultures, mentalities, histories and (church-religion) arrangements. In the absence of particular domestic legislation on issues such as religious time or refusal to shake hands, it is up to the judiciary to decide cases. And in the absence of such case law clarifications of the meaning of rights, due to 'passing' or 'covering' coping mechanisms, it is up to the shop-floor to adopt responses, which in light of political/societal ambivalences towards religion, religious diversity and integration, often reflect very local sensitivities bordering on intolerance towards minority religions and their 'strange practices'. These domestic experiences form the subject of Part II.

---

[229] Article 10.1 of the EU Charter of Fundamental Rights of the European Union (2010/C 83/02), binding since the entry into force of the Lisbon Treaty, is textually identical to Art 9.1 of the ECHR. See also Koenraad Lenaerts and Piet Van Nuffel, *Europees Recht* (Intersentia, 2011) 550 et seq.

[230] Pitt, 'Religion or belief: aiming at the right target?' n 64 above, 218.

PART II

Religion or Belief in the Belgian, Dutch and British Private Sector Workplace: Between Assimilation Demands and Reasonable Accommodation

European Country Studies: The Importance of Contextualisation

Vous songez à venir travailler en Belgique? Vous avez peut-être déjà pris la 'grande décision'? Nous, Belges, sommes heureux que vous veniez apporter vos forces et votre intelligence ... Nous vous le répétons: les travailleurs méditerranéens sont les bienvenus en Belgique.[1]

Part II analyses how issues of religion or belief in the workplace have been approached in three European countries, Belgium, the Netherlands and the United Kingdom, with commonalities as well as distinct features. For instance, all three are Western European liberal-democratic nations and (for the time being) Member States of the EU. However, the nature of the religious diversity in the respective countries is different; Belgium is predominantly Catholic, the UK is predominantly Protestant while there are roughly equal numbers of Catholics and Protestants in the Netherlands. It is said that '[w]ith the important exception of Northern Ireland, differences between Catholics and Protestants no longer give rise to significant tensions and discrimination in the employment field'.[2] In all three cases, after Christians and the unaffiliated, the largest religious minority is Muslim. Most Muslims in Europe have a migration background and—despite their internal diversity which often is substantial—are also ethnically distinct from the majority in the European country of settlement. Muslims are also said to be 'the single largest group of those who are the source of public anxieties'.[3]

The background of Muslims and other ethno-religious minorities differs somewhat across various EU Member States, reflecting differences in post-colonisation migration flows, 'guest-worker' programmes following the Second World War, family reunification movements and refugee flows. As a result of these various movements, the largest non-EU ethno-religious minorities within Belgium are of Moroccan, Turkish and Congolese origin. In the Netherlands, people of Moroccan,

---

[1] Institut belge d'Information et de Documentation, 'Vivre et travailler en Belgique' (1965) 3. Excerpt from brochure distributed in Morocco, Tunisia and Algeria in 1963 by the Belgian Ministry of Employment. See Y Lamghari, *L'Islam en entreprise: La diversité culturelle en question* (Editions L'Harmattan, 2012) 35–36.

[2] Pitt, 'Religion or belief: aiming at the right target?' in H Meenan (ed), *Equality law in an enlarged European Union: Understanding the article 13 directives* (Cambridge, CUP 2007) 203.

[3] T Modood, 'Muslims and the Politics of Difference' (2003) 74 *The Political Quarterly* 100 ('[I]t is clear that the estimated 15 million people in the EU who subjectively or objectively are Muslim, whatever additional identities they may have, form the single largest group of those who are the source of public anxieties').

Turkish, Antillean and Surinamer origin form the main minorities, who are also the subjects of Dutch minority and integration policies. People of Indonesian descent also have a significant presence as a minority group in the Netherlands but are considered largely 'assimilated' in Dutch culture and society and no longer subject to integration policies. Ethnic diversity is a prominent factor in the Netherlands, where Antilleans, Surinamers and Moluccans add 'colour' to the mix. In contrast, in the UK, Muslims come predominantly from India, Pakistan and Bangladesh, and Muslims from North Africa and Turkey form a much smaller group. The UK is also home to considerable numbers of Hindus and Sikhs.

Europe has historically been a continent of emigration. For instance, in 1950 Queen Juliana stated in her Queen's speech that 'the Netherlands is full, partially overfull' and half a million young Dutch workers were encouraged to emigrate to Australia and New Zealand.[4] Not long afterwards the Netherlands and other European countries started to actively recruit foreign guest workers to meet domestic labour shortages. Europe has also known considerable secularisation in recent decades. The ensuing changes in religious and philosophical make-up means Europe was not isolated from the challenges that immigration countries like the United States, Canada and Australia have long faced. Questions of integration/assimilation have become the site of important political and social struggles. Unlike in those countries though, Muslims have become the quintessential 'Others' in Europe. Connor writes that:

> Islam is not the only growing religious group to arrive on the European scene, but at least among the European popular media, it is the most prominent. With the Salman Rushdie, headscarf, and Danish cartoon affairs, not to mention the post-7/7/2005 world, some have described the religiosity of Muslim immigrants in relation to Europe's tradition of secularization ... as a 'clash of civilizations' ... Muslims have become the definitive outsider all so common in the discourse surrounding politics of immigration. Muslim identity is further complicated since, unlike the United States, religion is not a bridge but instead a barrier to incorporation within Europe.[5]

Younous Lamghari, who conducted fieldwork amongst the Human Resources staff, trade unionists and (predominantly Muslim) employees of the Brussels Intercommunal Transport Company MIVB-STIB ('Lamghari study'),[6] notes the tendency amongst company managers to conflate 'ethno-religious diversity' with the dichotomy Muslim/non-Muslim.[7] This conflation of religious and ethnic minorities with Muslims, despite the presence of many other non-Muslim

---

[4] Tijdelijke Commissie Onderzoek Integratiebeleid (Commissie Blok), *Bruggen Bouwen (onderzoek Integratiebeleid)* (2004) 250.

[5] Connor, 'Contexts of immigrant receptivity and immigrant religious outcomes: the case of Muslims in Western Europe' (2010) 33 *Ethnic and Racial Studies* 376, 380 (references omitted).

[6] Y Lamghari, *L'Islam en entreprise: La diversité culturelle en question* (Editions L'Harmattan, 2012). All translations from this work are my own. See also Y Lamghari, 'La neutralité à la STIB' in D Cabiaux et al (eds), *Neutralité et faits religieux Quelles interactions dans les services publics?* (Academia-L'Harmattan, 2014).

[7] Lamghari, *L'Islam en entreprise*, n 6 above, 101.

minorities, characterises the Belgian context to a much stronger extent than that of the Netherlands or the UK.

The political discourse across Europe has undeniably become more and more fiercely anti-Muslim, spreading stereotypes and instilling fear and concern in the majority population, which, as surveys show, become less comfortable with the presence of Muslims. Certain politicians and constituencies in the United States have, unfortunately, more recently started to follow a similar course. Following terrorist attacks in Paris (13 November 2015) and especially in Brussels (22 March 2016) much attention was paid to Belgium's 'poorly integrated immigrant population of mainly Moroccan and Turkish descent (41 per cent of the population of Molenbeek is Muslim)'.[8] But fear of and discomfort with Muslims[9] has been long present in Europe, even before 2001. In Belgium, the nationalist Vlaams Blok obtained its best election result in Flanders in November 1991 with a strong anti-Muslim programme.[10] Visible signs of difference in religious dress, in a context where socio-economic positions are highly unequal, have been 'seen to illustrate "unwillingness by Muslims to integrate" or an intention to "impose values at odds with European identity" ... issues such as forced marriage, perceived as a Muslim practice, have similarly been cited to corroborate these ideas'.[11]

In both Belgium and the Netherlands, the rise of political parties promoting anti-immigrant and anti-Muslim agendas is notable, and the impact of this on the issue of religious accommodation (in the broad sense) must be appreciated. In the Belgian 2004 regional elections, the Vlaams Belang received almost 25 per cent of the Flemish vote, meaning that one in four Flemish voters gave their vote to an extreme right-wing political party unequivocally hostile towards immigrants and Muslims. It was disconcerting that '[f]or Flemish voters, a vote for the Blok is already seen as a legitimate option'.[12]

In the Dutch 2012 general elections, the Partij voor Vrijheid (PVV) of Geert Wilders received 15.45 per cent of the vote, becoming the third largest party after the Volkspartij voor Vrijheid en Democratie (VVD) (liberals) and Partij van de Arbeid (PvdA) (socialists), making anti-immigration/anti-Islam parties hardly a

---

[8] eg R Cohen, 'The Islamic State of Molenbeek', *The New York Times*, 11 April 2016.

[9] See Z Strabac and O Listhung, 'Anti-Muslim prejudice in Europe: a multilevel analysis of survey data from 30 countries' (2008) 37 *Social Science Research* 268–86.

[10] After the 'Vlaams Blok' (ie the three associations affiliated with the Flemish nationalist party) was condemned for inciting racial hatred in 2004 by the Cour de cassation, its successor the 'Vlaams Belang' was set up which distanced itself from some of the most extreme earlier positions. In the 2007 general elections it obtained 12% of the votes, its highest percentage yet. With the success of the Nieuw-Vlaamse Alliantie (N-VA) party the popularity of the Vlaams Belang has dwindled, although the party has succeeded in pulling the political centre in Flanders to the right. J Erk, 'From Vlaams Blok to Vlaams Belang: The Belgian Far-Right Renames Itself' (May 2005) 28 *West European Politics* 493–502.

[11] Amnesty International, *Choice and Prejudice. Discrimination against Muslims in Europe* (2012) 12 (noting that political parties and the public sometimes throw problematic practices which violate human rights, such as forced marriages, into the same pile as issues which are covered under freedom of religion, including the right to wear religious dress).

[12] J Erk, 'From Vlaams Blok to Vlaams Belang: The Belgian Far-Right Renames Itself' (May 2005) 28 *West European Politics* 493–502.

fringe phenomenon but rather forming an additional 'pillar party'. This socio-political development, reinforced by persistent stereotypical portrayal of immigrants and Muslims in the media has led to increased 'lived hostility' which can hardly be conducive to the willingness of minorities to actively integrate in such societies. Yet, the dominant political reaction to this situation, reflecting a certain lack of patience despite considerable improvements and success stories, has been to emphasise the *obligations* of minorities to integrate and to give up aspects of identity which are seen as an obstacle to a more complete national unity. Otherness is seen as threatening unity and solidarity. This may be both a cause and consequence of the success of the right-wing, forming a vicious circle. Voters who feel threatened will be more likely to vote for anti-immigration parties. Even if such parties do not gain executive power,[13] it is undeniable that they move the party programmes of the mainstream parties further and further to the right, thus (re)shaping political options for all voters.[14] The causes that led to the white majority vocally expressing feelings of being 'threatened in their own country' may be real and need addressing, but 'solutions' channelling fears and hostilities towards minorities carry real consequences for groups which are scapegoated in society, the media and the political arena.

In the UK, one of the main reasons for the Brexit vote was discontent with immigration. Even if this did not necessarily relate to religious minorities so much as intra-European legal migration from Eastern Europe,[15] it has been argued that 'the EU referendum campaign was marked by divisive, anti-immigrant and xenophobic rhetoric.'[16] Britain's right-wing party, the United Kingdom Independence Party (UKIP), unlike the Vlaams Belang and the PVV, has repeatedly rebutted charges of racism and the prominent presence of black and ethnic minority members lends some support that the broader party line is about immigration rather than race. Still, the ensuing anti-immigrant atmosphere is not likely to reduce levels of xenophobia. Social research experiments have shown that even before the Brexit vote, there was considerable 'anti-Muslim hatred and hostility' in the British public space, in particular when using public transport.[17] For instance, the wearing of a veil has particularly pronounced connotations, including 'gender equality,

---

[13] See, eg, the *cordon sanitaire* in Belgium, a 1992 agreement between the mainstream political parties not to make any executive coalitions with the Vlaams Blok/Belang. See J Erk, 'From Vlaams Blok to Vlaams Belang: The Belgian Far-Right Renames Itself' (every party has critics who do not support the *cordon sanitaire*, especially following its re-branding into the Vlaams Belang in 2004). In the Netherlands, the PVV of Geert Wilders after the 2010 elections provided support for the liberal-conservative coalition's small majority in parliament.

[14] J Erk, 'From Vlaams Blok to Vlaams Belang: The Belgian Far-Right Renames Itself' ('Vlaams Blok has also managed to pull the political centre towards the right in Flanders. Mainstream Flemish parties have felt the necessity to incorporate aspects of the far-right agenda'). Various stances which were once 'uncompromising Vlaams Blok' positions were subsequently endorsed by the mainstream parties.

[15] A Taylor, 'The uncomfortable question: Was the Brexit vote based on racism?', *The Washington Post*, 25 June 2016.

[16] I Zempi and I Awan, 'What does Islamophobia feel like? We dressed visibly as Muslims for a month to find out', *The Conversation*, 12 October 2016.

[17] ibid ('The level of hatred and vitriol we experienced was startling').

religious extremism, lack of integration, and for some presents a threat to British and Western ideals.'[18]

Jurisprudential developments have not been isolated from socio-political developments. For instance, case law, sociological studies and NGO reports confirm a pattern in Belgium whereby religiously distinct workers are routed to the back-office or excluded altogether, a problematic tendency that may be symptomatic of a larger European discomfort with the existence or visibility of heterogeneity.[19] The unease of the white, native populations with immigration, Islam and 'multiculturalism' is recorded in the rise of the right-wing and the shifting of the centre to the right, but it also has exclusionary effects in the labour market. Right-wing politicians who question racism and discrimination as being a relevant factor or shrug their shoulders when asked for the causes of the undeniable socio-economic disadvantaged positions of ethno-cultural minorities should look in their own midst for part of the answer.[20] Neutrality, a spill-over from the public sector, or image-based arguments have been mobilised as arguments for restrictive dress policies, at times in response to the (discriminatory) prejudices of employers, (vocal) customers or the larger society. One can appreciate the unenviable position of many employers, who as gatekeepers or 'distributive agents' hold entrepreneurial discretion but ultimately need to respond to 'realities on the ground'. With the mainstreaming of right-wing ideology, customers feel vindicated in complaining about a grocery store saleswoman's headscarf, in asking for 'a doctor who is not visibly a Muslim', or requesting a temp agency to find workers who are 'one of our own'. In the UK, home to a very different political system and social model, extreme right-wing ideology has been less successful. Yet, the mariginalisation of the underclass—where ethno-religious minorities are disproportionately represented—has not been less problematic, another factor that played into the Brexit vote.

Each country study reveals its own dominant discourse or preoccupation when one reviews the issue from a broad societal perspective. In Belgium, the leading story is one of 'neutrality discourse—at times—gone wild' and correlated with this is the domination of Flemish nationalism as the defining feature of the country's future in various aspects: determining the relations with ethno-religious minorities in Flanders and determining the shape of the country's political future as a whole. The persistence and reach of discrimination, and the ineffectiveness/lack of application of the law, in the Belgian context is illustrated by the various temp agency controversies.

The leading story in the unitary Netherlands, on the other hand, focuses much less on federalism and nationalism, except that under an increasingly

---

[18] ibid.

[19] Significantly, Belgium followed France in banning the full-face veil so that this issue will not come up in the employment context.

[20] See, eg, interview with Liesbeth Homans, N-VA politician and then Flemish Minister for (amongst others) Poverty Reduction and Equal Opportunities; J De Ceulaer and W Pauli, 'Liesbeth Homans: 'Jammer dat men te pas en te onpas over racise spreekt', *Knackbe*, 21 May 2014.

anti-multiculturalist rhetoric, there are arguments that 'respect for the dominant Dutch culture' needs to be emancipated and demands on minorities need to include adherence to Dutch standards. The retreat from multiculturalism, with the shift in citizenship conception towards a thicker conception—while still reminiscent of the more typical liberal, accommodative approach—together with the acceptance and promotion of confrontational interpretations of the freedom of speech (as the Netherlands 'first freedom')[21] are core elements of the leading story in the Netherlands. These policy shifts and hardening political and societal discourses have had undeniable effects in various areas of life, legitimising exclusion and discrimination of Muslims and other 'foreigners'. With the rise of right-wing parties such as the Vlaams Blok/Belang and N-VA in Belgium, and the Lijst Pim Fortyn and Geert Wilders' PVV in the Netherlands, the political centre has been shifted to the right over time, making naming and blaming foreigners for social decay a more attractive prospect than seeking to find solutions for tensions in society. In the UK, the right had remained much more isolated, but the shift and retreat from multiculturalism has also been proclaimed. The leading story in the UK is thus of a somewhat different nature, and involves a generally progressive (minority) race policy in a post-colonial post-empire state which by utilising the prism of race/ethnic minority relations has triggered an *ethnification* of the oppressed working class. Indeed, the issue of class struggles plays a much more prominent role in the UK, a much more unequal society where opportunities are rigged in the favour of the (often white) rich middle and upper classes. Brexit will most likely not alter this.

The domestic case law must be placed in its appropriate socio-political context, which also can account for the level of emotional charge which cases carry in different contexts. Religious dress conflicts are thus clearly a charged, gender-relevant topic in Belgium and the Netherlands. Religious time conflicts overall carry fewer emotional connotations. Emotions also run high when it comes to some of the religious practices discussed under the final category, such as objections to 'hard' job duties (eg, handling pork/alcohol) or softer socialisation-related practices (eg shaking hands), to the extent that the perceived objectionableness of such practices bars even a priori consideration of protection under either legal framework. Most of these miscellaneous accommodations relate to Muslims, whose assertiveness is sometimes considered cause for concern.

Yet, the issues that have arisen in case law only represent a small batch of actual cases on the ground. In the case of shaking hands, for instance, there has not been a legal case in Belgium, but a number of controversies have been reported. If the mode of reporting on such controversies, and opinions published in newspapers are any indication, the workers involved are strategically wise not to bring their

---

[21] Netherlands Institute for Human Rights, *Onderzoek Mensenrechten* (2013), available at: www.mensenrechten.nl/publicaties/detail/18971. Research on human rights in the Netherlands revealed that the freedom of expression is the most well-known human right. 46% of respondents were able to name this human right; however, 30% of the Dutch were unable to name any human right.

claim in legal form. Such accommodation issues may be a sign of our time where countries are seeking appropriate ways to manage cultural and religious diversity, but religious people have been raising conflict issues in secular societies for a much longer time. In the case of Christians, 'old' accommodation requests have often already led to legislation or more established solutions,[22] eg healthcare workers' conscientious objections to abortion/euthanasia while newer ones, eg marriage registrars refusing to perform same-sex ceremonies, are still being negotiated.

---

[22] These can be accommodations or special protections. In the UK, blasphemy is a crime but only where the Christian faith is insulted; attacking this under Art 9 and 14 ECHR proved unsuccessful in *Choudhury v United Kingdom*, Application no 17439/90 (EComHR, 5 March 1991) (the applicant had sought criminal prosecution against Salman Rushdie as author of the book 'The Satanic Verses' and his publisher for blasphemy against Islam but the application was dismissed).

3

The (Non-)Accommodation of Religious Dress in the European Workplace

I. Introduction

Belgian, Dutch and British cases discussed in this chapter illustrate the approach taken in each country towards religious dress, in particular the hijab, in the workplace. The case law shows this to be a particularly gender-relevant area of the law, since Muslim women wearing headscarves have been the archetypal claimants. A 2012 Amnesty International report confirmed the gender-division of discrimination claims:

> [T]he nature of the complaints indicated women and men experience discrimination on the ground of religion differently. Cases involving Muslim men referred predominantly to accommodation of religious needs in the workplace, such as praying times or flexible working hours during Ramadan, the Islamic month of fasting. Most of the complaints introduced by women involved the wearing of religious and cultural symbols or dress.[1]

Wearing religious dress or exhibiting religious symbols has quickly turned into 'one of the key issues in the practical implementation' of the Employment Equality Directive.[2] The protection offered by domestic courts under the fundamental right to religious freedom has remained—far more—modest.

II. Religious Dress in the Employment Context in Belgium: Judgment-Proof Restrictive Employer Practices

Despite the overall rarity of case law on religious discrimination and accommodations in Belgium, a number of judicial decisions, all involving the Muslim

---

[1] Amnesty International, *Choice and Prejudice. Discrimination against Muslims in Europe*, n 11 above, 33–34.

[2] Chopin and Uyen Do, *Developing Anti-Discrimination law in Europe. The 27 Member States, Croatia, Former Yugoslav Republic of Macedonia and Turkey compared.* (comparative analysis of country reports) (Brussels, European Network of Legal Experts in the Non-discrimination Field, 2010) 39.

headscarf, show a judicial penchant for accepting dress restrictions which limit religious manifestations in the workplace, thus confining employment opportunities for Muslim women and other religiously visible employees. Broad dress restrictions have been considered legitimate under both human rights law and the Belgian Anti-Discrimination Act of 2007[3] based on arguments of company neutrality, customer preferences or corporate image, in particular when the job involves a front-office position. Written 'rules' against wearing religious dress and even unwritten 'practices' have been seen as non-arbitrary and justified. In particular, company 'neutrality policies' which have mushroomed in the private sector—as a spill-over effect of misguided and regretful developments in the public sector[4]—have been accepted as justifying *indirect discrimination* towards religious minorities, in particular Muslim women. Such policies are generally inserted into company policies or company 'regulations'. Despite their main goal to ban headscarves worn by female Muslim employees and thereby avoid this socially contentious issue, such policies prohibit a priori 'any religious, philosophical or political expressions' in the workplace for reasons of company neutrality or professional image, without linking such restrictions to any particular job function or work condition. Some cases illustrate the direct trigger for the adoption of such neutrality policies in discriminatory customer preferences (whether expressed or perceived) and/or as a strategy of conflict avoidance, but in the case law reasoning this background is often absent, thus disregarding the consequences of the *Feryn* decision[5] in the area of religion or belief discrimination.

The consequences of the *Eweida* decision[6] have also not yet been absorbed in the Belgian case law, but that is because the most important Belgian cases

[3] Wet van 10 mei 2007 ter bestrijding van bepaalde vormen van discriminatie, *Belgian Official Journal*, 30 May 2007 (hereafter 'Belgian Anti-Discrimination Act'). The precursor was the Anti-Discrimination Act of 25 February 2003 (Wet ter bestrijding van discriminatie en tot wijziging van de wet van 15 februari 1993 tot oprichting van een Centrum voor gelijkheid van kansen en voor racismebestrijding), *Belgian Official Journal*, 17 March 2003.

[4] Discussions regarding public sector dress restrictions have been prominent in Belgium and have allowed those objecting to religious dress or symbols to sharpen their discursive tools. In 2007, amidst public protest, the city of Antwerp banned all front-office city staff from wearing headscarves and all other religious or political symbols. See D Hermans, 'Scheldestad bant hoofddoek. 150 moslima's protesteren tevergeefs tegen verbod' ['Antwerp bans headscarves. 150 Muslim women protest to no avail'], *Het Nieuwsblad*, 16 January 2007 (it was subsequently reported that of the seven personnel members working at the city hall counter, three decided to take their headscarves off and other positions were sought for the others); US Department of State, *International Religious Freedom Report Belgium*, 2007. The Brussels regional government and a few other Flemish cities issued similar bans. At the federal level there are no specific directives on wearing religious symbols, with the notable exception of judges, police officers and other uniformed officials. In 2010, the Charleroi city council adopted a ban for teachers in the municipal schools following a dispute with math teacher Nural Topal. The Belgian Conseil d'Etat ruled in favour of the city: Conseil d'Etat, 21 December 2010, nr 210.000, A. 196.031/ g-117. Following years of discussions and protest, in 2013, the city of Ghent reversed its ban on religious symbols for civil servants.

[5] Case C-54/07, *Centrum voor gelijkheid van kansen en voor racismebestrijding v Firma Feryn NV* [2008] ECR I-5187.

[6] *Eweida and Others v UK*, Application nos 48420/10, 59842/10, 51671/10 and 36516/10 (ECtHR, 15 January 2013).

precede it. It is thus not excluded that the *Eweida* holding or elements of its reasoning will in time penetrate and influence Belgian jurisprudence. If fully acknowledged, both *Feryn* and *Eweida* should have important impact when it comes to the reasoning and outcomes Belgian religious accommodation cases.

More recent judicial decisions regarding religious dress, all involving Muslim women's headscarves on the job, have generally been subject to wide media circulations and thus led to extensive public messaging in Belgium. The predominant message broadcasted, however, has been that the freedom of religion and non-discrimination law is of little concrete use to veiled Muslim women who want to participate in the mainstream workplace, so that every case involves an uphill battle. This means that the *special effects* of anti-discrimination law (when it is being judicially enforced) likely have had effect on the shop floor of social life, leading to self-handicapping behaviour (not applying for front-office jobs, denying oneself certain educational choices, etc) and shaping the *general (non)effects* of the anti-discrimination law in this area.[7]

A. *HEMA*: Normalised Intolerance towards the Headscarf in Belgium?

In March 2011, the mainstream Belgian media reported extensively on the so-called HEMA headscarf case.[8] A Belgian branch store of HEMA, a Dutch retail chain, had dismissed a Muslim saleswoman for wearing a headscarf on the job. The young woman, 20-year-old Joyce Van Op den bosch, was a Belgian convert to Islam. Against expectations, her temporary contract had not been extended because of several complaints by customers who were unhappy or upset about seeing a saleswoman wearing a headscarf. Interestingly, the headscarf had not been an obstacle at the start of her employment and Ms Van Op den bosch was even given a headscarf in the company colours. This headscarf came from the Netherlands, where this formed an accommodative practice at HEMA branches.

Following the dismissal and in the midst of close media scrutiny, HEMA adopted an explicit ban on 'religious, ideological and political symbols'. This was accompanied by a peculiar press statement explaining why HEMA saw itself required to conform to 'local customs and preferences' because it was 'apparently' not customary to wear a headscarf at work in Belgium. The press release made clear that this

---

[7] For the distinction between general (the level of the shop floor) and special effects (in case of official enforcement) of the law, see J Griffiths, 'The social working of anti-discrimination law' in MLP Loenen and PR Rodrigues (eds), *Non-Discrimination Law: Comparative Perspectives* (Kluwer, 1999) 319, 321.

[8] See P Lesaffer, 'Hema ontslaat winkelbediende voor hoofddoek', *De Standaard*, 8 March 2011; X, 'Hema "schikt zich naar gewoonten van het land"' ['Hema "conforms to the customs of the country"'], *De Standaard*, 8 March 2011; Y Delepeleire, 'Hema voor rechter na ontslag voor hoofddoek' ['HEMA before the court after dismissal because of headscarf'], *De Standaard*, 6 March 2012. Discussed in Alidadi, 'From Front-Office to Back-Office: Religious Dress Crossing the Public–Private Divide in the Workplace'.

had triggered the decision to adopt a 'neutrality policy' in Belgium, in notable contrast to its company practice in the Netherlands where the headscarf had been incorporated in the work uniform. HEMA offered the dismissed employee a back-office position, but she rejected this because she enjoyed the contact with customers and did not see why she and her headscarf needed to be hidden.

The case was pursued in court, with the employee supported by the Belgian Centre for Equal Opportunity (CEOOR),[9] and led to the judgment of the Tongeren Labour Tribunal on 2 January 2013.[10] While this judgment was in the employee's favour, with six months' pay being awarded as compensation under the Anti-Discrimination Act of 2007, its reasoning remains problematic and means the case can hardly be considered a step forward for equal opportunities for Muslim women and other visible religious minorities. On the contrary, a patent defeat for the larger cause—the basic freedom to wear religious dress in the workplace, absent some pressing need—was buried behind the apparent (financial) win for the ex-employee.

The Labour Tribunal held that there had been direct discrimination in the case at hand (and there was no talk of justification via a genuine and determining occupational requirement) because *at the time of the dismissal* HEMA had no clear uniform policy banning religious dress. But the Tribunal also held that the subsequent company neutrality policy adopted would be considered legitimate and would block similar claims in the future from being successful. Indeed, the neutrality policy would effectively exclude all veiled Muslim women, turban-donning men or other visibly religious persons from employment at HEMA in Belgium, at least in front-office positions.

Interestingly, the Labour Tribunal said it had found inspiration for its decision in the quasi-jurisprudence of the Dutch Equal Treatment Commission (ETC). The Tribunal distinguished two situations: first, religious dress accommodation cases where the employer had no pre-existing dress policy at the time it dismissed an employee and, secondly, where there was such a policy to draw on. In the first case the analysis would involve assessing whether there was *direct* discrimination, which could only be justified in the case of a genuine occupational requirement. In the case of the saleswoman at HEMA, the Labour Tribunal could not possibly regard the non-wearing of a headscarf as such a genuine occupational requirement; it did state, obiter dicta, that such could be considered 'at most desirable or appropriate'. In contrast, if there had been such neutrality policy in place, a dismissal or refusal to hire someone because of religious dress would have to be assessed under an *indirect* discrimination analysis. This implies that the measure can much more easily be justified, so long as a 'legitimate objective' is pursued in a suitable and appropriate manner. And regarding these, the Tribunal foreshadowed

[9] In February 2016 the CEOOR, with two new co-directors Els Keytsman and Patrick Charlier, was renamed 'Unia'. However, considering its name at the relevant time, the designation CEOOR will be used in this section.
[10] Labour Tribunal Tongeren, 2 January 2013, AR 11/2142/A, Or. 2013/4, 109 (HEMA).

that such neutrality policies generally meet the test and thus can justify indirect distinctions.

However, the Tribunal took a cherry-picking approach towards ETC quasi-jurisprudence. The latter indeed distinguishes between two situations, and two corresponding tests, but they are different from what the Tribunal understood them to be. Situations such as the *HEMA case* where the dismissal was by way of direct reference to the headscarf clearly fall under the first test where headscarf dismissals are to be analysed under direct discrimination, with more limited justification possibilities. The second—indirect discrimination—analysis, in contrast, is required when the dismissal or rejection of the candidate is based on a *neutral reason*, which does not refer to the headscarf or other religious dress directly or even as pretext. This is not the test to be used when a pre-existing private sector *neutrality policy* is in place. The ETC would consider neutrality policies which refer—quite directly—to religious symbols as *direct discrimination*, and these therefore would as a rule fail to meet the first test under the anti-discrimination law framework.

Despite this substantial misconstruction, the Tribunal's holding stands and its message was conveyed loud and clear. The foreshadowing effectively was messaged not just to HEMA and other Belgian companies paying close attention, but also to the broader public, which received the confirmation that pre-emptive wide-spread restrictions on religious dress founded on a particular exclusionary understanding of the concept of neutrality (will) receive the judicial stamp of approval. In other words, Muslim women have no right to insist on wearing a headscarf on the job. This was all the more striking since HEMA's neutrality policy had been clearly adopted in response to flagrantly discriminatory customer responses.[11]

In the face of such judicial patronage of company neutrality policies, any job applicant is put on notice of his or her weak position when it comes to religious requests and the fact of imminent and legitimated exclusion from a very wide array of employment opportunities. In effect, the spill-over effect, the emulation of the same construction which has been utilised in the public sector is judicially approved for use by private profit-oriented companies not serving a public role but having a (local) customer base to please. Arguably, the endorsement of 'neutrality' policies—which have far-reaching effects—means a significant blow to the fundamental rights of employees in the workplace, as unilateral policies—as long as adopted a priori—are set to trump fundamental rights even if they are adopted to accommodate discriminatory customer preferences.

The case can be considered an important test for the EU-wide protection against religious discrimination. The CEOOR, which had voluntarily intervened in the HEMA case, had asked the Labour Tribunal to refer a number of questions

---

[11] The potential issue of harassment, by customers who had made derogatory comments towards the Muslim saleswoman, was not addressed.

for preliminary rulings to the European Court of Justice. However, the Tribunal—later confirmed by the Labour Court of Appeal—found that to be unnecessary to resolve the case at hand and refused to do so.[12]

While the Tribunal explicitly addressed the claims under the anti-discrimination framework (with the distinction between direct and indirect discrimination being key), it devoted only minimal attention to Article 9 arguments. It stated formulaically that 'on the basis of Art. 9.2 ECHR and the jurisprudence of the European Court of Human Rights, the Belgian employer can prohibit the wearing of a headscarf during work hours by way of a neutrality policy'. There was no concern in the judgment that HEMA was using the (real or supposed) bias of its customers to exclude vulnerable employees (cf *Feryn*), or that the fundamental rights of people were sacrificed in light of the majority's sentiments (cf *Eweida*).

B. G4S: Company Neutrality 'Practice' Suffices

The *HEMA case* does not stand alone. In fact, it should be considered a follow-up to another Belgian headscarf case which the CEOOR pursued unsuccessfully before the Antwerp Labour Tribunal and Labour Court of Appeal of Antwerp.[13] The so-called *Achbita v G4S* case was lost at the appeal level in 2011, the same year the HEMA controversy erupted.[14] However, the case was taken to the Cour de cassation, which has referred a question to the CJEU for a preliminary ruling.[15]

The employer was G4S Security Systems, a large multinational company that offers reception and security services and operates in, among other places, Antwerp. The company had dismissed a female Muslim employee who had been working for them for three years as a receptionist outsourced to different customers. Problems arose when the once valued employee, who wore a headscarf outside of work hours but took it off when starting her shift, one day informed her boss that, for religious reasons, she wanted to wear a headscarf in the workplace. She was told that a headscarf would not be tolerated since it violated the 'strict neutrality' the company strived for 'both internally within the company and externally towards customers'. Then, during a period of absence due to the woman's

---

[12] See art 267 TFEU, discussed above at Chapter 2, fns 173–175 and n 44 below.

[13] Both the summary proceedings as well as the proceedings on the merits were unsuccessful. The summary judgment proceedings (*action en cessation*) were dismissed by the tribunal and the Appeal court. The tribunal considered that the employee had no current interest to launch it because the discriminatory act (refusal to allow the wearing of the headscarf at work) had ceased and because there were really few probabilities that she could find herself one day in the same situation again, so the danger of repetition was not present. This decision shows the limits of the injunction procedure (*action en cessation*) enshrined under Belgian anti-discrimination law which does not foresee reintegration.

[14] *Achbita v G4S Secure Solutions NV*, Labour Tribunal Antwerp, 27 April 2010, Case nr AR/06/397639/A; confirmed by Labour Court of Appeal Antwerp, 23 December 2011, Case nr AR/2010/AA/453 and 2010/AA/467; See K Alidadi, 'Werkgever kan hoofddoek verbieden op basis van ongeschreven regels' ['Employer can ban headscarves based on unwritten rules'], *De Juristenkrant*, 26 May 2010, 1–2.

[15] Cass, 9 March 2015, AR S.12.0062.N.

illness, which may not have been unconnected to the headscarf issue, the conflict escalated and the competent company council (*ondernemingsraad*, which consists of representatives of the employees as well as of the employer) adopted a new dress policy, explicitly banning all staff from wearing 'visible symbols of their political, philosophical or religious convictions and/or any ritual connected thereto' in the workplace and instituting a uniform policy for receptionists.

Subsequent mediation attempts with the CEOOR and the liberal labour union intervening on behalf of the employee—Samira Achbita—failed as the parties held on tight to their respective stances and no accommodation options were pursued. Ms Achbita was eventually fired, but given a standard three-month severance payment. The new uniform policy for receptionists entered into effect the next day.

Ms Achbita, supported by the CEOOR which regarded it as an important test case, took the case to court.[16] On the merits, the Antwerp Labour Tribunal, for the purpose of deciding the claims of direct and indirect religious discrimination, considered the meaning of the term 'religion or belief' under the Belgian Anti-Discrimination Act. It was debated whether 'religion or belief' refers only to the *forum internum* or also entails manifestations of religion or belief by wearing religious dress and symbols—the latter being the position in the Netherlands and the UK. The CEOOR argued that an absolute ban imposed by a private employer on manifesting any religious convictions in the workplace amounted to unjustifiable direct discrimination.[17] G4S, on the other hand, contended that wearing a headscarf did not fall under the freedom of religion as it was not proven to be obligatory under Islamic precepts. The Tribunal held that the freedom to wear a headscarf may be a disputed precept of the Islamic religion and Muslims may take on different opinions on this, but it falls under the freedom of religion protected under Article 9 ECHR so long as the employee—who has the right to form her own opinion—genuinely considered it her religious duty. However, the Tribunal reiterated that under Article 9 ECHR manifestations of religion are subject to restrictions.

However, the protection against religious discrimination was significantly diluted in the decision. According to the Tribunal, and later confirmed by the Labour Court of Appeal, the 'wearing out' of religious symbols does *not* fall within the protected criterion 'religion or belief' under the Belgian Anti-Discrimination Act. This confines the notion 'religion or belief' under the Belgian Anti-Discrimination Act to the *forum internum*. Again this means that headscarf conflicts can only to be regarded under indirect discrimination with an open, more lenient possibility of justification.

---

[16] The summary proceedings had been unsuccessful, as the claim was dismissed by the Tribunal and confirmed by the Labour Court of Appeal because of procedural reasons (lack of standing), i.e. no risk of repetition of the alleged discrimination (Labour Court of Appeal Antwerp, 15 January 2008, *Sociaalrechtelijke kronieken* 2009, nr 2, 93–97).

[17] The CEOOR requested a preliminary ruling from the CJEU, but the Tribunal did not follow that request, arguing the case did not involve 'an absolute ban' on manifestations. The Labour Court of Appeal similarly refused to refer questions to the CJEU.

After all, it was reasoned, accepting that different treatments based on religious manifestations could amount to direct discrimination would negate the possibility of restrictions.[18] Therefore, since the employee was not fired because she was an adherent of Islam—the employer had known for years she was of the Islamic faith and had no problem with it—but because she had explicitly refused to abide by an 'instruction to dress neutrally', there was no direct discrimination on the basis of 'religion or belief'. This is a problematic stance. By limiting 'religion or belief' to the fact of *affiliation* to a religion or belief, and excluding practices that indicate/ manifest that religious belonging, the protection against (direct) discrimination is considerably deflated. As discussed, the Advocate General opinion delivered by AG Kokott adopts a similar stance, while AG Sharpston in her opinion on the *Bougnaoui* case argues that this is one way that EU anti-discrimination law offers a higher protection than Article 9 ECHR.

When it came to the direct discrimination claim, this failed since Ms Achbita was said to have failed to show that 'comparable employees' were treated differently. Here, the policy applied (formally at least) to all employees. Even though it was shown that other receptionists were in fact not wearing the uniform on the job *after* the uniform code was instituted, those employees were not considered 'comparable': surprisingly, believers (the employee) and non-believers (the other receptionists) could not be compared when it comes to treatment for wearing religious symbols, according to the Tribunal: a difference was noted that the other receptionists' failure to abide by the uniform rule was a one-time thing after which they had been 'reprimanded', while Ms Achbita had expressed her principled position on various occasions, thus justifying her dismissal for refusing to abide by the policy.

The employee's indirect discrimination claim failed because the ban on visible convictional symbols was considered proportionate to the legitimate aim of creating 'a neutral and discrete image towards customers' and to 'guarantee a peaceful and tolerant co-existence within the company', which according to the Tribunal can only be done through *showcasing* neutrality. The Tribunal considered that G4S was a 'multicultural enterprise' that hires people of all faiths, including 11 per cent Muslim employees.

The issue of discriminatory customer preference was the elephant in the room, since the receptionist was being outsourced and it had been the company she physically worked at that objected to her wearing a headscarf. Yet, the Tribunal rejected the assertion that the neutrality policy sought to give in to the discriminatory preferences of customers.[19] On the contrary, it noted that the 'neutrality aims to respect everyone's identity and convictions'. In addition, the Antwerp Tribunal did not accept that the restrictive dress code policy was merely adopted

---

[18] In case of direct discrimination, 'genuine occupational requirements' constitute the main justification.

[19] Case C-54/07, *Centrum voor gelijkheid van kansen en voor racismebestrijding v Firma Feryn NV* [2008] ECR I-5187.

by the company council (*ondernemingsraad*) to respond to this particular incident notwithstanding several red flags, but it found that an 'unwritten rule' (thus an 'unwritten neutrality policy') was already in place, and this on the disputable basis of the company's *diversity policy* and requirement for employees to be tolerant and not discriminate amongst co-workers. This unwritten rule was even considered 'validated' by the employee's previously abiding conduct.[20] Paradoxically it may seem, when an employer consistently refuses to hire visibly religious employees, it may actually gain a benefit in religious discrimination litigation by being able to assert the existence of an 'unwritten' neutrality policy. Consistent or 'non-arbitrary exclusion' of some applicants would thus seem to pay off in litigation.

The holding in this Belgian judgment can be contrasted with the Dutch approach where, for one, protection against religious discrimination unequivocally includes protection for religious manifestations though religiously mandated dress.[21] Under the Antwerp Tribunal's interpretation, the Anti-Discrimination Act's protective scope is considerably diluted, losing meaning for religious practices such as wearing religious dress, which have been shown to constitute a core testing ground for the Directive. Employer decisions, even if directly based on religious dress motives (in which case they would involve direct discrimination in the Netherlands) are then subjected to an indirect discrimination test with the wide possibility of open-ended justification. Further, there is no reference to anything approximating to a duty of reasonable accommodation under the protection against religious discrimination or genuine consideration for the religious interest of the employee in the workplace. The underlying position is that that religion is 'a thing of the mind' and does not belong in the workplace, plain and simple, without recognising that this essentially nullifies the notion of human rights and non-discrimination law applicable to employment relations.

The Cour de cassation's March 2015 reference for a preliminary ruling[22] will now allow the CJEU to have a say in the case.[23] Reporting on the case, Bribosia has called the formulation of the preliminary ruling 'very disappointing', regretting

---

[20] Contra *HEMA case*, where the employee wearing a headscarf on the job would rebut the existence of any such 'unwritten practice'.

[21] *Supra*: ETC 1995-31, 7 August 1995; see also District Court's-Gravenhage, 20 August 2007, *X v het college van burgemeester en wethouders van X*, Case nr AWB 06-4333 (LJN: BC3697) (the term 'religion' under the Dutch Equal Treatment Act needs to be understood broadly).

[22] The Cour de cassation, as a court of final resort, is under an obligation under Art 267 of the Treaty on the Functioning of the EU to refer a question which the CEOOR requested for a preliminary ruling. In contrast, the Labour Tribunal and Labour Court of Appeal, which are not courts of final resort, were not obliged to exercise the reference for a preliminary ruling and in fact ruled that the questions needed no referral to the CJEU.

[23] The question before the CJEU is formulated as follows: 'Can article 2.2.(a) of Council Directive 2000/78/EC of 27 November 2000 establishing a general framework for equal treatment in employment and occupation, be interpreted to mean that the prohibition for a Muslim to wear the headscarf at work does not imply any direct discrimination when the rule forbids all workers to wear any visible symbol expressing their political, philosophical or religious beliefs?'

that the issue of indirect discrimination was not taken up in the question.[24] However, it is submitted that, while the neutrality policy at hand certainly *also* raised concerns under indirect discrimination, the initial framing as direct discrimination could be regarded as fortuitous from the perspective of more robust accommodation for religion or belief in the workplace. Indeed, under the frame of direct religious discrimination—where a person is treated less favourably than another on *the grounds of religion or belief*—difference of treatment can only be justified by arguing a genuine and determining occupational requirement (Article 4.1 Directive 2000/78). The CJEU is then called to consider whether 'by reason of the nature of the particular occupational activities concerned or of the context in which they are carried out' the ban on display of religious symbols is to be considered a proportionate requirement to serve a legitimate aim. In short: does wearing the headscarf stand in the way of doing one's job as a receptionist?[25] Further, the company neutrality policy refers expressly to *religion*, so in that sense should not be seen as 'an apparently neutral provision, criterion or practice' under the indirect discrimination frame (Article 2.2.(b) Directive 2000/78). Expanding such provisions, criteria or practices, which are subject to an open justification scheme, to situations where there is a direct, express reference to a discrimination ground would expand the ambit of indirect discrimination substantially and bring under its frame instances of patent direct discrimination.

It is clear that much rides on the CJEU's upcoming decision, interpreting the Employment Equality Directive. It is hard to anticipate whether and how the current post-economic crisis context, with wide popular mistrust of the EU's working, will influence the CJEU as it decides a socially divisive issue. The CJEU could adopt a cautious, hands-off stance. Or it could take on this awaited opportunity (and the one offered by the *Bougnaoui* case) as an opportunity to contribute to a more harmonious interpretation of EU equality law in the area of religion or belief or even to explain the larger EU anti-discrimination framework, including the dichotomy between direct and indirect discrimination.

C. The *Club Case* in Brussels: Headscarves, Books and Shoes

The *HEMA* and *G4S* cases were not the first where a Belgian employer's attempts to outlaw religious symbols from a private workplace were validated.

---

[24] E Bribosia, European network of legal experts in gender equality and non-discrimination, Flash Report, 26 March 2015. Bribosia argues that this shows 'there is still a noticeable lack of knowledge of the anti-discrimination law by the professionals in charge of its implementation, especially of the notion of indirect discrimination'.

[25] The question formulated by the French Cour de cassation is even more focused on the issue of a genuine and determining occupational requirement as it asks whether 'Article 4 §1 of the Directive 2000/78 must be interpreted to mean that banning the headscarf because of the wish of a customer of an IT company to not have services performed by a [headscarf-wearing] staff member, with an engineering diploma, does not constitute a genuine and determining occupational requirement': French Cour de cassation (social chamber), n° 630, 9 April 2015 (13–19.855).

On 15 January 2008, the Labour Appeal Court of Brussels[26] held that 'the freedom to express one's religion is not absolute and can be limited when the religious practice is of a nature to disturb the order'. A well-known large bookstore chain, Club, had discharged a long-term female employee who—upon her first day after returning from an extensive (six-year) leave—wanted to wear a headscarf while shelving and selling books. The employee was fired without compensation or notice, for grave misconduct (*motif grave*). She launched judicial proceedings and lost her case before the Labour Tribunal of Brussels on 21 March 2006. On appeal, the Labour Court of Appeal confirmed the Tribunal's decision.

The Appeals Court based its ruling on several grounds. First, it held that the freedom of religion was not at stake in the case because the company had reprimanded its employee not for belonging to the Islamic faith but her coming to work while wearing an ostentatious religious symbol when there were 'clear company guidelines' which instructed workers to wear uniforms with the logo of the company as well as to refrain from wearing any symbols or clothes likely to undermine the corporate image (described as the 'open, available, sober, family-based and neutral' image of Club). Thus, the concept of 'religion or belief', here assessed under the human rights framework since the Anti-discrimination Act was not operative at the relevant time, was seen very narrowly—ie limited to the *forum internum*. Secondly, the Court emphasised that the freedom to manifest one's religion is not absolute and restrictions are allowed where the religious practices are 'likely to lead to chaos'. In the case at hand, the Court considered that Club could justify the dismissal on an objective consideration linked to its corporate image. Thirdly, the Court failed to see any discrimination, as the company policy applied to all workers without any distinction, ie a formally equal application sufficed.

Not only did the Brussels Labour Court of Appeal find the bookstore's workplace neutrality policy prohibiting non-neutral clothing for 'front-office personnel' to be based on objective criteria related to the company's 'open, available, sober, family-oriented, and neutral' image, but the employee was also chastised for her 'clear and open violation of this written company policy' by wearing a headscarf even following an earlier 'warning' on the phone that it would not be tolerated. This was considered to be 'an aggravating factor' adding to the 'grave misconduct' because the employee, in violation of the company policy, had failed to get in touch with the employer 10 days before the return date to make the practical arrangements. This behaviour of the 'insubordinate' employee caused a breakdown of trust and thus justified the immediate termination of the employment contract without notice or severance payment, according to the Labour Court of Appeal. The Muslim employee had, after her dismissal, stated she would have welcomed another position which did not involve customer contact but the company did not look into that option. The Court stated explicitly that the company had no duty to do so.

---

[26] Labour Court of Appeal Brussels (4th ch) nr 48.695, *EF v Club corp*, 15 January 2008, *Journal des tribunaux du travail* 2008, nr 1003, 140.

Again this is in contrast to the Dutch and UK case law, where the efforts of employers to look for alternative solutions are weighed, and a rejecting of any such options can tell against the employer. The Belgian judicial approach, by refusing to 'burden' the employer, effectively channels the religious employee to the unemployment agency.

Nevertheless, there have also been Belgian cases more sympathetic to the religious practising employee. In an older case, decided before the first Anti-Discrimination Act of 2003 entered into force, the Labour Tribunal of Charleroi (1992)[27] found the immediate discharge for 'grave reasons' of a shoe saleswoman who for religious reasons wore 'long and wide robes and skirts' to be 'abusive'. The employer had argued that the employee's dress did not fit in with the 'commercial lifestyle of the city'. The Tribunal, however, considered that the parties had not determined in advance any particular style of clothing that salespersons were to wear on the job, so that the woman was free to follow her personal taste and wear clothes that were comfortable for carrying out her work. The employer was found to have dismissed her out of a mere subjective fear that her appearance would hurt his business, even though there were no indications of actual financial loss, and no customer had ever complained. The Tribunal did not discuss what would be the outcome in case of customer complaints or proven financial repercussion.

III. Accommodation of Religious Dress in the Dutch Workplace: Illustrating the Divergent General and Special Effects of Anti-Discrimination Law

When it comes to the Dutch legal approach toward religious freedom, discrimination and accommodation in the workplace, a two-level analysis is called for: not only court decisions but also the quasi-judicial 'opinions' issued by the Equal Treatment Commission (ETC) must be discussed.[28] This is different to Belgium and the UK, where the national equality bodies do not have quasi-judicial competency, but rather provide victims and claimants with support and—the lucky few—legal assistance.[29] Before it morphed into the Netherlands Institute for Human Rights

---

[27] Labour Tribunal Charleroi, 26 October 1992, *Sociaalrechtelijke kronieken/Chroniques de droit social* 1993, 84–85.

[28] I refer to 'ETC' still since most of the cases precede the establishment of the College. Also, the College shifted its focus away from the quasi-judicial function of the ETC and towards prevention, research and awareness-raising. Often instead of issuing new opinions, the College will refer parties to older opinions dealing with the same matters.

[29] The ETC/College does not assist victims in pursuing their cases in court as this would conflict with the core task of considering complaints of unequal treatment in its quasi-judicial role; assistance is provided by local anti-discrimination agencies. In contrast, the CEOOR focused its advocacy and resources on a limited number of legal cases under the Belgian Anti-Discrimination Acts, and the British EHRC has maintained a lower profile in religion or belief cases, instead focusing efforts on research (coordination).

('College voor de Rechten van de Mens') in 2012,[30] the ETC had accumulated an extensive repertoire of opinions on the question of wearing religiously motivated dress and symbols on the job. ETC opinions are not legally binding, but there is a high degree of compliance by the parties[31] and, if the case is consequently pursued in court, its typically well-reasoned opinions are also genuinely considered, though this will not mean that they are necessarily followed by the courts.[32] One reason is that while the ETC focuses its analysis solely on non-discrimination law, in particular the Dutch General Equal Treatment Act (GETA), Dutch courts can also include in their reasoning the human rights framework or other dimensions of the dispute.

A. The ETC and Religious Dress Accommodation

A number of 'precedent opinions'[33] aptly illustrate the ETC's approach taken towards the accommodation of (minority) religious dress, which has been unequivocally open-minded and progressive on issues such as the Muslim headscarf. The widespread consensus amongst the commissioners is notable, contrasting with more divisive religious practices where the ETC's stance has changed over time.[34] This stance, however, is not necessarily rooted in societal attitudes on the ground towards visible manifestations of minority religions in Dutch society.

The ETC handled its very first case involving an employer-imposed ban on wearing headscarves on the job in 1995.[35] In that case, the ETC held that the term 'religion or belief' in the GETA includes the right to manifest one's beliefs, finding support in the Parliamentary documents, and found that the employer had

---

[30] Some ETC decisions have been controversial: Rita Verdonk, the then Dutch Minister of Integration, called for the abolition of the ETC in November 2006 following an issued opinion that a school cannot require a female Muslim teacher to shake hands with men. A 2007 bill proposed in the Dutch Parliament to this effect was not passed.

[31] J Goldschmidt, 'Implementation of Equality Law. A Task for Specialists or for Human Rights Experts? Experiences and Developments in the Supervision of Equality Law in the Netherlands' (2006) 13 *Maastricht Journal European & Comparative Law* 323, 325–27 (between 2001 and the first half of 2004 the compliance with opinions of the ETC went up from 60% to 84%; the compliance rates are attributed, among other things, to the way in which ETC hearings are handled).

[32] In the Supreme Court of the Netherlands, 13 November 1987, *St Bavo v Gielen*, NJ 1986/698, the Dutch Supreme Court (Hoge Raad) held that considerable weight must be given to a ruling and the recommendations of the Commission for Equal Treatment of Men and Women (one of the predecessors of the ETC) and sound reasons must be given to depart from these. The government did not follow the advice of the ETC to strengthen the authority of the opinions by amending the Equal Treatment Act to specify that courts must state the grounds for departing from its opinion: see ETC, *Het verschil gemaakt. Evaluatie AWGB en werkzaamheden CGB 1999–2004*, 95, available on the ETC website (between 2000 and 2004, 43 cases that the ETC had decided on came before courts: in 81% the opinion was given weight while in 61% the opinion was followed. Only in five cases did the court depart from the opinion without stating any grounds).

[33] These include opinions in disputes as well as advisory opinions.

[34] eg accommodating objecting marriage registrars; Muslims refusing to shake hands, discussed below.

[35] ETC nr 1995-31, 7 August 1995.

discriminated on the basis of religion. Thus, from the very start the ETC held that Dutch anti-discrimination law protects the *forum externum* as well as the *forum internum*.[36]

The ETC has repeatedly held that it is not required that the protected ground—for instance religious belief manifestation through dress—be the only or determining reason for the different treatment in question. This is crucial because it is extremely difficult to prove discrimination based purely on the wearing of a headscarf. It suffices that the protected criterion plays at least a role in the negative decision or different treatment. In 2001, the ETC considered a case where a Muslim female trainee who applied to a bailiff's office was refused a position after she made unequivocally clear during the interview that she wanted to wear a headscarf on the job.[37] Based on the circumstances of the interview, the ETC did not accept the employer's assertion that the wearing of a headscarf and the applicant's expressed religious beliefs in no way played a role in the decision to reject her traineeship application.

As discussed, Belgian courts are not suspicious of 'neutrality' policies or customer preference arguments being used by private companies. In comparison, on the rare[38] occasions that 'religious neutrality' arguments were presented to the ETC, they were summarily dismissed. Even in the case of a court clerk, the ETC regarded the neutrality argument as insufficient justification to prohibit the wearing of a headscarf.[39] It was held that even though the goal of independence and impartiality of the judiciary is itself a legitimate goal, the alleged means of achieving that goal were disproportionate considering the job functions of the court clerk.[40]

In its analyses, the ETC engaged extensively with the elaborate anti-discrimination framework in place in the Netherlands. Determining whether the actions of an employer are to be assessed as a direct or indirect distinction (*onderscheid*) requires attention to the set of circumstances in a specific case. In particular, it must be assessed whether the employer referred to the employee's religion when it prohibited the wearing of a headscarf (or other religious dress): 'In cases where

---

[36] In contrast, see Labour Tribunal Antwerp, 27 April 2010, Case nr AR/06/397639/A.

[37] ETC nr 2001-79, 6 August 2001.

[38] R Van den Boer, 'Een Open Doekje voor de Commissie Gelijke Behandeling?' in Rikki Holtmaat (ed), *Gelijkheid en (andere) Grondrechten* (Gelijkheid en (andere) Grondrechten, Kluwer 2004) 158–59; see also ETC advice of 12 August 2004 to Meldpunt Discriminatie Amsterdam, p 14.

[39] ETC nr 2001-53, 22 June 2001; this was a controversial decision. Dutch minister Korthals declared that it would not follow this (non-binding) opinion and the judiciary should refrain from expressing religious, political or other opinions. See M Kuijer, 'Vrouwe Justitia: blinddoek of hoofddoek? Noot onder Commissie gelijke behandeling 22 juni 2001, oordeel 2001–53' (2003) 26 *NJCM-Bulletin* 890, 890–902.

[40] The neutrality argument has also failed in other settings: ETC nr 1996-59: the bank could not rely on its 'religious neutrality' to stop one of its associates who was a Jehovah's Witness from proselytising in the area where the bank was situated and most of its clientele lived. The ETC held that the bank does not make clear what neutrality stands for, and suggests that neutrality could also be achieved through a pluriform composition of its staff.

the [employer] directly referred to the religion of the [employee], one talks of direct distinction on the basis of religion'.[41] Such direct distinction can only be justified by proving a genuine and determining occupational requirement, while indirect distinctions can more easily be justified under an open-justification system if they have a legitimate aim and their means towards that aim are considered proportionate.

(i) Direct Distinction Test: Rejection of Neutrality Policies

Thus, when employers refer to religion specifically and when it does so a priori in a workplace dress regulation, the case is considered one involving a *direct* distinction.[42] A 2010 case concerned a private foundation operating care and nursing centres with some 1400 staff members (90 per cent of them female, less than one per cent 'allochthone').[43] The organisation had adopted a ban on 'religious, political or philosophical dress, including head covers and buttons' in its dress regulations. A staff member of the foundation had contacted a local anti-discrimination bureau to see whether the provision was in fact in keeping with anti-discrimination legislation. The ETC opinion focused on the issue of the ban on 'religious head covers'. Although no specific job applicant or employee was involved, the ETC noted that 'because of this regulation, staff members who wear a headscarf because of religious reasons are not welcome to work for the foundation' and that in the past a temp cleaner—employed by another company which worked on its site—was rejected because she wore a headscarf, as the foundation did not allow staff members of other companies to wear head covers on its premises.[44] The only exception was that staff in the central kitchen, who had no contact with clients, were allowed to wear headscarves, and thus were not rejected for this reason.

To justify the restriction on religious, political and philosophical dress, the foundation had referred to the argument of neutrality, linking this up to the need for a 'healing environment' which was 'familiar, safe, friendly and recognisable' for elderly patients 'who still live in the past and often come from rural areas'. Beyond this, the image given of the elderly residents was hardly sympathetic; in the past one resident had refused to be assisted by an Afghani woman, and negative comments were received about a staff member wearing a chain of Bhagwan. The foundation argued: 'it can hardly be expected of demented, disoriented, elderly clients that they adjust themselves to—for them—foreign, non-recognisable circumstances. Staff must adapt to these clients. These vulnerable clients are entitled to that'. Also, the provision had been adopted by management after careful consideration and

---

[41] ETC nr 2008-144, 3 December 2008, para 3.9.
[42] Contra Belgian *HEMA case*, see above.
[43] ETC nr 2010-94, 28 June 2010 (own translations).
[44] A separate opinion addresses this case: ETC nr 2010-95 (direct distinction made based on the religion of the candidate).

with the agreement of the employees' council. The foundation argued it did not discriminate and offered opportunities for allochthone women to advance and integrate in society, but they needed to do so under the same conditions, accepting and respecting the dress code.

Based on its established case law, the ETC held that the case presented itself as one of *direct* distinction:

> The respondent has adopted a provision in its dress regulation that it is not permitted to wear religious, political or philosophical expressions, like a headscarf and buttons. *This provision refers directly to religion.* Considering the wording of the dress code, according to which wearing 'religious' expressions, like the headscarf, are explicitly banned, the Commission assesses that the respondent makes a direct distinction on the basis of religion ... The fact that the respondent does not exclude employees with non-visible religious expressions does not alter this (emphasis added).[45]

Therefore, the ETC found that the 'neutrality provision' at hand was not even 'apparently neutral' so as to call for an assessment under the *in*direct distinction framework. It found the provision itself discriminatory, not just its effects on certain groups. Under the direct distinction test, there are only limited legal justifications, and the ETC noted 'none of these are argued or appear here'. The issue of a potential genuine occupational requirement is not even discussed. It may have been that the foundation was taken by surprise by the assessment of direct distinction, but even if it had considered this, the argument that for *every* staff member it constituted a genuine occupational requirement to not wear religious, political and philosophical dress would be unconvincing.

Further, the ETC rejected the argument made by the foundation that the clause reflects their clients' wishes, noting that:

> The Commission understands the respondent's efforts to prioritise the interests of its client, of which many are disoriented and elderly ... the Commission understands that the respondent aims to hide the marks of identity of its staff so as to prevent problems of prejudice and presuppositions of the clients. The aim of equality legislation is precisely to fight and eradicate such prejudice and presumptions towards certain people and/or certain groups, in particular when such presuppositions have negative effects for certain groups.[46]

Thus no one—not even elderly, 'disoriented' nursing home dwellers—is relieved from the collective aims of equality legislation, marking a significant contrast to what is the case in Belgium. One should support the Dutch characterisation of neutrality policies as unacceptable direct religious discrimination; it is not merely their effect on certain groups which is problematic but rather their very being as general a priori exclusions arguably do more harm than singular or even repeated refusals to hire someone because of religious dress. The latter can still be justified for occupational reasons or safety or security concerns, while such blanket

---

[45] Paragraph 3.10 (own translation).
[46] Paragraph 3.12 (own translation).

policies—because of their generality—cannot. ETC's message discourages Dutch companies from adopting such 'losing' policies in the first place, even if meant to meet client wishes.

This is an important area where Dutch case law (ETC) and Belgian courts, responding under similar legal frameworks to largely the same societal developments on the ground, have adopted divergent approaches. The Belgian case law validates the exclusion on the ground, while the ETC's aim is to fight and reverse developments it sees as rooted in societal prejudice and presuppositions.

It can be noted that Belgian and Dutch approaches towards religious dress in the public sector, including public education, also differ markedly. While public school teachers in Belgium, with the exception of those who teach religion, cannot wear religious dress for neutrality reasons, in the Netherlands public school teachers are allowed to wear a headscarf or other religious dress on the job.[47] In the Netherlands, only in certain limited functions, civil servants can be restricted from wearing religious symbols (judges, uniformed police, military).[48] In an opinion which was subsequently rejected by the Dutch court, the ETC held in 2011 that a Muslim woman could not be rejected for a position as deputy clerk of a court (*buitengriffier*) because of her headscarf.[49] The ETC considered the motive for the dress code (the independence and the impartiality of the judiciary) as legitimate and non-discriminatory but found the exclusion of all Muslim applicants wearing a headscarf too drastic (ie disproportionate) and not necessary in light of the job functions of a deputy clerk. Even in highly sensitive public functions, such as staff and interviewers working for the Dutch Immigration and Naturalisation Service (*Immigratie en Naturalisatie Dienst*),[50] the ETC looks carefully to the objectives and the necessity of restrictions on religious dress to meet those objectives. When reasonable alternatives are available but not considered, outright restrictions will be disproportionate.

Clients' discriminatory demands act as a persistent player in private sector workplace cases, and were already at issue in a 1995 headscarf case before the ETC, concerning a cleaning company which asked staff not to wear headscarves to meet the needs of its own customers and had fired a Muslim woman of Turkish origin

---

[47] ETC nr 1999-103, 22 December 1999; See K Alidadi, 'Approches comparatives du débat sur la "neutralité": la liberté de culte des enseignants des écoles publiques et des fonctionnaires à travers l'Europe de porter des vêtements religieux' in D Cabiaux et al (eds), *Neutralité et faits religieux Quelles interactions dans les services publics?* (Academia-L'Harmattan, 2014).

[48] See HMAE van Ooijen, *Religious symbols in public functions: unveiling state neutrality. A comparative analysis of Dutch, English and French justifications for limiting the freedom of public officials to display religious symbols* (Intersentia, 2012), for a critique of some of these arguments used to justify these public sector restrictions.

[49] ETC nr 2001-53, 22 June 2001.

[50] ETC nr 2007-195, 6 November 2007. ETC Advisory Opinion, '*Neutraliteit, gezag en zichtbare geloofsuitingen bij de IND*' ['Neutrality, authority, and visible religious manifestation in the Immigration and Naturalization Service'], April 2012.

for her headscarf.[51] In that case the arguments of the employing cleaning company were set out extensively in the opinion, as follows:

> We as a company are guests on our customer's premises. We are repeatedly asked whether we employ foreign workers. The answer is yes. Then we are also asked whether foreign women can wear a headscarf, and we reply that some do. And we hear that some do not appreciate that. We ask them to put this on paper but they are not willing, it is too risky. So we ask our staff to take off their headscarf. If they do not, we don't fire them though, there may be some cowboy stories but that is not true … We base ourselves on the clients, if we didn't we would not be a good company. But it does not go so far that we take the wishes of the clients into account out of fear of not getting some assignment. But at the reception the coffee ladies have to wear clean work clothes, a clean skirt and clean shoes. You cannot work there as a woman with a headscarf, or a turban or in a kaftan. A police officer does not wear any headgear besides a police cap … we have to sometimes go ahead, respecting the wishes of customers regarding the headscarf. A customer will never terminate a contract because we disregarded such wish. They will always say price was the determining issue, even if you hear a half year later that that was not the issue. Customers can easily end the contract and find another company.[52]

Finally, the link between customer discriminatory pressures, avoidance strategies and neutrality policies was on display in a 2011 case, illustrating how the prejudicial demands of medical patients are also a problem on the ground in the Netherlands. A young Muslim woman applied for the position of a dental assistant.[53] The HR representative informed her that religious expressions were banned in the workplace and asked her if she would take off her headscarf on the job. When she declined, she was told she would not be considered for the job and the interview was discontinued. The employer was adamant that there could be no talk of discrimination; the applicant had been refused because of a 'neutrality protocol' which was in use in the clinic which banned all religious, philosophical or political opinions being expressed in the workplace. This protocol was adopted after a patient had refused to be assisted by a staff member with a headscarf, and persisted after the patient had been told that the staff member with a headscarf was just as capable as any other. The situation had deteriorated, with the staff member feeling threatened by the patient. The employer said he wanted to avoid situations like this in the future and prioritised the interests of and care of patients. The employer argued: 'The more neutral the staff, the less aggression is ignited amongst patients'. Also, the employer pointed to the fact that he employed a Muslim woman who did not wear a headscarf, and allowed her to 'participate in/observe Ramadan in the workplace'.

The ETC regarded this as a straightforward direct distinction case, which led to the determination of a violation:

> the fact that the underlying motivation of employer, that is the appearance of neutrality, is set out in neutral terms and in the eyes of the employer refers to an indirect distinction,

---

[51] ETC nr 1995-31, 7 August 1995.

[52] ETC nr 1995-31, 7 August 1995 (own translation).

[53] ETC nr 2011-92, 17 June 2011.

does not change [the fact that in the ETC's opinion it concerns direct distinction], considering that the specifications/declarations of the employer (in the job interview and in the dress regulation) do refer directly to religion.[54]

This line of jurisprudence should not only be regarded as good practice, but should be a requirement under EU anti-discrimination law standards.[55] Customer complaints about the religious dress of employees should not be seen as a justification for dismissal or other negative treatment. The employer should protect his staff against harassment and discriminatory behaviour, and despite hardships, disregard discriminatory beliefs, bias and intolerance. This interpretation of anti-discrimination gives employers an important role in fighting, or at least not giving in to, the sort of opinions and actions which are detrimental to equal opportunities and societal inclusion of minorities.

(ii) Indirect Distinction Test: Strict Proportionality and Search for Alternatives

When it assesses cases under indirect discrimination, the ETC carries out a rather strict scrutiny of the employer's decisions, which tends to favour the employee wishing to don religious dress. For instance, an employee of an Amsterdam hotel returned after his vacation in India baptised in the Sikh religion and came to work donning the five K's—*kesh* (uncut hair worn in a turban, and beard), *kangha* (comb), *kirpan* (dagger), *kara* (bracelet), *kachha* (underpants).[56] This violated the hotel employee dress code, and the employer was particularly concerned that the dagger the employee had informed him about would appear threatening to guests and other staff members. The employer sought to have the contract dissolved before the subdistrict judge (*kantonrechter*).[57] Discussing various elements of the case, and also clarifying its approach to determining the appropriate discrimination test, the ETC came to the conclusion that an indirect distinction was made based on a neutral dress code. For the hotel, the religious belief of the applicant was not as such the reason for the dismissal; rather his appearance was considered to be no longer in line with the clothing requirements of the hotel. However, the dress code did not pass the subsidiarity and proportionality test. The dismissal of the applicant was not proportionate to the aim that was pursued by the implementation of the clothing requirements, namely to uphold the image and

---

[54] At para 3.8.

[55] The Employment Equality Directive does not explicitly provide customer preferences are to be disregarded if discriminatory, but see Case C-54/07, *Centrum voor gelijkheid van kansen en voor racismebestrijding v Firma Feryn NV* [2008] ECR I-5187.

[56] ETC nr 1997-24, 25 March 1997.

[57] Under Dutch labour law, a permit must generally be obtained from the UVW (*Uitvoeringsinstituut Werknemersverzekeringen*) before a protected employee can be dismissed. Certain employees, eg those under temp agency contracts, are not covered. See Buitengewoon Besluit Arbeidsverhoudingen 1945 (Decree on Labour Relations) Another option is to have the employment contract dissolved before the subdistrict judge (*kantonrechter*).

the atmosphere in the hotel. The ETC was not convinced by the safety argument against wearing the dagger, because the dagger was not visible for others, being worn beneath the clothes. This case was subsequently confirmed by the Court of Haarlem.[58]

In a 2008 case,[59] a Muslim woman wearing a headscarf was refused an internship position with an optician store. The employer argued that his business catered to a fashion and brand-conscious clientele justifying a dress code that sought to ensure that staff would appear similarly fashionable. For the ETC this also presented an example of indirect distinction, since the policy though not directed towards the headscarf or religion, nonetheless placed Muslim women at a particular disadvantage. Again, the restriction on wearing a headscarf was not considered necessary and proportionate, since one can wear a headscarf and appear fashionable. In ETC opinions, one can see the efforts to fight and transcend stereotypes associated with Muslim women and the appearance of their headdress.

The same approach returns in other religious dress cases. A 2011 case involved a doctor's assistant of Islamic faith who in lieu of trousers wanted to wear a skirt or long dress in addition to the uniform hospital jacket.[60] After five years on the job, the employee requested a de facto accommodation because she considered that wearing trousers conflicted with her religious prescripts. However, the hospital provided and cleaned on a daily basis the white trousers and jackets which bore its logo and did not want to add a skirt or dress to its workwear range; it would also not allow the employee to wear her own long white skirt underneath the jacket. The arguments made for the refusal related to hospital hygiene (a long skirt or dress would be less hygienic than trousers), appearance (visibility and uniformity of dress) and cost/logistical burden (of extending the workwear range).

The ETC recognised the request as an expression of faith. It sought the advice of a healthcare infection prevention expert, to consider if the hygiene concern constituted an objective justification for the indirect distinction made by the hospital. It found that the arguments, while legitimate non-discriminatory aims, did not justify the distinction because the means to achieve those aims (the restriction) failed to meet (strict) requirements of subsidiarity and proportionality.[61] The ETC found no evidence that a long white skirt with the jacket with the company logo would affect the visibility and the uniform appearance of the staff. As far as logistics went, it noted that the hospital provided separate clothing to employees with special sizes and to pregnant employees. Providing a long skirt, or at least allowing a long skirt (to be bought in a medical store) and its industrial washing, would not

---

[58] President Rb (Subdistrict court judge) Haarlem, 18 March 1997.

[59] ETC nr 2008-14.

[60] ETC nr 2011-88, 10 June 2011 (Amsterdam Academic Medical Center (AMC)).

[61] For a critique of this case, see CW Noorlander, 'Godsdienst, levensbeschouwing en politieke gezindheid' in C Forder (ed), *Gelijke behandeling: oordelen en commentaar 2011* (Wolf Legal Publishers, 2012) 177 (arguing that the employer's professional-organisational autonomy was not duly recognised).

constitute an unacceptable burden. Essentially, the ETC held that by failing to reasonably accommodate the doctor's assistant (as it did with other some employees),
the employer violated its non-discrimination duty.

While religious dress cases often come out in the favour of employees, there are
exceptions. Self-exclusion by applicants, for one, appears to be a bad strategy if
one is then to subsequently challenge perceived discriminatory policies. In a 2008
case, a woman resigned from her position in a clothing store after she decided she
wanted to wear a headscarf, knowing that such was not welcomed in the store.[62]
The ETC found for the employer in this case since the woman had not actually
posed the question directly to the employer and thus had voluntarily resigned and
failed to prove an unjustifiable distinction.

In these indirect discrimination cases, the ETC essentially assesses a reasonable
accommodation duty. It subtly enquires into the negotiation process, assesses the
necessity of a restriction by exploring possible alternatives—proposed or not—
which do not involve a restriction (or less so), weighing respective burdens in the
process. There are numerous examples of this. In a 2008 case, a company producing
glass and metal amalgamations prohibited any headdress, including a headscarf
worn for religious reasons, citing justified safety risks.[63] The prohibition was written down in the company employee manual. The company had an equal opportunity policy and 40–60 per cent of its 80–110 employees were of foreign origin. A
woman was referred by a temp agency but was rejected as an applicant because she
had said that for religious reasons she would not take off her headscarf when asked
by the manager of the company. The case was assessed under the indirect distinction test, since the restriction was motivated by legitimate safety concerns (long
hair or a headscarf could get stuck in the machines on assembly lines). Nevertheless, the ETC found the 'measure'—the rejection of the applicant—unnecessary;
the applicant had offered to work with a bonnet instead of the headscarf, and also
offered to take off her 'upper headscarf' and only leave on a snug-fitting 'under
headscarf'. These proposals were rejected, citing safety concerns. The ETC thought
this to be 'curious' since employees with long hair were allowed to use hairpins
and hair elastics which can also come unfastened. Considering the employer did
not look into any of these alternatives and also indicated it would be unwilling to
consider these, indirect discrimination was found.

Another case is perhaps even more telling. In a 2006 case, a Muslim woman with
a headscarf was refused a job with a call centre,[64] because the company argued the
sound transmission over the headset would be of lesser quality when worn over a
headscarf, impacting the quality of the communication between phone operator
and customers. Here too, the indirect difference in treatment was found unjustified considering the availability of an—obvious and cost-free—alternative that

---

[62] ETC nr 2008-54.

[63] ETC nr 2008-144, 3 December 2008.

[64] ETC nr 2006-215, 27 October 2006; for cases of indirect distinction that were not justified, see
ETC nr 1996-85, 17 October 1996.

would satisfy both employer and employee, namely allowing the headset to be worn *under* the headscarf.[65] One can note that this understanding of the indirect discrimination test requires some good will, initiative and (at times) creativity from the parties, taking into account their respective interests, which essentially a reasonable accommodation framework seeks to do. It stands in stark contrast to the Belgian jurisprudence reviewed above whereby an employer need not show any willingness to consider reasonable alternatives, proposed or not by the employee.

The flip-side of this approach is that the employee's unyielding attitude will also be pertinent. For instance, the ETC found no violation by an employment mediation agency towards a Muslim woman who refused to alter the way she wore her (wide) headscarf to meet safety and hygiene requirements in the cleaning industry; in particular, the woman refused to tuck loose parts of the headscarf into her wide shirt because this would reveal her body's contours.[66] The agency had attempted to find alternatives before terminating the contract when all else failed. This approach is part and parcel of what one would expect under a *reasonable* accommodation framework, which has important potentials to provide opportunities and inclusion but also has its own limitations. One can see that at times a reasonable accommodation may not be enough to include an employee in a particular workplace, but even then the aggregate effect of an accommodating labour market—where making due efforts to respond to the religious needs of potential employees is mandated—would have significant inclusionary effect that would benefit all employees (including the unyielding employee).

Vermeulen and Overbeeke call dress and grooming an 'insatiable source of conflict' in the Netherlands.[67] While the ETC's approach has been commendable, the seemingly endless supply of headscarf/religious dress cases also points to a sociological fact, namely that while perhaps better accepted than in Belgium, the wearing of a headscarf—on the ground—is still not 'normalised' in the Netherlands, whether it be in the area of employment, education or sports.[68]

B. Dutch Courts and the Accommodation of Religious Dress

Dutch jurisprudence on religious dress in the private sector workplace exhibits the same 'active pluralist' approach, especially with regard to the Muslim headscarf. In a well-known case involving a Christian tram conductor (employed by

---

[65] According to the ETC, special circumstances can justify an employer instituting a strict uniform policy. The ETC ruled that the Amsterdam police could institute a uniform without allowing a headscarf for positions that require contact with the general public. However, in determining to which functions this strict policy should apply, a careful balance must be made. ETC nr 2008-123, 23 October 2008.

[66] ETC nr 2011-19.

[67] BP Vermeulen and AJ Overbeeke, 'Godsdienst, levensbeschouwing en politieke gezindheid' in C Forder (ed), *Gelijke behandeling: oordelen en commentaar 2010* (Wolf Legal Publishers, 2011) 153–54.

[68] ibid, 154.

the *Gemeentelijke Vervoersbedrijf*, GVB) who wanted to wear a cross on a necklace at work, the dress code restriction, however, was upheld. For various reasons, this 'GVB' case can be considered an outlier, and arguably a misguided one.

Already in 1986, a decade before the ETC Sikh hotel employee case, a lower Amsterdam court held that, in the light of the 'cosmopolitan' character of the city, employing a Sikh hotel worker who wore a turban and a beard would not harm the hotel's goodwill even if that goodwill was based on the hotel's 'Old Dutch' image.[69] The hotel was not allowed to terminate the employment contract because the employee's change in physical appearance was not considered to amount to the required 'change in circumstances'.

A reasonable accommodation, case-by-case approach—which is not a guarantee for an employee-favourable outcome—is apparent in a 2009 case involving a Muslim nurse who had been employed at a hospital for seven years and objected on religious grounds to a hospital dress code because it left the arms uncovered.[70] The dress code (short sleeves) was prescribed in the dialysis-ward, where the nurse would be working, for hygienic reasons and the health inspection service confirmed this to be a professional standard. While the nurse had offered to wear sleeves that left 15 centimeters/six inches of her arms uncovered, this proposal was not accepted and parties failed to reach an agreement. The hospital requested dissolution of the employment contract. The question the Court considered was: 'to what extent may a hospital through a dress code (ie wearing *short* sleeves) infringe the constitutional right of a Muslim nurse to dress according to her religious beliefs (ie wearing *long* sleeves or three-quarter length sleeves)? The Court found that the dress code was adopted on valid grounds and for good reason—in any case with regard to the dialysis department—and that an employee cannot require that the hospital provide scientific evidence for the fact that wearing three-quarter length sleeves entails greater risks of infection than wearing short sleeves. The aim is to minimise that risk as far as possible. The judge therefore found the dress code restriction necessary, proportionate and justified, *especially* since the hospital had examined alternative solutions such as wearing a gown during patient contacts or transferring to another department where long sleeves could be worn (to which the nurse objected).[71]

This case would be considered similarly if there had been an explicit legal duty to accommodate for religious practices under Dutch law. In the United States, when an employer faces undue hardship in accommodating an employee but has another job opening, an 'accommodation by transfer' is often appropriate. In the

---

[69] District Court, subdistrict judge Amsterdam (*Kantonrechter* Amsterdam) 24 January 1986, *Die Port van Cleve BV v J Singh*, *Rechtspraak Rassendiscriminatie* 1995, 171–73.

[70] District Court's Hertogenbosch, 13 July 2009, *Jeroen Bosch Ziekenhuis v X*, Case nr 620353, LJN: BJ2840.

[71] However, the employee was awarded damages (about €8,500) because the way the hospital had handled the conflict had inflicted psychological damage.

Shelton case,[72] a nurse who for religious reasons refused to assist in abortions in the labour and delivery unit was offered a transfer to another hospital unit. The hospital was found to have met its duty to reasonably accommodate, even though the nurse preferred to stay in the same unit and trade shifts with colleagues. So long as this reasonable accommodation test is effectively incorporated within the indirect discrimination framework, it could be argued that under the Dutch interpretation of the anti-discrimination framework, adopting an explicit reasonable accommodation duty would have negligible practical consequences in judicial cases, at least if the approach does not alter.[73] When it comes to the general effects of anti-discrimination law, however, it may well enforce the legitimacy of accommodation requests and help normalise the providing of religious accommodations.

As said, the GVB case, which received widespread media attention, can be considered somewhat of an outlier. This case concerned a tram conductor, Mr Mickel Aziz, who was fired for wearing a cross on a necklace, because that conflicted with the uniform code adopted by a recently privatised transportation company in Amsterdam (GVB).[74] The dress code was adopted in 2008 (one year after the privatisation) to display a more uniform and professional image. It included a ban on wearing visible neck chains over the uniform irrespective of their religious nature, as the concern was safety. Staff could wear a bracelet or ring with a chain 'of modest size and colour', but no necklaces. The tram conductor was a Coptic Christian, of Egyptian origin but holding Dutch nationality, who had been working at the company for 11 years while visibly wearing a golden cross of about five cm/two inches on a necklace. Upon the new uniform dress code being instituted, the tram conductor was asked to stop wearing the necklace or to wear it under his uniform. The company suggested a ring or bracelet with a cross, but after initially agreeing, Mr Aziz insisted on wearing the necklace in a visible fashion and was suspended.

Mr Aziz sought a declaratory judgment from the district court—he did not ask the ETC for an opinion—that his treatment had been discriminatory, in particular since the GVB *did* accommodate Muslim women who wanted to wear a headscarf on the job, by providing them a headscarf with the company logo. As a Coptic

---

[72] *Shelton v University of Medicine & Dentistry of New Jersey*, 223 F 3d 220, 226 (3d Cir 2000).

[73] See also L Waddington, 'Reasonable Accommodation. Time to Extent the Duty to Accommodate Beyond Disability?' (2011) 36 *Nederlands Tijdschrift voor de Mensenrechten/Nederlands Juristen Comit voor de Mensenrechten Bulletin* 186, 186–98 (arguing against the adoption of an explicit duty of reasonable accommodation for religion).

[74] Subdistrict Court (*kantonrechter*) Amsterdam, 14 December 2009, LJN: BK6378; Court of Appeal (*Gerechtshof*) Amsterdam, 15 June 2010 (LJN: BM7410); See Note by LC Groen, 'de kruistocht van de trambestuurder', *Annotaties bij Oordelen 2010*, 442–50. Because the GVB had been privatised in 2007 (the city of Amsterdam held 100% of the shares), there was some debate amongst commentators whether the relationship was a horizontal one or a vertical one involving the state, which would have some consequences regarding the human rights framework, see Groen, ibid, 449. Groen, however, presumes that a state must be involved before Art 9 ECHR is to be applied, quod non (see *Eweida* case, n 28 above).

Christian, he was struggling with this. He regarded the argument that the necklace was unprofessional as offensive.

However, his claim was dismissed by the Amsterdam subdistrict court judge as well as the Amsterdam Court of Appeal. The measure—the ban on necklaces—was assessed under an indirect discrimination test.[75] In light of the reasons argued by the employer, namely safety and the wish to reflect a professional image (but notably not 'neutrality') and the restriction on the right to manifest religious beliefs was considered to be necessary and proportionate to these legitimate aims. No doubt, the accommodation attempts undertaken by the employer worked in its favour: the company had paid for consultations with a psychologist and offered to have a bracelet or ring made for the employee. There can be some debate whether these can be considered *effective* accommodation (if they do not take away the conflict between the religious practice and work rules), but it is helpful that the Court values that a search for mutually agreeable solutions took place between the parties. The Court of Appeal rejected the 'double standards' argument, holding that the headscarf, which was integrated in the uniform with the colours of the uniform and GVB-logo—unlike the necklace with cross—'did not disturb the business-like, uniform and professional character of company dress'.[76]

One can certainly contest this latter reasoning, which distinguishes between two examples of religious dress/symbols—a Muslim and a Christian one—and the need to accommodate based on their treatment and facilitation *by the employer* when the issue at stake is precisely the employer's unequal treatment of comparable situations. The Dutch GVB case and the comparable British *Eweida* case are a sign of the spirit of our time. Efforts to counter hostility and stigmatisation of Islam and Muslims by seeking active accommodation of the headscarf are to be applauded, but the current approach leaves out other—religious minority—employees whose right to manifest their religion or belief in the workplace is not any less legitimate.

One can question whether the legal analysis would have been different under an explicit reasonable accommodation duty. I argue that is certainly possible; there remains a subtle but real distinction between assessing proportionality, even if the willingness to seek alternatives is considered, and directly assessing whether a duty to reasonably accommodate a particular employee in a given situation is met. The fact that extensive, collective accommodation for veiled Muslim women was possible points to the fact that an exception could have been made to the ban on necklaces for Mr Aziz who had served the company for 11 years while wearing a necklace without any safety incidents.

---

[75] Unlike the British courts in *Eweida* though, the Dutch courts saw GVB's measure as disadvantaging a group of Christians, to which the applicant belongs, who seek to visibly wear a cross. Similarly, however, neither of the two cases were duly analysed under the human rights framework.

[76] Court of Appeal (*Gerechtshof*) Amsterdam, 15 June 2010 (LJN: BM7410), para 3.16.

Groen has argued that the ETC would have assessed the proportionality differently as well.[77] While the Court too easily accepted the argument that wearing jewellery over uniforms violates a professional appearance, the ETC has opined that dress limitations cannot be justified by reference to presumed, unfounded feelings or thoughts of customers.[78] In addition, the 'good employment practices' (*goed werkgeverschap*) concept could require the employer to provide some transition arrangement for long-term employees.[79] Thus, reasonable accommodation may be one amongst various avenues to create more religiously accommodative workplaces for employees.

Despite the GVB case, in the Netherlands, both at the level of the ETC and the courts, the prevailing penchant is towards accommodating religious symbols and dress in the workplace, ie marking an 'active pluralist approach'. Saharso and Lettinga[80] regard the accommodative approach as fitting in the Dutch tradition of pillarisation: 'the legacy of pillarization makes religious identity claims highly legitimate in the Netherlands'.[81] Arguing that the framing and regulating of veiling reflect national traditions of citizenship, they see in the Dutch case that the relatively large presence of Muslim(a)s in the public debate and public opinion is also conducive to an accommodative approach. Even so, Saharso and Lettinga, looking at veil debates between 1999 and 2006, have noted two shifts in the Dutch debate. First, a shift from the neutrality frame (eg the veil being discussed in terms of state neutrality) towards a gender equality frame, with the veil being linked to debates on social cohesion, integration, and the moral limits of public behaviour. Secondly, they see the Dutch multicultural citizenship tradition being 'under pressure' and always contingent on 'power relations between political parties and political events on a national and international level'.

The constant flow of legal cases, however, also reveals that this is a *normative, aspirational tolerance* towards marks of 'otherness' in the Netherlands: while more accepted than in Belgium, the wearing of a headscarf in the Netherlands is hardly 'normalised' in the area of employment and while various large companies, such as Ikea or HEMA, are actively accommodating the headscarf, negative attitudes towards headscarves in the workplace are also a reality and arguments of 'representability', image and (to a lesser extent) neutrality are mobilised to restrict religious

---

[77] See Note by LC Groen, 'de kruistocht van de trambestuurder', *Annotaties bij Oordelen 2010*, 447.

[78] eg ETC nr 2010-10 and nr 2005-162.

[79] Groen, 448.

[80] S Saharso and D Lettinga, 'Contentious Citizenship: Policies and Debates on the Veil in the Netherlands' (2008) 15 *Social Politics* 455–80.

[81] One can question, however, whether pillarisation adds much to the perspective if one discusses issues where individuals seek to participate in a group where they differ in some ways from the norm; pillarization was essentially about the collective level, about giving groups of people space to live out their own ways of life, while sharing some common values. Pillarisation as an ideology also served as inspiration for the South-African apartheid regime, being an extreme example of how communities can be severed through policies. It can be somewhat molded and broadened in a general 'multicultural policy' but it is mostly rooted in a group-centered approach to diversity.

dress, particularly in front-office positions.[82] Thus, in contrast to Belgian case law, where the situation on the ground—the status quo—is legitimised, the Dutch country study reveals an institutional mechanism which uses anti-discrimination law to fight exclusions on the ground by—repeatedly—rejecting tenacious arguments to justify discrimination and exclusion. The deep divide between the normative 'golden veneer' of tolerance and the far more intolerant 'underbelly' of Dutch society was also apparent in the *Bruggen Bouwen* report (2003–2004), which reviewed and evaluated Dutch minority and integration policies.[83]

IV. Accommodating Religiously Distinct Dress in the British Workplace: Progressive Case Law and 'Flexible Tolerance' on the Ground

Unsurprisingly for a country which is often praised for its pragmatic and accommodationist stance regarding minorities and where even judges,[84] police officers and public teachers[85] are free to wear religious dress on the job, the UK's case law provides considerable space and legal protection for Muslim women and other religious minorities to display their faith in the workplace. Where restrictions have been accepted, it has been on the basis of health and safety (the scope of which is interpreted very broadly), not on the basis of an ideology of neutrality. However, the issues have been more controversial with regard to symbols of the Christian faith, illustrated by the *Eweida* and *Chaplin* cases.

---

[82] Amnesty International, *Choice and Prejudice. Discrimination against Muslims in Europe*, n 11 above, 51; referring to ETC (Equal Treatment Commission), 'Comments on the combined fourth and fifth Dutch report on The implementation of the International Covenant on Economic, Social and Cultural Rights: the headscarf and access to the labour market', November 2009, 8.

[83] eg Commissie Blok, *Bruggen Bouwen (onderzoek Integratiebeleid)*, n 4 above, 95. However, Vermeulen and Belhaj note that the liberal/accommodationist Dutch stance on religious dress also appears from the fact that even secular opinion-makers interviewed were open to finding 'reasonable solutions' to accommodate religious dress in the workplace. F Vermeulen and R El Morabet Belhaj, 'Accommodating religious claims in the Dutch workplace: Unacknowledged Sabbaths, objecting marriage registrars and pressured faith-based organizations' (2013) 13 *International Journal of Discrimination and the Law* 113.

[84] In 2003, Rabinder Singh QC became the first High Court judge to sit with a turban (as well as the youngest person to sit as a high court judge) C Dyer, 'High court judge will be first to wear turban', *The Guardian*, 23 March 2003. For judicial personnel the Judicial Studies Board has issued rather vague guidance in its Equal Treatment Benchbook, at chapter 3.3. (www.judiciary.gov.uk/Resources/JCO/Documents/Training/2009_etbb_3_religon.pdf).

[85] There is no general legislation in the UK mandating particular dress codes for school teachers or, more widely, those who work in public sector employment. Most school teachers work within state sector schooling, which includes schools that receive state funding on the basis that they have a faith-based ethos (eg Church of England, Jewish and Muslim schools).

A. Religious Dress and Grooming Disputes in Britain

Legal challenges to workplace dress requirements or prohibitions have arisen with greater frequency in public sector employment and in educational contexts, where uniforms are often required, but they are by no means absent in private employment contexts. Claims can be brought under the 2010 Equality Act, implementing the Employment Equality Directive, as well as under human rights law (the Human Rights Act 1998 allows British courts to rule on issues of compliance with the ECHR). Thus, the same dual legal framework can be utilised in Britain when formulating claims with regard to religious interests in the workplace. Also, some (piece-meal) dress accommodations has been put into legislative form, such as exemptions for Sikh motorcyclists and building-site workers,[86] which are relevant in a number of jobs such as goods delivery and construction. Employment disputes are handled by the Employment Tribunal (ET, formerly 'Industrial Tribunals') and the Employment Appeals Tribunals (EAT), but can go as high up as the Court of Appeal and the House of Lords/Supreme Court.

In practice, most cases involve a much more extensive analysis under the anti-discrimination framework than under the human rights frame. Davies has noted that

> in labour law, the HRA has not had a major impact because it has not been accompanied by the development of a human rights culture … it may take some time to transform the HRA from an underused statute into a major part of the United Kingdom's constitutional fabric.[87]

One reason for the under-utilisation of human rights is the historic dynamics between individual rights and collective action strategies in English labour law; trade unions and collective bargaining were traditionally the mechanism for the protection of workers. Individual legal rights were added starting in the 1970s,[88] but this was seen as 'creating a "floor of rights" on which collective bargaining could build'.[89] In the 1980s, individual rights were used to undermine the trade union movement, leading English labour lawyers to view the 1998 Human Rights Act with suspicion and fearing it would make collective reforms unfeasible.[90]

---

[86] The Motor-Cycle Crash Helmets (Religious Exemption) Act 1976 (exempts a Sikh who wears a turban from having to wear a crash helmet on a motorcycle); Employment Act 1989, section 11 (exempts a turban-wearing Sikh from any requirement to wear a safety helmet on a construction site. In 1998 the Health and Safety Executive issued a guidance note stating that Sikhs wearing turbans are exempt from the requirement to wear hard hats on construction sites, which applies to any construction site in Great Britain).

[87] ACL Davies, 'Worker's Human Rights in English Law' in C Fenwick and T Novitz (eds), *Human Rights at Work: Perspectives on Law and Regulation* (Oxford, Hart Publishing, 2010) 190.

[88] With the Industrial Relations Act of 1971 (unfair dismissal protection; now consolidated in the Employment Protection (Consolidation) Act 1978), Equal Pay Act 1970, Sex Discrimination Act 1975, Race Relations Act 1968 and 1976.

[89] Davies, 'Worker's Human Rights in English Law', 176, referring to Wedderburn, *The Worker and the law*, 3rd edn (Penguin, 1986) 6.

[90] ibid, 178.

This is mainly so for 'individual *rights in trade union law in particular*' (emphasis added),[91] and far less for the basic protection against discrimination and unfair dismissal, but it still explains the hesitation amongst some labour lawyers to mobilise human rights laws. Surely, the success of pursuing the *Eweida* case before the ECtHR may trigger the reconsideration of the Human Rights Act 1998 in the future.

The Equality Act 2010 superseded previously applicable legislation, notably the Race Relations Act 1976 and Equality Act 2006, and some secondary legislation. Before the enactment of the Employment Equality (Religion or Belief) Regulations 2003, which for the first time prohibited discrimination on the basis of religion or belief in employment settings, religious dress and grooming claims needed to be framed under the Race Relations Act as ethnic/racial discrimination. This was successful for groups such as Jews and Sikhs where religion and race largely overlap. In other cases, eg Muslims and Rastafarians, this strategy was unsuccessful since race and religion do not necessarily overlap in the same way. In *Crown Suppliers (Property Services Agency) v Dawkins*,[92] a Rastafarian who wore his hair in dreadlocks was refused employment as a van driver by a government agency when he indicated that he was unwilling to cut his hair. He complained of unlawful direct and indirect discrimination on the ground of his race, contrary to the provisions of section 1(1)(a) and (b) of the Race Relations Act 1976. An Industrial Tribunal upheld his complaint, finding that Rastafarians were an ethnic group, as stated in the leading House of Lords case of *Mandla v Dowell Lee*.[93] The Employment Appeal Tribunal, by a majority, allowed an appeal by the government agency and the applicant's appeal to the Court of Appeal was dismissed. The Court of Appeal considered that there was nothing to distinguish Rastafarians from the rest of the Afro-Caribbean community so as to render them a separate group defined by reference to their ethnic origins. Further, a 60-year history was not sufficient to amount to a 'long shared history', one of the essential criteria set out by the House of Lords in the case of *Mandla v Dowell Lee*.

Notably, workplace headscarf cases have been raised in rather unexpected settings. For instance, in *Noah v Desrosiers t/a Wedge*[94] a Muslim girl who habitually wore a headscarf for religious reasons was denied a job in a hairdressing salon. The owner of the salon argued it was necessary for stylists to display their own haircuts when at work in order to promote the salon's business. This argument thus basically came down to an occupational requirement. The Employment Tribunal considered this under the Employment Equality (Religion or Belief) Regulations 2003, in particular the provisions regarding indirect discrimination (having an

---

[91] ibid.
[92] *Crown Suppliers (Property Services Agency) v Dawkins* [1993] ICR 517; [1991] IRLR 327.
[93] *Mandla v Dowell Lee* [1983] 1 All ER 1062; [1983] IRLR 209.
[94] *Noah v Desrosiers t/a Wedge* [2008] ET Case No 2201867/07 (29 May 2008). See Peter Jones, 'Belief, autonomy and responsibility. The case of indirect religious discrimination' in G Levey (ed), *Authenticity, Autonomy and Multicultualism* (Abingdon, Routledge, 2015) 67–69.

open justification regime). While the Tribunal considered the hair salon's argued motivation to be a legitimate aim, it held that the salon sought to achieve this in a disproportionate way. The requirement for stylists to show off their haircuts was not a core requirement of the job and it would be up to the salon owner to carry out an actual assessment to show that her stylists not showcasing their own hairstyles would pose an actual risk to the business. Considering the arguments did not rise to such level, the job applicant was successful in her indirect discrimination claim.

In a widely reported case related to education,[95] *Azmi v Kirklees Metropolitan Borough Council,*[96] Ms Azmi, a bilingual teaching assistant of Islamic faith working at a Church of England school, was dismissed for refusing to remove her full-faced veil/niqab whilst teaching in the presence of male teachers. The Employment Tribunal dismissed her claims of direct and indirect discrimination under regulation 3(1)(a) and (b) of the Employment Equality (Religion or Belief) Regulations 2003 (applying Council Directive 2000/78/EC) and that decision was upheld on appeal by the Employment Appeal Tribunal.[97] The requirement to show one's face was motivated by the aim to provide effective education to the already vulnerable, disadvantaged children at the school, one considered very legitimate by the courts. Importantly, the evidence presented proved that obscuring the face and mouth impeded effective teacher–pupil communication. Thus, the requirement was necessary to meet that legitimate objective. Asking Ms Azmi to remove her face veil whilst teaching was also held to be a proportionate means of achieving that aim. In particular, Ms Azmi was only required to remove her veil when teaching the children but was free to wear it at all other times. While the *Azmi* case did not involve a typical private setting and the typical minority dress (the hijab), or precisely because of these two elements, it can be considered as revealing for the understanding of equality law as it applies to religious dress in Britain. For one, even the full-faced veil was initially accepted at a school associated with the majority Christian faith, even if it was later prohibited (for part of the employee's job functions). One could consider that a fortiori at least the same tolerance (and most likely more) would be given for less-inhibiting forms of religious dress (the hijab, the Sikh turban, the Jewish kippah…) in private sector settings.

---

[95] Another oft-discussed case related to religious dress in education is the British Sabina Begum case: *R (on the application of Begum (Sabina)) v Denbigh High School Governors* [2006] UKHL 15 (protecting other Muslim pupils from family and societal pressure to wear the more conservative *jilbab* considered an important goal). R Sandberg, 'The changing position of religious minorities in English law: the legacy of *Begum*' in R Grillo et al (eds), *Legal Practice and Cultural Diversity* (Aldershot, Ashgate, 2009).

[96] *Azmi v Kirklees Metropolitan Council* [2007] ICR 1154, UKEAT 0009/07/30003 (30 March 2007).

[97] Also, the EAT refused to make a reference to the European Court of Justice for clarification, inter alia, of whether a restriction on a manifestation of religion, in this case the wearing of a *niqab*, could constitute a form of direct religious discrimination.

Other interesting cases have been reported in local newspapers.[98] In a little-known case from 2010,[99] a bakery in the English town of Grimsby was found to have discriminated against a headscarf-wearing Muslim woman on religious grounds. The woman had agreed she would remove her headscarf at work for hygiene reasons and was willing to do so at the induction day at the bakery, but was then turned down. An Employment Tribunal in Hull found she had suffered religious discrimination since there was no other reason for her not being invited back.

In a 2011 Employment Tribunal case,[100] the discrimination and harassment claim of Hannah Adewole was rejected. Ms Adewole was a midwife who objected to wearing scrub trousers based on a biblical command that women should not wear men's clothing sought to wear scrub dresses while working in the operating quarters. Though it was recognised that the policy put her at a disadvantage in comparison with, for example, Muslim midwives who had no such religious objection to wearing scrub trousers (and who were allowed to wear hijabs over their uniforms), the Barking, Havering and Redbridge University Hospitals NHS Trust's dress code was considered justifiable as a proportionate means of achieving the legitimate aim of preventing infection in operating quarters.

The case of Nadia Eweida has already figured prominently in this analysis.[101] The devoutly Christian British Airways employee nearly lost her job at London's Heathrow airport for refusing to remove a cross on a necklace she wore on her uniform. The Court of Appeal ruled that she could not succeed in her claim of indirect discrimination because she could not prove that the measures had resulted in a *group* disadvantage (as she was seemingly the only one who made an issue out of wearing a cross) and that even if she could, the restriction was proportionate. However, the ECtHR, following a human rights analysis under Article 9 ECHR, effectively reversed that ruling, in her favour. In *Chaplin*[102] health and safety considerations were considered legitimate aims in a hospital setting and the restriction on wearing a cross-necklace—a risk if an elderly patient pulled or held on to it—was a necessary and proportionate means in light of that legitimate objective.

Grooming issues are a prominent issue in British case law, in contrast to Belgian and (to a lesser extent) to Dutch case law. Historically, employers were given some leeway to restrict employee facial hair when such was motivated by hygienic reasons (eg in the food industry). In a number of Employment Appeal Tribunal

---

[98] The case regarding a Latvian-born Muslim convert (Anastasija) who was awarded compensation as told by the local newspaper, is unreported. See www.thisisgrimsby.co.uk/story-14019822-detail/story.html. The reported case UKEAT/0310/10/JOJ concerns her husband—an Algerian-born Muslim, whose appeal against a decision by an employment tribunal dismissing his claim of discrimination on the basis of race failed—and did not touch on the issue of religious dressing.

[99] *Anastasija Bouzir v Country Style Foods Ltd* (2010) UKEAT (unpublished).

[100] *Adewole v Barking, Havering and Redbridge University Hospitals NHS Trust* [2011] ET (unreported): www.law.cf.ac.uk/clr/networks/lrsncd11.html.

[101] *Eweida v British Airways plc* [2010] EWCA Civ 80, [2010] ICR 890.

[102] *Chaplin v Royal Devon & Exeter Hospital NHS Foundation Trust* [2010] ET 1702886/2009.

cases from the late' 70s and early' 80s claims by Sikh employees (or prospective Sikh employees) in the food industry who did not want to shave their beards were rejected.[103] In *Singh v Rowntree Mackintosh*[104] and *Panesar v Nestlé*[105]—which were both decided within a few years of the Race Relations Act 1976—the Employment Appeal Tribunal and Court of Appeal, respectively, gave further deference to the employers' justifications for facial hair restrictions based on health and safety requirements in the food industry. Considering the substantial upgrades in legal protections for religious convictions and practices, and perhaps also evolved social acceptance standards in the British workplace, it has been argued that 'the court's reasoning in such cases is unlikely to be followed today given the development over the last thirty years of protection against discrimination on the grounds of religion or belief'.[106] However, in a 2007 case,[107] the dismissal of a Rastafarian driver for wearing dreadlocks was not considered discriminatory under the 2003 Employment Equality (Religion or Belief) Regulations. Placing the generally required standard of 'tidiness' for all drivers as a 'criterion or practice' under scrutiny, it was held that a requirement of tidy hair is a proportionate means of achieving the aim of a presentable appearance to customers and clients.

The diversity of religious issues, related to a variety of religions besides Islam, is characteristic of the British situation. As discussed in the introduction, what essentially were religious accommodation cases have been a feature of the UK social relations reality for some time, at least since 1969 when a ban on turbans and beards was retracted by the UK's Wolverhampton Transport Committee following a heated conflict with several of its Sikh conductors and drivers.[108] This dispute and many others have been resolved and never introduced in court. Just like the existence of cases, so the absence of case law may also reveal elements of what goes on on the ground. One can imagine that because of the more progressive mentalities on the ground, certain claims are simply not being raised since there is unproblematic accommodation for religious dress in practice. In this sense, the widespread general effects of legislation (eg where legislation codifies or only validates what already was the case before its adoption) may preclude the need for specific applications of anti-discrimination law. To the extreme, a law that is perfectly clear, accepted and complied with by all relevant actors would lead to no disputes or litigation whatsoever. However, a place where anti-discrimination

---

[103] See, eg, *Singh v Rowntree Mackintosh Ltd* [1979] IRLR 199, [1979] ICR 554 (EAT) (a Scottish case) and *Panesar v Nestlé Co Ltd* [1980] IRLR 64, [1980] ICR 144 (CA).

[104] *Singh v Rowntree Mackintosh Ltd* [1979] IRLR 199, [1979] ICR 554 (EAT).

[105] *Panesar v Nestlé Co Ltd* [1980] IRLR 64, [1980] ICR 144 (CA).

[106] Susanne Foster, 'Some light employment law relief, in support of Movember—what to do if your moustache gets up your employer's nose', 23 November 2010, at www.cm-murray.com/2010/11/23/some-light-employment-law-relief-in-support-of-movember-what-to-do-if-your-moustache-gets-up-your-employers-nose/.

[107] *Harris v NKL Automotive Ltd & Another* [2007] UKEAT/0134/07/DM (3 October 2007); 2007 WL 2817981.

[108] BBC, '1969: Sikh busmen win turban fight', *BBC Online* news.bbc.co.uk/onthisday/hi/dates/stories/april/9/newsid_2523000/2523691.stm.

law is 'obsolete' to this extent has not yet been created. Legal cases involving religious dress and other issues have become more frequent in recent years in Britain, in part because of the growing religious diversity and assertiveness amongst religious minorities but also because of developments in the legal protection available to claimants.

V. Comparison: Corporate Neutrality Policies and the Uneven Rooting of Reasonable Accommodation

In the absence of comprehensive direction from the ECtHR and the CJEU, the issue of religious dress in the private workplace remains, at least for the time being, in the hands of the Member States. National courts across Europe are dealing differently with the growing visibility of religious pluralism, and especially Islam, in the workplace with the general, abstract principles of religious freedom and non-discrimination on the basis of religion or belief as the essential guidelines. In the best case, the national court sees the challenge as finding a 'subtle balance' between the religious interests of the individual employee and other conflicting values, freedoms and rights.[109] An array of issues must be weighed to determine the necessity and proportionality of restrictions on employees' fundamental rights, an exercise which by its nature calls for an *in concreto* case-by-case assessment.

Needless to say, this assessment is embedded within particular legal cultures, including various models of church-state relationships and political/societal ambivalences towards religion, religious diversity and integration. It may be that considering this background, a uniform response is not warranted or desirable in countries so diversified with respect to historic contexts, religious composition, integration patterns and policies. However, in the area of employment, the issue of the legal protection for wearing religious signs in the European Union has been called 'particularly heterogeneous and confused'.[110] This divergent case law has consequences for EU law and for the EU project as a whole, since it greatly inhibits the free movement of workers based on their religious dress. But it would also be more in line with the EU 'fundamental rights revolution' to mobilise the freedom of religion or belief and the principle of non-discrimination towards more inclusive labour markets, by rejecting the idea that the alleged commercial interests of

---

[109] Point made by Lord Denning in *Ahmad v Inner London Education Authority* [1978] 1 All ER 574 at 578, namely that a subtle balance must be struck between protecting the rights of the religious employee without placing an undue burden on the employers or additional responsibilities on co-workers.

[110] Bribosia, Chopin and Rorive, *Rapport de synthèse relatif aux signes d'appartenance religieuse dans quinze pays de l'Union européenne* (2004) 24.

employers[111] generally trump those of the employee to dress in accordance with her religious beliefs and practices.

While with regard to religious dress, legal controversies in Belgium have centred around the headscarf, in the Netherlands and Britain both the religions involved and the dress/grooming issues involved in legal cases have extended wider.

Even though the Employment Equality Directive has introduced a convergence in terminology and framework in EU Member States' laws, it has not produced a uniform or consistent level of protection for employee rights to manifest religion or belief in the workplace. Indeed, the different results achieved in Belgium, the Netherlands and Britain in comparable headscarf scenarios illustrate that a common non-discrimination *framework* does not necessarily ensure harmonisation of *protection* throughout the EU. Where in the Netherlands the concept of indirect discrimination has allowed the ETC and Dutch Courts to see the absence of attempts to find reasonable accommodations as an element in the assessment of necessity and proportionality of restrictions under the indirect discrimination test, Belgian case law rejects the idea that employers should have to explore accommodations, disconnecting the non-discrimination inquiry from the search for reasonable accommodations. In various Dutch cases, the efforts of employers to look for solutions to keep the employee on the job are considered central, and alternative avenues are even proposed by the ETC. In Britain, similarly, such efforts on behalf of employers are considered mandated under the prohibition of indirect discrimination. In contrast, Belgian courts have held in unequivocal terms that the prohibition of indirect discrimination does *not* entail any duty for employers to offer employees (eg who request to wear religious dress in violation of expectations or policies) any form of accommodation, including offering an alternative position with the company where that would be feasible.[112]

A recent empirical study on the de facto practices of religious and cultural accommodations in Belgian companies concluded that the current case-by-case and employer discretionary method of dealing with claims for religious and cultural accommodations leads to legal insecurity, unequal treatment and arbitrariness.[113] The study also reveals that labour unions do not always have an incentive to support religious claims (which sometimes contradict other union goals),[114] in particular if there was no group of employees behind the request. But

---

[111] It can be noted that it can be in the employer's (long-term) interest to allow headscarves as well.

[112] Labour Court of Appeal Brussels, 15 January 2008, *Journal des tribunaux* 140 (case regarding the 'Club' bookstore chain); Labour Court of Appeal Antwerp of 23 December 2011, AR nrs 2010/AA/453 and 2010/AA/467, unpublished (G4S).

[113] Ilke Adam and Andrea Rea, *Culturele diversiteit op de werkvloer: praktijken van redelijke aanpassing in België* (Brussels, CEOOR, 2010).

[114] For instance, the request of Muslim employees to skip lunch break during Ramadan and go home earlier is not supported by the labor union, as the right to reasonable breaks has been fought for a long time and is considered too important to compromise. *ibid* (*Culturele Diversiteit op de werkvloer*) 114. Under the EEOC Guidelines workers 'use of lunch time in exchange for early departure' is mentioned as a type of reasonable accommodation by way of flexible scheduling. 29 CFR § 1605.2(d)(1)(ii). However, the divergent interests of individual religious employees and labour unions is not unique

introducing a legal duty of reasonable accommodation for religious observance and practice in Belgium remains highly contested,[115] and the CEOOR has taken a stance against adopting a reasonable accommodation duty in Belgium, instead seeking to rely entirely on voluntary concessions by employers.[116]

Thus, despite similar legal frameworks and the absence of any explicit duty of reasonable accommodation for religion or belief under either the Belgian Anti-Discrimination Act, the Dutch General Equal Treatment Act or the UK Equal Treatment Act 2010, the concrete applications in the practice of domestic courts—the special effects of legislation—and the situation 'on the ground' is considerably different in these European countries.

The Dutch and British approaches are preferable both from an equal rights perspective as well as from an economic efficiency line of argumentation. The Belgian approach fails to recognise that offering an existing employee some accommodation can also be to the employer's advantage (eg someone familiar with and already trained in the company can remain a valued employee in an alternative position within the firm).

Introducing an explicit duty of reasonable accommodation for reasons of religion in Europe would signify a 'levelling up' of protection in certain 'restrictive jurisdictions' like Belgium, a consolidation in progressive jurisdictions, and overall a more effective convergence in the interpretation of the shared legal framework across Member States.

When it comes to the specific issue of company 'neutrality policies', the situation is also very different. In contrast to the Netherlands and Britain where arguments based on 'neutrality' are rarely accepted, Belgian courts have readily taken sides with private sector employers who stand behind an exclusive interpretation of this mystifying concept in eradicating any 'pluriformity', ironically sometimes in the name of tolerance towards diversity. The mushrooming of company neutrality

---

in Belgium, as in the US labour unions are a major force in blocking legislation aimed at strengthening the reasonable accommodation duty under Title VII of the Civil Rights Act (Workplace Religious Freedom Act) beyond the de minimis standard because of fears that in some cases to accommodate employees' Sabbaths will mean overriding seniority systems (T Berg, 'Religious Liberty in America at the End of the Century' (2001) 16 *Journal of Law & Religion* 187, 214).

[115] See the final report of the Belgian *Rondetafels van de Interculturaliteit* presented to the Federal Minister of Work and Equal Opportunities, Milquet, on 8 November 2010, which speaks of an irreconcilable difference of opinion within the reporting committee on workplace reasonable accommodations for religious practices, and therefore only recommends that 'one should consider more in-depth the potential advantages and disadvantages of the extension of the concept of reasonable accommodation' (report available at: www.interculturalite.be). See also K Alidadi, 'Studie over redelijke aanpassingen voor religie op Belgische werkvloer', *De Juristenkrant*, 12 January 2011, 6–7. (discussing the CEOOR's debatable stance against the introduction of a legally binding reasonable accommodation duty and instead choosing to rely solely on social dialogue procedures).

[116] For a critique, see K Alidadi, 'Redelijke aanpassingen voor religieuze praktijken op de Belgische werkvloer: van "goodwill" naar afdwingbaar recht?' ['reasonable accommodations for religious practices in the Belgian workplace: from "goodwill" to enforceable right?'] in M-C Foblets and JP Schreiber (eds), *Les Assises de L'interculturalité: Regards Croisés/ De Rondetafels van de Interculturaliteit: Een Terugblik* (Brussels, Larcier, 2013).

policies, supported by broad social intolerance and judicially embraced, has considerable harmful exclusionary effects on religious minority groups. Neither in its understanding nor in its effects, can this neutrality be considered neutral or value-free.

Of course, 'neutrality' need not be interpreted in the exclusive fashion that it has tended to be seen: an inclusive understanding would yield very different results (and render the debate on employment opportunities somewhat pointless). Interpretations are not set in stone and always subject to debate. As Pierre Legrand has stated,

> an interpretation is the outcome of an unequal distribution of social and cultural power within a society as a whole and within an interpretative community in particular (judges *vis-à-vis* professors, and so forth) and operates, through repeated articulations, to eliminate or marginalize alternatives. Ultimately, what interpretation prevails amongst the array of competing interpretations—and what interpretation endows the rule with a relative fixity of meaning—is a function of epistemic conventions produced as a result of power struggles that are themselves non-epistemic (which means that the other interpretations on offer would also have promoted understanding of the rule if they had been adopted, albeit not in the same way.[117]

One way of addressing the topic thus may be to challenge the understanding of neutrality as necessitating bans on religious dress (thus the exclusive interpretation). Such debates are taking place with regard to the public space and sphere (civil servants, state school teachers and pupils). Unlike the public sector, the private sector need not stay 'neutral', and this comes with considerable (entrepreneurial) freedoms. Private sector employers do need to respect human rights and cannot discriminate against people for reasons amongst others of their religion or belief. In this sense, they need to abide by and pursue anti-discrimination policies, not 'neutrality policies', so that the debate arguably should centre on that topic.

In the area of religious dress, it has thus become urgent to mobilise the full protective potential of *existing laws* to halt the exclusionary effects on visible religious minorities. Proposing reasonable accommodations as a way forward complements, rather than contradicts, this.

A. Legal Assessment of Private Neutrality Policies: Bias Hidden in Plain Sight

To conclude this chapter on religious dress in the workplace I want to focus on one of the key issues—private company 'neutrality' policies. Such policies are mushrooming in the private sector for various reasons. Some policies no doubt are a thin cover for discrimination. But it may also be explained by the conflict-avoiding

---

[117] P Legrand, 'What "Legal Transplants"?' in D Nelken and J Feest (eds), *Adapting Legal Cultures* (Oxford, Hart Publishing, 2001) 58–59.

strategies of businesses, in particular when it comes to polarising issues of religion in the public sphere. This latter reason seems more legitimate at first glance but it is ultimately misguided.

The comparative analysis showed that such policies are treated fundamentally differently across the EU. In Belgium, courts have played into this development by lending legitimacy and, through the judicial seal of approval, de facto have *promoted* broad and a priori restrictions on employment opportunities for Muslim women and other visible religious minorities. In this sense, the law *fortifies*—instead of combating—societal pressures on minorities to conform via 'passing' and 'covering' or to face far-reaching consequences. For Muslims and religious minorities in an already problematic labour market situation this constitutes an additional and hardly trivial barrier to participation.

I argue that from a legal point of view the judicial legitimating of private sector 'neutrality' policies—for instance in Belgium—is flawed and I see at least four reasons. Elsewhere I have written that despite a number of judicial defeats, the Belgian equality body Unia, NGOs and trade unions should push for a rectification of existing Belgian jurisprudence on private sector neutrality policies.[118] Clearly, a Europe-wide banning of this *bottleneck*[119] by the CJEU would be preferable since Belgium will not be the only Member State faced with a surge in discriminatory company neutrality policies.

First, under anti-discrimination law, neutrality policies cannot be considered justified as they effectively constitute (and should be framed as) *declaratory discriminations*, a form of direct discrimination. In the absence of special circumstances justifying it (eg health and safety concerns), general bans on religious dress in so-called 'neutrality policies'—unduly and disproportionately restricting freedom to manifest religion—should not be accepted. Belgian jurisprudence is too willing to accept neutrality under an exclusive understanding as being possible, good, necessary and proportionate. This is even more the case where the link between discriminatory preferences and neutrality is either open and palpable (eg *HEMA case*) or more concealed/cloaked but still present (eg *G4S case*). Seeing neutrality policies as effective forms of *declaratory discrimination statements*, and thus *direct discrimination* on the basis of religion or belief, means only genuine and determining occupational requirements can offer justification. Since this can only be done on a case-by-case basis, such *general policies* would thus by definition fail the test even if in particular cases restrictions could be seen as justified.

In the CJEU's *Feryn* decision[120] there was direct discrimination under the Racial Equality Directive prohibiting discrimination on the basis of so-called race and

---

[118] K Alidadi, 'Geloof en levensbeschouwing op de Europese en Belgische arbeidsmarkt: juridisch kader en recente ontwikkelingen' (2015) 4 *Tijdschrift voor Mensenrechten* 7–11.

[119] See J Fishkin, *Bottlenecks: A New Theory of Equal Opportunity* (Oxford, Oxford University Press, 2014).

[120] Case C-54/07, *Centrum voor gelijkheid van kansen en voor racismebestrijding v Firma Feryn NV* [2008] ECR I-5187.

ethnicity. The CJEU accepted that employers can directly discriminate by declaration. As discussed above, that case involved the CEO of a Belgian company (specialising in the sale and installation of doors) announcing in public interviews that he would not employ Moroccans to fill open vacancies because of customer preferences. The Belgian equality body argued that even if there was no specific victim, the company had discriminated against a group based on their ethnicity; by stating that Moroccans would not be hired, it was sure this group would not apply for the open posts at the company. The CJEU, responding to a number of prejudicial questions referred by the Brussels Labour Court of Appeal, held that (real or implied) discriminatory preferences of customers are no justification for discriminating against (future) employees on the basis of their ethnicity and that this could be described as 'discrimination by declaration', prohibited under Directive 2000/43.

There same can be argued with regard to an open declaration that a company will not hire any persons who wear, amongst other things, religious symbols such as the headscarf; the only difference is the reference to the notion of neutrality, which gives it an aura of legitimacy. The exclusionary employment practice involved in the *Feryn* case obviously hurt minorities substantially, and there are signs that such practices are widespread in Belgium. The employer organisation 'UNIZO' acknowledged that Belgian employers routinely refuse to hire 'allochthones' because of fears of the adverse customer reaction, but advised employers not to give in to such pressures and instead stand by their allochthone workers and defend their work.[121] There are other signs of sugarcoating the 'hesitance' of Flemish employers to hire ethnic minorities as 'fear of getting their feet wet' since they are 'unfamiliar with the work ethic' of an ethnic minority group.[122] A large section of Belgian employers thus errs on the side of caution by not giving ethnic minorities a chance to disprove widely-held stereotypes. The exclusion of a partially overlapping religious minority, protected under anti-discrimination law, is exacerbated by neutrality policies. It should be clear that 'neutrality' in various circumstances purely forms a cloak for intolerant (under)currents in society. But even if such policies are adopted in good faith, meaning without the express will to exclude or to 'avoid conflicts', their effect remains the same. Effective anti-discrimination law in such circumstances can only be unsettling in both its special and general effects and to do so it must challenge such normalised instances of intolerance and discomfort with the presence of religious expressions. Indeed, 'fundamental rights ultimately exist to protect minorities, unpopular minorities in particular, against the tyranny of the majority'.[123]

---

[121] G Fransen, 'Klanten hoeven geen Marokkanen. Firma Feryn vindt geen valabele werknemers', *De Standaard*, 28 April 2005.

[122] VDAB Studiedienst, *Kansengroepen in Kaart: allochtonen op de Vlaamse arbeidsmarkt*, 2nd edn (VDAB, 2012) 15–16. An HR study showed 7 out of 10 Belgian employers were of the opinion that allochthone workers did not show adequate input and motivation. This was even though only half had ever employed allochthone workers.

[123] J Flo and J Vrielink, 'The Constitutionality of the Belgian Burqa Ban', *openDemocracynet*, 14 January 2014.

Belgian courts have accepted this argument in other areas of anti-discrimination law. In a 2013 decision, the Labour Tribunal in Bruges[124] found the rejection of a worker because of his alleged disability or physical or genetic characteristic (an additional ground covered under the 2007 Anti-discrimination Act) was unjustified. The case concerned an employee who had a condition known as congenital syndactyly, where some of his fingers were fused together. The employer had hired him as a temp worker in a computer business and was intent on offering him a permanent employment contract. But because some customers and co-workers found the employee's hands to be 'unpresentable', the employer had retracted its offer (and admitted this to the worker's parents). The Labour Tribunal in Bruges found a case of direct discrimination based on disability and physical or genetic characteristics. The Court referred to the *Feryn* case, expanding that decision's reach to the protected ground of disability, for the position that an employer cannot justify direct discrimination in order to meet (discriminatory) preferences of either customers or co-workers.[125] The need to have 'presentable hands' (not having congenital syndactyly) was also not considered to constitute a genuine and determining occupational requirement or even a legitimate aim. This decision is to be applauded. Indeed, an important responsibility lies with the employer, who as a distributive agent has a say in the distribution of scarce goods like jobs and, in its role of mediating between its workers, customers and the outside world, must seek to help realise anti-discrimination objectives.

Secondly, the human rights framework too can bolster arguments against judicially legitimating neutrality policies, in particular in the form of ramifications of the ECtHR's *Eweida* decision. This is despite the fact that Article 9 ECHR routinely only receives a passing mention in such cases.

Importantly, company neutrality policies cannot be considered to *automatically trump* Article 9 ECHR fundamental rights of employees any longer. There has to be an effective and genuine balancing of the various rights and interests at stake, including the fundamental right of the employee to express his or her religious beliefs and practices, which must be given adequate weight in the exercise. It must be recognised that restrictive dress policies imply real restrictions on the employee's rights and critically impact on the opportunities of (visible) minorities in the employment market. This does not mean restrictions on dress are not allowed in the workplace in any circumstance: a ban was, for instance, accepted (but not mandated) in the *Chaplin* case because of safety and security considerations and this can indeed, under certain circumstances, justify some restrictions. But in *Eweida*, the corporate image concerns of British Airways (even if legitimate) proved insufficient to warrant overstepping employee rights to manifest their freedom of religion in the workplace. It is clear that after *Eweida*, where the European

---

[124] Labour Tribunal Bruges, 10 December 2013, AR nrs 12/25521/A and 12/2596/A.
[125] Thus the Labour Tribunal expanded the *Feryn* holding to different discrimination grounds, but also added that preferences of co-workers (not at stake in the *Feryn* case) were no justification.

Court closely links pluralism, democracy, and the protection of religious freedom together, a more effective consideration of employee rights under Article 9 is due. What's more, while in *Eweida* the ECtHR considered the corporate image argument of BA as legitimate, this need not be the case with a neutrality policy which is motivated by meeting discriminatory customer preferences.

Additional arguments can bolster the anti-discrimination and human rights based arguments against the acceptance of neutrality policies in the private sector.

There is a textual argument which makes the parallel with the exception provided under Article 4(2) Employment Equality Directive regarding religious-ethos employers. The provision allowing religious-ethos employers to select staff on the basis of religion or belief is an exception to the general rule protecting against religion or belief discrimination and must thus be interpreted (very) narrowly. A general requirement that all employees should be part of a certain church or of a certain faith is regarded as a clear violation of the limited exemption. Instead, whether a certain faith requirement is allowable depends on the context and the job function in particular.[126] Thus, the so-called organic approach has been discredited in favour of a functional approach, which minimises the exclusionary effects of religious-ethos company hiring policies while allowing for organisational autonomy regarding key posts. One can argue that the same need to justify (non)faith must also—at the very least—be applied in the case of non-religious ethos or 'neutral' employers. There too, a *general* policy applying a (non) faith requirement to all staff (organic approach) is unacceptable; any such requirement must seek to meet a 'specific need' considering the context and job functions, thus requiring a case-by-case analysis. Holding otherwise means that private commercial companies—'secular organisations'—are given more leeway than religious ethos companies, and that arguably was not the purpose of including a specific provision on religious-ethos employers in the Employment Equality Directive.

Finally, in this context it is paramount to address the spill-over effect of neutrality policies adopted in the public sector in countries like Belgium and France. If it is good for the government to adopt a neutrality policy, how can it be wrong for a private company to do so as well? However, the spill-over of 'neutrality' to the private sector only exacerbates the problem of exclusion by transferring a misguided policy to even greater segments of the labour market, here without any clear link to basic rights or underlying state principles and values. It must be stated that the legitimacy and appropriateness of such policies with regard to the public sector is also contested,[127] and my point here is not to argue that public sector neutrality

---

[126] See Y Stox, *Discriminatie en Identiteit. Identiteitsgebonden Werkgevers in het Belgisch en Europees Arbeidsrecht* (Brussels, Larcier, 2010); L Vickers, *Religious freedom, religious discrimination, and the workplace* (Oxford, Hart Publishing, 2008); M-C Foblets and K Alidadi, 'The RELIGARE Report: religion in the context of the European Union: engaging the interplay between religious diversity and secular models' in M-C Foblets et al (eds), *Belief, Law and Politics What Future for a Secular Europe?* (Aldershot, Ashgate, 2014).

[127] See, eg, van Ooijen, *Religious symbols in public functions: unveiling state neutrality. A comparative analysis of Dutch, English and French justifications for limiting the freedom of public officials to display*

policies should enjoy less scrutiny or require less context- and job-specific justi-fication. However, the French example shows that what goes for the public sector need not be accepted in private sector employment. Indeed, while the situation of French public servants with regard to religious dress has been clear with formal bans, the Cour de Cassation has resisted such policies with regard to private com-panies. French public civil servants, without exception, are required to abide by the principle of *laïcité*, which, in the interpretation of the Conseil d'Etat, implies abstaining from showing one's religious affiliation through distinct dress or sym-bols in either back-office or front-office functions.[128] But *laïcité* does not apply and cannot be made generally applicable to private companies. In the *Baby-Loup* affair, subject of prolonged and messy litigation, the French Cour de cassation courageously dismissed the application of the *laïcité* doctrine to the private sector. In 2013 the French Cour de cassation found for a Muslim carer and co-director who had been dismissed for wearing a headscarf by the Baby-Loup day-care cen-tre, and held that *laïcité* could not be extended to the private sector by an employer which was not a faith-based organisation (*entreprise de conviction*).[129] It remanded the case to the Paris Court of Appeal. However, in June 2014— after the Paris Court of Appeal found for the employer—the Grand Chamber of the Cour de cassation confirmed the Appeal judgment on a limited ground related to company internal policies, while reiterating that *laïcité* only relates to the state and that an employee's freedom of religion can only be restricted to the extent that it is justi-fied by the nature of the job duties and if proportionate to the objective sought.[130]

One can question the relevance of arguments based on (political) secularism, routinely used to justify restrictions on religious expressions, in the context of this research, which focuses on private sector employment. After all, secularism relates to the relationship between religions and the state and—unless one overstretches the sphere of the political to cover all social life—has little to do with the situation

---

religious symbols, at 260, distinguishes six arguments offered in support of dress restrictions in the Netherlands and also offers compelling counter-arguments for each one. (the six 'points of contention' being: equal treatment of the public official, personification of the state, public officials' bias, risk of proselytism, image of the state, separation of church and state).

[128] In France, the principle of *laïcité* applies to civil servants but also to agents, who have 'only' a fixed-term contract—of public law—with the state or local public authorities. The French Law No 83/634 of 13 July 1983 Act on the rights and duties of civil servants is relevant here, and the Conseil d'Etat has clearly set out what this and other legal provisions mean for public servants in a 2000 ruling (CE, Avis, Mlle Marteaux, 3 May 2000, n° 217077; Avis rendus par le Conseil d'Etat sur des questions de droit posées par un tribunal administratif ou une cour administrative d'appel). This advice of the Conseil d'Etat, addressing three questions, has become a reference in this matter.

[129] French Cour de cassation (social chamber), 19 March 2013, n 11-28.845, *Bull* 2013, V, n° 75; On this date, the French Cour de cassation issued its first Baby-Loup decision, holding that the internal regulations of the day-care centre which prohibited staff from wearing the hijab and other religious symbols were unjustified.

[130] French Cour de cassation (grand chamber), *Mme A c Association Baby Loup*, Arrêt n° 612, 25 June 2014; A Jouan, 'Baby-Loup: la Cour de cassation confirme le licenciement de la salariée voilée', *Le Figaro*, 25 June 2014.

of employees in the private sector[131] workplace. Therefore, drawing on neutrality and secularism arguments when issues of religion in the labour market are discussed adds little to the debate and often is confusing. Obviously, in a general way the relations between a state-religion regime will affect various social areas and societal developments (and vice versa) as messages are continuously sent out, exchanged and reframed. But this hardly makes the spill-over defensible.

---

[131] In the case of public employment, one can argue (some of) the civil servants 'represent' the state and must remain neutral. Secularism—'the separation of church and state'—would then lead to this neutrality mandate. This is a misleading argument, because in none of the three countries is there a separation of church and state, and a misleading one, since a concept of which the goal is protection of freedom of religion and non-discrimination is subverted into legitimations for violating exactly those fundamental rights and freedoms.

4

Conflicting Religion-Worktime Demands: Is Europe Keeping Up with the Times?

'A culturally homogeneous society whose members share and mechanically follow an identical body of beliefs and practices is today no more than an anthropological fiction'.[1]

I. Introduction: Intersection of Human Rights and Working Time Regulation

Religious time accommodation requests—requesting time-off for religious holidays, weekly Sabbath, prayer time—are the most common accommodation category after religious dress requests. This is borne out by the available case law as well as by sociological studies.[2] Working time protections, largely because of labour union action, have been 'central to labour law since its inception'[3] and are a focus of the modernisation of labour law. The right to 'observe days of rest and to celebrate holidays and ceremonies in accordance with the precepts of one's religion or belief' is also a recognised aspect of the fundamental right to freedom of religion or belief.[4] Thus, there are different areas of law that should be considered, even if there are no lucid lines to be drawn.[5]

---

[1] B Parekh, *A Commitment to Cultural Pluralism* (Paris, UNESCO, 1998) 3.

[2] eg see Ilke Adam and Andrea Rea, *Culturele diversiteit op de werkvloer: praktijken van redelijke aanpassing in België* (Brussels, Centrum voor Gelijke Kansen en voor Racismebestrijding, 2010) on religious time requests within various sectors in Belgium.

[3] ibid, 510.

[4] See Declaration on the Elimination of All Forms of Intolerance and of Discrimination Based on Religion or Belief, Proclaimed by General Assembly resolution 36/55 of 25 November 1981, Art 6(h).

[5] Some aspects of labour law may be regarded as part and parcel of what human rights are about ('labour rights as human rights', an approach strengthened since the Declaration of Philadelphia of 1944) and particular working time protections can be considered a component of non-discrimination law (which itself can be seen as falling under human rights) since they address the situation of certain vulnerable employees. However, many ILO Conventions on working time (Convention no 1, 1919; Convention no 14, 1921, Convention no 47, 1935) preceded the post-Second World War human rights revolution and had particular goals to protect domestic workers against some of the effects of

In Europe, the temporal organisation of society, including 'the rhythm of working life', remains by and large embedded in Christianity:

> Thus, Sunday is a non-working day for the majority of workers in all the Member States and most public holidays coincide with major mainstream Christian festivals. To turn that statement around, a Christian worker is unlikely, most of the time, to find that the demands of normal work schedules conflict with the requirements of religious observance in any European Union country. The same is not true for other religions, whose holy day may fall on Friday or Saturday and whose major religious festivals are not recognised in national calendars.[6]

Public holidays in many European countries are a mix of religious days and other significant days without explicit religious connotation. This is the case in Belgium,[7] in the Netherlands[8] and the United Kingdom.[9] Even the public holiday systems in France and Turkey, known for their strong secularism, reflect the majority religion in those countries. These public holiday schedules can therefore entail a significant inconvenience and disadvantage for minority religionists who follow another calendar or observe other holidays. Muslims, Jews and Seventh-Day Adventists have faced worktime conflicts when they sought to participate in the mainstream workplace while staying committed to their religious convictions and practices. 'Neutrality' is clearly lacking in this area of social regulation. Minorities who do not practise the majority Christian religion are generally expected to adapt to the dominant schedule legislation, although some accommodation may be embedded in legal instruments.

Unsurprisingly therefore, this appears to be a particularly minority-relevant area of law and society since, despite the secularisation of large segments of the European population, 'many aspects of social and cultural life are rooted in Christianity'.[10]

---

international competition. Overall, the interactions between human rights, anti-discrimination law and labour law remain unexplored: see McCann, 'Decent Working Hours as a Human Rights: Intersections in the Regulation of Working Time' in C Fenwick and T Novitz (eds), *Human Rights at Work: Perspectives on Law and Regulation* (Oxford, Hart Publishing, 2010) 520, 522.

[6] ibid, 204.

[7] The religious days are Easter, Easter Monday, Ascension, Pentecost, Pentecost Monday, Assumption of Mary, All Saints and Christmas; the non-religious days are New Year's Day, Labour day, National Holiday and Armistice Day. See Act of 4 January 1974 concerning the legal holidays (*wet inzake de feestdagen*). In addition, the days of the three communities are holidays for their civil servants and for employees of institutions controlled, supervised of financed by them (eg municipalities, universities) and may also be observed by banks in the relevant community. King's feast is a holiday observed by all (ie federal, community or regional, provincial and local) administrations.

[8] Easter, Easter Monday, Ascension Day, Pentecost, Pentecost Monday, Christmas and Boxing Day; New Year's Day, King's Day (formerly Queen's day) and Liberation Day (once every 5 years) are non-religious holidays.

[9] New Year's Day, Good Friday, Easter Monday, Early May Bank Holiday (May Day), Spring Bank Holiday, Summer Bank Holiday, Christmas Day, Boxing Day.

[10] Pitt, 'Religion or belief: aiming at the right target?' in H Meenan (ed), *Equality law in an enlarged European Union: Understanding the article 13 directives* (Cambridge University Press, 2007) 204.

However, globalisation[11] and 'flexibilisation'[12] demands have altered the landscape and today Christians are also facing challenges in reconciling work and religious observation. The effect of labour market 'flexibilisation' on working time standards is illustrated by various religion-worktime cases in Europe involving Christians. In the Netherlands and in the UK[13] practising Christians object to working on Sundays have filed legal cases. In fact, it may be that white majority workers are in a better position to raise such claims considering their societal and employment status. Conversely, when (minority) workers find themselves in more tentative employment situations, they will be less inclined to raise accommodation issues, which explains the lack of relevant case law in some areas.

II. Belgian Case Law on Religion-Worktime Conflicts

The Belgian Constitution of 1831 devotes a separate clause—Article 20—to the issue of religious time, stating that '[n]o one can be obliged to contribute in any way whatsoever to the acts and ceremonies of a religion or to observe its days of rest'.[14] Courts have held that neither this provision nor Articles 9 and 10 ECHR stand in the way of establishing Sunday as the weekly day of rest; Sunday rest seeks to contribute to the physical and mental well-being of employees and does not force employees to abide by religious traditions connected to Christian traditions nor force upon them any form of religious belief.[15]

Article 20, 5° of the Belgian Employment Contracts Act of 1978 mandates employers to give their employees the necessary time off (without pay) to meet their religious commitments.[16] Parliamentary debates reveal that the legislator sought to give protection to all religions, and not to limit it to specific religions (eg the officially recognised religions) or to certain holidays.[17] But the protection was

---

[11] McCann, n 5 above, 509 ('responses to the pressures of globalization embrace a paradigm of flexibility that valorizes unhealthy and antisocial hours').

[12] Indeed, the notion of 'flexibility' was invented not so much to accommodate workers and their schedules, but to allow companies to meet market demands posed by globalisation and international trade. See European Trade Union Confederation, *The Flexicurity debate and the challenges for the trade union movement* (ETUC, 2007). Of course, the time demands touch all workers, irrespective of any religious affiliation or practice. Women and men with caring duties often face hardships due to time demands.

[13] eg *Copsey* case, n 64 below; *Mba* case, n 68 below.

[14] Article 20 Belgian Constitution.

[15] eg Court of Bergen on 9 December 1994, *Journal des tribunaux* 1995.

[16] Article 20, 5° of the Belgian Employment Contracts Act of 3 July 1978 (*Arbeidsovereenkomstenwet*); See M Claes, *De plichten van de werknemer en werkgever* (Antwerp, Maklu, 2000) 84–85; P De Pooter, *De rechtspositie van erkende erediensten en levensbeschouwingen in Staat en maatschappij* (Ghent, Larcier, 2003) 60.

[17] *Hand Kamer*, 1889–99, 28 March 1899, p 966.

not to be 'absolute', since that could result in a 'disruption' for the company.[18] This accommodation provision has been part of Belgian law since 1900 but has given rise to little case law.[19] Recent case law decisions applying the rule are particularly rare. It seems that few employees (or trade unionists) know about this black letter rule, which has been subject of a minimalistic judicial interpretation.

For instance, in 1989 the Labour Court of Appeal of Antwerp held that Article 20, 5° and 16 (a general good faith provision) of the Employment Contracts Act do not require that a teacher is given time off to exercise his individual religious duties. A teacher was dismissed after missing work on several occasions for religious reasons and relied on Article 20, 5° to argue that his dismissal was abusive. The Court, however, held that this provision did not entitle the teacher to a 'separate holiday arrangement to fulfill individual religious duties'.[20]

A review of post-2010 cases shows that employment termination disputes related to worktime conflicts are rarely taken to the Belgian labour courts. In 2014, one such case did make it all the way to the Cour de Cassation.[21] The case involved a dismissal of a blue-collar worker with a contract of indefinite duration who was dismissed by his employer who cited 'repeated absences' over the course of 10 years' employment. The employee sued the employer for abusive dismissal (ie one which is manifestly unreasonable)[22] and, after initially losing the case, prevailed before the Court of Appeal of Mons and before the Cour de Cassation. The employer argued that various (justified) absences over the course of the employment period, mostly for medical reasons and a large number following a workplace accident, had harmed the company, since co-workers had had to fill in for the employee. However, the facts revealed that absenteeism was likely used as pretext in an attempt to dismiss a long-time employee—who was no longer needed—without a termination payment. The employer was unable to meet his burden of proof to show the disruption of the business organisation as a result of the employee's absences; the employee was considered arbitrarily dismissed and was awarded damages in the amount of six months' pay.

The general rule under Belgian labour law is termination with notice or payment in lieu for employees who have a contract of indefinite duration. Justified absences need to be shown to have genuinely harmed the company before—very exceptionally—an immediate dismissal without payment is accepted. Justified

---

[18] Ann Parl, Senate, 1898–1899, 230.

[19] Act of 10 March 1900; see Roger Blanpain, *Principes de droit du travail* (Bruges, La Charte, 1984) 116.

[20] Labour Court of Appeal Antwerp, section Hasselt, 18 April 1989, *Limburgs Rechtsleven* 1989, 105. For an overview of cases, see D Cuypers, C Meeusen and M Kempen, 'Culturele minderheden in het sociaal recht' in Centrum Grondslagen van het recht-UFSIA (ed), *Recht en verdraagzaamheid in de multiculturele samenleving* (Antwerp, Maklu, 1993), 256 (case law references in fn 95).

[21] Cour de Cassation, 3 February 2014, AR S.12.0077.F.

[22] Under Art 63 of the Law of 3 July 1978 an abusive dismissal (*licenciement abusive/willekeurig ontslag*) is one which is motivated by reasons unrelated to the conduct and ability of the employee or the company's needs.

absences can only exceptionally lead to immediate dismissals when there are real harmful effects on the company.[23]

No recent case addresses the specific issue of religion-worktime conflicts in the context of a dismissal, yet there are a number of relevant Belgian cases concerning *unemployment benefits*.[24] These cases involve jobseekers who refuse jobs because of conflicts with their religious time commitments; or they involve employees who were dismissed from their job for a similar reason. Their application for unemployment benefits is subsequently rejected, because they are considered to have refused a 'suitable position' and become voluntarily unemployed.

To determine the existence of a 'suitable' employment, a number of reasons are listed under the Royal Decree of 25 November 1991 concerning rules on unemployment.[25] The Cour de Cassation has held that these reasons are not exhaustive; and religious objections made by an unemployed person, even when not listed, can form such criteria to take into account to assess whether the position involved was in fact suitable employment.[26] When an employment position makes the practice of a religion impossible or disproportionately hinders religious practice, the court assumes a moral compulsion (*morele dwang*) which justifies refusal of a job offer.[27] When a jobseeker makes—justified—objections to a job offer based on religious grounds, the job in question was not a 'suitable job' so that the jobseeker cannot be penalised for the refusal to work. But overbroad refusals are problematic and a jobseeker can be sanctioned for not inquiring into the job specifics as well as *possible accommodations*.[28] Indefinite exclusion from unemployment benefits is possible when an applicant makes him or herself de facto 'unavailable for the

---

[23] See a number of unemployment cases holding that job seekers are entitled to refuse job offers or resign from existing positions when they face irreconcilable demands because of their religion. Eg Labour Court of Appeal Bergen/Mons, 8 November 1985 (job which made the observing of Saturday worship by a Seventh-Day Adventist impossible not considered a 'suitable job'). For a more detailed discussion of unemployment disputes pertaining to religion or belief, see K Alidadi, 'Religion at the Intersection of Employment Law and Unemployment Insurance in Belgium, the Netherlands and Britain' (forthcoming 2017) *European Labour Law Journal*.

[24] eg Labour Court of Appeal Ghent, section Bruges, 24 April 1998, AR 96/373 (*RVA v Vanexem*); Labour Court of Appeal Antwerp, section Antwerp, 17 March 2011, AR 2010/AA/246 (*Bleichfeld v RVA*); appeal against judgment of the Labour Tribunal Antwerp, 29 March 2010, AR 09/4923/A.

[25] With regard to this area are relevant: arts 51, 52bis, 53, 53bis, 141, 142, 144 and 146 of the Royal Decree of 25 November 1991 concerning rules on unemployment, *Moniteur Belge*, 31 December 1991, p 29888. (predecessor: Royal Decree of 20 December 1963); arts 22–33 of the Ministerial Decree of 26 November 1991 concerning the application of the rules on unemployment, *Moniteur Belge*, 25 January 1992, p 1593. [arts 51 and 52 § 1 of the Royal Decree of 1991 states that a worker who is dismissed because of his or her 'faulty attitude' (foutieve houding) is considered unemployed because of circumstances dependent on his will (voluntarily), and can be excluded from benefits for 4 to 26 weeks.

[26] See Cour de Cassation, 28 March 1973, *Arresten van het Hof van Cassatie* 1973, 761, *Rechtskundig Weekblad* 1973–74, 1069; Cour de Cassation, 30 January 1984, *Arresten van het Hof van Cassatie* 1983–84, 643, *Rechtskundig Weekblad* 1984–85, 1636. The same was held under the predecessor Royal Decree of 20 December 1963, see Labour Court of Appeal Ghent, section Bruges, 24 April 1998, AR 96/373 (*RVA v Vanexem*).

[27] See Labour Court of Appeal Ghent, section Bruges, 24 April 1998, AR 96/373 (*RVA v Vanexem*).

[28] Labour Court of Appeal Ghent, section Bruges, 24 December 1998.

general labour market', which could be done by placing too-gratuitous require-ments on any jobs one is willing to accept.[29]

Legal disputes regarding religion or belief in the unemployment context in Belgium have also involved, amongst other things, the issue of the Sabbath and involved members of the Seventh-Day Adventist Church and the Jehovah's Wit-nesses. The issue of resting on the job at Ramadan has also come up.

A. Sabbath and Religious Service

A case, which was appealed to the Labour Court of Appeal of Antwerp in 2011, involved Ms Bleichfeld, a Seventh-Day Adventist who had rejected what the state unemployment service (*Rijksdienst voor Arbeidsvoorziening/Office National de L'emploi* (RVA/ONEM)) regarded as a suitable job as a housekeeper.[30] She had told the employer she was merely applying for the job because the employment agency directed her to do so and that cleaning was not her preferred line of work. She had also made religious reservations against working on Saturdays, having stated 'it is hard to find work as a saleswoman, since I cannot work on Saturdays (for religious reasons). The RVA suspended her from unemployment benefits for a period of 20 weeks[31] but also excluded her indefinitely because her religious reser-vations against working on Saturdays were considered to amount to unavailability for the labour market under article 56 § 1,1 of the 1991 Royal Decree. These sanc-tions took into account the fact that the applicant, apart from short work stints, had been receiving benefits for almost 13 years.

The Labour Court of Appeal confirmed the appellant's suspension for the implicit refusal of the housekeeping position, where it was shown that she could have worked around the religious time requirements, but reversed the indefinite exclusion from benefits. The Court held that 'the Appellant, who makes a reserva-tion for labour on Saturdays for religious reasons, is not unavailable for the labour market; she remains available for employment during the remaining workdays (from Monday to Friday)'.

Another case, decided by the Labour Court of Appeal Ghent in 1998, involved Ms Vanexem, a Jehovah's Witness who was excluded from benefits because of a stated unwillingness to work during weekends 'for personal reasons' meaning reli-gious duties to attend Sunday public meetings, watch tower study meetings, and making house visits.[32] The employment agency had proposed a part-time bakery

---

[29] ibid. Indefinite exclusion, unlike temporary suspension, is however a very exceptional sanction, and in religious objection cases is rarely accepted as being appropriate.

[30] Labour Court of Appeal Antwerp, section Antwerp, 17 March 2011, AR 2010/AA/246 (*Bleichfeld v RVA*); appeal against judgment of the Labour Tribunal Antwerp, 29 March 2010, AR 09/4923/A.

[31] See limits on suspension periods set under Art 51 and art 52bis, § 1, 2° of the Royal Decree of 1991.

[32] Labour Court of Appeal Ghent, section Bruges, 24 April 1998, AR 96/373 (*RVA v Vanexem*).

job under a schedule (25 hours a week, spread over 5 half days, including the weekend) which may have included weekend work. The RVA had adopted a similar sanction as in the Bleichfeld case: a suspension for 26 weeks and an indefinite exclusion.

Ms Vanexem prevailed before the first instance Labour Tribunal in Ieper,[33] which found the bakery job to be unsuitable because it conflicted with applicant's religious duties. Also, the proposed schedule was considered not to conform with a 'generally common work schedule' since it entailed weekend work. In contrast, the Labour Court of Appeal of Ghent reversed this finding, and in a rather exceptional move, found even the indefinite exclusion from benefits justified in this case. First, it scrutinised more closely both the actual religious commitment of the applicant as well as the proposed work schedule, failing to find any conflict between the two. Secondly, it reassessed the consequences of refusing all weekend work. The Appeal court first discussed the nature of applicant's religion, finding that all religions fall under the protection of Article 9 ECHR which has direct vertical effect:

> No distinction can be made in this respect according to the religion the unemployed person practises. It is not up to the judge to make reservations regarding religious convictions with a *possibly sectarian character* as long as 'public order, health or morals or the protection of the rights and freedoms of others' is not endangered. However, it does not suffice to merely state one adheres to a certain religion: the court should be able to verify whether the unemployed person has thus far taken seriously the principles which he is now asking the government to take seriously (emphasis added).

In this case, Ms Vanexem was found to be a genuine religionist, evident in part by her signing a declaration that she does not wish to undergo blood-transfusions.[34] But in the next step, assessing the extent of the religious commitments involved, the Court accepted the duty to attend Sunday afternoon 'public meeting' and 'watch tower study' explained in a brochure offered into evidence, but found it made no reference to a duty to make house visits on Saturday or on Sunday-morning. In addition: 'These house calls cannot be considered on the same footing as the activities on Sunday afternoon. It is clear that this *proselytism does not belong to the nucleus/core of the religious praxis* (emphasis added)'.[35] What's more, the bakery job, which the applicant had blankly rejected without asking about the specifics, in fact may or may not have included a Sunday afternoon shift or even weekend work:

> On the contrary, since the position was only for 5 half days, it is very likely that this [having to work on Sunday afternoon] would not have been required. It is even possible that the applicant only would be scheduled in one of the two mornings or none at all. *It is*

---

[33] Labour Tribunal of Ieper, 7 June 1996.
[34] Jehovah's Witnesses are best known for their door-to-door preaching and distribution of literature (*The Watchtower* and *Awake!*), refusing blood transfusions and military service and perhaps also for not celebrating birthdays and Christmas.
[35] Judgment, 6.

also possible that she would have been able to negotiate an agreeable arrangement with the employer (emphasis added).[36]

The Labour Court of Appeal also disagreed with the Labour Tribunal that weekend work was not part of today's standard work schedules. Because she had objected to any weekend work without the religious commitments to back this up, Ms Vanexem was seen to have made herself unavailable for the labour market; the fact that she was willing to accept any work during the weekdays could not discount the fact that she was excluding herself from a range of suitable positions.[37]

Juxtaposing the *Bleichfeld* and the *Vanexem* cases may yield an interpretation that refusing Saturday work is ok, but refusing all weekend work is going too far. However, on closer examination the reason why Ms Vanexem was found to be unavailable for the labour market was not because not enough positions remained available when setting reservations against any weekend work (in fact, for the court sufficient positions did remain), but rather because it was considered unwarranted to refuse *any and all* weekend work in her circumstances. In other words, a real conflict with her religious obligations was lacking. Such conflict must also be proven in case of requests for accommodation; and despite the fact that it is not up to courts (or employers) to assess the concrete details of religious duties, in order to provide accommodation the extent of the conflict must be known in order to be able to work towards an effective accommodation. The question is: what happens if justified religious commitments are so stringent that very few positions remain available? In Great Britain, sincerely held religious/conscientious beliefs or objections are good cause for restricting one's availability for some positions *as long as* there remain 'reasonable prospects of employment'.[38]

It is not entirely clear to what extent religious time requests *should* be accommodated, eg which business reasons form acceptable grounds for refusing religious time requests, yet if jobseekers could be penalised if they do not explore accommodation options, certainly, it would seem contradictory to then insist that employers have no duty whatsoever to provide certain accommodations. Yet, this seems to be the situation indeed: accommodations by employers would be entirely voluntary (and could thus be outright refused) but jobseekers must still engage in accommodation negotiations or else run the risk of being denied unemployment benefits.

An explicit duty of reasonable accommodation would also strengthen the Court's/RVA's argument that the employee should have tried to negotiate an accommodation and not simply presume that they would not be hired because of religious dress or duties on the Sabbath. Denying the duty of employers to make any reasonable accommodations for staff on the basis of religion or belief stands

---

[36] Judgment, 7.

[37] Article 51 Ministerial decree requires availability for 'all suitable positions', so setting conditions that are not justified taking into account the criteria for suitability means making oneself unavailable for the labour market).

[38] Jobseeker's Allowance Regulations 1996, section 13(2).

in stark tension with the argument that the applicant should not have presumed he/she would be rejected for a position (eg because of a headscarf or a conflict with a religious time commitment) and is rightly sanctioned for such a self-handicapping 'presumption' to avoid rejection.

B. Resting During Ramadan

A 2011 case before the President of the Labour Court of Antwerp involved the issue of resting during Ramadan.[39] The RVA had suspended a Muslim blue-collar worker from unemployment benefits for eight weeks after he was dismissed by his previous employer, with notice, for allegedly sleeping on the job.[40] The man said he was merely resting on a couch, because he was not eating or drinking during Ramadan, but the President of the Labour Court held that 'the individual religious creed (*geloofsbelevenis*) of the worker, some Muslims do eat and drink at work, cannot justify not doing one's work'. However, because the applicant had been employed for four years, the president reduced the suspension to the minimum of four weeks. The decision had little regard for the position of the worker and the potential for accommodation, which would have avoided dismissal of an employee with four years' work history. The lack of accommodation left a tired Muslim worker who has to perform physically challenging labour during Ramadan in a bind, arguably unnecessarily, since allowing reasonable rest breaks or shifting working time might have prevented the unemployment situation.

Overall, what these cases indicate is that religion-worktime conflicts do lead to dismissals but that employees are hesitant to challenge the dismissal on this ground in court; they instead apply for unemployment benefits and may appeal the negative decisions of RVA/ONEM.

Although such unemployment benefits disputes are handled by the labour courts (where an employer representative sits on the panel), employers are not party to such cases: it is a case between the unemployed person and the RVA/ONEM. Consequently, employers do not feel the effects of such litigation and may be oblivious to the ramifications of a potentially discriminatory dismissal. If a religious employee or jobseeker is denied benefits, one may argue that he or she faces a double exclusion, both on the European labour market and when it comes to entitlement to state unemployment benefits. Yet 'accommodating' too much in the area of unemployment benefits, while having the benefit of providing a safety net which can be crucial in the short term, may end up legitimising (and subsidising) forms of employment exclusion in the long term.

---

[39] President of the Labour Court Antwerp, 6 June 2011, AR 11/673/A (*Said v RVA*).

[40] Reference was made to arts 51 and 52 § 1 of the Royal Decree of 1991 which states that a worker who is dismissed because of his or her 'faulty attitude' (*foutieve houding*) is considered unemployed because of circumstances dependent on his will (voluntarily), and can be excluded from benefits for 4 to 26 weeks.

III. Dutch Case Law on Religion-Worktime Conflicts

The Dutch Working Time Act of 1995, which aims to protect employee health, safety and well-being while allowing a 'healthy combination of work, private life and caring responsibilities',[41] establishes Sunday as the day of rest. Article 5: 6 of the Act prohibits Sunday work and requires employers to organise the work so that employees are free on Sundays, unless the nature of the work requires it (eg hospitals, restaurants and the fire service) *and* the employee has agreed to work on Sundays.[42] Sunday work is also possible when company circumstances render it necessary and the employer obtains the approval of the works council, as long as the employees involved give their consent as well.[43] Thus, employees can never be forced to work on Sundays. What's more, the employee therefore need not refuse for religious reasons. A number of Dutch judgments relate to this strict Sunday rest protection.[44]

Other cases involve the days of rest of minority religions and show the contrast in legal protection with that of Sunday rest. The Supreme Court of the Netherlands (*Hoge Raad*)—in a 1984 landmark case that first applied the fundamental right to freedom of religion and non-discrimination to a private dispute—has held that an employer may not refuse a timely request for time off to celebrate an important religious holiday, unless the running of affairs would be seriously hampered.[45] In the case, a Muslim employee had asked for a day off because he wanted to celebrate the Islamic sugar feast (*Eid al Fitr*). The court, noting the difference between 'generally recognised Christian holidays' and religious holidays of other faiths,[46] acknowledged the individual and societal interests in observing religiously significant days. Since this case, provisions regarding Ramadan and other minority religions have been collectively negotiated and included in collective labour agreements. Also, this has led to an employee-favourable body of case law.[47] For instance, a court held that a Jewish salesman whose request for time off during the Sabbath was rejected and who

---

[41] Dutch Working Time Act (*Arbeidstijdenwet*) of 23 November 1995.

[42] Article 5: 6. 1. Working Time Act. This right to free Sundays has been enshrined in Dutch law since 1907. See WA Zondag, *Religie in de arbeidsverhouding. Over religieuze werkgevers en religieuze werknemers* (Uitgeverij Paris bv, 2011) 9 et seq.

[43] Article 5: 6. 2. Working Time Act.

[44] District Court, sub-district judge Gouda of 12 December 1996, Prg 1997/4697; District Court Rotterdam, 6 February 2006, *Jurisprudentie Arbeidsrecht* 2006/7; District Court Assen 1 July 2002, *Jurisprudentie Arbeidsrecht* 2002/189 (*Stichting De Thuiszorg Incare*).

[45] Supreme Court of the Netherlands, 30 March 1984, *Inan/de Venhorst*, NJ 1985, 350.

[46] It held that the generally recognised Christian holidays are days which Dutch society accepts as days of rest irrespective of the faith of the employee. See discussion and critique in Zondag, *Religie in de arbeidsverhouding. Over religieuze werkgevers en religieuze werknemers*, n 42 above, 15.

[47] Contra District Court Gravenhage (The Hague),19 January 2000, JAR 2000/97 (request rejected of an employee who sought to either start later or have the late Sunday shift or take leave so that he could participate in church service twice on Sunday).

then failed to show up on a Saturday he was scheduled to work should not have been summarily dismissed.[48]

Religious time conflicts have also figured prominently in the quasi-jurisprudence of the Dutch Equal Treatment Commission (ETC) and its successor, the Netherlands Institute for Human Rights. The ETC has repeatedly held that the Sabbath of religious employees, including Jews and Seventh-Day Adventists, needs to be protected.

The ETC routinely performed a detailed assessment to see if an employer's time demand or a refusal to accommodate is justified. Illustrative of its reasoning was the case of a devout Christian who was denied a lock-keeper position because he would not be available for work on Sundays.[49] He claimed this treatment amounted to indirect discrimination on the ground of his religion, and the ETC agreed so that the employer needed to put forward an objective justification to justify the requirement for staff to be available for work on all days of the week. The objective justification test, as it often does, turned on the 'necessary' element; the employer was not able to provide a convincing argument why the accommodation of a single lock-keeper who does not wish to work on Sundays would give rise to operational problems. Though this judgment leaves room for a different outcome in other cases, depending on the actual possibilities for the employer to accommodate the needs of an employee without running into operational difficulties, the message is clear: a worker has a presumptive right to be accommodated so he can observe his Sabbath or day of rest. An employer who cannot put forward compelling reasons for not accommodating this need discriminates on the ground of religion. Accommodation thus allows the rule which has an indirectly discriminatory effect on particular religious groups to be maintained.

While the demand that workers be available for both early and late shifts constitutes indirect distinction as well, in certain situations (and for a limited amount of time) this can be justified.[50] Another case involved a Muslim applicant who was refused by a temp agency for a three-week assignment as a warehouse employee because he would not be available every Friday, when he planned on attending Friday prayers at a mosque. He had asked whether he could leave early or start later on Friday once every two weeks. The case also mentions that the applicant prayed five times a day but that this did not form a problem since he would be able to utilise break time and make use of an available on-site prayer space (the employer also adjusted breaks for Muslim employees during Ramadan). However, the employer regarded the availability for both shifts during the short time-frame to be a 'fixed requirement'. The ETC assessed the availability requirement under an indirect distinction test; there was no direct reference to the applicant's religion

---

[48] District Court, subdistrict judge Haarlem, 2 July 2004, *Jurisprudentie Arbeidsrecht* 2004/176.
[49] ETC, nr 2006-147.
[50] ETC nr 2010-101. The two shifts were Monday to Fridays from 5.30 am to 2.00 pm and from 2.00 pm to 10.30 pm.

but the rule did place Muslims who wanted to attend Friday prayers at a particular disadvantage. The ETC held that this requirement served a legitimate aim and that it was necessary and proportional considering that 30 temporary workers were being hired for a special project to be completed within a short time-frame and staff presence from beginning to end of one of the shifts was need for a smooth transfer of tasks.

It was 'technically' impossible to take individual requests into account during this period but the employer had indicated he would be willing to accommodate reasonable time requests afterwards. Interestingly, there had been a lack of clear communication; the applicant said that had he known complete availability was only needed for three weeks, he would have been willing to forfeit the Friday mosque visits for that limited time period. The ETC, however, held that it was up to the person asking for accommodation to clarify the scope of the request, and not up to the employer or temp agency to look into this for every individual candidate. One can question, however, whether a better outcome would have been possible: particularly, if more information had been given at the time the man required into potential time adjustments. As far as accommodation dialogue is concerned, one would hope there is some back and forth as far as information sharing is concerned, and it is not entirely up to the candidate to (re)formulate requests without knowing the legitimate needs of the employer.

The reason for requesting time off should actually be based on a religion or belief. In a 2010 case the applicant had refused to work on Second Easter day (Easter Monday) not because of religious reasons but because he 'was of the opinion that Second Easter day should be a free day one gets to spend with family'.[51] The ETC stated that for a 'belief' to be covered, there needed to be a 'somewhat coherent system of ideas, related to fundamental convictions about human existence'.

On 2 February 2012, the ETC confirmed an implied reasonable accommodations duty in a religious time off request. The case involved a saleswoman of a travel company who wanted to have Sundays off to observe her religious duties.[52] The employer was found to have discriminated on the basis of religion by refusing to offer her a subsequent employment contract because of the refusal to work Sundays. Even if there were good reasons for requiring staff to work on Sundays (to meet client demands in the travel industry), the employer had some 150 employees and only wanted to be open eight Sundays a year under a new scheduling system. In these circumstances, the request of a single staff member to be exempt from work on Sundays could easily be met.

Soon after its establishment in 2012, the Netherlands Institute for Human Rights confirmed this approach in three opinions involving a Jewish applicant who was refused an internship at a security company—which required 24/7 availability from its security staff—because he was unavailable for work on

---

[51] ETC nr 2010-160 (no 'belief' at stake).
[52] ETC opinion nr 2012-24, 2 February 2012.

Saturdays.[53] The complaint was filed by a mother and her son who were Orthodox Jews and observed the Sabbath. The son wanted to enroll in a training programme for airport security, which included a full-time internship with an airline security firm for 20 weeks (40 hours/week). The problem was that all four companies offering such internship had a requisite that interns be available 24/7, a requirement that the son would not be able to meet. The Institute held that the Sabbath can be considered a direct expression of religious conviction, so that it falls under the protection of the General Equal Treatment Act. Balancing the parties' interests in the given circumstances, it found the Jewish applicant's interest weighty enough to justify an accommodation:

> Considering that [religion] concerns a ground protected under equality legislation, [the security company] can be expected to make some additional efforts to allow the boy to complete a mandatory internship. Such efforts have not been shown. The interest of the boy weighs more than that of the company. He is an intern who has to fulfill a mandatory internship for his programme and is dependent on a limited number of internship companies. It concerns a short internship, the company takes on a small number of interns compared to a large number of regular employees and only schedules in one intern per shift. Therefore, the co-workers will not be taxed and the company can assure complete coverage across the airport. The fear that the company will also have to make exceptions for other employees is unfounded, considering that this involves an intern.

While one can applaud the emphasis on reasonable accommodation efforts, the case in fact downplays a clearly indirectly discriminatory rule (24/7 availability) which is allowed to stand as long as an individual exception is made. In addition, the argument used to dismiss the 'floodgates' concern, supposedly because this concerns an intern and not a regular employee, is hardly convincing. If a rule, practice or provision disproportionately disadvantages a certain group, the rule itself should be reassessed and reformed. Certainly, as long as that is not the case, exceptions should be anticipated. The fact that the case concerns an intern is a foreteller of future challenges: what happens when he and others in his situation apply for a permanent position? One way the rule can be reformed is by including an explicit reference to possible exceptions or accommodations, at least if the legitimate aim and necessity of the rule itself can be shown. However, if there are no compelling reasons to maintain the rule, the rule itself should be scrapped.

In conclusion, Dutch law currently provides very generous—though not equal—protection for the majority and the minority when it comes to religious time requests. Sunday rest enjoys a very high level of protection so that employees—whether religious or not—only work on Sundays if they agree to do so. Conflicts do arise, including when applicants inform an employer that they object to Sunday work during the recruitment phase or in negotiating a contract renewal.

---

[53] Netherlands Institute for Human Rights, 19 November 2012, nr 2012-175; nr 2012-176 and nr 2012-177. See R Holtmaat (ed), *Gelijke Behandeling 2012: Kronieken en Annotaties* (Wolf Legal Publishers, 2013) 211 et seq.

In these cases, courts and the ETC hold *any* penalisation to be discriminatory. The Dutch Sunday rest protection is somewhat of an 'absolute' protection, a variant of which in the United States was struck down by the US Supreme Court in the case of *Thornton v Caldor* (1985)[54] since it was considered to exceed a reasonable accommodation and to unduly promote religion contrary to the Non-Establishment Clause of the First Amendment to the US Constitution. This protection can be seen to promote practising Christians over religious minorities who observe another day of rest (eg Seventh-Day Adventists and Jews). Non-believers may also object to such regulation which they consider unjustified in a secular society.

The protection for religious minority days of rest or time accommodations is not identical, but still elevated. In principle, religious time accommodation requests should be granted as long as they do not seriously disrupt the running of the organisation or business. Dutch employers are required to show flexibility in this regard. In addition, the Dutch dismissal permission system (*ontslagtoestemming*) adds a procedural guarantee to enforce these rights. Under this system, the permission of the Minister of Social Affairs and Employment—via the regional labour office *UWV WERKbedrijf*—is to be obtained before a contract for an indefinite period can be terminated (at least for certain categories of workers).[55] Therefore, the rules are bound to be applied rather effectively, as dismissal permits are denied if the underlying reason is a refusal to work Sundays or on other religiously significant days. This, however, does not apply to the most vulnerable categories of worker who will need to rely on employer goodwill.

IV. British Case Law on Religion-Worktime Conflicts

Long before Brexit, the UK stood apart in the European Union when it came to the issue of working time since it opted-out of the EU Working Time Directive, which caps the working week at 48 hours and includes other worker protections.[56] Average working hours in the UK are high compared to other EU countries (in fact, they are only higher in Romania and Bulgaria).[57]

In contrast to the Netherlands, where Sunday rest is greatly protected for all employees, the UK Employment Rights Act 1996 gives only 'shop and betting workers' the right to refuse to work on Sunday and this irrespective of religion.[58]

---

[54] *Estate of Thornton v Caldor, Inc*, 472 US 703 (1985).

[55] A dismissal which is not preceded by a request and award of such permission is voidable. See Art 6 of the Decree on Labour Relations of 1945. Uitvoering van de werknemersverzekeringen (UVW).

[56] Owen Jones, *Chavs. The demonization of the working class* (Verso, 2012) 160.

[57] ibid, 160.

[58] Employment Rights Act 1996, Part IV, ss 36–43. These workers are covered unless they were specifically hired to work only on Sundays.

Other employees have no particular enforceable rights to refuse Sunday work,[59] notwithstanding some potential ramifications of human rights and non-discrimination law. Requests for time off to observe religious obligations are addressed under the indirect discrimination framework, but under a more lenient justification test than in the case of religious dress.

The ECHR framework had been ineffective in addressing the needs of religious (minority) employees. In fact, ECHR law in this area was considered controlled by a number of cases from the UK,[60] where rather modest accommodations were denied and where the ECtHR refused to extend protection under Article 9 ECHR under the then-dominant 'freedom to resign' doctrine.

In contrast, the example of sex discrimination law, which has been interpreted to allow mothers to adjust their working schedules so they can reconcile their job with caring duties, shows that non-discrimination law has indeed been 'a source of rights for individual workers to influence the scheduling of their working hours'.[61] In the leading UK sex discrimination case of *London Underground Ltd v Edwards* (1997)[62] a veteran female train operator and a single mother faced hardships following the overhaul of the London Underground rostering system. Ms Edwards was forced to resign and sued her employer under the Sex Discrimination Act 1975. Both the Employment Appeal Tribunal and the Court of Appeal found in her favour because the proportion of female train operators who could comply with new rostering arrangements was 'considerably smaller' than the proportion of male train operators (20 of the 21 total female operators versus all 2,023 male operators). Ms Edwards' personal inability to comply was thus sufficient to prove a disparate impact on women.[63]

The Court of Appeal held that employers can adapt work schedules but need to be attentive to potential hardships for their staff. The court clearly would have wanted to see a reasonable time accommodation and found the employer's inflexible approach towards Ms Edwards indefensible. Linking the two, it held that 'the more clear it is that the employers unreasonably failed to show flexibility in their

---

[59] See also Sunday Trading Act 1994 and the Christmas Day (Trading) Act 2004 (restrictions on opening hours of 'large shops'). There is an exception on Sunday trading restrictions for Jews (and no other religious group) previously under the Shops Act 1950, section 53, and under the Sunday Trading Act 1994, Schedule 1, section 2(2)(b) *iuncto* Schedule 2, Part II.

[60] *Ahmed v United Kingdom* (1982) 4 EHRR 126: Muslim school teacher seeking time off to attend Friday prayers at local mosque; *Stedman v United Kingdom*, Application no 29107/95 (EComHR, 9 April 1997) (Christian travel agent refusing to work Sunday shifts).

[61] Deirdre McCann, 'Decent Working Hours as a Human Right: Intersections in the Regulation of Working Time' in C Fenwick and T Novitz (eds), *Human Rights at Work: Perspectives on Law and Regulation* (Oxford, Hart Publishing, 2010) 521.

[62] *London Underground Ltd v Edwards (No 2)* [1997] IRLR 157.

[63] The Court of Appeal held that 'It is not appropriate to lay down a rule of thumb defining what amounts to a proportion which is "considerably smaller" for the purposes of determining the potentially discriminatory nature of a requirement or condition'. Here, one woman being affected (the complainant) was sufficient. However, corroborating elements included the fact that no man was apparently inconvenienced and the sociological fact that women are more often single parents.

employment practices, the more willing the tribunal should be to make a finding of unlawful discrimination'.

Interestingly, the new rostering scheme could also have created problems for Christian workers since under the new system Sunday had become part of the working week. At the time of the dispute (in 1992), there was no legal protection against indirect religious discrimination in the UK, so that the fundamental right to religious liberty would have been the only framework for religious employees to turn to. However, the then-standing 'freedom to resign' doctrine stood in the way. Thus, had Ms Edwards objected to the Sunday as a workday or to the shift based on religious reasons, she most likely would not have prevailed. What's more, even today, it is not crystal clear that a religious Ms Edwards would in fact prevail in court, even though the legal instruments and case law have considerably advanced.

Religious time conflicts have involved both Christians and religious minorities, notably Muslims and Jews. Perhaps the most well-known recent religion-worktime conflict case in the UK is *Copsey v WWB Devon Clays Ltd* (2005).[64] The case, called a 'bellwether for future developments'[65] in the area of religious time conflicts, concerned a Christian shop worker who did not want to work on Sundays. Following an increase in work demand, the employer had introduced a shift change, from a traditional Monday to Friday schedule to a seven-day schedule. This eventually led to the constructive dismissal of Mr Copsey, a practising Christian.

Copsey was not a discrimination case since at the relevant time the Employment Equality Directive had not yet been implemented in the UK. The Court of Appeal reviewed the case under the law on unfair dismissals and human rights law (Articles 9 and 14 ECHR). The Court of Appeal found no unfair dismissal; the dismissal was considered justified due to the employer's economic needs and the same condition applied to all employees (formal equal treatment). Further, the Court of Appeal—with three Lord Justices issuing their own reasoning—held that the requirement to work on Sundays was not in violation of Article 9 ECHR, adopting the argument that Mr Copsey was not dismissed because of his religious beliefs, but rather because he had refused to agree to the new employment terms and conditions. Lord Justice Mummery explicitly referred to the 'freedom to resign' argument used by the ECtHR. It was, however, also noted that the employer had consulted widely and tried to find alternatives for Mr Copsey. The Court of Appeal left explicitly open whether the issue would be different under the forthcoming EU non-discrimination regulation.

The *Copsey* case outcome was unfortunate as it failed to consider the employee's religious needs, but in light of the 'freedom to resign' doctrine, hardly surprising.

---

[64] *Copsey v WWB Devon Clays Ltd* [2005] EWCA Civ 932; [2005] IRLR 811. Mr Copsey was represented by Paul Diamond, a controversial religious rights barrister who has been involved in various significant cases including *Eweida* and *McFarlane*. *Eweida and Others v UK*, Application nos 48420/10, 59842/10, 51671/10 and 36516/10 (ECtHR, 15 January 2013); *McFarlane v Relate Avon Limited* [2010] EWCA Civ 880, [2010] IRLR 872.

[65] McCann, 'Decent Working Hours as a Human Rights: Intersections in the Regulation of Working Time', n 5 above, 525.

Commentators argued that the outcome would be different under the (indirect) discrimination framework. For instance, Pitt wrote that '[i]t is inconceivable that the same approach could be taken under the [Employment Equality] Directive'[66] and anticipated a different outcome under a fairly strict objective justification test:

> The stipulation that the employer should have to show that the practice having an adverse effect is objectively justified as an appropriate and necessary means of achieving a legitimate aim suggests that a fairly high standard of objective justification will be required. This further implies that national courts and the CJEU should not follow Convention case law in this particular context.[67]

However, in a 2013 case which received wide media coverage, the Court of Appeal rejected the indirect discrimination claim of Ms Celestina Mba, a practising Baptist employed by the south London borough of Merton.[68] Ms Mba was a childcare worker who provided respite care for children with severe learning difficulties in a home run by the London Borough of Merton Council.[69] When she had taken up her position in 2007 a manager agreed to exempt her from any Sunday duty, but she was later pressured to take up Sunday shifts or face disciplinary action. She offered, to no avail, to take up night shifts and Saturdays. The dispute over Sunday work led to Ms Mba resigning from her job and suing the Council for religious discrimination under the UK Employment Equality (Religion or Belief) Regulations 2003. Her claim was dismissed by the London Employment Tribunal, which referred to her contractual obligation to work on Sundays and failed to see Sunday observance as a core component of the Christian faith. Her argument that Muslim workers were treated more favourably and given time off for Friday prayers was rejected.[70]

The Employment Tribunal (ET) decision was essentially confirmed by the Employment Appeal Tribunal although it was said that part of the ET decision was 'inelegant in its phraseology'. Ms Mba, supported by the Christian Legal Centre, then appealed to the Court of Appeal. She objected to the arguments that the Merton Council had made efforts for two years to accommodate her, despite her contractual commitment towards weekend work, so that she was able to attend Sunday worship, and that the Sunday observance was not a core component of the Christian faith even if it was deeply held.[71] She argued that she had a verbal agreement with her employer that she would not be scheduled on Sundays but that a

---

[66] Pitt, 'Religion or belief: aiming at the right target?', n 10 above, 217.

[67] ibid, 217.

[68] *Mba v Mayor and Burgesses of the London Borough of Merton*, [2013] EWCA Civ 1562. While this is a public sector case, its holding would not change on the mere fact that it involved a private sector employer.

[69] O Bowcott, 'Christian care worker who did not want to work on Sundays loses legal fight', *The Guardian*, 5 December 2013: www.theguardian.com/law/2013/dec/05/christian-care-worker-sundays-legal-fight.

[70] www.bbc.co.uk/news/uk-england-london-17143627; www.cm-murray.com/2012/02/23/sunday-working-%E2%80%93-a-day-of-rest/.

[71] According to Elias LJ, these objections raised by Ms Mba were 'essentially makeweight considerations in the justification analysis of the Employment Tribunal'.

management change had led to her being given Sunday shifts despite her offer to take unpopular shifts and work anti-social hours. The Court of Appeal confirmed the outcome of the ET and EAT decisions, even if it did find certain legal errors in the reasoning. Significantly, the Court of Appeal held, contrary to the Employment Tribunal, that Sunday observance should be considered 'a core component of the Christian faith',[72] making the case partially victorious for both parties.[73]

However, the employer had adequately shown that the—indirectly discriminating—measure was necessary and proportionate towards a legitimate aim of having sufficient employees to fill its work rotas.[74] There was no other viable or practicable way of running a children's care home effectively and the fact that Ms Mba's job description included a specific weekend work provision bolstered this.

Thus, unlike in the Netherlands, a UK employer can adopt a provision or institute a practice requiring its workers, despite their religious objections, to work on Sundays as long as there is a legitimate aim and the requirement is justified and necessary in that context. A contractual provision may bolster the employer's case, but this is neither necessary nor sufficient. In the end, the outcome depends on an ad hoc balancing exercise where the discriminatory impact on the employee must be weighed against the reasonable needs of the employer's business.

The Mba Court gave consideration to the interplay between the human rights and non-discrimination law frameworks; the question was whether the justification hurdle should be less onerous because only a relatively small group would be affected. Lord Justices Elias and Vos both found that the issue whether the belief was widely shared (thus affecting a large group of people) may be relevant to the question of justification under the aspect of proportionality. However, how widely held a belief might be or whether it is a 'core belief' is irrelevant for the purposes of determining proportionality, since Article 9 does not require any test of group disadvantage and concentrates only on the religious freedom of the individual, and domestic anti-discrimination legislation must be interpreted in a way which is compatible with Convention rights under section 3 of the Human Rights Act 1998.

Following the announcement of the outcome, the counsel for Ms Mba (Andrea Minichiello Williams of the Christian Legal Centre) told journalists that

> if the court of appeal had been prepared to consider the facts according to the correct test, Celestina would have won. The onus should be on the employer to reasonably accommodate their employee ... However, this judgment is a big step forward for proper treatment of Christians and is an important victory. At last the courts are beginning to

---

[72] This may be considered largely a dated debate, since under *Eweida* there is no need for a protected religious practice to be a 'core' element of one's faith.

[73] O Bowcott, 'Christian care worker who did not want to work on Sundays loses legal fight', *The Guardian*, 5 December 2013 ('Mba—who wore a wristband declaring "Not ashamed of the Gospels"—described it as a "victory"').

[74] E Slattery and E Bowyer, 'Court of Appeal confirms contractual requirement to work on some Sundays was justified', 9 December 2013, www.lexology.com.

demonstrate greater understanding of what it means to be a Christian. Many Christians will now be able to argue their employer must respect their rights of Sabbath worship.[75]

In contrast, the National Secular Society president (Terry Sanderson) said that a win for Ms Mba would

> have potentially brought chaos to the workplace with those of all religions having their day off too. Religious requests should only be accommodated at work *where it is practicable and fair to all*. Employers should be able to refuse accommodation where it would impede efficiency and indeed, viability of their business or result in discrimination against other workers, for example on weekend working or holidays (emphasis added).[76]

The latter response may overlook the fundamental rights implications of religion-worktime requests and prioritise business necessity, but formulated as such it is pro accommodation since economic viability appears to be the only limit. The reticence (or suspicion) regarding the concept of reasonable accommodations, then, seems to mainly derive from a disbelief that all that is required are in fact *reasonable* accommodations. If *reasonable* accommodations are explained and understood properly, perhaps some 'antagonists' could be convinced of their merits.

A good number of religious time claims have been brought under the Employment Equality (Religion or Belief) Regulations 2003 and, subsequently, under the Equality Act 2010.[77] Overall, these cases reflect a pragmatic approach; as long as there is a compelling business interest and certain efforts towards accommodations were made, the employer will prevail. Attempts at finding alternative solutions serve a useful purpose in showing the proportionality of the measure. For instance, *Cherfi v G4S*[78] concerned a Muslim security guard who was refused permission to leave his work premises on Fridays during lunch time to attend a prayer at a nearby mosque. The employer argued business necessity for the refusal, since their customer contract required there to be a certain number of security guards on site during operating hours. Mr Cherfi argued that this requirement placed practising Muslims at a disadvantage and amounted to indirect discrimination. The employer prevailed in his justification defence. The Employment Tribunal and the Employment Appeal Tribunal found the requirement to be necessary and

---

[75] O Bowcott, 'Christian care worker who did not want to work on Sundays loses legal fight', *The Guardian*, 5 December 2013.

[76] ibid.

[77] *Cherfi v G4S Security Services Ltd*, [2011] UKEAT/0379/10 (24 May 2011); *Thompson v Luke Delaney George Stobbart Ltd* [2011] NIFET 00007 11FET (15 December 2011); *Edge v Visual Security Services Ltd* [2006] ET/1301365/06; *Estorninho v Zoran Jokic t/a Zorans Delicatessen* [2006] ET/2600981/06; *James v MSC Cruises Ltd* (ET case no 2203173/05); *Williams-Drabble v Pathway Care Solutions Ltd* [2005] ET/2601718/04; *Mayuuf v Governing Body of Bishop Challoner Catholic Collegiate School & Another* [2005] ET Case no 3202398/04; *Fugler v Macmillan London Hair Studios*, [2005] ET Case no 2205090/04.

[78] *Cherfi v G4S Security Services Ltd* [2011] UKEAT/0379/10/DM (24 May 2011). See also *Mayuuf v Governing Body of Bishop Challoner Catholic Collegiate School & Another* [2005] ET Case no 3202398/04 (refusal to allow a Muslim time off for Friday prayer was justified and not indirectly discriminating, considering the school's teaching schedule demands).

proportionate to a legitimate aim, that is, the operational needs of the business. The employer's proportionality argument was bolstered by showing that it was impossible to find a replacement for Mr Cherfi during the Friday prayer break and reasonable efforts were made to find an alternative solution. In particular, Mr Cherfi had been offered an alternative shift schedule which would allow him to be home on Fridays and there was the possibility to use a prayer room on site, both of which Mr Cherfi rejected.

In cases where the employer prevails, the issue often revolves around showing that (sometimes substantial) efforts have been made to find alternatives which meet both parties' interests. When this is not done, the measure cannot be considered proportionate under the circumstances. The nature of the work and contractual agreements, showing a compelling business need, can also play in the employer's favour. All three factors played a role in *James v MSC Cruises Ltd*,[79] which held that the requirements of occasional Saturday work did have an adverse effect on Seventh-Day Adventists such as the employee, but that this contractually agreed requirement was justified in light of the business need of providing customers' service (selling cruise holidays) and the showing of efforts to find alternative solutions.

In contrast, the employer in *Thompson v Luke Delaney*[80] was unable to show why it was not possible to have other employees cover a Sunday shift from noon to 4.00 pm so as to allow a Jehovah's Witness employee to attend worship services at that time. Here, the employee prevailed in his claim of indirect religious discrimination. The same failure to make efforts towards finding viable alternative solutions was the reason the Employment Tribunal found for the employee in *Edge v Visual Security Services Ltd*.[81] *Edge* involved a Christian employee who objected to Sunday work. While this was flagged at the job interview and presented no problem at the original work site, the problem arose after transfer to another company site where Sunday work was required. The employer showed little effort to find a solution indicating instead that this would be 'simply too much trouble'.[82] The same was the result in *Fugler v Macmillan London Hair Studios*, where the employer made no efforts to allow a Jewish employee to take time off on Yom Kippur, which coincidentally fell on a busy Saturday.

Making no efforts whatsoever towards alternative solutions will significantly weaken an employer's case. On the other hand, employers prevail when such

---

[79] *James v MSC Cruises Ltd* (ET Case no 2203173/05).

[80] *Thompson v Luke Delaney George Stobbart Ltd* [2011] NIFET 00007 11FET (15 December 2011).

[81] *Edge v Visual Security Services Ltd.* [2006] ET/1301365/06.

[82] *Estorninho v Zoran Jokic t/a Zorans Delicatessen* [2006] ET/2600981/06 concerned a similar case with a similar outcome. (Christian chef refusing Sunday work, employer cannot point to particular efforts to find alternative despite existence of a legitimate reason for requiring Sunday shifts; there was a failure to 'discuss the matter with the other chef or look at other ways of covering Sundays'). See also *Williams-Drabble v Pathway Care Solutions Ltd* [2005] ET/2601718/04 (Practising Christian, who objected to a permanent—and non-negotiable—work rota requiring occasional Sunday shifts after having informed the company of her faith commitments when hired, won unfair dismissal indirect discrimination claim).

efforts towards finding a viable alternative can be demonstrated, and can bolster their case by adding the requirement to the employment contract since British courts still have a tendency to give primacy to contractually agreed commitments.[83] Indeed, the British cases reflect a tendency to see employment cases as matters of contract and to accept arguments calling for a flexible workforce and labour market. The challenge is to integrate human rights considerations within this framework, and one can now convincingly maintain that employee protection in religion-worktime conflicts must be stepped up, not only under the anti-discrimination framework, but also under the ECHR since the *Eweida* decision overruled the 'freedom to resign' doctrine.

The Equality and Human Rights Commission advises employers to be generous and flexible when faced with a religious time accommodation request:

> [I]f a Muslim employee requests to use their annual holiday entitlement for the purposes of celebrating Eid, the EHRC Code suggests that the employer accommodates that request where it is reasonable for the employee to be ... it would also need to go on to show that there was no other, more proportionate, way in which that aim could be achieved, for example, by arranging for other employees to cover the work.[84]

In sum, similarly as in cases involving religious dress and grooming, British courts have incorporated a *de facto duty of reasonable accommodation* under the existing anti-discrimination legal provisions so that employers cannot argue it is 'simply too much trouble' to consider alternative solutions. A significant difference is that time demands are still viewed as a contractual matter, while employers cannot justifiably restrict religious dress under contractual provisions (eg a 'neutrality' policy). There is a recognition that religious dress raises human rights concerns, which cannot be abrogated through contractual stipulations. Religious time requests arguably are not considered as such, but more as a practical matter where compelling business interest can be routinely upheld. This affects both Christians and religious minorities in Britain, since only 'shop and betting workers' are protected from having to perform Sunday work. The fairly lenient approach towards employer scheduling policies would not be justified if it were not for the—at times substantial—efforts employers make to accommodate employees who observe certain days of rest or who want religiously significant holidays off. An explicit duty of reasonable accommodation would be a useful addition to British law since it builds on and adds support and clarity to the existing jurisprudence.

---

[83] See, eg, *Mba* case, n 68 above; *James v MSC Cruises Ltd* (ET Case no 2203173/05).

[84] Caroline Stakim and Ian Johnston, 'Religious Discrimination and Muslim Employees' (2013) 25(12) *Employment Law Commentary* 2–3 ('The EHRC Code does not impose legal obligations and it is not an authoritative statement of the law. However, tribunals and courts must take relevant sections of the EHRC Code into account when deciding discrimination claims brought by employees'). The Employers' Forum on Belief (EFB) advises its members similarly: 'It is ... important to be able to demonstrate that other potential solutions were properly considered and that the working hours were not just unilaterally imposed, especially if an employee has previously expressed concerns based on a religious belief'.

V. Conclusion

Modern working time regulation allows individual workers to influence their work schedules for personal, family or societal reasons. Parental leave schemes which allow adjustment or reduction of hours over a certain period are a good example.[85] The case of religious time accommodation, where working time protection is being linked up to a substantive civil-political fundamental right, shows much affiliation with such arrangements as well as differences:

> The working time laws are more direct, however, in that their primary purpose is to enable employees to alter their schedules. They thereby sidestep any question of whether such accommodation is required, which can arise under religious rights ... When this initial hurdle is overcome, however, a number of similarities emerge between claims for hours adjustments that are framed as religious rights and those brought under working time laws.[86]

There can also be significant differences in the scope of application and approach. For instance, the generous accommodation regime under the Dutch Act on Work Hours Adaptations (*Wet aanpassing arbeidsduur* (WAA)) only applies to employers with 10 or more employees[87] and only when an employee has worked for a given employer for at least one year. Also, the employee needs to request the change four months in advance, and there are limits as to how many times an employee can request changes in working time. Such arrangements may be useful for religious employees as well, but various conditions make it less attractive and show the limits in the specific case of religious time conflicts. First, not all religious employees will be able to utilise the above scheme, ie if they work for small employers or have not worked there for at least one year. In addition, if an employee seeks time off during an annual religious holiday it does not make sense to ask for a long-term change in schedule months ahead of time. Religious employees may seek one-off, occasional or repeated shift changes in the cases of a conflict with a religious holiday instead of a structural change in work (like working part-time with significant loss of salary); they should not be forced into the same mold that was not designed with their particular needs in mind. General working time accommodations may thus in some circumstances be useful but they are not tailored instruments which can adequately meet the interests of European employees who seek to reconcile work and religious commitments.

All workers can benefit from protective regulations and protections and thus have an interest in a 'floor of rights', and in the best case these general protections

---

[85] McCann, 'Decent Working Hours as a Human Rights: Intersections in the Regulation of Working Time', n 5 above, 522–23. In the UK since 2003 parents can ask for reduced hours and for working from home. Employment Rights Act 1996 pt VIIIA. But some arrangements apply to all workers; in the Netherlands, see the *Wet op de aanpassing van de arbeidstijd* of 2000.

[86] McCann, ibid, 523.

[87] Article 12 WAA.

and built-in accommodations can—largely—meet the needs of religious minorities. But general, non-specific, protections or accommodations may be either unavailable or insufficient.[88] Also, certain techniques of time regulation will be more useful than others for religious employees: for instance, a right to refuse overtime hours[89] for religion or belief reasons will be more helpful than criteria and maxima for overtime hours or a wage premium for a worker who wants to be able to observe religious days of rest, religious holidays or festivals, or to attend religious services. An employee then needs to turn to *specific* tools under labour law, non-discrimination law, or human rights for a tailored accommodation on the basis of religion or belief. The need for *specific* religious accommodation rights thus depends on a number of factors, including the level or nature of protection available to all workers under the relevant national regime. Under a less protective working time regime, requests from religious workers may come up more frequently, but this may have to do with the general lack of protections for all workers. On the other hand, in a relatively highly protective system, such as in continental Europe, the occurrence of religious time accommodations may point to the inadequacy, from the point of view of religious minorities, of the general majoritarian-oriented labour law protections or it may point to exclusions of certain categories of workers from that general high level of protection.

Under a reasonable accommodations framework, the mandate of religious (time) accommodations may or may not be applicable to very small employers. Under Title VII of the US Civil Rights Act, the reasonable accommodation duty applies to employers with 15 or more employees. In Canada every employer has a religious accommodation duty under the federal and provincial Human Rights Codes, although the size of the employer and other circumstances (such as whether the employee asks for adjustment well in advance or at the very last minute) will figure in when deciding whether or not there is undue hardship.[90] However, there should be no conditions as far as concerns length of existing employment relations or strict time frame within which to request accommodations.

It would be possible to anchor such a right under either EU non-discrimination law, the European Convention (extending the ramifications of the *Eweida* case to religious time accommodations) or general labour law. There are, however, also

---

[88] eg, in the United States the cases of *Trans World Airlines, Inc v Hardison* 432 US 63 (1977) and *Ansonia Board of Education v Philbrook* 479 US 60 (1986) illustrate this; for Canada, see *Central Okaganan School District No 23 v Renaud* [1992] 2 SCR 970 and *Central Alberta Dairy Pool v Alberta (Human Rights Commission)* [1990] 2 SCR 489 (collective labour agreements did not facilitate religious accommodations, but rather impeded them).

[89] This right of refusal is in some countries restricted to particular categories of employee, McCann lists eg pregnant workers, workers with health problems, those with caring duties or young workers; McCann, 'Decent Working Hours as a Human Rights: Intersections in the Regulation of Working Time', n 5 above, 520.

[90] See *Alberta Dairy Pool* case, n 89 above; Christian Brunelle, 'The Growing Impact of Human Rights on Canadian Labour Law' in C Fenwick and T Novitz (eds), *Human Rights at Work: Perspectives on Law and Regulation* (Oxford, Hart Publishing, 2010).

other proposals which would allow for structural accommodation for minority groups. Perhaps a more audacious proposal involves adapting and updating public holiday schedules to reflect the reality of considerable religious and philosophical diversity in European societies. Recognising the most important religious minority holidays would allow at least some employees hassle-free observance of religious duties and reconciliation with work life and would have an additional awareness-raising effect. Constructive proposals for amending laws have been made by expert commissions set up to offer recommendations on how to manage multiculturalism. For instance, the Staci Commission in France and the Roundtables for Interculturalism[91] in Belgium have made such proposals to 'pluralise the holiday schedules', so as to create more systematic ways to accommodate minorities. However, these suggestions were hardly readily accepted and even faced outright rejection and hostility.[92]

Other—more modest—ways for a state to advance this issue include the adoption of generous accommodations for civil servants and publishing the dates of the most important religious holidays of the most common minority religions (eg on an annual basis, in circular letters or other government information methods).[93] A duty of reasonable accommodation, implying a presumptive right to leave for observance of religious duties, forms a necessary 'catch-all' addition to these more structural proposals.

In this context, it can also be noted that the review of the EU Working Time Directive[94] offers an important window of opportunity to address the issue of religion-worktime conflicts, despite the considerable reticence to address a 'sensitive issue'. The 2003 Working Time Directive has a stated aim to 'meet the needs of employers and workers in the twenty-first century, while securing effective protection of workers' health and safety' has (minimum standard) provisions on daily

---

[91] See MC Foblets and C Kulakowski, *Final report Roundtables of Interculturalism (Rondetafels van de Interculturaliteit)* (Brussels, 8 November 2010). One of the most audacious proposals related to the public holiday schedule. It was proposed that the current system be replaced by a better balance between secular holidays (eg Labour Day), Catholic holidays and holidays associated with other religious/ideological traditions.

[92] Some European countries do have systematic accommodation for minorities. This includes Italy (but only for Jews and Seventh-Day Adventists). In Spain there are Agreements with the Holy See, the Protestant Federation, the Jewish Community Federation, and the Islamic Commission allowing for religious time accommodations but this requires the previous agreement between the parties (employee and employer) so that it can remain dead letter if the employer does not agree. Also, the working hours must be made up by the employee without any compensation.

[93] This is notably done in France, see F Fregosi and D Kosulu, *Secular Law, Religious Diversity and Public Space. Controversies, areas of tension and actors' contributions: the case of France* (French sociological report RELIGARE project, 2012).

[94] Directive 2003/88/EC of the European Parliament and of the Council of 4 November 2003 concerning certain aspects of the organisation of working time, [2003] OJ L299, 18.11.2003, pp 9–19 ('Working Time Directive'). The Directive has two forerunners. In December 2010, the Commission issued a second-stage consultation paper asking social partners for their views on changes to be made to the Directive. Communication COM(2010) 801: Reviewing the Working Time Directive (second-phase consultation) of the social partners at European level, Brussels, 21.12.2010.

rest breaks, weekly rest, maximum weekly working time (maximum 48 hours, derogations allowed for, eg religious leaders), annual leave/holidays and aspects of night work, shift work and patterns of work. It remains silent on the issue of religious time, observances and days of rest, despite the fact that no doubt religious diversity adds to the challenges of workers in the twenty-first century. The 2010 European Commission Communication on Reviewing the Directive reveals some of the considerations in favour of *not* addressing this sensitive topic[95] at EU level:

> The question of whether weekly rest should normally be taken on a Sunday, rather than on another day of the week, is very complex, raising issues about the effect on health and safety and work-life balance, as well as issues of a social, religious and educational nature. However, it does not necessarily follow that this is an appropriate matter for legislation at EU level: in view of the other issues which arise, the principle of subsidiarity appears applicable.[96]

Today, labour law protections in Europe and across the world struggle to protect workers in the area of working time. Allowing religious employees to find a balance between religion and work, in particular in the context of globalisation,[97] should be recognised as part of the labour law modernisation challenge. The failure to address the issue in a long-term EU instrument is therefore a missed opportunity.

---

[95] We can observe that religious time accommodations tend not to raise the same type of fundamental rights clashes as religious symbols and requests touching upon the relations between men and women, such as refusals to shake hands and may thus be less 'sensitive' than anticipated. The employee asks to be excused from work to observe religious duties or celebrate a religious holiday. The celebration or observance thus happens elsewhere, away from the workplace (prayer in or near the workplace being an exception). Nonetheless, religious time accommodations face resistance and objections: 'special arrangements' are seen as privileging minorities; they can conflict or compete with other employees' time accommodation requests, including those necessitated by caring duties.

[96] Communication COM(2010) 801: Reviewing the Working Time Directive (second-phase consultation) of the social partners at European level, Brussels, 21 December 2010, 11.

[97] For instance, overtime can be disruptive for parents and those with childcare duties, but can also impact on employees with religious commitments. Deirdre McCann, 'Decent Working Hours as a Human Right: Intersections in the Regulation of Working Time' in C Fenwick and T Novitz (eds), *Human Rights at Work: Perspectives on Law and Regulation* (Oxford, Hart Publishing, 2010) 520.

5

Religious Affiliation Discrimination and Miscellaneous Accommodation

I. Introduction

Issues related to religious dress and religion-worktime conflicts are the most recurrent religion or belief matters that currently arise in the European workplace today. These were discussed in the previous two chapters. This, however, leaves out of the equation a wide array of matters which can arise for employees who hold their religion or belief dear and want to reconcile it with their professional life. At times, issues of religious dress or time can coincide with other accommodation requests, and it may even come as a surprise that multiple issue accommodation does not occur more frequently, since practising religionists will seek to live out their faith in the workplace in various ways.

For instance, an orthodox Jewish employee may want to wear a yarmulke on the job as well as to observe the Sabbath, eat kosher food and avoid physical contact with members of the opposite sex. A Muslim woman wearing a headscarf or a bearded Muslim man may have similar objections to shaking hands with members of the opposite sex, may avoid contact with alcohol or pork and request prayer time and space.[1] A devout Christian may want to make his or her faith visible by wearing a cross and by observing Sunday as a day of rest.[2] Seventh-Day Adventists may object to eating pork or other foods regarded as unclean, or to smoking, while Rastafarians may object to pork but not to all smoking, Buddhists may object to any meat products,[3] and members of the Church of Jesus Christ of Latter-day Saints may object to (some) hot and caffeinated drinks. Other taboo food, drink or social behaviours may conflict with general work conditions or the demands of modern Western life. These may lead to problems with job duties (touching, handling, selling the product) but will also be reflected in more social aspects of

---

[1] See, however, ETC nr 2000-75, 29 November 2000 (objection to serving alcohol by a Muslim woman, who did not wear a headscarf).

[2] See, eg, the *Eweida* case which at the level of the Employment Tribunal also raised the issue of Sunday rest. *Eweida and Others v UK*, Application nos 48420/10, 59842/10, 51671/10 and 36516/10 (ECtHR, 15 January 2013).

[3] *Jacóbski v Poland*, Application no 18429/06 (ECtHR, 7 December 2010).

the workplace (sharing lunch in the canteen, socialising at a work party). While a number of cases have raised such multiple issues, the 'single issue case' still is paradigmatic. Perhaps this points to the fact of considerable 'accommodation' on the side of the employee prior to approaching the employer with an accommodation request. Despite all issues being important to a religious person it may be that he or she decides to 'pick her fight' focusing on what matters most. An obdurate practitioner who rejects any and all compromise and rejects the idea of 'wearing one's religion lightly' will have difficulties fitting into most modern workplaces and may decide at some point to find alternative employment opportunities or pull out of the workforce altogether.

We cannot possibly exhaustively list all 'miscellaneous issues'; though the case law of the Member States offers us interesting and eclectic examples,[4] workplace field studies, NGO reports and other data reveal glimpses of still rare but emerging issues on the ground.[5] For instance, despite there being no cases with regard to objections of female nurses to washing male patients this is a real challenge, at least in the Netherlands[6] and in Belgium[7] and most probably in other countries. The lack of case law on requests for prayer facilities in the employment sphere similarly does not mean the issue is not raised in practice in the Netherlands (where case law has addressed the issue in the education context), Belgium and the UK. Closely connected to prayer facilities is the issue of ablution practices and facilities, one that is equally absent from current case law. Finally, we collected no case law regarding dietary needs, while for many employees, requests for workplace canteen food to take into account religious diets (eg kosher/halal

---

[4] Countries with an equality body which can deliver opinions are a notable source of 'miscellaneous religious issues'. This is the main reason the Netherlands has the widest 'repertoire' of miscellaneous accommodation cases. For a list of such recent accommodation cases across Europe, see Alidadi, 'Reasonable Accommodations for Religion and Belief: Adding Value to Article 9 ECHR and the European Union's Anti-Discrimination Approach to Employment?' (2012) 37 *European Law Review* 693–715 at 697–98.

[5] See, eg, Y Lamghari, 'La neutralité à la STIB' in D Cabiaux et al (eds), *Neutralité et faits religieux Quelles interactions dans les services publics?* (Academia-L'Harmattan, 2014); Tzadik, 'Jewish Women in the Belgian Workplace: An Anthropological Perspective' in K Aldadi, M-C Foblets and J Vrielink (eds), *A Test of Faith? Religious Diversity and Accommodation in the European Workplace* (Aldershot, Ashgate, 2012); S Jonlet, 'Les discours des musulmans sur la place de leur religion au travail' in D Cabiaux et al (eds), *Neutralité et faits religieux Quelles interactions dans les services publics?* (Academia-L'Harmattan, 2014).

[6] See ETC nr 2000-75, 29 November 2000, where a nursing centre intern initially raised the issue that because of her Islamic convictions she could not wash male patients, or serve pork or alcohol. She later changed her stance on the two first issues, and the issue in the case focused on the serving of alcohol to patients. The Dutch Ethics Committee of Nurses and Caregivers in the Netherlands has issued an advisory opinion on this subject in 2010 (*Omgaan met gewetensbezwaren: wie moet de gevolgen dragen?*) [Dealing with conscientious objections: who should bear the consequences?] This advice takes the position that washing patients is a 'core business', which it need not be, and advocates a rather far-reaching exclusionary 'solution' (not admitting candidates into programmes), which obviates the need to request accommodations.

[7] Based on my conversation with a director of a large elderly care facility in Belgium, during training on how to manage diversity for civil servants.

food) will considerably affect their well-being.[8] The fact that these various issues frequently 'stay under the legal radar' is due to coping mechanisms on the ground. At times, such matters do trigger public debate. For instance, in March 2013, a small outrage arose when traces of pork were found in the sandwiches served in the company canteen of the STIB-MIVB, the Brussels Intercommunal Transport Company.[9] The company had ordered an investigation to see whether any horse-meat had found its way to the food in its canteen, but instead found pork gelatin in various sandwich spreads (including tuna salad and chicken salad). Something which usually would not have been a cause for concern was in fact alarming for the many Muslim employees who consciously had opted for such sandwiches think-ing it was halal.[10] The company immediately decided to (temporarily) stop selling these products in its canteen. The union CSC, member of the confederation of the Christian trade unions, was said to be 'outraged and requested compensation for the staff'.[11] The support of the trade union for staff in this matter no doubt relates to the fact that many Muslims work at the STIB-MIVB.[12]

Despite the impossibility of exhaustiveness, it is, however, possible to separate 'miscellaneous accommodation issues' in two main categories and proceed to address some characteristics, challenges and experiences. A first category involves requests for exemptions from or changes to particular job duties. A second category is more loosely tied to concrete job duties, here the (often implicit) expectations that the employee has difficulty meeting (and which employers find problematic) revolve around work circumstances, including socialisation expectations and the use of certain facilities or space. The line is not entirely lucid, and some cases can fall in-between.

A thorough discussion of the topic of religion or belief in the workplace must, however, include two more crucial issues which, strictly speaking, cannot be con-sidered part of (miscellaneous) accommodation issues. These are religious affilia-tion discrimination and religious harassment, the latter relating to social relations

---

[8] Sociological research conducted within the RELIGARE project indicated that in Turkey there are pressures and inconveniences for non-believers/practitioners who wish to eat/drink during the day during Ramadan in some workplaces. Tuğba Tanyeri-Erdemir, Muharrem Erdem and Theresa Weitzhofer-Yurtışık, *Challenges of Religious Accommodation in Family-law, Labour-law and Legal Regu-lation of Public Space and Public Funding*. (Turkish Socio-Legal Research Report RELIGARE project, 2012).

[9] X, 'MIVB zoekt paard en vindt varken in eigen sandwiches' ['MIVB searches for horse and finds pork in its own sandwiches'], *Brussel Nieuws*, 5 March 2013.

[10] The food was thus also not kosher but it was not reported whether there were any Jewish employees.

[11] The request for compensation was attacked in the online comments section as being out of place. Some comments also minimised the issue, or argued that it is up to people to inform themselves about what is in the food they consume.

[12] This consideration dovetails with the sociological research findings of Adam and Rea that groups of religious employees are more easily supported by the trade unions than when the (accommodation) issue involves a few or single 'out of place' religious employees. See I Adam and A Rea, *Culturele diver-siteit op de werkvloer: praktijken van redelijke aanpassing in België* (Brussels, Centre for Equal Opportu-nities and Opposition against Racism (CEOOR), 2010).

in the workplace but with legal specificities meriting a separate discussion. The following sections address these two topics, before proceeding with the miscellaneous issues related to religion and belief in the European workplace.

II. Religious Affiliation Discrimination: The Thin Heart of the Matter?

The concept of religious employment discrimination may conjure up images of a person being treated adversely in the workplace on account of his or her affiliation or beliefs, for instance a job applicant being rejected or a worker being fired because he is a Muslim, a Jew, a member of the Jehovah's Witnesses or the Church of Scientology. Interestingly, such 'straightforward' cases are extremely rare if one looks at the case law in Europe.

Religion is an invisible trait, but one which intersects and overlaps with the more visible characteristics of so-called race and ethnicity. Apart from manifestation of characteristic practices and observances which (serve to) show one's affiliation and beliefs, there are other ways to find out or at least second-guess a person's religion or belief. Of course, some people can more easily hide their religious affiliations than others and many people are presumed to belong to certain religions when in fact they do not. For instance, ethnic minorities from Muslim countries often are presumed to be Muslims.

In one particular area of employment law, the issue of religious affiliation (and often a level of practice) is central. When it comes to recruitment and hiring by religious-ethos companies, religious affiliation may be one of the core requirements for a job position and giving up or not properly maintaining membership status may lead to dismissal.[13] The same religious requirements which may be standard and largely accepted for religious-ethos companies would constitute straightforward cases of direct discrimination on the basis of religion or belief in a mainstream private sector context. It is clear that jobseekers should not be rejected for, and employees may not be disadvantaged because of, their religious

---

[13] See Art 4.2 Employment Equality Directive; Y Stox, 'Religious-Ethos Employers and Other Expressive Employers under European and Belgian Employment Law' in K Alidadi, M-C Foblets and J Vrielink (eds), *A Test of Faith? Religious Diversity and Accommodation in the European Workplace* (Aldershot, Ashgate, 2012); Various ETC and Dutch court cases concern the issue of religious affiliation within religious-ethos companies. eg ETC nr 2012-126, 24 july 2012 (Catholic employee rejected from a protestant school, no violation of the General Equal Treatment Act (GETA) found); ETC nr 2012–156, 28 September 2012 (employee without religion refused at Christian care organisation, no violation of the GETA found); ETC nr 1999-16, 8 February 1999 (religion requirement for a timberman/furniture maker regarded as disproportionate, violation of GETA found); District Court, subdistrict judge Groningen, 18 October 2012, LJN: BY4910 (dismissal of education and administrative assistant because she gave up her membership in the Reformed Church had a legitimate aim but was disproportionate considering her age and length of employment).

affiliation or identity in the strict sense. The most minimalistic protective regime would prohibit discrimination on the basis of religious affiliation; eg the argument that the employee is 'free to resign' doesn't cut wood in such cases. This explains why the ECtHR found a violation of Article 9 ECHR under its old jurisprudence in religious affiliation discrimination cases such as *Ivanova*.[14] The European Court held that 'at the heart of the applicant's case was whether her employment had been terminated solely ... because of her religious *beliefs*'.[15]

Similarly, if the concept of 'religion' under non-discrimination law is regarded as excluding the right to wear religiously distinct dress or to manifest religion in an outward way, direct discrimination would (only) be found in cases where an employer rejects, dismisses or refuses promotion to a person based on his or her religion or mere belief. This is the implication of certain Belgian case law decisions as well as AG Kokott's opinion in the *Achbita* case before the CJEU.[16] In this sense, both human rights law and non-discrimination law protect against such blatant forms of direct discrimination.

Yet it is exceptional that such clear cases can be proven; more 'sophisticated' discrimination has replaced blatant discrimination, at least when it comes to religion or belief.[17] This observation may be considered positive or rather hide an ugly underbelly.[18] The persistence and widespread nature of discrimination in the Belgian employment context, combined with lack of mechanisms which hold discriminating employers responsible, can perhaps best be illustrated by the various temp agency affairs.[19] As significant instances of discrimination, they did not relate to *religious* discrimination as such but had and have significant impact on religious minorities, in particular Muslims. In 2001, the so-called '*Adecco affair*' surfaced after a whistleblower disclosed disturbing practices within this large temp agency: in its internal information systems Adecco maintained separate lists for native Belgians and for foreigners or those with immigration backgrounds ('allochthones'), with the former being coded 'BBB' ('*Blanc-Bleu Belge*', which refers to 'pure-bred' Belgian cows). This system allowed Adecco to carry out employer requests

[14] *Ivanova v Bulgaria*, Application no 52435/99 (ECtHR, 12 April 2007). The claimant was a member of a Christian Evangelical Group known as 'Word of Life' and was fired from her position as a swimming pool manager at a public school after refusing to resign or renounce her faith under pressure.
[15] *Ivanova v Bulgaria*, Application no 52435/99 (ECtHR, 12 April 2007), para 81.
[16] Case C-157/15, *Samira Achbita and Centrum voor gelijkheid van kansen en voor racismebestrijding v G4S Secure Solutions NV*, Opinion of Advocate General J Kokott, 31 May 2016.
[17] The Canadian Supreme Court used such considerations to abolish the distinctions between direct and indirect forms of discrimination in the *Meriorin* case of 1999. *British Columbia (Public Service Employee Relations Commission) v British Columbia Government Service Employees' Union (Re Meiorin)*, [1999] 3 SCR 3 (case on a fitness test for firefighters).
[18] For instance, in the Belgian case there are statistical indications of widespread and structural discrimination in the labour market and various surveys reflect negative opinions of the majority towards ethno-cultural minorities. Employment disparities along ethno-religious lines are a reality in all European countries.
[19] See T Kenis and I Maly, 'Racisme in de interimsector: een straatje zonder einde?' *DeWereldMorgenbe*, 16 December 2010.

for BBB's only; more than a hundred businesses were involved in making such requests, often companies with diversity charters. This was hardly an isolated incident and the same issue has reappeared from time to time but allowed to go on unpunished. In fact, the 2012 Amnesty International report 'Choice and Prejudice' notes that according to a large temporary employment agency with a special unit which records discriminatory requests from customers, 'in one third of such requests, clients expressed a refusal to hire Muslims in general.'[20]

There are a few instances of religion or belief affiliation discrimination. The ETC has handled at least one such incident. In a 2010 case,[21] a member of a very small new Christian religious movement—the 'Orde der Transformanten' in relation to which at one time there was a criminal investigation into the acts of two other members[22]—worked as a legal-administrative assistant for a city, but her contract was not renewed and there were various indications that it was because of her affiliation with the 'Orde der Transformanten'. At first, she had been given a temporary contract instead of a fixed contract, and during evaluations she was informed her contract might not be renewed; reference had been made to her eating habits and her ringtone. At the ETC hearing the city argued that its decision was due to spending cuts as well as alleged problems with her functioning within the team. The ETC found neither convincing: the spending cuts were announced only subsequently to the case and there were no indications of the employee's poor functioning. Since the employer was unable to discharge the shifted burden of proof and convince the ETC that the woman's religious affiliation was *not* a reason for its negative employment decision, direct discrimination was established.

Considering the close ties between religious affiliation discrimination and ethnic/racial discrimination, the *Feryn* case[23] may be seen as on point. The legal battle was initiated by the Centre for Equal Opportunities and Opposition against Racism (CEOOR) following explicit statements in the press made by the CEO of a company installing garage doors that he would not hire any Moroccan employees since his customers did not want a Moroccan entering their home and handling their security installation. Replace the word 'Moroccan' with 'Muslim', which is not a great stretch in the Belgian context, and you get religious affiliation discrimination, an incidence of direct discrimination.

In the Netherlands, a recent—rather bizarre—incident raised the same issue. In 2014, the owner of a small cleaning company (Mr Wesley de Laat of 'Budget Cleaning Brabant') had published a job notice in a local soccer association paper

[20] Amnesty International, *Choice and Prejudice. Discrimination against Muslims in Europe* (2012) 36 ('In the agency's view such requests often stem from a lack of awareness on diversity and non-discrimination').

[21] ETC nr 2010-188.

[22] This movement was set up in 2003 in Hoeven, Noord-Brabant which according to Wikipaedia has a mere 100 members, most of them nudists living in a commune. It can be noted that the Netherlands does not have a sect-watchdog organisation.

[23] Case C-54/07, *Centrum voor gelijkheid van kansen en voor racismebestrijding v Firma Feryn NV* [2008] ECR I-5187.

hoping to recruit 'true Dutch' employees. This attracted widespread attention, indignation and even led to death threats towards Mr de Laat, who appeared on the well-known tv talkshow Pauw & Witteman and defended his stance; he said he operates a 'Dutch company with Dutch employees' and that his own 'market research amongst 10,000 households' indicated that 80 per cent of households preferred Dutch cleaners coming to their house. Citing 'customer needs' in the particular market in Brabant (as opposed to Rotterdam where the 'mentality is clearly different') for a hiring practice which he failed to see as discriminatory, he bragged that his business approach was highly successful—a 'hole in the market'—and he was able to hire nine employees. He argued in favour of openly discriminatory vacancies, saying 'the advantage to such clear job positing is that Khaled or Ahmed often would not apply for the job in the first place'. Instead he considered it hypocritical that some companies give people hope and make them waste time and expense when in the end they reject them under the pretext that they 'don't fit with the company profile'. The affair appeared to have been a hoax[24] but it did get people thinking about the economic incentives for persistent discriminatory practices.

The few instances of direct discrimination on the basis of religious affiliation serve to show that if the limits of human rights and non-discrimination protection are confined to this type of religion or belief discrimination alone, the scope, meaning and significance of the legal protection is rendered extremely narrow.

III. Negative Work Environment and Harassment; Proselytising in the Workplace

Anti-discrimination law protects against various kinds of discrimination, including harassment. Article 2.3 Directive states:

> Harassment shall be deemed to be a form of discrimination within the meaning of paragraph 1, when unwanted conduct related to any of the grounds referred to in Article 1 takes place with the purpose or effect of violating the dignity of a person and of creating an intimidating, hostile, degrading, humiliating or offensive environment. In this context, the concept of harassment may be defined in accordance with the national laws and practice of the Member States.

The core of harassment, including on the ground of religion or belief, is a negative—'intimidating, hostile, degrading, humiliating or offensive'—work environment which violates an employee's dignity. Bullying and hostilities may come from

---

[24] A week after the interview, Mr de Laat argued it had all been a 'publicity stunt', allegedly inspired by the European week against discrimination, and served to show that the media 'just copy everything' without doing their research on a story. T Lankreijer, '"Discriminerende" Wesley de Laat misleidde Pauw & Witteman', *The Post online*, 13 April 2014.

co-workers or customers, but it is the employer who will be held liable if he fails to act appropriately towards such a situation. For further elements, the Directive defers to Member States' law and practices, anticipating different approaches.

Reports and social science research indicate that many religious employees are made to feel uncomfortable when negative comments are directed towards their religion, but often choose to let things lie or address it with their boss, but rarely turn to the courts.[25] Overall, religious harassment case law is rare. One case before the ETC, involving an employment discrimination complaint of a Hindu woman, shows that various forms of discrimination tend to overlap in the case of harassment. In 2011, a Hindu woman argued she was being discriminated/harassed/bullied by her colleagues based on race, disability, gender and religion, by receiving various derogatory comments in the IT recruitment company where she was the sole woman and the only employee of non-Dutch origin (Surinamer) and of Hindu religion.[26] The tensions led to her calling in sick and developing health issues, which upon her return only made the situation worse as they led to insinuations and more harassment. The ETC found harassment based on race and gender to exist since the employer had failed to adequately address the issues raised by the woman, but not on the basis of disability and religion since the witness reports produced did not speak of those forms of comments or discrimination.

In another instance, the ETC also found the harassment of a Muslim employee when, following the September 11 events, a direct supervisor of the employee had said to him 'you are all the same' and the employer had failed to investigate the matter.[27]

Employees can become victims of a negative work environment because of their religion or belief. Conversely religious employees at times can be seen to contribute to such negative environment when their behaviour crosses the acceptable limits of proselytism in the workplace. In the Netherlands, there are two cases involving workers discussing/advocating their faith on the job. One 1997 case involved a Christian hospital employee being dismissed following warnings that he should not share his Christian religious beliefs with the patients (handing out booklets and leaflets, singing hymns, speaking with patients, warning them against specific treatments such as yoga and acupuncture).[28] A 1999 case involved a physiotherapist of Christian faith who expressed her faith at work, inter alia by discussing faith with patients.[29] The employer prohibited the applicant from discussing her faith any longer with patients, former patients and colleagues, and also transferred her to another branch. The employee argued the 'gagging order'

---

[25] eg E Tzadik, 'Jewish Women in the Belgian Workplace', n 5 above, notes several Jewish women receiving negative comments about Judaism and Israel, particularly around the times that conflicts and incidents in the middle-east region are reported.

[26] ETC nr 2011-33, 14 March 2011.

[27] ETC nr 2004-08, 29 January 2004.

[28] ETC nr 1997-148, 23 November 1997.

[29] ETC nr 1999-19, 11 February 1999.

constituted direct discrimination on grounds of religion, but the ETC found that it was not the employee's religious belief as such that was the decisive reason for the measures, but complaints by patients about the way the applicant propagated her belief. The ETC reviewed the case under indirect discrimination on grounds of religion, because the prohibition affected those who propagate their belief in the same manner as the employee affected, finding this indirect distinction, based on the facts and circumstances, objectively justified.

Workplace proselytising cases have also arisen in Britain, but notably not in Belgium. In a public sector case, *Chondol v Liverpool City Council* (2009),[30] the city council was not found to have unfairly dismissed a social worker who had promoted his religious beliefs to service users by proselytising and, in one case, by distributing a Bible. And in an interesting case against a local YMCA, *Monaghan v Leicester Young Men's Christian Association* (2004),[31] it was not considered direct discrimination under the Employment Equality (Religion or Belief) Regulations 2003 to instruct an employee of a multiracial, multi-religious organisation (even one with a Christian ethos) that he should not attempt to convert clients to Christianity. Going by these examples, there is very limited space for employees to proselytise in the European workplace, and employees are expected to 'wear their religion lightly'.

IV. Objections to Job Duties Grounded on Religion or Belief

Religiously or philosophically motivated objections to certain job duties can be 'traditional conscientious objections' or new objections relating to new legal and societal developments ('modern conscientious objections') or formulated primarily by newly immigrated minorities ('multicultural conscientious objections'). Particularly for the traditional kind, specific accommodative legislation has been adopted. For instance, the 1967 British Abortion Act provides an exemption for health personnel who have conscientious objections to carrying out or assisting in abortions.

A. Traditional Conscientious Objections

There is widespread support for such 'traditional' accommodation: when the European Values Study (1999)[32] tested public opinion across Europe on this issue.

---

[30] *Chondol v Liverpool City Council* [2009] UKEAT/0298/08 (11 February 2009).
[31] *Monaghan v Leicester Young Men's Christian Association* [2004] ET Case no 1901839/2004 (26 November 2004).
[32] The European Values Study 2008, however, no longer included this question.

60 per cent of respondents either agreed or strongly agreed with the statement that 'if a nurse were asked to help perform a legal abortion, she should be allowed to refuse on religious grounds'. In the UK, this figure was almost 70 per cent. Other 'traditional' conscientious objections include objections by medical professionals to treatments relating to euthanasia.

In a 2000 ETC case, a female member of the Reformed Congregations—an Orthodox Protestant Church with members mainly in the Netherlands—was interviewed by a hospital for a training/employment position.[33] She had indicated on her written application that she was a conscientious objector and would refuse to participate in abortions or euthanasia as well as other activities related to abortion or euthanasia. During the interview, this was elaborately discussed and she was presented with various situations and asked how she would handle these. She clarified that she would not want to partake in the general care of a woman who was about to undergo or just had an abortion at the hospital (the issue of euthanasia was not discussed), for instance she would not want to shave the woman prior to the procedure or transport her away from the operation room, but would be fine once she was back in the post-op room. The applicant was subsequently refused the position, even though the hospital considered her highly competent. During a phone conversation, she was told the reason for the refusal was that she was 'insufficiently flexible' due to her refusal to partake in the general caring of all patients. The woman argued that the refusal amounted to an unjustified distinction on the basis of her religious convictions. At the ETC hearing it appeared the only issue in dispute concerned her indication that she did not want to transport a woman who had had an abortion from the operation room. The hospital had no issue with the conscientious objections to activities directly related to euthanasia and abortion (in fact 10–20 per cent of its staff were conscientious objectors) and she would not have been asked to partake in any such activities (including shaving women prior to an abortion). Interestingly, at the hearing the woman said that upon consideration she would have no objections to transporting a woman from the operation room as that would not relate to the abortion itself but constitute part of general care and the employer replied that in that case there were no objections to hiring her.

The ETC, however, found that the hospital was justified to take her refusal of post-abortion care into account and doubt the willingness of the applicant to commit to caring for all patients. The ETC hospital had an arrangement for conscientious objectors, which the applicant could make use of, but the ETC failed to see a direct link between the refusal of post-abortion transportation and the religious convictions of the woman. The ETC took advantage of the case to formulate a recommendation to the hospital, which dealt with conscientious objections on a regular basis. The ETC advised the hospital to draft and deliver to applicants *prior to* job interviews a guide clearly stating what is expected of nurses who have

---

[33] ETC nr 2000-13, 21 March 2000.

conscientious objections so that they are informed and can consider their positions in advance.[34]

B. Modern Conscientious Objections

Besides such long-standing conscientious objector cases, advances in LGBT rights (in the form of anti-discrimination laws, same-sex partnerships or marriage)[35] have created new areas of conflict for employees with strongly held religious beliefs. These issues have been most prominent in the public sector, with cases such as *Ladele* in the UK and the *'weigerambtenaren'* affairs in the Netherlands. The ECtHR has held that it falls within the state's margin of appreciation to refuse to exempt conscientiously objecting marriage registrars from having to perform same-sex partnership/marriage ceremonies.[36] The Dutch case shows that in the domain of such sensitive conflicts, the last word has not been said.

In 2008[37] the ETC changed its opinion concerning marriage officers who have religious objections against same sex-marriages, allowing non-discrimination of sexual minorities to trump the right to religious freedom of objecting civil servants. The ETC advised municipalities to adopt a rule against hiring or accommodating objecting registrars in light of the goal to protect gay couples against discrimination by state representatives. Until then, the ETC had considered the lack of accommodation of objecting marriage registrars to be indirect discrimination and inquired into potential alternatives which would allow the objecting registrar to stay on board. Since 2008 though, the ETC considers it objectively justified and proportionate ('as there are allegedly no other less discriminating means available') to exclude marriage registrars who raise conscientious objections to performing marriages and partnerships between same-sex couples. This is a notable and unfortunate shift. Floris Vermeulen notes that Mr Casterman, the chairman of the Commission in the 2008 decision, referred to the earlier stance as 'a pragmatic one in which the CGB just looked at the availability of alternatives rather than take a balance of basic interests'.[38] Ben Vermeulen and Adriaan

---

[34] ETC nr 2000-13, 21 March 2000, see § 4.6.

[35] In 2000, the Netherlands became the first country to legalise same-sex marriages; Belgium as the second country followed suit in 2003 (statutory cohabitation had been possible since 2000) while in England, Wales and Scotland (but not Northern Ireland) this option became reality in 2014.

[36] *Eweida and Others v The United Kingdom*, Application nos 48420/10, 59842/10, 51671/10 and 36516/10 (ECHR, 15 January 2013).

[37] Compare ETC nr 2002-25 (the first such *'weigerambtenaar'* case finding unjustified—disproportionate—indirect distinction and calling for respecting the conscientious objection of a public marriage registrar against same-sex marriages) with nr 2008-40, 15 April 2008 (the legitimate goals pursued by the city justified the far-reaching restrictive measures against conscientiously objecting registrars). The ETC's change of heart was explained in an Advisory Opinion: *Trouwen? geen bezwaar!* (Marriage? No objection!). See CGB Oordelenbundel 2007, 126.

[38] See F Vermeulen and R El Morabet Belhaj, 'Accommodating religious claims in the Dutch workplace: Unacknowledged Sabbaths, objecting marriage registrars and pressured faith-based organizations' (2013) 13 *International Journal of Discrimination and the Law* 113.

Overbeeke criticised the ETC's 2008 reasoning,[39] disagreeing that the earlier decision was made on purely pragmatic grounds: 'Seeing whether alternatives are feasible is not only a pragmatic decision, but also includes striking a balance between different interests and rights'.[40]

Vermeulen and Overbeeke also note that while the ETC attempted to bolster its argument with a human rights argument, this fails. Neither the 'the right to marriage' enshrined in Article 12 of the ECHR nor the equality standards laid down in the ECHR and ICCPR—Vermeulen and Overbeeke note—pertain to same-sex marriages, and while states recognising same-sex marriages are obliged to ensure everyone can get married in the municipality where they live, that does not necessarily imply that all marriage registrars in the municipality should be ready and willing to perform such marriages. Indeed, impromptu marriages are rare; usually some scheduling takes place, allowing for the pragmatic avoidance of confrontational situations. And rarely would so many registrars object as to render the situation of accommodation untenable. Finally, Vermeulen and Overbeeke poke a hole through the ETC's final argument based on EU Directive 2000/78/EG, since this directive only contains a prohibition of discrimination on grounds of sexual preference in *employment cases*, and does not touch on the issue of same-sex marriage. In the end, the ETC's stance is based on moral grounds,[41] and on a shaky legal argumentation.

In contrast, Oldenhuis argues that in (particular public) employment, a level of 'toning down' (*dempen*) is justified and expected; for him that implies that

> a civil servant should officiate at gay marriages, even if he personally, due to his religion, has objections. His 'core business' after all is the officiating at marriages; like that of a notary is to register an act transferring immoveable property.[42]

Agreeing with Vermeulen and Overbeeke, it seems highly arbitrary to depart from the general Dutch approach in indirect discrimination cases—which appropriately looks at the availability of alternatives—for an ideological and hierarchical stance, particularly striking in an instance where state neutrality is considered crucial. The rejection of reasonable accommodation in the name of sexual orientation equality in the case of conscientiously objecting civil servants, and the automatic trumping of one fundamental right over another right, is bound to have—unproductive—effects on the private sector handling of similar conflicts.

When it comes to the private sector, religiously-motivated objections to providing various services to same-sex couples have been similarly raised. Such refusals,

---

[39] ETC annual report 2008, 95 et seq.

[40] See also Vermeulen and Belhaj, 'Accommodating religious claims in the Dutch workplace: Unacknowledged Sabbaths, objecting marriage registrars and pressured faith-based organizations', n 37 above.

[41] The same was said by Flora Lagerwerf, a former CGB member and a former senator for the Dutch Christian Democratic party (CDA): 'The commission expressed its own moral opinion by saying that the behaviour of the civil servant was hardly justifiable. Well, I don't think you should ever do that, your own opinion is not relevant at all'. See ibid.

[42] FT Oldenhuis, *Religie op de werkvloer* (Heerenveen, Protestantse Pers, 2013) 9.

for instance in the frame of a wedding/partnership celebration or in another context, have frequently focused on the business owner(s) but here I am mainly interested in the objecting employees' position and rights. In this sense, *McFarlane v Relate Avon Limited*,[43] involving an employee who raised objections to certain job duties (providing relationship counselling to same-sex couples) can be seen as a foreteller of future developments.[44] Sandberg argued that *McFarlane* is an illustration of the tension between 'new religion law' in the UK and older religion-related laws on the books. The former is facilitative and applies equally to all religious and non-religious beliefs—'seeking to protect religious freedom mainly as an individual right which needs to be balanced against other rights'— while older laws on the books protect(ed) Christianity in the UK while providing some toleration for minority faiths, but with a characteristic 'lightness of touch'.[45] Indeed, the idea behind many 'new religion laws', including the Human Rights Act 1998 which incorporated Article 9 ECHR into British domestic law and the prohibition of religious discrimination under subsequent instruments, is not to protect religion per se but facilitate the free exercise of religion by individuals in different areas of social life. In this sense, this is a positive development. However, the risk is that the 'mechanical' balancing exercise being performed does not fully acknowledge the place that religious convictions take on in the life of an employee. The result in *McFarlane*, the twin case to the equally unsuccessful *Ladele* case,[46] can attest to this: the Employment Appeal Tribunal held that Gary McFarlane, a relationship counsellor who was dismissed for refusing because of his Christian beliefs to counsel same-sex couples on sexual matters, did not suffer discrimination under the then-applicable Employment Equality (Religion or Belief) Regulations 2003 nor was there a violation of Article 9 ECHR. The *Ladele/ McFarlane* twin cases show that there is a de facto exception carved out when it comes to the accommodation of a person whose objection conflicts with sexual minority rights. The laudable British flexibility is abrogated in this case and a hierarchy of rights and values is adopted.

As discussed above, the reasonable accommodation framework allows the balancing of various competing interests and rights, the rights of employees on the one hand and the rights of employers and other parties on the other. There is no reason why some accommodation issues should be exempted from such ad hoc balancing, in particular as an easy, but unsatisfactory, way out of a modern human rights dilemma. The British case, however, shows that concerns over the *Ladele/ McFarlane* scenario have led to a broader abandonment of the reasonable accommodation duty idea. In a July 2011 public statement accompanying its application

---

[43] *McFarlane v Relate Avon Limited* [2010] EWCA Civ 880; [2010] IRLR 872; 29 BHRC 249.

[44] See R Sandberg, 'Laws and Religion: Unravelling *McFarlane v Relate Avon Limited*' (2010) 12 *Ecclesiastic Law Journal* 361, 361–70 (noting that the 'Blair and Brown years', 1997–2010 with the Labour Government in power, produced a large number of 'new religion laws' subsequently resulting in an 'abundance of case law').

[45] ibid, 361.

[46] *Islington London Borough Council v Ladele* [2009] EWCA Civ 1357.

to intervene in the *Eweida* et al cases at the ECtHR, the British equality body, the Equality and Human Rights Commission (EHRC) stated that if given leave to intervene, it would argue for more robust protection of freedom of religion or belief and for 'reasonable accommodations'.[47] The EHRC argued that '[j]udges have interpreted the law too narrowly in religion or belief discrimination claims' and that 'courts have set the bar too high for someone to prove that they have been discriminated against because of their religion or belief'. A staff member (John Wadham, legal group director) was quoted in media reports as saying

> Our intervention in these cases would encourage judges to interpret the law more broadly and more clearly, to the benefit of people who are religious and those who are not. The idea of making reasonable adjustments to accommodate a person's needs has served disability discrimination law well for decades. It seems reasonable that a similar concept could be adopted to allow someone to manifest their religious beliefs.[48]

However, this proposal soon stirred controversy as the cases referred to also included instances of discrimination on the ground of sexual orientation by (Christian) public sector employees. The position pro reasonable accommodation was subsequently dropped, as an obligation to accommodate religious beliefs was seen to jeopardise the rights and status of sexual minorities, prejudicing the ultimate goal of the Equality Act:

> [I]n an indication of the volatility of public debate on the *Ladele* and *McFarlane* cases, the EHRC ... in July 2011 felt it necessary to issue a statement to its stakeholders clarifying that 'under no circumstances would the Commission condone or permit the refusal of public services to lesbian or gay people'.[49]

In the UK setting, growing concerns surrounding the clash with sexual orientation equality in the recent decade have also led to implicit objections to a possible right to reasonable accommodation for religion or belief. At the turn of the millennium, the Parekh Commission recommended

> that legislation be introduced in Britain prohibiting direct and indirect discrimination on grounds of religion or belief. Employers, schools and other institutions should be under a duty to make reasonable adjustments to accommodate a person's religious observance or practice, provided that this can be achieved without undue adverse effects on the employer's business or on the general conduct of the school or other institution. Since many employers and schools do already make reasonable adjustments, the good practice they have developed should be evaluated and shared more widely'.[50]

[47] See D Woods, 'Equality and Human Rights Commission seeks European test of UK law on religious discrimination', 14 July 2011: www.hrmagazine.co.uk/hrc. This followed earlier statements by then chairman of the EHRC, Trevor Phillips, in favour of more robust protection against religion or belief discrimination and reasonable accommodations. J Wynne-Jones, 'Trevor Phillips wades into the debate on religion in modern society', *The Telegraph*, 19 June 2011.

[48] ibid.

[49] See A Donald, *Religion or belief, equality and human rights in England and Wales* (London, Equality and Human Rights Commission, 2012) p 4, fn 6.

[50] The Commission on the Future of Multi-Ethnic Britain, *The Future of Multi-Ethnic Britain* (Profile books, 2000) 240–41. The Parekh Commission was set up by the Runnymede Trust in 1997 'to

In contrast, the Commission on Religion and Belief in British Public Life (in many ways considered a successor to the Parekh Commission) convened in 2013 by the Woolf Institute, failed to address the key issue of reasonable accommodation for religion or belief in its report.[51]

Mr McFarlane's dismissal relied on the new Equal Opportunity and Professional Ethics policy adopted by his employer, Relate (a charity which provided various types of counselling, mediation and training services). However, it was noteworthy that Mr McFarlane was not unwilling to providing counselling to same-sex couples, he only raised conscientious objection when it concerned the discussion of sexual matters. Rather than trying to find ways to reconcile the employee's convictions with the quality provision of its services, the employer decided to put him on the stand. After four years on the job, Mr McFarlane was asked to sign a declaration that he agreed to counsel in same-sex relationships through psycho-sexual therapy in accordance with the Equal Opportunity policy, and went through a disciplinary hearing where he confirmed he would provide such services. However, months later he told his supervisor that he would have difficulties if asked to do so (ie the issue had not arisen in practice in that time). This led to his dismissal. His claim for discrimination and harassment was rejected by both the Employment Tribunal[52] and the Employment Appeal Tribunal. The latter referred to the now well-known paragraph by Lord Bingham in the House of Lords decision in *R (Begum) v Denbigh High School*, that paraphrased the ECtHR's 'freedom to resign' argumentation.[53] Indeed, under that argumentation, nothing stopped Mr McFarlane from resigning and finding alternative work where he would not have to counsel on same-sex sexual matters. In that sense, no real balancing of rights was done at the level of the domestic courts. An appeal was made to the Court of Appeal, but this was refused.[54] The application was supported by a witness statement from Lord Carey of Clifton, the former Archbishop of Canterbury, who rejected the idea that Christian teaching on same-sex unions was discriminatory or homophobic and instead expressed concern that:

> It is, of course, but a short step from the dismissal of a sincere Christian from employment to a 'religious bar' to any employment of Christians. If Christian views on sexual

---

consider the political and cultural implications of the changing diversity of British people'. For a more elaborate discussion, see K Alidadi, 'On Reasonable Accommodations for Religion or Belief: Charting and Linking Perspectives, Positions and Recommendations in Four "Managing Diversity" Commission Reports' in K Alidadi and M-C Foblets (eds), *Ethnic, Religious and Cultural Diversity in Four National Contexts: The Role of Expert Commissions* (Abingdon, Routledge, 2017 forthcoming).

[51] Based on conversations with Tariq Modood and Maleiha Malik, members of the CORAB Commission.

[52] The claim of wrongful dismissal was, however, accepted on procedural grounds.

[53] 'The Strasbourg institutions have not been at all ready to find an interference with the right to manifest religious belief in practice or observance where a person has voluntarily accepted an employment or role which does not accommodate that practice or observance and there are other means open to the person to observe his or her religion without undue hardship or inconvenience'.

[54] *McFarlane v Relate Avon Ltd* [2010] EWCA Civ 880; the application was refused in the judgment of 29 April 2010.

ethics can be described as 'discriminatory', such views cannot be 'worthy of respect in a democratic society'. An employer could dismiss a Christian, refuse to employ a Christian and actively undermine Christian beliefs. I believe that further judicial decisions are likely to end up at this point and this why I believe it is necessary to intervene now.[55]

Such balancing was done subsequently at the level of the ECtHR (*Eweida and Others v United Kingdom*), since the Court abandoned its former 'freedom to resign' doctrine, but a very deferential test was applied considering the 'fundamental rights conflict' situation at hand. One can argue the *Eweida* decision lacks internal consistency since it fails to exercise the sort of careful balancing act with regard to the *McFarlane* case that it proscribes in its *Eweida* decision. A more thorough analysis may have led to honouring Mr McFarlane's conscientious objection.

Case law on non-religious belief has been largely absent, but conscientious objection is one area where philosophical belief could come in.[56] Indeed, people can object to various job duties because of deeply held, nonreligious belief. In the *Nicholson v Grainger* case in the UK, environmental convictions (a genuinely held belief in anthropogenic climate change) was considered to be of 'sufficient cogency, seriousness, cohesion and importance' and 'worthy of respect in a democratic society' to qualify as 'philosophical belief' for the purposes of the Employment Equality (Religion or Belief) Regulations 2003. Mr Nicholson, who was head of sustainability at Britain's largest residential landlord, argued he was unfairly dismissed for following his moral imperatives.[57] In particular, he believed that people must cut carbon emissions to avoid catastrophic climate change. After the plaintiff was allowed to proceed with his case under the Employment Equality (Religion and Belief) Regulation 2003, the dispute was settled out of court, but there were some indications of disagreement about the issue of using aviation to travel to meetings,[58] which could be a potential objection for persons who hold such deeply-held beliefs as Mr Nicholson.

C. Multicultural Objections

In a number of situations Muslims and other minorities have objected to particular job duties. Such 'multicultural' objection cases typically involve refusal to come

---

[55] *McFarlane v Relate Avon Ltd* [2010] EWCA Civ 880. Also discussed is the UK case of *Eunice & Owen Johns v Derby City Council*, High Court of Justice, 28 February 2011, para 50.

[56] *Grainger plc v Nicholson* [2010] ICLR 360 (EAT) (Appeal No UKEAT/0219/09). Nicholson had argued that his beliefs were 'not merely an opinion, but a philosophical belief which affects how I live my life including my choice of home, how I travel, what I buy, what I eat and drink, what I do with my waste and my hopes and my fears'.

[57] R Verkaik, 'Green beliefs win legal protection', *The Independent*, 3 November 2009.

[58] ibid. Mr Nicholson stated he no longer travels in aeroplanes and he argued Grainger's chief executive of showed 'contempt' for his concerns and allegedly having a staff member fly from London to Ireland to deliver a forgotten BlackBerry.

into contact with pork and/or alcohol, for instance a Muslim shop worker who refuses to stock shelves with bottles of alcohol.[59]

There is even an (old) Belgian case on this issue, although it does relate to the unemployment sphere. In the 1974 case before the Brussels Labour Court, A Muslim applicant had refused a job at a butcher shop since it required him to come into contact with pork.[60] The Tribunal did not consider his subsequent imposition of penalty by the State Unemployment Office, which had suspended his unemployment benefits, to be justified. Considering the job task, the court held the position could not be considered 'suitable' and the man had legitimate religious objections to refuse the job offer.

The ETC has considered cases where Muslim medical professionals object to serving alcohol to residents. In a 2000 case,[61] a female Muslim nursing student (not wearing a headscarf)[62] was working as an intern at a care centre. She ended her internship because she was asked to pour alcoholic beverages for the residents (she had indicated at the interview that because of her religion she could not wash male patients, or serve residents pork or alcohol, but later she objected only to the serving of alcohol). She argued her school had provided insufficient support in resolving the issue, instead making denigrating comments[63] and trying to redirect her into another area of study. The ETC found there to have been an unjustified direct distinction in the case. Underlining that 'religion or belief' under the General Equal Treatment Act (GETA) includes religious practices and not merely the holding and expressing of beliefs, the ETC found the refusal to serve alcohol on the basis of Islamic beliefs to constitute a protected direct expression of faith ('*rechtstreekse uitdrukking geven aan de godsdienstige overtuiging*'):[64] even if there are differences in opinion and practice within these religious precepts on the use and offering of alcohol, it was a generally known fact that the use of alcohol is prohibited in Islam. It also appeared that the religious convictions of the applicant for not serving alcohol to residents have partly been the reason for the care centre to require her to perform all nursing activities, so the care centre in fact went out of its way to confront the student instead of finding ways to accommodate her religious objections to serving alcohol. This amounted to direct distinction since the treatment was motivated by her faith. In addition, the ETC noted that the serving of alcohol appears to be merely 'incidental' to the job and an objection would most likely not lead to substantial difficulties.

---

[59] For an interesting German case, see Federal Labour Court of 24 February 2011, n 2 AZR 636/09. X, 'Controversial Court Ruling: Muslim Shelf Stockers Can Refuse to Handle Alcohol', *Spiegel Online*, 25 February 2011.

[60] Labour Tribunal Brussels, 5 December 1974, *Journal des tribunaux* 1986, 293.

[61] ETC nr 2000-75, 29 November 2000.

[62] Various comments were made asking her why she was persisting on the issue of serving alcohol when she was not wearing a headscarf.

[63] She argued the internship coordinator had asked her 'would you get a heart attack if you had to serve alcohol?' 'is your religion then more important than your studies?' and she was told to stop making a fuss since no-one would hire her if once she graduated. Some of these comments were denied by the relevant persons, so the ETC was unable to draw up a conclusion on this issue: ETC nr 2000-75, 29 November 2000, para 3.6.

[64] ibid, para 4.4.

In the UK too there have been a number of private sector cases where employees have refused to handle 'unclean' products, and this issue has created a divide in British grocery store policies. In *Ahmed v Tesco Stores Ltd* (2008),[65] a Muslim warehouse worker wanted to be exempted from the handling of alcohol and argued the requirement to handle alcohol amounted to indirect discrimination.[66] The Employment Tribunal, however, found for the employer (Tesco) since it considered a legitimate aim to exist (the supplying of alcohol to customers) and the requirement that the employee handle alcohol necessary and proportionate to that aim. Despite the fact that no accommodation was provided, when the employee raised the grievance, he was heard and the process was duly handled within a reasonable time frame. Much importance was given to the fact that the employee was made aware of the requirement and job duties during his recruitment interview, characteristic of the British 'contractual approach' in non-dress cases.

The 'Tesco approach', however, was not shared by other British retailers. In 2013 Marks & Spencer was reported to have an explicit policy of accommodating its Muslim and other religious minority employees, by allowing them to 'politely decline to serve customers [buying alcohol or pork] for religious reasons'.[67] A representative from M&S, however, stated that their policy is rather 'to work closely with our member of staff to place them in a suitable role, such as in our clothing department or bakery', so as to avoid the customers being offended.[68] It appeared that grocery store chains could be placed in two opposite camps:

— Sainsbury's guidelines state there is no reason why staff who do not drink alcohol or eat pork for religious reasons cannot handle them. Tesco said it made no sense to put staff on a till if they refused to touch certain items for religious reasons.

— Asda said it would not deploy any Muslims on tills who objected to handling alcohol, while Morrisons, which is based in Bradford where there is a large Muslim community, said it would 'respect anyone's wishes not to handle products for religious or cultural reasons'.[69]

From a market economy perspective, both the formal equality as well as the accommodative stance have their benefits and pitfalls in the British context. Under a profit-maximising approach, the benefits of accommodating and building goodwill amongst some minorities should be balanced against expected protest and backlash from a part of the customer base.[70] From a reasonable accommodation standpoint, the practical and flexible stance of M&S makes much sense.

---

[65] *Ahmed v Tesco Stores Ltd and Others*, ET Case no 24 1301492/08.

[66] Claims of direct discrimination and harassment were also raised, but summarily dismissed.

[67] SJ Evans, 'M&S tells Muslim staff they CAN refuse to serve customers buying alcohol or pork', *Daily Mail*, 22 December 2013.

[68] L Salkeld, 'M&S faces boycott as it lets Muslim staff refuse to sell alcohol or pork', *DailyMail*, 23 December 2013.

[69] ibid.

[70] ibid. (One shopper had posted on the M&S Facebook page: 'I shan't be shopping in M&S anymore. The quintessentially British retailer bows down to Muslim beliefs. And in turn alienates the majority of Christian and non-religious customers. Outrageous').

The Dutch ETC handled a (public sector) case with a very interesting spin in 2008. An educational institution and a city was found to have discriminated against a Muslim woman who had applied to teach Dutch as a second language but indicated she refused to encourage the students—long-term unemployed who have a language other than Dutch as their main language—to dress 'neutrally, or less ostentatiously religiously' to improve employment chances.[71] The ETC saw the refusal to declare something which the applicant saw as contrary to her religion as a religious expression covered under the GETA. Also, one could doubt whether this advice would be accepted when given by a teacher who herself does not abide by it.

An issue which lies somewhere between an objection to a job task and an objection to a work related circumstances concerns religiously motivated objections against immunisations.[72] The ETC has on various occasions held that an employer discriminates indirectly on grounds of religion when he adopts a vaccination-requirement as appointment policy.[73] In a 2005 case, involving a member of the Reformed Congregations, the same outcome was reached.[74] In the case, a woman had applied for a job as a trainee nurse at the hospital, but was rejected because she conscientious objected to a required Hepatitis B vaccination. The ETC saw the hospital's aim, namely to protect workers and patients from infection with the Hepatitis B virus, as a legitimate one but saw sufficient alternatives which would not indirectly discriminate on grounds of religion. In addition, there was no legal basis for a vaccination obligation for hospitals, unlike in the case of the military which has a compulsory vaccination programme and includes a possibility for military staff members to obtain an exemption.[75]

V. Let's Shake on it? Social and Gender Relations in the Workplace

Besides objections to actual job duties, some cases involve religious (or non-religious) employees who object to or are highly uncomfortable with particular workplace standards, circumstances and expectations. These issues can relate to socialisation standards or expectations and could be considered trivial in other

---

[71] ETC nr 2008-91 and 2008-92.

[72] The modern anti-vaccination movement is in fact quite diverse: people have objections against vaccinations (for their children) for health concern reasons or environmentalism, but also because of distrust of the pharmaceutical companies, capitalism or the government. Vaccination is said to be as much about social issues as it is medical. See Eula Biss, *On Immunity: an Inoculation* (Graywolf Press, 2014)

[73] ETC nr 2001-89, 1 October 2001; ETC nr 2003-9, 16 January 2003; ETC nr 2003-10, 16 January 2003.

[74] ETC nr 2005-31, 1 March 2005.

[75] Immunization of the Military Act, 7 August 1953.

contexts or at other times, in particular since the concrete performance of a job is not, or is only very minimally, affected. An interesting European case, which occurred in Denmark, concerned the request by an employee to be excused from an office birthday party.[76] The employee was a Jehovah's Witness and did not celebrate birthdays and felt uncomfortable attending one at work. Since one could expect that attending such party is not part of one's job duties and would not negatively affect the employee's performance, one can argue such requests should be honoured. The 'accommodation' may not make them popular in the workplace but certainly it would not affect their appraisals, their prospects, or their pay and the employee should not be penalised in any other way.[77] The question is, however, if an employee needs an 'accommodation' for something that as such does not fall within his or her actual job description or duties. The risk is that by problematising non-conforming social behaviours in the workplace, we extend exclusions towards employees who are perfectly capable of being productive workers.

Some of these work circumstance objections or accommodation requests, however, are considered to raise fundamental issues, in particular because they are said to challenge the equality between men and women. From amongst the various 'religion in the workplace' issues, objections to shaking hands as well as refusals to serve same-sex couples has arguably been subject to the most heated debates. The controversy regarding handshaking is not so much due to the act (or rather abstention) itself, but due to the particular connotation routinely given to a refusal by a Muslim to shake the hands of members of the opposite sex. Indeed, there may be good reasons to *not* shake hands with any person, at least during certain times, and this may be a policy in some workplaces. Hospitals have at times instituted such policy for medical or public health reasons. Also, in many Asian cultures greeting does not need to involve physical contact. It is hardly uncommon for Western business men to brush up on culturally sensitive business etiquette and adapt to different cultural greeting standards when conducting international business negotiations.[78] But when the act is motivated by religious beliefs and implies gender-based distinctions, things are viewed in a different light.

The 'shaking hands' debate has triggered wide societal considerations of the position of women in Islam—even if restricting physical contact between men and women is not only an issue in Islam—of the parameters of politeness and 'respectful' greeting, and of the integration or assimilation of newcomers. The proposal by a religious objector to treat all persons the same by not shaking hands

---

[76] Eastern High Court (Denmark) 3 January 2008, OE2008.B–821–07.

[77] One could, however, argue that during such friendly work parties work-related or work-relevant issues may be discussed, some brainstorming may be going on, information and ideas could be exchanged, etc. So the 'anti-social' person is not only excluded from social contacts, but is sometimes also cut off from other workplace aspects including at times work tasks that get distributed at such time. Accommodation would then not only require the person be exempt, but would also affect the ways work gets distributed.

[78] eg: www.venturejapan.com/japanese-business-etiquette.htm ('Do not grab your host's hand when first meeting and give it a hearty shake—many Japanese seldom shake hands and can be so uncomfortable doing so as to avoid meeting again!')

with anyone is rarely considered helpful, confirming that the problem is not the practical (non) act of not shaking hands per se, but the *beliefs* behind it. Controversy has been most amplified in the Netherlands, less so in Belgium, and the issue has been the subject of a considerable more relaxed laissez-faire attitude in the UK.

A. Redefining the Parameters of Politeness? Refusal to Shake Hands in the Netherlands

A public incident in 2004 involving Minister Rita Verdonk, then sitting Dutch Minister of Integration and known for her staunch stance against multiculturalism, shot the shaking hands debate into the Dutch imaginary and vernacular. On the occasion of a meeting with Muslim religious leaders, one of the (many) Muslim leaders refused to shake her hand, something that took her (and many others) by surprise.[79] With the image of the Minister's outstretched hand being refused by a Dutch imam as a front-page introduction for the general Dutch audience to an aspect of Islamic gender relations, the political, legal and societal debate took off. The issue divided politicians, opinion makers and the Dutch public. On one side, some people including Minister Verdonk considered such behaviour and 'attitude' towards women unacceptable. On the other hand, multiculturalist proponents argued society should respect minority religious beliefs and practices in this instance. The then Mayor of Amsterdam, Job Cohen, conversely argued in 2008 that civil servants such as Muslim 'street coaches'[80] are free to not shake hands with members of the opposite sex as long as they do their jobs well.[81] Cohen argued shaking hands constitutes merely a social custom (not a legal requirement) and an abstention was not to cause offence to women; rather it was motivated by respect towards instead of lack of regard for women.

The ETC had a prominent role in this debate. At one point, its very existence seemed to be hinging on this point. In 2006, following two 'accommodative' ETC opinions in shaking hands cases,[82] Minister Verdonk and others called for the ETC's abolishment.[83] While other political parties did not support his call, they did agree that the ETC opinions on shaking hands should be disregarded.[84]

---

[79] The accompanying picture shows the Minister holding out her hand while the imam holds his hand on his heart (sometimes with subtitle saying 'with all due respect, I cannot shake a woman's hand'). This would not be the only time an imam refuses to shake the Minister's hand, see J Kooistra, 'Opnieuw weigert imam hand Verdonk', *Elsevier*, 26 April 2006.

[80] 'Street coaches' [*straatcoaches*] are part of a strategy in Amsterdam to address social disturbances by youths. These coaches (recognizable through their dress, available 7 days a week, fluent in 'the language of the street') fill a gap between youth work and the police. For more information, see http://www.aanpakoverlast.nl/.

[81] See, eg, B Peeters, 'Cohen heeft gelijk, hand schudden hoeft niet', *Elsevier*, 22 February 2008.

[82] ETC nr 2006-220 and 2006-221, 7 November 2006 and ETC nr 2006-202.

[83] X, 'Verdonk: Schaf Commissue Gelijke Behandeling af', *Elsevier*, 6 November 2006.

[84] www.discriminatiezaken.nl/doc/Factsheet%20handen%20schudden.pdf (at 4: 'De oproep van Verdonk om de CGB af te schaffen werd door PvdA, D66, GroenLinks en het CDA resoluut afgewezen, maar zij waren wel eensgezind van mening dat de oordelen van de CGB betreffende het "handen schudden" niet opgevolgd dienen te worden').

The ETC's significant change in jurisprudence, as well as the notable divergence between the ETC and Dutch courts in this matter, exemplify a broader societal divide on such matters which relate to human rights, minorities, integration, Dutch values and gender equality. Most cases have addressed the handshaking issue with regard to the public sector, in particular in schools, but the same analysis and balancing would largely apply to private sector cases. In 2002, the ETC had found that a Rotterdam high school did not discriminate when it dismissed a Muslim reprography employee for refusing to shake hands with women. The school argued that not shaking hands with women ran counter to mainstream Dutch norms and values, and was itself offensive and discriminatory.[85] The ETC considered first that the practice involved, refusal to shake hands or otherwise have physical contact with members of the opposite sex, is a legitimate expression of religious belief. Even if the practice is not followed by the majority of Muslims in the Netherlands, it still falls under the protection provided by the GETA, a stance it would repeat in subsequent cases. The ETC held that the demand that all employees (or students) should (be willing to) shake hands can have discriminatory effect on a group because of their religion (eg orthodox Muslims). The question, however, is whether an unjustifiable distinction is made by penalising a student or staff member because of such refusal. The outcome thus depends on the justification test for indirect distinction and which alternatives the ETC considers are available that could be adopted in lieu of a negative decision. In the 2002 case, the school was found to have a consistent policy explicitly pursuing gender equality. And the refusal to shake hands, irrespective of whether it is motivated by a lack of regard for women or not, *can be perceived* as a denial of the equality between men and women. In light of these factors, the requirement and the dismissal were considered justified.

In 2006 the ETC reconsidered its earlier decisions, saying 'some nuancing' was called for. The case involved a Muslim woman who wanted to register for a training programme to become a teacher's assistant. During the intake interview she informed the school that she did not shake hands with men (older than 12 years old) and the school went out of its way to explain that this was not acceptable under its policy. The woman asked the ETC for an advisory opinion whether this constituted discrimination on the basis of her religion. Here again, the ETC reiterated that a direct expression of someone's faith was at stake and that the requirement to treat men and women the same by shaking hands with both served a legitimate aim. However, in contrast to its earlier decisions, it held that the requirement was not 'necessary' since there was 'at least one alternative'. The school, in particular since it aimed to create an environment of equal opportunity for its students and staff, could suffice by requiring the woman and others in her situation to greet all persons in an equally respectful way without any physical contact. As long as she was willing to do this, she should be able to enrol. Thus, a simple (re)consideration

---

[85] ETC nr 2002-22, 5 March 2002.

and a stricter proportionality test tilted the outcome the other way. In 2008, 2010 and 2011, the ETC held on to this position, despite considerable public and political opposition. Ben Vermeulen wrote that he did not see a clear reason why the ETC changed its stance on this matter.[86] The change with regard to shaking hands is the mirror image of the ETC's decision regarding marriage registrars, and arguably inconsistent with those decisions since alternatives are also possible there. In the end, much depends on the connotation one gives to such religiously motivated refusal to shake hands with men or women, with regard to various stakeholders (the employee, the teacher, the student, the colleague, the employer, the customer), each potentially holding different, conflicting understandings of the gesture. Vermeulen does not consider that the ETC justifies sufficiently why it gives priority to the religionist's perspective in the newer cases. What is clear though is that using the gender equality argument to exclude Muslim women from educational or professional opportunities because of expressions of faith is inherently problematic. In effect, Muslim women are regarded as unable to exercise personal autonomy. It is equally contradictory for institutions or organisations which emphasise the values of diversity and equality to effectively exclude minorities from opportunities by insisting on majoritarian conformist social behaviour.

In the same year, an Utrecht school (Vader Rijn College) and a female Muslim economics lecturer were embroiled in a heated conflict and asked the ETC for an opinion.[87] The lecturer was employed at an 'ethnic' public high school, where the majority of the 700 students were of Turkish or Moroccan descent. When starting what would have been her second year teaching at the school she had emailed her colleagues on the first day of school to 'give them a heads up' that she would not shake hands with male colleagues because of religious objections. She wrote in the email that this was her personal and well-considered decision,[88] that she was exercising her rights, and that she hoped her colleagues would not feel personally offended or that this would affect their relationship.[89] This email set a train of events in motion and eventually led to her suspension and dismissal for 'serious reasons' ('*redenen van gewichtige aard*'); the principal appeared particularly agitated that the instructor had not come to him or the board first but instead had directly contacted colleagues.

Officially, the school board's dismissal was not due to religious reasons; rather 'the behaviour' (sending the email and announcing that one refuses to shake hands with member of the opposite sex) was seen as in breach of the school's 'Code of Conduct concerning Intimidation, Discrimination and Violence'. The

---

[86] BP Vermeulen, '2006-220 Handenschudden op school?' in Commissie Gelijke Behandeling (ed), *Gelijke behandeling: oordelen en commentaar 2006* (Nijmegen, Wolf Legal Publishers, 2007) 367.

[87] ETC nr 2006-220, 7 November 2006.

[88] Later in court she explained that she considered shaking hands with adult men under her religion as sexual harassment.

[89] Indeed, the reason employees announce in advance that they will not shake hands with members of the opposite sex is to connect this to their religious beliefs and to avoid such unpleasant situations. See, eg, ETC nr 2011-139, para 3.27.

employer was willing to offer the lecturer generous financial compensation, but she argued there were no 'serious reasons' for the dismissal since the employer was (indirectly) discriminating against her based on her religion.

The ETC found for the lecturer, holding that the working conditions that the tutor shake hands with members of the opposite sex constitutes indirect distinction and the two justification arguments advanced by the school were insufficient. Certainly, respectful greeting in the school setting is of importance, but enforcing a uniform way of greeting derived from the dominant culture is not the only way to achieve this. The school's second argument was that it was preparing pupils, many of ethnic minority origin and thus facing considerable discrimination and disadvantage, for the internship or job market. It wanted these pupils to learn the customary Dutch ways so they would know how to handle job interviews and the like, and lecturers function as role models in that regard. The latter was considered a legitimate goal (even though the ETC noted that the Netherlands is a diverse country and various sectors have their own customs as well) but it failed to establish the necessity of imposing a uniform mode of greeting on teachers and staff. The instructor was prepared to greet men with a friendly nod, and this should have sufficed.

The case led to much public debate and further litigation, after the ETC opinion was criticised for its overly lenient approach.[90] The controversy was one of the reasons that the school did not want the lecturer back, even though the attention drawn to the issue was to a large extent facilitated by the school's public announcing and handling of the matter. The school, disagreeing with the ETC, took the case to the Utrecht District Court. The lecturer appealed the decision to the Central Appeals Tribunal (*Centrale Raad van Beroep*, which handles public sector employment appeals). The Utrecht District Court on 31 August 2007[91] decided that the conflict between the teacher and the school board was in itself sufficient reason for dismissal, but did not give a ruling on the issue of (religious) discrimination. It found an alleged 'breach of trust' due to the sending of an email without consulting the employer and held because of the extensive media attention for the case and the intense debate at the school that a return of the lecturer to work would cause much disturbance and unrest.

The instructor had argued that she was suspended because of actions which were motivated by her religious beliefs and that the employer gave no reasons for failing to follow the ETC opinion. In a remarkable move, the District Court held:

> In the opinion of the court, in the named circumstances, neither the freedom of religion nor any other legal norm is at stake. Further, so far as the applicant refers to the opinion of the ETC, the question the ETC addressed—briefly assess whether the employer had acted

---

[90] See, eg, nieuws-uitgelicht.infonu.nl/mens-en-samenleving/36539-handen-schudden-weigerende-moslim-docente-terecht-ontslagen.html ('Het advies van de commissie is duidelijk een schrijftafeladvies').

[91] District Court of Utrecht, 31 August 2007(LJN: BB2648).

in violation of the Equal Treatment Act—is different from the test the court is to execute, namely whether there were acceptable grounds [for the suspension/termination].[92]

This is a peculiar reasoning; if the employer had discriminated on the basis of employee's religion, there would be no 'serious ground' to suspend and terminate the contract. Finding a 'serious ground' for the termination implies a rejection of the discrimination claim, and the ETC had given its expert (non-binding) opinion. Thus, the issue of the shaking hands was avoided and the ETC opinion disregarded.

The 'elephant in the room' was addressed in the appeal, but again the decision came out in the favour of the school. The Central Appeals Tribunal on 7 May 2009 found a justification for the indirect distinction on the basis of the employee's religion: the legitimate aim was to adhere to a norm of greeting 'which prevents segregation and promotes clarity in a multicultural school community in which uniformity [is]… placed above diversity'.[93] In its considerations, it struck the balance between the various interests involved very differently than the ETC:

> The refusal to shake hands and the reason [the female teacher] provides for that—she considers shaking hands with adult men from her religious convictions as sexual intimidation—can be seen by others as confrontational and unpleasant ['*confronterend en onaangenaam*'] and puts pressure on mutual relations. In the situation of [this female teacher] this is not only the case with male colleagues and students, towards whom she functions as a role model—but also externally, towards parents and third parties involved with the school. In relation to these last groups, the teacher is first and foremost the representative of the school and in that sense the greeting rule relates directly to her functioning as a civil servant. In the given circumstances, the Tribunal is of the opinion that the interest of the school to prevent segregation and promote clarity in a multicultural school community by prioritising, as it did, uniformity over diversity weighs heavier so that the uniformity in way of greeting is appropriate and necessary.

The requirement to shake hands with everyone, in particular for someone with the function of a civil servant, was thus necessary and proportionate and the refusal to abide by this constituted the 'serious reason' needed to justify the dismissal. The Central Appeals Tribunal summarily dismissed the claim based on the religious freedom provision of the Dutch Constitution (article 6); this was considered 'absorbed' into the Equal Treatment Act, so that the result of the analysis would be the same under either framework. The human rights framework was essentially rendered toothless.

While the 'cultural relativist' approach of the ETC was criticised, one could also refute the 'cultural dominance' reasoning of the courts in this case. There are various problems with the latter and the result it justifies, even if it should be recognised that no position on this issue is free of normative considerations. First, the 'requirement' that an employee shakes hands with colleagues, superiors,

---

[92] District Court of Utrecht, 31 August 2007 (LJN: BB2648), para 2.26.
[93] Central Appeals Tribunal, 7 May 2009 (LJN BI2440), para 7.10.

customers etc is in most cases not a job function and quite rarely would be a key job task, and rarely would a court accept there to be a 'genuine and occupational requirement' in the sense of article 4.1 of the Employment Equality Directive. Rather, it concerns an implied social expectation, which is why the 'announcing' of a refusal comes across a bit awkwardly. This distinction can play a determining role in the assessment of discrimination (or freedom of religion) claims.[94] Dismissals based on non-core job tasks should be considered suspect and justify an elevated review test, since the risks of socially motivated exclusion need to be confronted. Indeed, the less of a (core) job task a request concerns, the more likely a dismissal or other negative treatment seems disproportionate and unjustified. Accommodation in such situations will often be particularly productive.

Secondly, the court accepted the argument that in a multicultural context it is justified, and perhaps even more so, to impose uniformity 'to prevent segregation and promote clarity'. The approach is also not in line with the long-held aspiration model of 'pluriformity' in the Netherlands, but more importantly the accommodation with regard to handshaking is associated by the court with a risk of segregation. This is clearly unwarranted. An 'accommodation' (the relaxing of social conformist expectations) would not have promoted segregation, but rather inclusion, not both in real terms when it comes to the direct parties but also in symbolic terms. The dismissal of a female Muslim lecturer (meaning, one female minority role model less) for a religiously motivated request and the message sent out to (future) staff and students is hardly conducive to the integration and participation of Muslims and other religious minorities.

More fundamentally, the idea that we need to privilege uniformity for clarity's sake in a multicultural context implies that there is such (unproblematic) uniformity amongst the dominant group; that minorities are simply asked to abide by 'the Dutch customs'. It hides the fact that there is much intra-diversity and that the particular customs enforced may be highly excluding towards minorities. Greeting customs differ considerably by country, by region, by class, by social setting and by gender, at the very least and physical contact is one aspect of this social phenomenon. In some regions a kiss on the cheek *particularly* between members of the opposite sex is customary. Could such *gender-differentiating* greeting methods, which can certainly make some feel uncomfortable, also be justified?

Finally, underlying any approach is the implied answer to the question 'whose perspective is most pertinent when it comes to the refusal to shake hands?' Should the employee's perspective be determinative or should we consider and give weight to third party perspectives, including potential insult suffered by third parties including parents? Taking the subjective approach clearly can be problematic but considering the lack of better alternatives it is often preferred in anti-discrimination law. The perspectives of third parties are certainly relevant, but giving too much weight to those can be dangerous as those may cloak not only bias and prejudice but also misunderstandings. Judicial decisions can utilise the

---

[94] See below, discussion of Mr Enait's case.

opportunity a case provides to challenge dominant preconceptions about minority groups and their practices. Also, allowing a 'confrontation' between different perspectives can give anti-discrimination law a broader appeal and effect in social life.

Another high-profile handshaking affair in the Netherlands concerned Mr Mohamed Faizel Ali Enait, a controversial (public) figure who considers himself an 'orthodox Muslim' and who does not shy away from public controversy. The dispute between Mr Enait and the city of Rotterdam started in 2005 when he applied for a position as 'client manager' with the city's social service but was rejected.[95] The controversy ended in 2012,[96] after the Court of Appeal confirmed the judgment of Rotterdam District Court and found his discrimination claim without merit.[97] Similarly to the female economics lecturer whose case was discussed above, Mr Enait was able to convince the ETC[98] but not the Dutch courts.

The District Court in Rotterdam held that the city had not made an unjustified distinction in rejecting Mr Enait as applicant for the position of client manager because he refused to shake the hands of women.

The justification centred around the city's wish not to make a distinction based on gender, and the court accepted that this was a legitimate aim and the measure taken was necessary and proportionate towards that aim. The court considered that, on the one hand, shaking people's hands in the Netherlands is a generally acceptable form of greeting; 'the refusal to shake a hand can be seen as impolite or offensive, especially if the refusal is motivated by the fact that the other person is of the opposite sex'.[99] On the other hand, it considered the job function at hand: the position of client manager, required meeting and discussing with clients, both men and women, of different religions (though most would be Muslim) not only in the office but also in their homes. The court considered that 'for a substantial part of these clients at least, shaking hands will be considered an appropriate and polite way of greeting'. The court did not take into account the proposal made by Mr Enait to not shake hands with *men or women*:

> The city could choose to prescribe that client managers, or a certain client manager, like the applicant, would shake no-one's hand. In this way, the inequality between men and women would also be prevented. However, if the city were to take a measure like this, this

---

[95] While his rejection for that position was primarily motivated by his refusal to shake (eligible) women's hands because of his religious beliefs, the issue of religious dress played a role, albeit a more minor role. Mr Enait attended the job interview with a long beard, coordinated head cover and *djellaba*.
[96] The applicant announced he would pursue his case before the European Court. He subsequently obtained his law degree and came into the public debate again in 2008 when he refused to stand up for a judge for religious reasons citing Muslim 'fundamental egalitarianism'. Marcel Haenen, 'Orthodoxe moslim hoeft niet op te staan bij de rechter', *NRC Handelsblad*, 5 September 2008.
[97] District Court Rotterdam, 6 August 2008 (LJN: BD9643); Court of Appeal, The Hague, 23 August 2011 (LNJ: BW1267); Court of Appeal, The Hague, 10 April 2012 (LNJ: BW1270).
[98] ETC nr 2006-202. The ETC found an unjustifiable indirect distinction in that the City had failed to consider alternative ways of greeting which could be equally respectful; not shaking anyone's hand would make the treatment of men and women equal.
[99] District Court Rotterdam, 6 August 2008, para 5.2.2.

would mean he would no longer be willing to adopt a greeting and politeness form which is generally accepted in the Netherlands.[100]

By leaving out the discussion about alternative and respectful ways of greeting, the court disregards an essential element of the case which should be brought under a proportionality test. Why stick with 'the' dominant form of greeting, even if it leads to exclusion of an apparently otherwise competent employee for the job because of his/her religion, when an alternative is available? The real issue though may be whether the alternative in this particular situation, where the shaking of hands requirement moves more towards a job task, is really reasonable.

The Rotterdam court assessed the case under the GETA, the Dutch equal treatment act, and in particular the prohibition of indirect discrimination. The plaintiff also argued a violation of Article 9 ECHR, Article 18 ICCPR and Article 6 of the Dutch Constitution but the Court considered a separate analysis under this framework obsolete after dismissing the anti-discrimination claim, holding in a sweeping statement that these provisions do not offer any further protection beyond the GETA.[101] The implied usurpation of human rights by the GETA would mean that the fundamental right to freedom of conscience, thought and religion has no other implications beyond the prohibition of discrimination in the Netherlands. This is, however, not a unanimously followed approach as illustrated by another handshaking case where a District Court,[102] referring to The Hague Court of Appeals' decision regarding Mr Enait, considered another handshaking dispute in the frame of the request for a dismissal permit.[103] The case involved a Muslim youth worker who refused to shake hands with women and worked for a community organisation which had 'a strong suspicion that he has a radicalising influence on the youths'. The court assessed the matter solely under the generic 'freedom of religion' (*godsdienstvrijheid*), and did not consider the General Equal Treatment Act or the prohibition of (indirect) distinction. It found that the fundamental rights are not absolute and may be restricted in case of objective justification, which it found present in the case at hand.

On appeal from the Rotterdam court, the Court of Appeal[104] confirmed the lower judgment regarding Mr Enait, while rejecting the city's new arguments that the refusal to shake hands cannot be considered a protected expression of a belief under the General Equal Treatment Act or Article 9 ECHR and that Islam does not

---

[100] District Court Rotterdam, 6 August 2008, para 5.2.3.

[101] District Court Rotterdam, 6 August 2008, para 5.3.

[102] District Court, subdistrict judge Midden-Nederland, 9 January 2013, LJN: BY8858.

[103] Since the employee's contractual status benefiting protection, the employer was required to submit a request to be able to dissolve the agreement. It is generally very difficult for employers to dismiss such protected employees, See District Court, subdistrict judge Rotterdam, 20 June 2012, LJN: BX4414. The apparent ease for an employer to dismiss the employee relying on the reason of refusal to shake hands may thus be seen as striking.

[104] Court of Appeal of The Hague, 10 April 2012 (LNJ: BW1270).

strictly prescribe this behaviour. The Court of Appeal considered that a judicial organ has to restrain itself when considering the religious motives behind certain acts, but

> In the case the appellant has made it sufficiently clear that in certain orthodox inter-
> pretations of Islam the shaking of hands with women of marriageable age is considered
> 'impure' and that he follows such interpretation. The court sees no reason to appraise
> the religious importance for the appellant as so minor that it would need to be placed
> outside the scope of the [GETA] and the ECHR.[105]

The Court of Appeal likewise assessed whether there was an indirect distinction based on religion and whether the restriction was necessary and appropriate, this time in light of the suggestion of the appellant to avoid shaking hands with *any* clients on the job and to greet all respectfully. Mr Enait tried to bolster his posi-tion by referring to the situation in the city of Amsterdam, where the Mayor had said that social services staff members were allowed to refuse shaking hands with women as long as they performed their job adequately. The Court of Appeal con-sidered that the city needs to show a level of neutrality towards all citizens irre-spective of gender, the client manager being seen as the representative of the city who should accommodate the clients by greeting them in 'a way which cannot be regarded as lacking in respect and offensive'. While the Court of Appeal was will-ing to accept—or at least did not find either way—that one can respectfully greet another without shaking hands when one takes the initiative, it foresaw a real possibility that in fact the client would take the initiative and the client manager would then be required to reject a hand which has been extended—in that case many would regard this as hurtful and offensive, which would harm the rela-tionship between the social services users and the city, and could be particularly upsetting to women since

> refusal of an extended hand of a female user/client is unacceptable, since that refusal can
> be felt as a denial of equality between men and women, and thus as extra hurtful. Such
> experience is made worse if the background to the refusal is the religious conviction that
> shaking the hands of women is 'impure'; not shaking the hands of male clients/users does
> not attenuate this concern.[106]

In the end, even in a traditionally tolerant Netherlands, such accommodation was considered to be a bridge too far. However, it is important that the courts looked into the specific job functions at hand, and the situations the employee would reasonably frequently be placed in were particularly relevant to the requirement. The job of 'client manager' involved an 'externally oriented position' representing the city and entailed extensive contact with outside beneficiaries of services. The judgments regarding this case should not be taken to mean that a refusal to shake hands would not be accepted for *any* position.

---

[105] Court of Appeal of The Hague, 10 April 2012, para 4.
[106] Court of Appeal of The Hague, 10 April 2012, para 15.

Other hand-shaking cases led to ETC opinions in 2011[107] and 2012.[108] In the 2012 case a Muslim man applied for the position of parking controller (*parkeer-wachter*) with a company providing services in the municipality of Amsterdam. He was rejected because he informed the employer that he had religious objections to shaking hands with members of the opposite sex and the company expected all its parking controllers to treat each other and the citizens in an equal, respectful manner, including by shaking hands. The ETC held there was an indirect distinction on the basis of the man's religion; the applicant, a Muslim, was in fact particularly affected by the handshaking requirement. However, in the circumstances of this case, the ETC considered the distinction justified. In particular, the function in question was largely set in the public space where contacts with citizens arise spontaneously and cannot be arranged in advance. The contacts are brief and non-recurring. In addition, the work of a parking controller could evoke negative emotions in citizens. Because of the context and nature of the work it was not clear whether there was any reasonably acceptable alternative is available.

Thus, the ETC finds the requirement of shaking hands justified when the job circumstances move the shaking hands requirement more towards a core job function rather than a standard related to the social work environment. While in the case of teachers, outside contacts (eg with parents) occur more intermittently, in the case of a parking controller it will be daily. A school has an opportunity to educate the school community (students, other teachers and third parties) about different cultural practices and the values of diversity and tolerance, but it may be practically much more difficult to do for an employer when there is no such relatively contained environment. The nature of the job and the context in which it is exercised is thus key; in that sense, one could look to the test for establishing a 'genuine and occupational requirement' for inspiration in case of indirect distinction on the basis of social job standards and expectations such as shaking hands.

In the sociological interviews conducted in the frame of RELIGARE, the issue of shaking hands was widely discussed. Some respondents argued civil servants should have the right to refuse to officiate at same-sex marriages because colleagues could do the job instead, but should not be allowed to refuse to shake hands with the opposite sex. Others argued that civil servants should not be allowed to refuse to officiate at same-sex marriages since it was a job function, while shaking hands is only a social custom for which there are alternatives. Yet other respondents answered in the positive or in the negative for both issues. Based on these sociological interviews, including with some religious leaders and ETC commissioners

[107] ETC nr 2011-139, 16 September 2011 (dismissal of a young Muslim who was to intern at a school as geography lecturer because he did not want to shake hands with women constituted forbidden discrimination on the basis of religion (short 10-week internship for one day a week). The young man subsequently discontinued his education following the choice 'shake hands or leave', but still wanted the decision of the ETC on the matter for reasons of principle. The ETC was also not convinced other alternatives were offered/discussed)

[108] ETC nr 2012-54, 22 March 2012 (a Muslim man applying for the position of parking controller at a company that is responsible for the parking policy in the municipality of Amsterdam).

in the Netherlands, Floris Vermeulen concludes that various arguments, including the neutrality argument, are utilised in contradictory ways to come to different results. Also 'there lacks consensus as to when this is applicable. In addition, opinions can change within a relatively short period of time'.[109]

B. Shaking Hands in Belgium

While the issue is hardly 'resolved' in the Netherlands, two polar opposite responses can be found in Belgium and the United Kingdom. In Belgium, the responses indicate a rather unanimous rejection of culturally strange practices such as a religiously motivated refusal to shake hands with members of the opposite sex. The perspective of the dominant majority is not merely prioritised but effectively *monopolises* the debate. The Belgian approach does not differ from the Dutch approach in the justification of indirect discrimination per se (the legal site of struggle where the Dutch shaking hands debate is mainly situated), but rather in a preliminary matter, namely whether shaking hands is an expression of religious faith. At the core, this is a fundamental difference. Many Belgian commentators fail to see an issue of freedom of religion or religious discrimination when an employee, and a fortiori a civil servant, is dismissed for refusing to shake hands with women (or men).

However, there have been no legal cases in Belgium with regard to the issue of refusal to shake hands at work.[110] This is clearly not because the issue does not arise, reports and media controversies prove that it does. Rather, the lack of legal pursuance may find an explanation in the treatment of such issues in the media and in the court of public opinion, which would seem to foreshadow the result of a potentially lengthy and costly lawsuit. Also, considering the Belgian jurisprudence with regard to neutrality policies (implying a ban on the expression of one's faith by refusing to shaking hands in the workplace) as well as the political climate, it is highly unlikely that the equality body Unia would pick this fight to pursue in the near future.

In 2013, an incident occurred where a street sweeper in Elsene, Brussels, refused to shake the hand of the city's Alderwoman for Public Cleanliness (*Schepen van Openbare Reinheid*), the liberal politician Viviane Teitelbaum.[111] He was disciplined by losing one week's salary and was warned that 'next time the penalty would be

---

[109] Vermeulen and Belhaj, 'Accommodating religious claims in the Dutch workplace: Unacknowledged Sabbaths, objecting marriage registrars and pressured faith-based organizations', n 37 above, 129.

[110] But see Labour Tribunal Verviers, 29 May 1989, JLMB 1989, 1410 for a far broader refusal by a Muslim jobseeker to work with members of the opposite sex. The Tribunal held that the woman, who had expressed that she was only willing to work with a veil and in a department where only women were employed and working, had made herself 'unavailable' for the entire labour market and was thus not entitled to unemployment benefits.

[111] D Vileyn, 'Standpunt BDW: Verboden?', *Brussel nieuws*, 21 August 2013.

harsher'. The case received minor—and one-sided—media attention. Reporting on this issue, local city newspaper reporter Danny Vileyn's piece reads like a condemnation of the man and 'his like' of which there are 'too many' in Brussels. There is no understanding for the position of the street sweeper, who 'has placed himself outside of our community'. The religious motivation is considered 'absolutely irrelevant, even if the man apologised with his hand on his heart'. It is equally unfathomable to the reporter that the man 'persists in his anger' (*volhardt in de boosheid*) since he risks losing his job in case of 'repeated infringements'.[112] The penalty is considered 'light' and there is no consideration for potential financial hardship for the man involved and his family. Instead, the focus is on how many of these 'strange cases' *we* can afford in *our* society. While this single reporter certainly does not represent the entire Belgian society, the lack of alternative reporting and absence of the defence of the man by any minority organisation remain problematic.

The reporter noted that this is not the first time the issue has come up, nor will it be the last. In April 2013, a Brussels city museum employee was dismissed after he had refused to shake the hand of a female politician.[113] The man was a convert to Islam working at the Museum of Brussels where female socialist politician Karine Lalieux was attending a party. It was said the refusal to shake hands was the 'last straw' after the man had also refused to wear a uniform, to carry around trays with alcoholic drinks and allegedly had tried to convert co-workers. He was said to have indicated he would not give mouth-to-mouth to women in an urgent situation (though it is questionable whether this was a likely situation for the job in question). The vote to dismiss the employee had been almost unanimous: 43 of the 49 council members had voted for, two voted against and four did not vote. The fact that the director of the Belgian equality body (Jozef de Witte) stated that the dismissal was justified is very revealing.[114] Unlike in the Netherlands, there was no outcry or long political, societal and legal debate. Unlike in the UK, no minority organisations tried to defend or explain the actions of the museum employee. In Belgium, the only expressed opinions argue that a refusal to shake hands *is* an insult to women, and does not fall under the freedom of religion 'since the freedom of religion is obviously not absolute'.[115]

Interestingly, the refusal to shake hands has recently come up in an entirely different context; after an 'allochthone' police inspector revealed disturbing racist behaviour in the Antwerp police force, it was reported that various police officers

---

[112] ibid. 'In addition, he risks landing in societal marginality. How many people placing *themselves* in marginality can *we* afford?' (emphasis added).

[113] X, 'Stad ontslaat bekeerde moslim die vrouwen geen hand geeft', *Brussel nieuws*, 13 May 2013.

[114] ibid. Belgisch Centrum voor gelijkheid van kansen en voor racismebestrijding (CGKR)

[115] Some striking readers' comments on the dismissal story included: 'Well. There can be little discussion about it. The freedom of religion is not limitless' ('Jelle'). And 'Even though I would also not want to shake Karine Lalieux's hand (do your work well first man!) the city acted correctly in this case!' ('Yasmin'). Other comments note the need for civil servants to adhere to the duty of neutrality in the workplace ('he can do whatever he wants at home') and discuss whether the man would be entitled to unemployment benefits following the dismissal.

in Antwerp refused to shake hands with the (few) allochthone officers on the corps. This behaviour was accompanied by other unwelcoming and bullying behaviour displaying racist sentiment.[116] When seven allochthone Antwerp police officers—anonymously—talked about their experiences, they all stated that that some white Belgian officers refused to shake their hands or to go on patrol with them.[117] Yet, even when these officers come forward with complaints, the issues are minimised and ignored. Thus, this problematic behaviour, revealing a sense of superiority and hostility towards others, was not problematised in this context. While another (clear) wrong need not make another right, it sheds light on the interpretation of a foreign practice as 'wrong' in the first place. And in addition, it points to a patent case of double standards. This points to the fact that it is not the greeting by other ways than physical contact that is at stake, but rather the interpretation of a refusal to shake hands which is done *only* according to 'Western' frames.

C. Shaking Hands in the UK

Similarly to Belgium, there has not been a hand-shaking legal case in the UK. But the issue has appeared in the news, reflecting—on the surface at least—a vastly different approach. In 2007 a female Muslim police officer refused the hand of Commissioner Sir Ian Blair, the head of the Metropolitan Police, at a passing out ceremony in South West London for newly qualified recruits marking the end of an 18-week recruit training course.[118] She was standing—wearing a hijab—in the line-up of 200 recruits. The behaviour was questioned by Scotland Yard and Sir Ian but 'Muslim groups defended the police officer, saying her beliefs would not affect how she carried out her job and called for greater understanding of different cultures'.

One Islamic leader, chairman of the London-based Islamic Human Rights Commission Massoud Shadjareh, argued: 'I don't think shaking hands is something that makes or breaks a relationship. I don't think in any sort of job that is something that becomes an obstacle to one performing one's duties'. Muslim leaders also reassured people that in case of urgency, eg when a man has been shot,

---

[116] H R T, series on minorities in the Antwerp police force: 'Allochtone agenten getuigen over racisme in het Antwerpse politiekorps', *De Standaard*, 30 May 2014 (when an 'allochthone' police inspector in Antwerp, Nourddine Abarkan, revealed widespread racism within the Antwerp police corps in an interview with *De Standaard* on 21 May 2014, he was first discredited and threatened with sanctions; after some public scrutiny, more investigation into the matter was ordered).

[117] E Bergmans, 'Allochtone politieman voelt zich geviseerd binnen Antwerpse politie, "Ik geef diejen bruine geen hand"', *De Standaard*, 21 May 2014; E Bergmans, 'Racisme bij de Antwerpse politie "Ik wil niet bij die makak in de auto"', *De Standaard*, 31 May 2014. (There are only about 40 allochthone officers amongst the 2,600 police officers in Antwerp, this while 30% of people living in Antwerp are of non-European origin).

[118] BBC news, 'Muslim Pc refused to shake hands', *BBC news*, 21 January 2007; see also S Marsden, 'Police recruit's refusal to shake hand defended', *The Guardian*, 21 January 2007; 'I cannot shake your hand, sir. I'm a Muslim and you're a man', *London Evening Standard*, 20 January 2007.

the officer would have no problems helping immediately: 'If she has to resuscitate that dying person, Muslim law will then change and allow her all sorts of physical contact because a life is at risk and life is so precious'. A police spokeswoman confirmed: 'The officer maintains that she puts the requirements of being a police officer above her personal beliefs and only exercises the latter when she has choice to do so'. It was also said that

> Sir Ian was informed on his arrival of the officer's request. This has never happened before and he was bloody furious. But he agreed to go along with it so as not to cause a scene. He went out and shook the hand of every single new recruit apart from her. It was very obvious and very embarrassing.

However, taking distance from this initial sentiment, it seemed the concern turned on the real matter at hand: 'There was a great deal of discussion about it afterwards. People were asking "how the hell is she going to make an arrest if she refuses to touch men?"'.

The incident reportedly led to top-level discussions at Scotland Yard, which stated that the woman would be fired if she failed to fulfil her duties. But this was because 'her attitude towards men might impede her ability to detain offenders'. An inquiry was launched to see whether the woman's 'strict religious beliefs prevent her performing *as an effective police officer*'.

However, concern about gender equality in Islam was not raised. Rather the worry was the other way around, it was about 'political correctness' towards minorities: 'senior commanders are worried that dismissing her would deepen the atmosphere of mistrust between the police and the Muslim community'. Indeed, despite some measures to recruit more minorities including ethnic minority women, such as allowing Muslim female police officers to wear an adaptation of the hijab since 2001, the numbers of Muslims, and Muslim women in particular, are very low: 300 Muslims and 20 Muslim women in a police corps of 35,000.

In 2014 there was another minor but peculiar incident. Mr Shneur Odze, an Orthodox Jewish politician running for Member of European Parliament on the list of the Eurosceptic ring-wing UKIP[119] refused to shake hands with women.[120] He had told party members his Orthodox Judaism forbids him from physical contact with women other than his own wife. While some party activists were reportedly offended, since the stance 'threatens to alienate half the electorate', 'senior officials have rebuked these activists as "rude" and "wrong" for refusing to respect Odze's beliefs'.[121]

---

[119] UK independence party. UKIP's former leader Nigel Farage became somewhat notorious after insulting the new president of the European Council Herman Van Rompuy in 2010 by saying 'you have the charisma of a damp rag and the appearance of a low-grade bank clerk' (for which he was fined 10 days' pay). The party campaigned heavily for Brexit.
[120] S Payne, 'Jewish UKIP MEP Candidate Refuses to Shake Hands with Women', *IB Times*, 17 February 2014.
[121] S Payne, 'Jewish UKIP MEP Candidate Refuses to Shake Hands with Women', *IB Times*, 17 February 2014.

Apart from in particular circumstances and jobs, shaking hands is a work condition that is not core to most jobs. It is an incidental job expectation in most situations. In that sense, assessing the context and nature of the job in question to see if alternatives could reasonably be allowed seems the best legal approach. The overarching question remains whether the objecting person can nonetheless be 'an effective' employee. From a culturally sensitive perspective, people should always be allowed some leeway, for religious, cultural, or personal reasons on how to greet others. Holding otherwise would justify oppressively excluding practices. One could redefine 'refusal to shake hands' as using alternative ways of greeting, without physical contact, but with respect. In that sense, the parameters of politeness can be (and have to be continuously) redefined to allow for more inclusive practices. The willingness to discuss such matters could also allow for a development of simple etiquette to prevent awkward situations. The same way that women who want to avoid a kiss on the cheeks from a man have learned to preemptively bring out their hands for a handshake instead, when men or women do not want to shake hands they can place their hands on their heart, and the other party can take a cue for that. A disregard for the reasons indicated by the person in question, in particular a woman who sees shaking hands with strange men as sexual harassment, is particularly problematic. When a female politician shook the hand of the new Belgian Prime Minister instead of kissing on the cheeks, she was hardly criticised for that choice (although it was unclear if there was any 'choice' involved and if so on whose part).[122] In contrast, some other demands go too far and besides raising objections of principle also are not practicable in the modern workplace. For instance, a demand from an employee to not be in the same room with male or females is much more difficult to accommodate in most circumstances.

Distinctions between how people treat men and women in greeting in the end remain a staple of Western society. In that sense, there may be little difference between Mr Enait making a distinction by shaking hands with men but greeting women otherwise and Belgian Prime Minister Charles Michel who during the inauguration on October 2014 shook hands with the male Ministers on his government while he gave the female Ministers a kiss on the cheek. In fact, the latter even made a distinction between the female Ministers by kissing three of them and shaking hands with the fourth female member of the government, Elke Sleurs, who later explained she is not inclined to kiss on the cheeks a person she does not know very well. And in the same sense that it is her choice to prefer a handshake over a kiss on the cheeks, a woman with a different comfort level can politely defer by greeting without physical contact, whether that be religiously motivated or not. In the end, any disagreement is about the interpretation of certain gestures, which is a highly cultural exercise. The question then is whether Mr Enait's refusal to shake hands with women, or rather to have physical contact with unfamiliar women, amounted to a lack of regard for women? Or does the fact that Mr Michel

---

[122] X, 'Elke Sleurs krijgt geen kus van Charles Michel', *De Morgen*, 11 October 2014.

doesn't greet men with a kiss on the cheeks say something about his stance towards women as opposed to men?

VI. Religious Prayer and Dietary Considerations in the Workplace

The issue of religious prayer in the workplace is connected to both religious time as well as facilities, and is one which often involves groups of employees rather than a sole worker. It is an issue which has been raised only sporadically in litigation, most likely since it is—if at all—handled pragmatically on the ground. When a chapel, meditation room or other appropriate facility is already available, often minority religious employees are able to use those. In the UK, the EHRC Code calls for employers to be flexible and to accommodate, where possible, requests for a suitable place to pray.[123] In 2013, a group of Muslim employees won a case against Tesco supermarkets before the Employment Tribunal. After two years of lobbying for a prayer room at the Tesco distribution centre in Crick, Northamptonshire, Tesco managers allowed workers access to a security office. However, they restricted the access in 2012, keeping it locked when not in use. The Employment Tribunal found a case of indirect discrimination against Muslims by Tesco.[124]

In the Netherlands, the issue of prayer space was one aspect of an employer's request for a dismissal permit (which the court refused to issue).[125] The employer had instituted proceedings to be able to lay off the employee who had been employed at the company for 16½ years, citing negative appraisals due to repeated tardiness, loss of motivation, bad customer service and a problematic attitude towards colleagues (unwillingness to clean shared space and especially toilets saying 'there are enough women' for that). However, all these arguments were rejected (eg there was no tardiness when the employee failed to show up at work 'at least 15 minutes' before the start of his shift). The employer also reprimanded the employee for praying during work hours and in the visible presence of customers, but it was found (collaborated by witnesses) that he only did so during legitimate break time and had created a warehouse space, in between curtains, where customers had no access. With regard to the prayer issue, the court stated:

> Even if strictly taken it cannot be stated that—in the current state of affairs—an employer is obliged to provide a space to the employee to pray in case there is no such suitable space within the business, 'good employment practices' (*goed werkgeverschap*) do imply

---

[123] C Stakim and I Johnston, 'Religious Discrimination and Muslim Employees' (2013) 25(12) *Employment Law Commentary* 2, 4.

[124] Evans, 'M&S tells Muslim staff they CAN refuse to serve customers buying alcohol or pork', n 67 above.

[125] District Court, subdistrict judge Rotterdam, 20 June 2012, LJN: BX4414.

that when such space is available or can be created without particular burden or cost, the employer should not prohibit the employee from making use of it.[126]

In the case at hand, the long-term employee had essentially found a coping mechanism and accommodated his own praying without any explicit demands, convinced that he was doing it during his own breaks and not bothering anyone in a warehouse space. The employer in fact had no problem with the fact of prayer in the workplace, but there had been misunderstandings regarding the modalities. A more open dialogue to find reasonable accommodation no doubt could have been helpful to both parties in this regard. Apart from the prayer issue, this case illustrates the extensiveness of argumentation and action which is required of employers in the Netherlands to be able to dismiss protected employees, even in case of a breakdown of the relationship or malfunctioning of the employee. This protection goes much beyond what anti-discrimination law has to offer in such cases. However, because they do not have the benefit of working under such beneficial protective contracts (or are refused such employment in the first place), many religious employees find themselves obliged to turn to anti-discrimination law for protection.

In Belgium, a 1994 case before the Labour Tribunal of Nivelles touched on the use of prayer facility, discouraging employees from 'practising their religion in the workplace'.[127] The Labour Tribunal held that an employer may regulate (and even prohibit) a religious practice if it is internal, during working hours or on certain company premises. Dismissal after warning was not unreasonable since it was up to the Muslim workers to practise during breaks and not in reserved anti-contamination rooms. While it is true that the practice of a religion outside the company has no connection 'with the conduct of the worker or the operational requirements of the enterprise', it is otherwise when the worker practises his religion within the company, according to the court.

The issue of prayer facilities has come up more frequently on the ground. We were able to look into the file related to a case in which the Belgian equality body (then CEOOR) intervened and had posted on its website as an example of a 'success-story'.[128] The employer was a Belgian branch of an Asian multinational where there were tensions between a number of Muslim employees (temp workers) and Belgian workers (with more secure contracts, and enjoying the union's backing). The request of the Muslim employees to have a praying room was not supported by the union, and according to the equality body's public story it helped bring the parties to a solution by having a 'silent space' meant for 'praying in silence, meditation, rest or reading something'. However, such 'success' came after

---

[126] District Court, subdistrict judge Rotterdam, 20 June 2012, para 4.10.

[127] Prayer facilities: Labour Tribunal of Nivelles, 11 March 1994, *Revue de Jurisprudence de Liège, Mons et Bruxelles* 1994, 1400.

[128] Under the heading 'Praying at work' ('*bidden op het werk*'), as well as in its annual 2012 and 2011 discrimination and diversity reports.

years of negotiation, during which the Muslim workers had been pestered significantly (eg forced to go and pray in their cars) and ultimately laid off.

In fact, the main reason that the prayer demand was not entirely dismissed was because the management did not support calls for a neutrality policy (the unions did) because it was out of step with their business model. Considering the time it took to come to a 'mutually agreeable solution' and the sacrifices that were made in the process, this is perhaps not the best incidence of success in negotiating religious accommodations. More than illustrating that such prayer requests can be negotiated, it shows the rigidity in such processes and the inequality that is maintained when the union uses its position to advocate (only) for the more privileged workers and works against the interests of religious minorities who incidentally enjoy a much lesser employment protection. It is telling that in the end, the only way the union agreed was because the space was not designated as a prayer space, but rather as a 'general leisure room', and any activity was to be done 'in silence', which in itself can become a source of tension and conflict.

What has been said for prayer facilities applies to large extent to the issue of dietary considerations in the workplace, these are being handled pragmatically and have rarely led to litigation. In the British case of *Khan v Direct Line Insurance plc*[129] the question was whether incentivising sales staff with alcoholic drinks amounted to discrimination of Muslim employees who do not drink alcohol on account of their religious beliefs. The Employment Tribunal held that it did not. Having an incentive system to encourage sales was found to be a legitimate aim and giving alcoholic drinks was an appropriate way to do so. In addition, the company had in practice replaced the alcohol with gift vouchers where an employee did not want the alcoholic drinks.

---

[129] *Khan v Direct Line Insurance plc*, [2005] ET/1400026/05.

6

Country Study Insights and Reasonable Accommodation

I. The Limits of the Law

The previous chapters have focused on a variety of religious accommodation issues recurring in the European workplace, including religious dress, religion-worktime conflicts and refusal to shake hands with members of the opposite sex based on religious beliefs. Collectively, these cases provide a wealth of information about *which issues* occur in practice as well as *how* employees, employers, European and domestic courts deal with such (legal) conflicts.

At the supranational level, EU law and the ECHR are the legal instruments to address religious requests related to the workplace. While EU law has been considered the most appropriate framework for addressing most issues and the CJEU's role may be bolstered by the two religious discrimination cases currently pending before it, the CJEU has been on the warming bench and been unable to influence the scope and extent of the protection against religious discrimination in the workplace in the first 16 years of the operation of the Equal Treatment Directive. At its end, the ECtHR has only recently resuscitated Article 9 ECHR in *Eweida v United Kingdom* (2013), the full implications of which would create a small revolution in the law of many Member States such as Belgium. Indeed, the ECtHR has created momentum to turn the positive duties under Article 9 ECHR into a de facto reasonable accommodation duty, but whether and when this happens depends on a variety of factors and is likely influenced by criticism of judicial activism expressed regarding other areas of the Court's jurisprudence. In any event, by encapsulating the issue at the supranational level, whereas before it was relegated to the domestic/local level under the freedom to resign doctrine, the ECtHR's *Eweida* decision implies an upgrading of the human right to freedom of religion or belief: what is worth protecting on a 'uniform' level is thus 'fundamental' enough to mandate shared, minimum standards.

Considering the vacuum left by the limited supranational guidance and oversight, much remains to be decided at the domestic level. The Belgian, Dutch and British examples highlight particular aspects of the human rights and anti-discrimination law frameworks shared with other European countries. Legal rights, incorporated in abstract and principled legal instruments, have to be shaped and reshaped through case law decisions. The comparative consideration of the issue of dress codes illustrates that the proper limits of religious freedom and non-discrimination in the workplace are not well-established in Europe, but that reasoning and decisions are influenced by highly normative, ideological debates and positioning. These frameworks are highly susceptible to dilution though interpretative minimalism. For instance, while freedom of religion or belief can be said to cover both the *forum internum* as the *forum externum*, a considerable hollowing of the fundamental right in practice ensues when it is limited to beliefs, and the manifestations which are most recurring are excluded from the same level of protection. Article 9 ECHR too can be reduced to a mere window-dressing tool.

Belgian labour courts have approved restrictive policies towards religious dress, especially when coated in 'indistinct' formal equality and neutrality language. Restrictive, exclusionary practices and developments in the labour market were given a judicial stamp of approval and led to the disqualification of large pools of minority job applicants including Muslim women wearing a headscarf. But considering the political context this is unlikely to be addressed in the short-term in Belgium.[1] What's more, regressing from existing anti-discrimination protections is quite imaginable.[2]

In the Netherlands and the United Kingdom, the *judicial* approach towards religious dress has been consistently accommodative, predominantly by employing the anti-discrimination law framework. This is not to say that these countries have not struggled, and are struggling, to appropriately address this and other accommodation issues, such as refusals to officiate at same-sex marriages or to shake hands with members of the opposite sex. Even when it comes to religious dress and other visible symbols of faith, persistent recurrence of the issue of religious dress restrictions and penalisations in particular in the Netherlands shows that the substantial notions of equality promoted at the discourse level have not been realised as better inclusion on the ground (yet). Challenges also include appropriately addressing the claims of individuals belonging to the *majority* religion, who have at times presented notable illustrations of double standards.

It goes without saying that only a small minority of cases reach the courts. Sociological and NGO reports can provide insights into the salience of these issues addressed above as well as other *issues* that play a role in the particular national or local contexts.[3] Ethnographic studies are particularly apt at illustrating

---

[1] Aziz has called the current Belgian government 'the most right-winged since World War II', see R Aziz, 'Waarom protesteren we eigenlijk nog?', *De Standaard*, 16 October 2014.

[2] The Belgian federal coalition agreement prescribed a 're-evaluation' of the Anti-Discrimination Act in the future and a staunch opponent of anti-discrimination law was appointed to the board of the Interfederal Centre for Equal Opportunities (now Unia) in October 2014, see J Van Horenbeek, 'N-VA'er aangesteld bij Gelijkekansencentrum: "Discrimineren is een fundamentele vrijheid". Matthias Storme (N-VA): controleur of saboteur?', *De Morgen*, 25 October 2014.

[3] eg Y Lamghari, *L'Islam en entreprise: La diversité culturelle en question* (Editions L'Harmattan, 2012); I Adam and A Rea, *Culturele diversiteit op de werkvloer: praktijken van redelijke aanpassing in België* (Brussels, Centre for Equal Opportunities and Opposition against Racism (CEOOR), 2010); Amnesty International, *Choice and Prejudice. Discrimination against Muslims in Europe* (2012); Sociological studies conducted within the RELIGARE framework.

the complexity and ingenuity of individual and collective 'coping mechanisms' at play.[4] Litigation—requiring significant resources—remains the exception, and in certain circumstances is seen as a 'loss of face' in the community or counter-productively 'kicking up a fuss' in society.[5]

Any legal analysis thus primarily looks at the 'tip of the iceberg'. While this method has its limitations, it also has strengths in this context. In particular, a comparative legal perspective—indeed, looking at various 'tips of icebergs'—can produce a better understanding of how challenges on the ground interact with and are mediated by judicial interpretations and actions. Courts in three European countries with comparable high-quality human rights and anti-discrimination laws have given significantly different interpretations to concepts such as indirect discrimination/distinction, proportionality, neutrality, religious expressions, freedom of religion or belief and so on, and have affected the situation in diverse ways. The 'sociological sphere' and the 'legal level' cannot be neatly separated; they interact and to some extent are dependent on each other. Negotiations often occur in the shadow of the law, which in turn cannot ignore but only seek to guide social developments on the ground. Case law that consistently shoots down company neutrality policies sends a powerful message to labour market stakeholders and helps shapes the state of play when it comes to toleration or accommodation of religious practices in the workplace. Jurisprudence proclaiming such neutrality policies to be legitimate, necessary and proportionate has general effects[6] beyond the case before the bench, with notable effects on employers, employees, labour organisations and society as a whole.

Reasonable accommodation already runs through the case law of the Member States, for instance when a Dutch court, in the frame of an indirect discrimination action, assesses whether any alternatives were available which could have reconciled the parties' interests and allowed the employee to keep his or her job. In the UK too, courts have considered the (in)flexibility of employers and their willingness to adopt measures to allow the inclusion of employees who wear religious dress or have certain religious objections. Both legal scholars and policy-makers, including Lisa Waddington, Lucy Vickers and Andreas Stein, have argued that if interpreted broadly or 'dynamically' the prohibition of indirect discrimination

---

[4] For accounts of Jewish women who adopt various coping strategies in the face of difficulties and hostilities in the workplace in Belgium, see, eg, Tzadik, 'Jewish Women in the Belgian Workplace: An Anthropological Perspective' in K Aldadi, M-C Foblets and J Vrielink (eds), *A Test of Faith? Religious Diversity and Accommodation in the European Workplace* (Aldershot, Ashgate, 2012).

[5] See above; A Hoque and P Shah, *UK Report On Fieldwork* (RELIGARE project, 2012).

[6] When it comes to the effects of legislation, John Griffiths makes an apt distinction between special and general social effects of legislation. The latter refers to general effects in society, without any official or judicial actions taken. Special social effects, in contrast, refer to effects of legislation in conflict situations where official or judicial actors become involved, in other words when equal treatment commissions or courts decide on particular claims of discrimination. J Griffiths, 'The social working of anti-discrimination law' in MLP Loenen and PR Rodrigues (eds), *Non-Discrimination Law: Comparative Perspectives* (Kluwer, 1999) 319.

already includes (or at least *should* include)[7] a right to reasonable accommodation of deeply-held beliefs and religious practices, making explication obsolete. But despite positive signs testifying to the aptitude of the anti-discrimination framework to address particular issues, the 'reasonable accommodation approach' is not shared by all European countries, nor adopted in all areas where it could be useful. There is also no guarantee that this approach will continue; public and political sensitivity to the issues involved could make courts change course. In that sense, an explicit and separate duty for European employers to provide reasonable accommodations (and a corresponding right for the employee) on the basis of religion or belief would not be wholly novel when it comes to religious rights in Europe. However, such duty of reasonable accommodation would have considerable added value in the current European state of affairs, making a vital difference to help foster a more promising substantive equality for religious minorities and others in the area of employment.

II. The Added Value of Reasonable Accommodation for Religion and Belief in the European Context

The idea of reasonable accommodation entails a mentality switch with regard to the role of religion in the workplace. The ex-ante legitimacy and recognition it affords requests for accommodation can have important effect on the shop-floor level and in the lives of employees. I therefore argue that, in light of the often problematic socio-economic status of ethno-religious communities—low participation rates, high unemployment, occupational segregation—across Europe, it is justified to look beyond the existing legal frameworks in Europe to law and policy practices and instruments that work towards a more substantive notion of equality for individuals belonging to these various vulnerable groups, and to explore the transformative capacities of a legally explicit mandate. Hardships faced today by sizeable disadvantaged and excluded groups have adverse effects on the European economy and on the society of today and tomorrow.

In the United States, soon after the adoption of the 1964 Civil Rights Act, the Equal Employment Opportunity Commission (EEOC) interpreted the prohibition of religious discrimination under Title VII of that Act to imply a duty of reasonable accommodation on the employer. When the EEOC's position was dismissed in a number of court cases, such duty was explicitly included in the Civil

---

[7] Both Vickers and Stein seem to argue for integrating a duty to accommodate within the prohibition of indirect discrimination, see Vickers, 'The relationship between religious diversity and secular models: an equality-based perspective' in M-C Foblets et al (eds), *Belief, Law and Politics What Future for a Secular Europe?* (Aldershot, Ashgate, 2014); A Stein, 'Reasonable accommodation for religion and belief: can it be accommodated in EU law without an express duty?' in M-C Foblets et al (eds), *Belief, Law and Politics What Future for a Secular Europe?* (Aldershot, Ashgate, 2014).

Rights Act in 1972.[8] Since then, American employers with more than 15 employees have a legal duty to reasonably accommodate the practices, observances or beliefs of their employees unless doing so would amount to an 'undue hardship'.[9] An employee who feels his request was unduly rejected or was even entirely ignored can turn to the EEOC and potentially file a suit alleging the failure to accommodate. It must be stated that the concept of 'undue hardship' has been interpreted by the US Supreme Court as very low a de minimis standard.[10] An statutory 'absolute' religious time accommodation was struck down *In Re Estate of Thornton v Caldor*.[11] The US Supreme Court held that a Connecticut State statute, stating that an employee cannot be required to work on his day of Sabbath or be dismissed for refusal to work on that day, was unconstitutional under the Establishment Clause of the First Amendment. Because of the de minimis standard, the duty of reasonable accommodation is not considered especially strong. An employer retains substantial discretion in deciding how far to accommodate, but need not do so if it exceeds minimal cost or inconvenience.[12] But it is a workable right and employers often go beyond what is minimally required for a variety of reasons, including the cost of defending a lawsuit and the generally positive regard for religion and employees with faith.[13] Often the cost or inconvenience of providing religious accommodations will not exceed the cost of potential lengthy and expensive litigation, even if it would exceed the de minimis standard (which the repeatedly proposed Workplace Religious Freedom Act (WRFA)[14] seeks to overrule). Though the de minimis rule formally still stands, in the most recent highprofile reasonable accommodation case, involving a Muslim student who wanted to wear a headscarf and was refused a position at the clothing store Abercrombie & Fitch in Tulsa, the Supreme Court in an opinion by the late Justice Scalia found

---

[8] The EEOC interpreted the prohibition of discrimination on the basis of religion to *imply* a duty of reasonable accommodation on the employer. See, however, *Dewey v Reynolds Metal Co* 429 F 2d 324 (6th Cir 1970); cf Emmanuelle Bribosia, Julie Ringelheim and Isabelle Rorive, 'Aménager la diversité: le droit de l'égalité face à la pluralité religieuse' (2009) 78 *Revue trimestrielle des droits de l'homme* 319.

[9] 42 USCA s 2000 (e)(j).

[10] *Trans World Airlines, Inc v Hardison*, 432 US 63 (1977).

[11] *In Re Estate of Thornton v Caldor* 472 US 703 (1985).

[12] See Fredman, *Comparative study of anti-discrimination and equality laws of the US, Canada, South Africa and India* (European Network of Legal Experts in the non-discrimination field, 2012) 50.

[13] This explains why atheist and non-believing employees in the American setting succumb to discrimination in the workplace; see my chapter entitled 'The Limits of State Law in an Organized Secular-Humanist Community in the Southern Bible Belt: Model Behaviour Shaping Restraint Law Use' published in the collective article K Alidadi, J Bernaerts, P Burai, M-C Foblets, K Kokal, M Riedel and E Steyn, 'Which Law for Which Religion? Ethnographic Enquiries into the Limits of State Law vis-à-vis Lived Religion' (2016) 3 *Rechtsphilosophie: Zeitschrift für Grundlagen des Rechts* 237–82.

[14] This Bill, which has been repeatedly introduced in Congress, including in 1999 by then Senator John Kerry, proposes amendments to Title VII of the Civil Rights Act of 1964 to limit employers' discretion to decline to accommodate employees' religious practices, effectively overruling the *Hardison* decision and the de minimis rule.

for the employee, saying this was 'really easy'.[15] The right to reasonable accommodation was resuscitated, as it was held that an employer may not refuse to hire an applicant if the employer is motivated by avoiding the need to accommodate a religious practice.

While in the US, Congress (and State legislatures) as proponent(s) of broad religious liberty have responded to restrictive holdings of the US Supreme Court with protective legislation, in Canada it was the Supreme Court[16] which adopted a right to reasonable accommodation. Today, there are significant differences,[17] as the Canadian Supreme Court considered this a 'transversal' right which applies to all discrimination grounds, though it was first decided in a case involving religious discrimination in employment.[18] The standard for assessing undue hardship also differs; the Canadian approach is purposive, as the Supreme Court explicitly rejected the de minimis standard and adopted a more demanding standard aimed at removing entry barriers to the employment market and instituting substantive equality.[19]

Thus, with a later start the Canadian courts have caught up with their North American neighbour and even (far) surpassed it. Amongst other things, employer's justification arguments for non-accommodation are scrutinised much more strictly by Canadian courts. But these judicial developments towards greater equality, accommodation, and inclusion have not been unanimously well-received in this officially multicultural nation; notably, the 'crisis of accommodation' in Quebec led to appeasement attempts and the setting up of the Bouchard-Taylor Commission which issued its report in 2008.[20] However it must be stated that this crisis and the Commission's report did not relate to religious accommodation in employment, but rather in public education and health.[21] The backlash may also

---

[15] US Supreme Court, *Equal Employment Opportunity Commission v Abercrombie & Fitch*, 575 US _ (2015); A Liptak, 'Muslim Woman Denied Job Over Head Scarf Wins in Supreme Court', *New York Times*, 1 June 2015 ('"This is really easy" Justice Antonin Scalia said in announcing the decision from the bench').

[16] Before the 1970s the US Supreme Court was considered a pioneer in advancing substantive equality rights and the Canadian Supreme Court was far less responsive to equality claims until the Charter of Rights and Freedoms was adopted in 1982. In Canada, human rights codes/non-discrimination laws have been given 'quasi-constitutional' status by the Supreme Court, so that these codes have primacy over laws such as employment laws and collective labour agreements. Supreme Court of Canada, *Quebec (Commission des droits de la personne et des droits de la jeunesse) v Communauté urbaine de Montréal (City of Montréal)* [2004] 1 SCR 789, 799 (s 15: 'Section 52 unquestionably gives the Quebec Charter a preeminent, quasi-constitutional stature in relation to other Quebec legislation').

[17] Another issue is the (barring of) cross-fertilisation between constitutional equality protections and anti-discrimination statutory protection. The US Supreme Court has refused to adopt Constitutional protections in parallel to what is mandated under the Civil Rights Act, while Canada has extended the approach under the Human Rights Codes to the Charter's equality guarantee.

[18] *O'Malley v Simpsons-Sears* [1985] 2 SCR 536.

[19] See *Central Okanagan School District No 23 v Renaud*, [1992] 2 SCR 970.

[20] G Bouchard and C Taylor, *Building the Future. A Time for Reconciliation (report)*, (Government of Quebec, 2008).

[21] I have discussed the Commission report (and those of three other national 'managing diversity' commissions) more elaborately in K Alidadi, 'On Reasonable Accommodations for Religion or Belief: Charting and Linking Perspectives, Positions and Recommendations in Four "Managing Diversity" Commission Reports' (forthcoming).

have been much more pronounced in Quebec than elsewhere in Canada since it has been said that 'one of the most striking features of the politics of accommodation is an increasing gulf between public attitudes in Quebec and those in the [rest of Canada]'.[22]

The concept of reasonable accommodations is not inherently linked to one particular characteristic or 'discrimination strand', though is a particularly appropriate way to address disadvantages or obstacles related to religion or belief, disability and gender. In Canada the right to accommodation is transversal, meaning it is linked to all characteristics under non-discrimination law, including religion, disability, gender and race.[23] In the US, the accommodation duty on the ground of disability was included in the 1973 US Rehabilitation Act and in its successor act, the 1990 Americans with Disabilities Act.[24] The latter is credited with having 'brought the issue of reasonable accommodations for individuals with disabilities to the attention of policy-makers and disability activists on a global scale'.[25]

Under EU law, an enforceable right to reasonable accommodation is reserved for people with disabilities in the area of employment and occupation, where it is recognised that to achieve full inclusion of persons with disabilities, effective individualised measures or supportive adaptations of the social environment are crucial and much-needed.[26] The UN Convention on the Rights of Persons with Disabilities (2006) also makes extensive use of the concept, bringing the denial of reasonable accommodations under the definition of discrimination on the basis of disability[27] and extending the right beyond the area of the labour market.[28]

---

[22] S Choudhry, 'Rights Adjudication in a Plurinational State: the Supreme Court of Canada, Freedom of Religion, and the Politics of Reasonable Accommodation' (2013) 50 *Osgoode Hall Law Journal* 589 (discussing findings from a public opinion poll in 2007).

[23] See S Day and G Brodsky, 'The Duty to Accommodate: Who Will Benefit?' (1996) 75 *La Revue du Barreau Canadien* 433; Waddington, 'Reasonable Accommodation. Time to Extent the Duty to Accommodate Beyond Disability?' (2011) 36 *Nederlands Tijdschrift voor de Mensenrechten/Nederlands Juristen Comit voor de Mensenrechten Bulletin* 186, 191 on the 'unitary approach' in Canada, where the *de minimis* standard applicable in the United States has also been rejected in favour of a more generous, purposive approach. *Central Okanagan School District No 23 v Renaud*, [1992] 2 SCR 970 (Canada Supreme Court).

[24] Americans with Disabilities Act 1990 42 USC s 12101 et seq. In order to establish a prima facie case of failure to adopt reasonable accommodations under the ADA, a plaintiff must show that: (1) the individual is disabled within the meaning of the Act; (2) she is otherwise qualified for the position, with or without reasonable accommodation; (3) her employer knew or had reason to know about her disability; (4) she requested an accommodation; and (5) the employer failed to provide the necessary accommodation. *Johnson v Cleveland City School District* 443 Fed Appx 974, 982–83 (6th Cir 2011).

[25] L Waddington, 'Chapter six: reasonable accommodation' in D Schiek, L Waddington and M Bell (eds), *Cases, materials and text on national, supranational and international non-discrimination law* (Oxford, Hart Publishing, 2007) 630–31.

[26] See Article 5 and recital 16 Employment Equality Directive. see also Article 4 Proposal for a Council Directive on implementing the principle of equal treatment between persons irrespective of religion or belief, disability, age or sexual orientation COM(2008) 426 final (hereafter 'Proposed Horizontal Directive'). Interestingly, a denial of reasonable accommodation is considered a form of discrimination under the Proposed Horizontal Directive, following the UN Convention on the Rights of People with Disabilities 2006.

[27] Article 2 UN Convention on the Rights of Persons with Disabilities 2006.

[28] See, for instance, Art 24 UN Convention on the Rights of Persons with Disabilities 2006, with regard to reasonable accommodation in education.

Few explicit reasonable accommodation duties extending beyond disability have been adopted in Europe,[29] but various countries do have specific legislation and measures in place which—without using the term explicitly—de facto amount to particular instances of (reasonable) accommodations for certain (religious) groups in employment and beyond.[30]

The diverging meanings of the concept of indirect discrimination in the case law practice of the Member States are an important consideration in light of the objective of effective freedom of movement of workers within the EU, a fundamental objective of the EU Treaty. Considering this divergence, one could argue that introducing a legal duty at the EU level would have the advantage of levelling the playing-field across the EU labour markets, eg creating more uniformity in the legal practices of the Member States,[31] which would aid the free movement of workers. This is not to say that a reasonable accommodation duty will *guarantee* a *uniform* approach in all Member States, as it arguably has also not done so in the case of disability,[32] but it is bound to discredit and brush away some extreme limiting approaches which are incompatible with the idea and purpose behind reasonable accommodations. Further consistency in approaches can be promoted, eg, by adopting clear guidelines on possible types of accommodations, the standard to be used in assessing the 'reasonability' and the burden/hardship test, and by various 'soft law' measures.[33]

Despite its promising beginnings, the achievements brought about *in practice* through the concept of indirect discrimination have been called disappointing.[34] While there is the potential to unmask taken-for-granted rules that in effect are structurally disadvantageous to some, indirect discrimination merely means

---

[29] See, eg, Article 5.4. Flemish Decree on Proportionate Participation on the Labour Market of 8 May 2002, applicable in the area of Flemish education and employment mediation, contains a general duty of reasonable accommodation for various 'risk groups' (*kansengroepen*). This provision has not been tested in practice with regard to religious minorities.

[30] See the Law allowing the Jewish minority in Italy time off on important Jewish religious holidays in *Sessa v Italy* Application no 28790/08 (ECtHR, 3 April 2012). In the UK, s 11 of the Employment Act 1989 exempts turban-wearing Sikhs from having to wear safety helmets on a construction site. An instance of accommodation on the basis of gender is the right for new mothers to take (un)paid breastfeeding breaks on the job. There are also examples outside of employment. In many countries there are exemptions to animal slaughtering laws to accommodate Muslim and Jews. Again in the UK, Sikhs are exempt from the requirement to wear motorcycle helmets under s 2A of the Motor-Cycle Crash Helmets (Religious Exemption) Act 1976.

[31] In this context it is important to note that EU Directives generally 'shall be binding, as to the result to be achieved, upon each Member State to which it is addressed, but shall leave to the national authorities the choice of form and methods'). Art 288, para 3 of the Treaty on the Functioning of the European Union.

[32] Waddington, 'Chapter six: reasonable accommodation', n 25 above, 629 et seq.

[33] The term proportionality is probably more appropriate in the European context, as opposed to 'undue hardship' in the US context. On guidance: in the US the Equal Employment Opportunity Commission (EEOC) issues compliance manuals and guidelines; in the UK there is also experience with such tools (British Equality and Human Rights Commission and Acas).

[34] Schiek, 'Chapter three: Indirect discrimination' in D Schiek, L Waddington and M Bell (eds), *Cases, materials and text on national, supranational and international non-discrimination law* (Oxford, Hart Publishing, 2007) 332–33.

'a prohibition to exploit existing inequalities and to stabilize further or even increase them'.[35] For that reason it has been said that it will 'never bring about the changes required to eliminate structural discrimination, but only allows individuals to challenge the results of such practices in limited circumstances'.[36]

But the concept is also unduly complex, and knowledge of this legal concept is lacking on the shop-floor, contributing to its misapplication or a 'dead letter' status. In 1999, Woldringh and others conducted socio-legal research on the effects of equal treatment law in the Netherlands (the 1994 Equal Treatment Act, but also sex equality legislation going back to the 1970s). They contacted 1,309 employers (both public and private, large and small) and talked to the Human Resources managers. One question was meant to test the familiarity with the concepts of direct and indirect discrimination ('distinction' in the Dutch jargon).[37] While the familiarity with equal treatment law in general was broad, when asked about the difference between direct and indirect distinction, 90 per cent of the respondents had never even heard of this. The small group which indicated knowledge was then asked about the difference. Only a few were able to correctly state the difference; many respondents thought that direct distinction refers to 'clear and visible discrimination' while indirect distinction refers to concealed discrimination or discrimination via some backdoor.[38] Woldringh and others noted that knowledge in this area had not improved in the five years since 1994, when another researcher[39] looked into the same issue.

III. Arguments Against Reasonable Accommodation and Rebuttal

Is it a good idea to give employees across Europe an explicit and legally enforceable right to reasonable accommodation for reason of religion or belief? What are the potential benefits, trade-offs and burdens for the parties directly involved—current or prospective employees and employers—as well as for co-workers, labour unions, customers and the broader society? While this basic question has generated considerable—and at times polemic—debate in legal and policy circles and beyond, some find the idea so objectionable that any dialogue or study is rejected forthright.

Some academics have argued against adopting such provision, with different—complementary and contradictory—reasons advanced. An explicit duty of reasonable

---

[35] ibid, 332–33.
[36] ibid, 332–33.
[37] C Woldringh, 'Arbeidsorganisaties en gelijke-behandelingswetgeving' in IP Asscher-Vonk and CA Groenendijk (eds), *Gelijke behandeling: regels en realiteit* (The Hague, Sdu, 1999) 341 et seq.
[38] C Woldringh, 'Arbeidsorganisaties en gelijke-behandelingswetgeving', n 37 above, 351.
[39] ibid. JAH Blom, *De effectiviteit van de Wet gelijke behandeling m/v: tweede deelonderzoek* (The Hague, Vuga 1995).

accommodation for religion or belief (they say) would hold little added value in light of what is already there. It would be confusing and counter-productive, considering the existing prohibition of direct and indirect discrimination and such right for persons with disabilities under EU law.[40] The fact that claims of religious employees have the potential to conflict with other democratic values and (human) rights ('clashing rights') is a pivotal reason for discarding the idea.[41] Some people lump reasonable accommodation together with other (progressive) protection against discrimination, and favour an overall inferior protection for the ground of religion or belief,[42] while others focus on the undesirability or inaptness of the accommodation approach in particular.

Positions in favour of extending reasonable accommodation have also been articulated. Some authors focus on religion or belief while others advocate an encompassing accommodation mandate covering all discrimination grounds or potential sources of disadvantage. For instance, Bader has argued 'for as much accommodation as is compatible with the standards of moral minimalism'.[43] This would allow considerable space for accommodation as

> only some ethno-religious practices of non-liberal minorities conflict with the core of minimal morality, or of minimal liberal-democratic morality. The broad variety of practices, which do not involve such conflicts (even if they require considerable accommodation) should be easier to resolve.[44]

Somek regards accommodation as a remedy for the 'normative deficiency' of EU anti-discrimination law. He writes that

> accommodation concerns all protected groups equally ... It is difficult to imagine some justification [for limiting it to individuals with disabilities] ... The broad sweep of accommodation comes to encompass potentially all impediments to participation in markets that unduly compromise the integrity of one's life.[45]

This issue is complicated by the fact that reasonable accommodations is so strongly affiliated with anti-discrimination law and human rights protections that some

---

[40] See L Waddington, 'Reasonable Accommodation. Time to Extent the Duty to Accommodate Beyond Disability?', n 23 above; A Lester and P Uccellari, 'Extending The Equality Duty to Religion, Conscience, And Belief: Proceed With Caution' (2008) 5 *European Human Rights Law Review* 567, 570.

[41] See Malik, *Religious Freedom in The 21st Century (Westminster Faith Debates)* (focusing on the *Ladele* case).

[42] McColgan, 'Class wars? Religion and (in)equality in the workplace' (2009) 38 *Industrial Law Journal* 1; A Lester and P Uccellari, 'Extending The Equality Duty to Religion, Conscience, And Belief: Proceed With Caution' (2008) 5 *European Human Rights Law Review* 567, 570. (McColgan argues that in light of the potential clashing rights perspective 'inherent in the prohibition of discrimination on grounds of religion or belief with the regulation of discrimination on other grounds', it is 'a mistake to protect religion and/or belief in like manner to grounds such as sex, race, sexual orientation and disability').

[43] Bader, *Secularism or democracy? Associational governance of religious diversity* (IMISCOE/Amsterdam University Press 2007) 129.

[44] ibid, 153.

[45] Somek, *Engineering Equality. An Essay on European Anti-Discrimination Law* (Oxford, OUP, 2011) 183–84.

authors have argued that freedom of religion and non-discrimination are 'empty' and 'nugatory' without a corresponding duty of reasonable accommodation.[46] Other scholars remain cautiously open to the idea of reasonable accommodations playing a useful role in the European context.[47]

Reasonable accommodation can be considered an *aspirational* right as it can be considered to tie in with notions of pluralism, inclusion and equality, but it is also possible to see it as a *corrective* right similar to what was the case in the United States and Canada. As an aspirational 'model' it squarely falls in the ambit of normative political theories on minorities, Islam and multiculturalism, and one could discuss the merits without much regard for the realities on the ground or the particular (geographical) setting. However, to argue that reasonable accommodation not only makes general sense, but is particularly called for in a given context requires particular attention to the current state of play. Reasonable accommodation is a corrective right if it is needed to address particular needs that arise on the ground. These two aspects are obviously often lumped together, but the distinction may be useful to bear in mind when discussing various arguments pro and contra: is the position defended based on normative ideas (alone) or also by reference to current legal and social developments?

When I advocate for an enforceable right to reasonable accommodation for European employees, irrespective of religious minority status, I certainly defend certain normative stances. But I also proceed from—my understanding of—the legal and sociological state of play in Europe today. My position is thus formulated against a particular backdrop: the current European and national (judicial) approaches towards religion in the workplace, in particular the findings in the previous chapters on religious dress, religion-worktime conflicts, religious affiliation discrimination and the variety of other accommodation issues.

The preceding chapters, looking at *current court practices* dealing with claims and requests that often could be framed in terms of reasonable accommodations, set up the necessary background. Indeed, the current frameworks show various cracks and holes. Certainly the law, both at the European level as well as at the domestic level, is in flux and positive developments may be conceivable. But in light of the current political, economic and social context in Europe, the human rights regime embedded in the ECHR, as well as the anti-discrimination law perspective as it stands—and despite huge progress made—have undeniable shortcomings. It is not justified to sit patiently and idly until the tide turns. There are also inherent limitations and causes for concern which will not dissipate with all

---

[46] Somek, *Engineering Equality. An Essay on European Anti-Discrimination Law*, ibid, 182; Lori G Beaman, 'Religion and Rights: The Illusion of Freedom and the Reality of Control' (2005) 6 *Culture and Religion* 17, 20. See also Christine Jolls, 'Antidiscrimination and Accommodation' (2001) 115 *Harvard Law Review* 642, 652–66 (arguing that traditional antidiscrimination law, especially disparate impact, is best understood as accommodation requirements, so that the two are not so easily distinguishable).

[47] eg in the UK, see B Hepple, *Equality: The New Legal Framework* (Hart Publishing, 2011) and Vickers for a more cautious position: L Vickers, *Religion and Belief Discrimination in Employment—the EU law* (Brussels, European Network of Legal Experts in the Non-Discrimination Field, 2006) 20.

the luxury of time or in the best socio-political circumstances. Reasonable accommodation is not only a good idea, it becomes essential to the proper and just handling of many challenges that religious employees are facing today and will continue to face in a Europe they too want to call home. In addition, reasonable accommodation is a modest yet effective corrective with merits and appeal that go beyond the mere enforceability it introduced; it offers a much-needed *positive paradigm* in the European vocabulary.[48]

Accordingly, one must highlight both 'tangible' benefits of reasonable accommodation, in the sense of the legal-technical shortcomings under human rights and indirect discrimination (which could lead to more appropriate outcomes in particular cases), as well as more 'intangible' reasons that relate to the appropriateness of the *language* and *framing* to address the situation and claims of religious individuals in secular workplaces (even if such does not necessarily lead to different outcomes). Indeed, framing claims of religious employees in terms of requests for reasonable accommodations has the potential to move the debate away from and beyond the dominant and pejorative 'discrimination talk', which is likely to trigger defensive reactions from 'perpetrators'. The fact that 'words matter' in the search for equality must be acknowledged: this is clear to People First disability advocates, having discussions whether the people-first terminology ('individual with disability') is preferable over terms that fit better in the social model ('disabled person' recognises better that a disability may be due to external societal factors).[49] In the same way that words describing people can help alter attitudes about those people, words that describe how those people's situation in society should be addressed can effectuate a useful change in paradigmatic treatment.[50]

In what follows, I identify five commonly heard objections. These objections are: (A) reasonable accommodation is obsolete in light of existing anti-discrimination law protections, (B) the adoption of such a right is undesirable and/or politically unfeasible, (C) 'voluntary accommodations' render a legally enforceable right obsolete, (D) settling for reasonable accommodations short-sells minority concerns, and (E) reasonable accommodation is a legal transplant and would not fit in the European culture. While I offer rebuttals to these wide-ranging objections, I do consider that much is to be gained from engaging in dialogue and taking the opportunity to address critical concerns.

---

[48] See ibid, 185, shift in terms of a 'decommodifying' shift in EU non-discrimination law.

[49] www.disabilityisnatural.com/explore/pfl.

[50] Recently, illustrating the importance of language used in reporting and public discourse with regard to ethno-religious minorities, the Belgian newspaper *De Morgen* decided to ban the use of the term '*allochtoon*' in its reporting commonly used to describe residents of foreign origin for reasons that this term is stigmatising and excluding. W Verschelden, 'Waarom wij, De Morgen, "allochtoon" niet meer gebruiken (opinion)', *De Morgen*, 22 September 2012. For a critique (because no better alternatives are available and utilising categories is required to be able to show that discrimination is reality and equal opportunities are not) see D Jacobs, 'Waarom ik 'allochtoon' voorlopig blijf gebruiken', *De Morgen*, 22 September 2012.

A. Comprehensive EU Anti-discrimination Law Makes Reasonable Accommodation Obsolete

The importance of the Employment Equality Directive, prohibiting discrimination *on the basis of religion or belief under EU law*, cannot be overstressed. The Directive closed many gaps in legal protection for vulnerable parties across the EU. Change in the legal framework of Member States altered the prospects of success for some considerably. In some aspects it was a game changer. For instance, in the UK there was no cause of action available against *religious* discrimination before the Employment Equality Directive was implemented in the Employment Equality (Religion or Belief) Regulations 2003. There was legal protection against racial or ethnic discrimination under the UK Race Relations Act 1976 and this allowed some but not all persons belonging to religious minorities to successfully frame their discrimination claims accordingly.[51] This turned to be in particular a problem for Muslims, faced with a 'legal anomaly'.[52] The fact that a EU Directive closed this gap was significant since it allowed Member States cumulatively to dodge charged debates on religious rights, Islam and minorities.

The anti-discrimination law framework certainly had positive effects and it remains promising in some respects. Why then adopt a new tool when what we have is still operational, even if grossly under-utilised?

The logic of EU anti-discrimination law is centred around the dichotomy of direct and indirect discrimination. There is an undeniable *crowding-out effect* of the (indirect) discrimination approach towards other progressive measures. Meenan aptly noted that as long as indirect discrimination is considered the principal tool for achieving substantive equality, positive action[53] will have an 'image problem'.[54] The same goes for reasonable accommodation, which shares some of the goals and values of indirect discrimination, but does not necessarily operate according to the same model or approach. If the protection against discrimination seeks to realise a 'good enough' equality,[55] reasonable accommodation may be considered to aim for an 'excessive' form of equality (which some, admittedly, find inappropriate).[56]

---

[51] Hepple, *Equality: The New Legal Framework*, n 47 above, 40.

[52] In *Mandla v Dowell Lee*, the House of Lords saw religion as one element for identifying an ethnic group, and found the Sikh community to constitute such a distinct racial/ethnic group protected under the Race Relations Act 1976. Jews were also protected under the Race Relations Act as well, but Muslims (who range from a large variety of ethnic backgrounds) still were not. See *Mandla v Dowell Lee*, [1983] 2 AC 548.

[53] The more current term in the US is affirmative action. In the US, the debate (in particular with regard to college admissions) has been fierce, see R Kennedy, *For Discrimination: Race, Affirmative Action, and the Law* (Pantheon, 2013).

[54] See Helen Meenan, 'Introduction' in H Meenan (ed), *Equality law in an enlarged European Union: understanding the article 13 directives* (Cambridge University Press, 2007) 23–24.

[55] See O'Brien, 'Equality's false summits: new varieties of disability discrimination, "excessive" equal treatment and economically constricted horizons' (2011) 36 *European Law Review* 26 (arguing that the EU formal equality model aims at a 'good enough' equality instead of a more complete substantive equality).

[56] ibid.

Reasonable accommodation can also share in some of the criticisms directed towards positive action; by going beyond banning negative treatment, reasonable accommodation—like positive action—may be seen as a preferential treatment that causes disadvantage to or discrimination against others.[57]

But it is precisely because of its comparatively audacious approach that reasonable accommodation can avoid some of these pitfalls of 'discrimination talk' or even 'human rights talk'. Indeed, reasonable accommodations besides addressing socio-economic and distributive justice concerns, also provide—or at least have the effect of providing—a certain 'recognition'[58] that is significant in Western Europe's multicultural context. In this context, raising concerns of inequality and exclusion require effective and swift actions.[59] By stressing the legitimacy of *differential treatment* on the basis of religion or belief, reasonable accommodations challenge the classic non-discrimination mantra requiring equal treatment of people *despite* differences in characteristics.

By its prospective orientation and operative nature reasonable accommodation emphasises the importance of procedural fairness when it comes to employee requests. Reasonable accommodation is there to be *applied*; indirect discrimination is to be *avoided* by the employer, who can be penalised ex post for exceeding certain boundaries. A perverse effect of anti-discrimination law is the shifting of the battle ground; overt discrimination tends to dissipate and exclusion is effected in more complex, and harder to prove, ways. And the incentive to avoid even talk about such a sensitive matter as religion in the workplace may be considerable.

The reasonable accommodation approach has some non-tangible effect— arguably a benefit. Allowing space 'for the articulation and legitimacy (and illegitimacy) of dealing with certain kinds of claims in ways that are deemed acceptable and satisfactory'[60] may well be one of the key contributions of an explicit and legally enforceable reasonable accommodations framework in Europe.

(i) Religion is not disability

Under the EU law framework, a right to reasonable accommodation exists for persons with disabilities. This has had mixed results in the jurisprudence of the Member States and is subject to significant development.[61] Paradoxically, the existence of the parallel right on the basis of disability can be and has been constructed by some as an obstacle rather than a facilitating factor for its extension

---

[57] Meenan, 'Introduction', n 54 above, 14, on the other hand, the critique of privileging group rights over individual rights should not be applicable in the case of reasonable accommodation.

[58] C Taylor, 'The politics of recognition' in C Taylor and A Gutmann (eds), *Multiculturalism: Examining the Politics of Recognition* (Princeton University Press, 1994) 25–73.

[59] EU Fundamental Rights Agency, *Data in Focus Report 2: Muslims* (FRA, 2009) (providing data on how Muslims across 14 Member States experience discrimination and victimisation).

[60] Modood, 'Is There a Crisis of Secularism in Western Europe?' (2012) 73 *Sociology of Religion* 130, 136.

[61] See A D'Espallier, *Redelijke aanpassingen, evenredigheid en rol van de rechter* (Bruges, Die Keure, 2016).

to other grounds, in particular religion or belief. Whether in favour of disability accommodation or not, some seek to conscientiously guard the right from what they consider undue expansion. The intra-equality law rivalry may in part be due to the single-axis structure[62] of anti-discrimination law and policy which encourages competition between advocates of various vulnerable groups who defend the rights of one minority in ways that can harm other groups' interests in achieving social justice.[63]

Despite the history behind reasonable accommodation in the US, some construe the concept as inherently adapted to the situation of persons with disabilities and inappropriate in the case of personal characteristics which are subject to volition and change.[64] A lower protection is argued to be appropriate, since religion or belief is said to be different from 'individuals' immutable physical features or personal characteristics—such as gender, age or sexual orientation' and is rather concerned with 'modes of conduct based on a subjective decision or conviction, such as the wearing or not of a head covering'.[65] One can dispute the neat division in immutable and mutable characteristics, but the question is whether the distinction should necessarily mandate a lower level of protection for religion or belief. In the end, the exclusion mechanisms at play can be similar irrespective of the immutability of a characteristic and no less problematic from an equality perspective. The notion of 'outsider' is multi-faceted so inclusion measures must seek to address this complex reality rather than setting up barriers.

B. Adopting such Right is Undesirable and/or Politically Unfeasible

This objection lumps two assertions which upon cursory review seem to differ starkly from one another. Yet, there is often a connection between arguing that a legally enforceable reasonable accommodation right is a bad idea and arguing that the chances of it being adopted in the foreseeable future are slim. In order to move

---

[62] See the landmark article by K Crenshaw, 'Demarginalizing the Intersection of Race and Sex: A Black Feminist Critique of Antidiscrimination Doctrine, Feminist Theory and Antiracist Politics' (1989) 1 *University of Chicago Legal Forum* 139.

[63] European Commission, *Green Paper on Equality and Non-discrimination in an Enlarged EU* COM(2004) 379 final (2004), 17 ('some organizations that have a tradition of working with particular target groups have found the transition to this [integrated approach to the five grounds of discrimination] challenging'). Clearly, there are overlaps between the various grounds, giving rise to cross-cutting loyalties which the law fails to adequately address, eg individuals with disabilities can have deeply-held beliefs; sexual minorities can belong to ethno-religious minorities, a woman can be Muslim, have the Belgian nationality, Moroccan roots, and [be] mother of disabled children.

[64] J Huys, 'Het niet voorzien van redelijke aanpassingen voor de persoon met een handicap is een vorm van discriminatie' (2003) 91 *Tijdschrift voor Sociaal Recht* 391.

[65] This is the argument used in the opinion delivered on 31 May 2016 by AG Kokott in the *Achbita* case (Case C-157/15), para 45. This regards protection under the current anti-discrimination law, but the argument applies a fortiori to a discussion *de lege ferenda* on reasonable accommodation.

the discussion in a more productive direction, it remains necessary to continuously untangle the two.

That the current political climate is not favourable bears little doubt.[66] The
lack of an extension of the duty of reasonable accommodation to other grounds
besides disability in the Horizontal Directive is a telling sign.[67] In its 2004 green
paper accompanying the proposed horizontal directive, the European Commission expressed its wish to 'complete' the European non-discrimination framework, but reasonable accommodation for reason of religion or belief[68] was notably
omitted from the 2008 Proposal for a Horizontal Anti-discrimination Directive.[69]
That the European Commission has also failed to address a particular aspect of
religious accommodation in the Working Time Directive was discussed above.
What also plays a role is that (a) real advocate(s) for reasonable accommodations
on grounds of religion or belief is absent; the European Network on Religion or
belief (ENORB, started in 2011) is still a fledgling organisation, and churches and
religious organisations are not necessarily well-placed to make the case for reasonable accommodation.[70]

The political and economic circumstances in the EU have changed considerably
since the time when the anti-discrimination directives were adopted. The Union
has been substantially enlarged, so the unchanged requirement of unanimity under
Article 19 TFEU renders the political decision-making process challenging to say
the least. Concerns about religious fundamentalism and terrorism, the 'refugee
crisis', and now Brexit are key challenges for the EU today. European anxiety about

[66] See T Heneghan, 'EU sees faith bias problem, but not sure of solution' *Reuters* 7 December 2012
(quoting Andreas Stein, head of the equality law unit in the European Commission as saying during
the two-day RELIGARE conference on 4–5 December 2012 on the topic of reasonable accommodations 'These are already not easy times for defending (what) we currently have in place' and 'There is
a non-negligible political risk in reopening these directives. Trying to improve them may achieve the
opposite in the end').

[67] Proposal for a Council Directive on implementing the principle of equal treatment between
persons irrespective of religion or belief, disability, age or sexual orientation COM(2008) 426
final (hereafter 'Proposed Horizontal Directive'); this proposed horizontal directive is stalled, see
L Waddington, 'Future prospects for EU equality law: lessons to be learnt from the proposed equal
treatment directive' (2011) 36 *European Law Review* 163.

[68] The horizontal anti-discrimination directive does seek to strengthen and expands reasonable
accommodation for persons with disabilities into other domains of social life such as housing and
public transportation are included, see Art.4 Proposal Horizontal Directive.

[69] European Commission, *Green Paper on Equality and Non-discrimination in an Enlarged
EU*, COM(2004) 379 final, p 20; Council Communication from the Commission to the European
Parliament, the European Economic and Social Committee and the Committee of the Regions,
Non-discrimination and Equal Opportunities: a Renewed Commitment. COM(2008) 420 final; ibid, 4.

[70] While Churches and religious organisations may want members of their faith to be accommodated, and may support them in specific instances, as employers they would not (want to) have to
provide reasonable accommodation to potential employees of different faiths working in their organisations. ENAR (European Network Against Racism) has shown interest and organised some events
on reasonable accommodation, but there is a risk of alienating part of its backing and it may feel its
priorities should be elsewhere.

Islam[71] is an undeniable obstacle, since a right to reasonable accommodation is seen—to some extent justifiably so—to favour Muslims and religious minorities.

As this analysis showed, religion-workplace issues not only involve Muslims in Europe. This is particularly clear when one expands from the headscarf as a religious symbol par excellence to religious time and miscellaneous—both older as well as modern multicultural—accommodation issues. Still, it cannot be denied that in Europe, Muslims remain at the forefront of incidences revealing tensions between liberalism and religion, secularism and diversity. As the data on labour participation and unemployment shows, Muslims are also the group for which cultural disadvantage and socio-economic disadvantage coincide, adding to compound levels of disadvantage and exclusion. Yet, some 'subtleties' surrounding the accommodation debate can get lost in more public debates, resulting in accommodation being seen solely as an issue for Muslims, and more specifically Muslim immigrant communities. This is not the case: freedom of religion *or belief*, non-discrimination based on religion *or belief*, and reasonable accommodations can be vital for religionists and non-believers alike, depending on the societal and economic context.

Nonetheless, the European Commission has limited incentive to propose progressive initiatives to upgrade the anti-discrimination framework in this context, instead opting to let the current protections 'run their course'. It can also be noted that until now, the enforcement efforts of the European Commission with regard to non-discrimination directives has mainly gone into securing full implementation of the directives (as well as awareness raising and skills training for judges and legal professionals through the PROGRESS Programme); they have only just embarked on the application verification phase.[72] The lack of CJEU case law on discrimination on the basis of religion or belief bolsters this; there is too little experience with the existing rules and it is not yet clear how CJEU case law can affect legal developments.

A call for the law to rise to a new, more inclusive register with the adoption of reasonable accommodations must take into account the current European context and zeitgeist, without being conditioned or limited by this. In the long-term, Europe will not be able to shy away, hiding behind subsidiarity to avoid such core

---

[71] A recent Ipsos Mori survey found that in many countries, including Belgium, people overestimate the number of Muslims and migrants, while they underestimate people of Christian backgrounds. Surveyed Belgians thought 29% of the population are migrants, when the number is 10%, and thought 29% of people are Muslim while the actual number is much lower (6%). In the UK, those surveyed thought Muslims in the UK constituted 21% while the actual percentage of is 5%. See J Temmerman, 'Weet u hoeveel moslims er in België wonen?', *De Morgen*, 29 October 2014; A Nardelli and G Arnett, 'Today's key fact: you are probably wrong about almost everything', *The Guardian*, 29 October 2014.

[72] See European Commission, *Joint Report on the application of Council Directive 2000/43/EC of 29 June 2000 implementing the principle of equal treatment between persons irrespective of racial or ethnic origin ('Racial Equality Directive') and of Council Directive 2000/78/EC of 27 November 2000 establishing a general framework for equal treatment in employment and occupation ('Employment Equality Directive') from the Commission to the European Parliament and the Council, Brussels, 17.1.2014*, COM(2014) 2 final, with all infringement proceedings now being closed off.

questions that all European societies face and which affect the European project as a whole. Certainly, at the national level, a duty of reasonable accommodation could be adopted: this would certainly be allowed under EU law[73] and is consistent with the idea that Member States have the freedom of means to achieve the same end results set by an EU Directive, in this case effective protection against religious discrimination in the workplace. But it can be expected that adopting such a duty would be most difficult in precisely those countries where a jurisprudential rebuffing of a reasonable accommodation duty was described. A robust *EU-wide* protection is therefore essential in moving forward (and preventing any regression in) the fight against intolerance and discrimination in the EU as a whole.

C. 'Voluntary Accommodation' Renders Legal Enforceability Redundant

Another argument often heard is that *a duty* of reasonable accommodation is obsolete because employers are already providing their employees with various accommodations without a law forcing them to do so. Voluntary accommodations on the ground are thus said to be making legally enshrined rights obsolete.

In practice, many pragmatic and workable solutions are sought and found on the ground and these practices may in part explain why some issues do not, or rarely, come up in the case law of certain countries. It is not only the law that can provide workable solutions. 'Trouble-less cases' or 'non-cases' in this field are a potentially rich source of illustrations showing that arrangements need not be—explicitly—grounded in legal talk to meet parties' interests. For instance, a kindergarten may provide kosher food for children and staff or a workplace (or prison) canteen can serve *halal* dishes or a fish dish on Fridays to meet the request of Italian Catholics who make up a large portion of the workforce.[74] A hospital may arrange shifts and assignments so that nurses and doctors who conscientiously object to assisting in abortions or other medically sensitive procedures need not work during the times or at the departments where these procedures are scheduled.[75] Even a registrar's office may draw up a schedule to accommodate a registrar who has conscientious objections to officiating over same-sex partnerships or marriages.[76] These examples can be considered as pragmatic (often bottom-up) tools to manage religious diversity in a given organisation and as vectors to ward off tensions before they escalate into conflicts. While it is difficult to gain insight into their operation on the ground (apart from some examples reported in the media) the

---

[73] Recital 28 Employment Equality Directive.

[74] Example provided in study by Adam and Rea, *Culturele diversiteit op de werkvloer: praktijken van redelijke aanpassing in België* (Centre for Equal Opportunities and Opposition against Racism, Brussels, September 2010).

[75] Dutch ETC opinion nr 2000-13, 21 March 2000.

[76] See discussion of the *Ladele* case.

non-(legal) conflict mode in which they are to be situated can be expected to offer many examples of 'good practices'.

One can imagine employers provide such accommodations for a variety of reasons, including economic efficiency, image concerns, moral reasons, and understanding of good faith standards or their understanding of what the law requires. In the case of some employers, such accommodations may fit in within an inclusive or equal opportunities employment policy which is more than mere window-dressing. Certain employers may have realised that reasonable accommodation can 'pay for itself in the greater productivity of the worker', as well as 'have externalities beyond that particular worker', eg by increasing other workers' productivity or by attracting an additional customer base.[77] Indeed, some accommodations fit well within 'the model of economic efficiency'.[78] This means there is experience on the ground of making every day adjustments for the benefit of workers and for the sake of good work relations, even in countries and in areas where no explicit reasonable accommodation duties have been enacted.[79]

The Canadian Bouchard-Taylor Commission, appointed to look into the 'accommodation crisis' in Quebec,[80] coined the terms 'concerted adjustments' and 'harmonization practices' to refer to 'non-legal accommodation' as opposed to reasonable accommodation *sensu strictu*. Yet, such distinction should not distort the fact that these 'voluntary solutions' too are *embedded* in the law and often are negotiated 'in the shadow of the law' though they remain fragile as they often depend on the goodwill of stakeholders and can alter as conditions change. Some 'anchoring' of good practices in the law is thus justified.

A 2010 Belgian sociological study on de facto practices of religious accommodations, which sought to document as many instances as possible of such negotiated reasonable accommodations for religious reasons in a number of segments of the Belgian private and public sector, concluded that such adjustments are being awarded on a case-by-case basis by various Belgian public and private employers.

[77] Waddington, 'Chapter six: reasonable accommodation', n 25 above, 725–27, referring to K Wells, 'the impact of the Framework Employment Directive on UK disability Discrimination Law' (2003) 32 *Industrial Law Journal* 264.

[78] ibid.

[79] See, eg, for Belgium: Adam and Rea, *Culturele diversiteit op de werkvloer: praktijken van redelijke aanpassing in België*, n 74 above. See also M-C Foblets and C Kulakowski, *Final report Roundtables of Interculturalism (Rondetafels van de Interculturaliteit)* (Brussels, 8 November 2010) 18–19: this Committee was set up by the Belgian government to offer advice on various multicultural challenges: because of disagreements within the steering committee, the Roundtable's report did not advance a definite recommendation on reasonable accommodation for religion or belief in the workplace (except that the issue merits further research). The Belgian Centre for Equal Opportunities has argued against adopting a reasonable accommodation duty, instead seeking to rely entirely on voluntary concessions by employers. Alidadi, 'Studie over redelijke aanpassingen voor religie op Belgische werkvloer', *De Juristenkrant*, 12 January 2011, 6–7.

[80] See Gérard Bouchard and Charles Taylor, *Building the Future. A Time for Reconciliation* (Government of Quebec, 2008) (chaired by the sociologist Gérard Bouchard and the philosopher Charles Taylor)

Assessing the situation on the ground, the authors argue that the employers' discretionary way of dealing with requests 'leads to arbitrariness, unequal treatment of employees within the same organisation and legal uncertainty'.[81] In particular, the study found that employers are more inclined to consider accommodation requests made by groups of employees (who often can rely on the support of the labour union as well), and less likely to respond to requests made by individual workers. Also, while reasons to reject (or allow) accommodation requests are frequently 'market-related', there are a variety of ideological reasons listed as well, including the wish to have a 'neutral' or 'secular' workplace and the position that religion has no business in the workplace.

One worrying observation made in the study was that particular religious requests, such as the request to wear a headscarf on the job or to make use of an available space for prayer during break times, can trigger restrictive responses even if they do not actually impede or disturb the running of the business, but because of the 'uncomfortable situation' they create. Restrictive measures include adopting a formal rule in the company regulations, which effectively block potential similar requests in the future, giving them an a priori illegitimate character. These 'solutions' not only impede current employees from reconciling faith and profession but they also discourage religiously observant individuals from applying for jobs. Many employees and co-workers in Belgium are uncomfortable with the idea of having to confront religion in the workplace (eg seeing colleagues praying in the dressing rooms can be disturbing or even 'shocking' to some) and seek to avoid tensions and conflicts. Also, the idea that accommodations for reasons of religion or belief 'privilege' religious employees remains persistent. The discomfort sometimes experienced by employer, fellow employees and labour union members, is in part due to the unfamiliarity with (minority) religions and a lack of religious literacy, and the easiest response is to wipe 'the problem' off the table by a priori delegitimising the visibility of faith in the workplace. In some cases, there could be conflicts between individual interests and more collective employee interests, for instance when it comes to seeking individual exemptions from standard break-times rights (which have been long struggled for by unions), which will create tensions.[82] In this regard, labour unions can play a constructive but also an obstructive role. When collective bargaining offers no solace, there may be a particular need for individual counter-balancing measures to adequately protect certain employees from being disadvantaged or targeted.

While lessons can be learned from studying incidents of bottom-up and pragmatic good practices, one should still bear in mind that seemingly *voluntary*

---

[81] Adam and Rea, *Culturele diversiteit op de werkvloer: praktijken van redelijke aanpassing in België*, n 74 above, 134. The authors also point to what they see as a positive consequence of the lack of legal enshrinement of a right to reasonable accommodation: namely, that a number of conflicts were resolved without the need to refer to legal routes. Their argument that a legally enforceable duty would have a counter-active effect on such conflicts is, however, speculative and unconvincing.

[82] ibid, 134.

adjustments remain fragile, as they ultimately depend on the goodwill of stakeholders.[83] Fostering goodwill is commendable, and there may be various 'soft law' ways of encouraging such practices in companies, but it is no substitute for 'hard' legal remedies. Several cases illustrate that initially agreed accommodations can be retracted. In principle, nothing prevents a change of heart and reversal of a voluntary accommodation, even at the whim of the accommodating party. This is a crucial difference compared with *legally* enforceable rights: even if the entitlement to accommodations is not absolute and offers much leeway in practice, the legal enforceability of reasonable accommodations means remedies are available in case accommodations requests are ignored, outright rejected or suddenly retracted.

The introduction of reasonable accommodations does not mean that pragmatic, voluntary accommodations would become moot, meaningless or ineffective. Rather, the negotiation between parties (often one 'weaker' than the other) will then be transformed and placed 'in the shadow of the law'.[84] In case of a rejected request or later change of heart, legal recourse will be available to the employee and a court will assess whether granting accommodations would be reasonable and proportionate under the circumstances. Another advantage to confirming the right to reasonable accommodations on the basis of religion or belief is that it would add legitimacy to employee requests, which can be useful for employers wanting to avoid tensions between employees in the workplace. In one Belgian company, management sought to accommodate a number of Muslim employees by opening up an available conference room for prayer so that employees would not have to pray in the presence of other workers (as that had led to tensions). The labour union objected to this accommodation. In its view, it would 'privilege' certain religious employees (Muslims with low seniority) and it insisted that any space would have to be opened up to every employee in the company. By the time the issue was resolved, most of the Muslim employees were no longer employed at the company. Here, a duty to reasonably accommodate enshrined in the law would have allowed management to point to its legal obligations as support for its will to accommodate.[85]

The law could thus be seen to offer certain incentives to both employer and employee to negotiate accommodations, in the same way as protections against non-execution of a contract operate: the availability of legal action stimulates parties to negotiate in case of a problem. In addition, an explicit duty, in particular if complemented by clear guidelines, including examples on the most common

---

[83] European Network Against Racism, *Reasonable Accommodation of Cultural Diversity in the Workplace. Report of the Third Equal@Work Meeting* (December 2011) 7.

[84] This term is borrowed from M Galanter, 'Justice in Many Rooms: Courts, Private Ordering, and Indigenous Law' (1981) 19 *Journal of Legal Pluralism and Unofficial Law* 1, 25, and R Mnookin and L Kornhauser, 'Bargaining in the Shadow of the Law: The Case of Divorce' (1979) 88 *Yale Law Journal* 950.

[85] Case file reviewed by author at the Belgian Centre for Equal Opportunity in May 2012. A duty of reasonable accommodation in the United States and Canada also applies to trade unions, and this is certainly recommendable if a reasonable accommodation duty were to be adopted in Europe.

'good practices', would also be to the advantage of employers, who in the current perceived legal vacuum are unsure how to deal with accommodation requests and sometimes seek assistance from unions, religious leaders or other experts.[86]

D. Settling for Reasonable Accommodation is Short Selling Minorities

It has been argued that the requirement of reasonable accommodation forms an important facet of substantive equality.[87] However, the idea that reasonable accommodation fits within a substantive equality approach or is even conducive to substantive equality (going to 'the heart of the equality question') has also been challenged by progressives. This is most apparent in some debates in Canada on the topic of reasonable accommodation.[88] Indeed, despite reasonable accommodation concessions being considered to go too far for some, an important question is whether the reasonable accommodation approach is in fact too modest, and perhaps counter-productive in terms of achieving more genuine equality in the long term.

Day and Brodsky, seeking to go beyond accommodations in addressing underlying power imbalances and 'discourses of dominance, such as racism, able-bodyism and sexism, which result in a society being designed well for some and not for others',[89] argue for a reconsideration and redesigning of the rules of the game instead of advocating for accommodations. Similarly, Beaman argues this in terms of 'deep equality'. Accommodations are seen not as challenging the rules made for the normative majority but as further entrenching these:

> It allows those who consider themselves 'normal' to continue to construct institutions and relations in their image, as long as others, when they challenge this construction are 'accommodated'.

> Accommodation, conceived this way, appears to be rooted in the formal model of equality. As a formula, different treatment for 'different' people is merely the flip side of like

---

[86] ENAR, *Reasonable Accommodations and Cultural Diversity in the Workplace. Report of the Third Equal@Work Meeting*, n 83 above, 4.

[87] S Fredman, *Comparative study of anti-discrimination and equality laws of the US, Canada, South Africa and India*, n 12 above, 55, referring to Supreme Court of Canada, *Eaton v Brant County Board of Education*, [1997] 1 SCR 241, at paras 66–67.

[88] This idea against accommodations is not only advanced by those who seek to go further, but also by those who do not necessarily advocate a 'difference-sensitive approach'. A prominent example is political philosopher Brian Barry who dismisses reasonable accommodations. See B Barry, *Culture and Equality: An Egalitarian Critique of Multiculturalism* (Cambridge MA, Harvard University Press, 2001). Also Belgian philosopher Patrick Loobuyck argues that reasonable accommodation as an exception to the rule should only apply in extraordinary cases (and should be a matter of goodwill of employers rather than enforceable rights), most other cases leading either to rule change or to implementation for all. See P Loobuyck, 'Critical remarks on the pro-religion apriority of the RELIGARE project' in M-C Foblets et al (eds), *Belief, Law and Politics What Future for a Secular Europe?* (Aldershot, Ashgate, 2014).

[89] Day and Brodsky, 'The Duty to Accommodate: Who Will Benefit?', n 23 above.

treatment for likes. *Accommodation does not go to the heart of the equality question*, to the *goal of transformation*, to an examination of the way institutions and relations must be changed in order to make them available, accessible, meaningful and rewarding for the many diverse groups of which our society is composed. Accommodation seems to mean that we do not change procedures or services, we simply 'accommodate' those who do not quite fit. We make some concessions to those who are 'different', rather than abandoning the idea of 'normal' and working for genuine inclusiveness.

In this way, accommodation seems to allow formal equality to be the dominant paradigm, as long as some adjustments can be made, sometimes, to deal with unequal effects. Accommodation, conceived of in this way does not challenge deep-seated beliefs about the intrinsic superiority of such characteristics [as mobility and sightedness]. In short, accommodation is assimilationist. Its goal is to try to make 'different' people fit into existing systems (emphasis added).[90]

Notwithstanding its potential to address existing shortcomings in human rights, non-discrimination, labour law and voluntary accommodations frameworks, when it comes to addressing the needs of religious employees in secular workplaces, the concept of reasonable accommodations thus has to face its own limits: this is essentially due to the 'rule and exception' and individual justice approach it adopts towards social processes of exclusion. By settling for mere exceptions, 'deep equality' is forfeited. The underlying power asymmetries in a majority-biased society remain unchallenged, the legitimacy of structural taken-for-granted rules is accepted. This in turn necessitates—repeated—requests for accommodation.

With minorities and outsiders holding *a right to ask* for accommodations and only under certain *conditions to receive* such accommodations, the reasonable accommodation 'solution' leaves untouched the issue of majority-biased organisation of society on various levels:

[So-called] universal norms and rights [in Western Europe] are inflected by particular historical traditions and national cultures which give distinctive interpretations to ideas such as individual and group, public and private, rights and obligations and so create a de facto second-class citizenship for those who do not identify with that culture or are not privileged within it.[91]

Beaman and other scholars[92] therefore have argued for 'going beyond (toleration and) accommodation'[93] and looking at 'deep equality', finding this particularly appropriate in the Canadian context (with a multicultural mandate in the Constitution, with existing duties and higher standards of reasonable

---

[90] Day and Brodsky, ibid, 462; It can be noted that the *Meiorin* Court cites this segment [1999] 3 SCR 3 at para 41.

[91] Modood, 'Is There a Crisis of Secularism in Western Europe?', n 60 above, 136.

[92] Beaman, 'Deep Equality: Moving Beyond Tolerance and Accommodation': www.luthercollege. edu (undated) and references cited; Day and Brodsky, 'The Duty to Accommodate: Who Will Benefit?', n 23 above.

[93] Beaman, ibid. 'Although tolerance has been a bit less "tolerated" recently, reasonable accommodation has gained status as the mode of framing any discussion of the everyday negotiation of religious diversity'.

accommodation etc).[94] The concept of 'deep equality', which is proposed as a way to move beyond this impasse, is said to be 'still a bit nascent':

> [T]he parameters of this concept [of deep equality] are still under construction, but its core element is a commitment to a complex understanding of diversity that emphasizes similarity (...) on the conceptual continuum of sameness and difference ... The idea of a continuum recognizes the shifting possible interpretations of equality, which can range from formal equality emphasizing sameness (a model perhaps most starkly represented by the laïcité approach of France) to substantive equality with its emphasis on difference.[95]

From a theoretical standpoint, such quest for 'deep equality' should not be easily dismissed as it has the potential to break down existing exclusions, making ex post accommodations obsolete. The equality project, as opposed to the accommodations quest, seems to have no bounds: '[w]hile it is easy to talk about "too much accommodation", "too much equality" is less comprehensible'.[96]

The argument here is thus that minorities are selling themselves short by taking comfort in 'mere' accommodations, accepting small handouts instead of pressing for more radical and transformative equality.

These compelling (deep equality) arguments, however, go beyond the judicial sphere of assessing particular cases and also to some extent the employment area, where the power imbalance as between employer and employee is an inherent feature of the relationship. But they have—through Day and Brodsky amongst others—already influenced the Canadian Supreme Court, which advises (public) employers to go beyond merely *responding* to individual accommodation requests and which also includes consideration regarding the proactive rule design in its consideration of whether or not an employer (or service provider) has duly discharged its accommodation duty. In *Meiorin* (1999), the Canadian Supreme Court held that employers

> must build conceptions of equality into workplace standards. By enacting human rights statutes and providing that they are applicable to the workplace, the legislatures have determined that the standards governing the performance of work should be designed to reflect all members of society, insofar as this is reasonably possible ... The standard itself is required to provide for individual accommodation, if reasonably possible.[97]

---

[94] Beaman, ibid. ['Similarly, the point can be made that tolerance and accommodation are better than nothing. Veit Bader (2011), for example, argues that "Gritted teeth tolerance and collective tolerance are part and parcel of any minimalist morality and of any decent polity". So, if those who argue that tolerance and accommodation are better than nothing mean that it is better than outright hatred or refusal to engage at all with those who are marked as being "other", then they are probably correct. My argument, though, is that in the Canadian context we might want to argue that tolerance and accommodation are not good enough, especially given our constitutional commitment to multiculturalism, approaches to human rights and emphasis on equality'.]

[95] Beaman, ibid.

[96] ibid.

[97] In *British Columbia (Public Service Employee Relations Commission) v British Columbia Government Service Employees' Union* [1999] 3 SCR 3.

No doubt going beyond accommodations, which should be seen as a genuine improvement in its own right, is the broader horizon for genuine equality.

To be sure, a spin on the same debate—ie advocating more cautious, piece-meal and more feasible strategies *versus* rejecting that approach and instead striving for a more radical transformation of society which will be less feasible—has not only taken place in the area of protection and inclusion of religious minorities but also when it comes to other social movements including feminism,[98] anti-racism,[99] and the LGBT rights movements.[100] In many of these movements, the 'accom-modationists' have prevailed over more radical-minded advocates. In part this relates to the inherent tendency within movements because of internal divisions and dynamics to settle for the most 'feasible' solution or strategy. But the internal divisions and disagreements have somewhat undermined some movements' dyna-mism. For instance, in the case of the feminist movement, Bell Hooks, in discuss-ing the history of the women's movement, notes that women who did not face additional barriers because of class, race, disability or sexuality favoured the less radical strategy: '[f]rom the onset of the movement [white] women from privi-leged classes were able to make their concerns "the" issues that should be focused on in part because they were the group of women who received public attention'.[101] Hooks sees the divisions as undermining feminist politics: 'When women acquired greater class status and power without conducting themselves differently from males feminist politics were undermined. Lots of women felt betrayed'.[102]

In fact, she notes that 'the freedom of privileged-class women of all races has required the sustained subordination of working-class and poor women'.[103] Absorbing some lessons for the case of religious minorities may imply that one

---

[98] B Hooks, *Feminism is for everybody: Passionate politics* (South End Press, 2000) 37 'Conflict arose between the reformist vision of women's liberation which basically demanded equal rights for women within the existing class structure, and more radical and/ or revolutionary models, which called for fundamental change in the existing structure so that models of mutuality and equality could replace the old paradigms. However, as the feminist movement progressed and privileged groups of well-educated white women began to achieve equal access to class power with their male counterparts, feminist class struggle was no longer deemed important'.

[99] Another example is the critical race movement in the United States, which advocates a more radi-cal approach to societal transformation and favours a race-conscious approach as opposed to a more cautious, colour-blind, liberalist approach.

[100] Indeed, the tension between the movement for modest improvements of the situation (some-times called the assimilation strategy) and a more radical one of 'deep equality' such as we see in this area is not unique to this area. Notably, in the areas of LGBT rights the same divergent and at times competing strategies are present: eg Julie Mertus with regard to the two strategies LGBT rights in the US, J Mertus, 'The Rejection of Human Rights Framings: The Case of LGBT Advocacy in the US' (2007) 29 *Human Rights Quarterly* 1036, 1051 ('For LGBT activists in the United States, the 1970s were marked by a struggle between assimilation-oriented activists and confrontational strategists. Some activists made a point of emphasising their radicalism.' The so-called 'veterans of the homophile movement' were considered 'old-fashioned accommodationists'); E Marcus, *Making Gay History: The Half-Century Fight for Lesbian and Gay Equal Rights* (Harper Perennial, 2002) 121 ('in the end mainly assimilation style strategy remained with sporadic bursts of radical liberation projects').

[101] Hooks, *Feminism is for everybody: Passionate politics*, n 99 above, 37.

[102] Hooks, ibid, 42.

[103] ibid, 41.

should not too easily give up on more transformative proposals. When majority standards or even formal equality—which can be seen as equality with built-in advantages for some and disadvantages for others—is not addressed but channelled through 'mere' reasonable accommodations and thereby deeper entrenched, this indeed constitutes a problem with the 'remedial approach' to reasonable accommodation (as opposed to a perspective on reasonable accommodations which incorporates calls for more substantial transformations, see the *Meiorin* Court above). One could argue though that pursuing more transformative changes may be more the purview of political organising than legal rights-based approaches. Also, in the current context of anxieties about the place of religion in European societies, with some feeling intensely disconcerted by ongoing changes, arguing for more profound transformation may certainly not be the most viable way forward in advancing the interests of religious minorities, and rights-based approaches may offer the most realistic advances, at least in the short-to-medium term.

E. Reasonable Accommodation in Europe is a Misfit

When it comes to the debate on the merits of reasonable accommodation, a number of obstacles have been formulated. These concern the expediency (anti-discrimination law), the sufficiency (deep equality), the necessity (voluntary accommodations) and the feasibility (socio-political context); this last argument focuses on the suitability of reasonable accommodation as a response to European challenges. According to this argument, reasonable accommodation is a legal transplant and therefore rejected from the body of European law.

To some extent, as was discussed above, reasonable accommodation may be considered an American concept and approach. Indeed, US courts have developed a predilection for reasonableness and balancing tests since the 1960s.[104] Also, the term itself may have an American 'ring' to it. Perhaps a concept so foreign to our legal culture would not be functional here (and perhaps this explains some problems in applying the reasonable accommodation framework in the case of disability). Accordingly, one could ask whether reasonable accommodations should be seen as a 'legal transplant'.[105]

There are undeniable differences between the US, Canada and Europe when it comes to relevant law and society developments. For instance, the role of religion in society and in government is valued differently, and so is the general approach

---

[104] This is when, for instance, US courts started to abandon the rule-based territorial approach to choice-of-law questions. See W Reese, 'Conflict of Law and the Restatement Second' (1963) 28 *Law and Contemporary Problems* 680.

[105] The term 'legal transplant' is generally attributed to the Scottish-American legal scholar WAJ 'Alan' Watson: A Watson, *Legal Transplants: An Approach to Comparative Law* (University of Georgia Press, 1974). Defending the idea of diffusionism, Watson argues that developments in legal systems are primarily due to borrowing. Pierre Legrand has been a vocal opponent of the idea of legal transplants, dismissing the notion of 'law' which underpins it.

towards minorities, integration and citizenship.[106] Religion, overall, in the US is seen as a positive force rather than a primitive, disruptive and unsettling phenomenon, although there is an increasing unease with Islam in the US. But the basic right to religious liberty resonates with a public which is still predominantly religious in the US. In contrast, Europe is secularised (paradoxically though, government and religion remain far more entangled on the continent). In many European countries, the relevance of religious liberty is no longer evident and in some respects a (militant) secularism is seen as the guarantor of equal rights and emancipation in a difference-blind republican system. If this broader apprehension about the visibility of (minority) religion in Europe is reflected in the debate on reasonable accommodations, the latter appear a misfit.

This may contain some truth, but is not to say that *the idea* of reasonable accommodations for religious individuals or groups is foreign to—internally diverse—European jurisdictions. Various European countries have specific legislation and measures in place which—without using the term reasonable accommodation or its equivalent in the local language explicitly—de facto amount to particular instances of (reasonable) accommodations for certain (religious) groups in employment[107] and beyond.[108] The discussion of the case law examples also shows that many 'good practices' constitute de facto reasonable accommodation approaches.

When it comes to the overarching area of human/civil rights and non-discrimination, there has been much convergence and 'cross-pollination'[109] between European and North American jurisdictions. In particular, the concept of disparate treatment is a close cousin of indirect discrimination.[110] The US has been a fertile ground for legislative and jurisprudential developments in this

---

[106] See N Foner and R Alba, 'Immigrant Religion in the U.S. and Western Europe: Bridge or Barrier to Inclusion?' (2008) 42 *International Migration Review* 360, 360–92.

[107] See, eg, Art 5.4. Flemish Decree on Proportionate Participation on the Labour Market of 8 May 2002, applicable in the area of Flemish education and employment mediation, contains a general duty of reasonable accommodation for various 'risk groups' (*kansengroepen*). This provision has not been tested in practice with regard to religious minorities. Also under Art 13(2) of the Bulgarian the Protection against Discrimination Act, employers should provide employees with time off to meet religious commitments or days off on their religious holidays. Under Art 173 of the Bulgarian Labour Code employees with religion other than the Eastern Orthodox Christianity have a right to use their annual leave when their denomination has a holiday or take up unpaid leave 'but not more than the number of days for the Eastern Orthodox Christian holidays'. Thanks to Maya Kosseva for this information.

[108] See the Law allowing the Jewish minority in Italy time off on important Jewish religious holidays in the ECtHR case *Sessa v Italy*. In the UK, s 11 of the Employment Act 1989 exempts turban-wearing Sikhs from having to wear safety helmets on a construction site. An instance of accommodation on the basis of gender is the right for new mothers to take (un)paid breastfeeding breaks on the job. There are also examples outside of employment. In many countries there are exemptions to animal slaughtering laws to accommodate Muslim and Jews; again in the UK, Sikhs are exempt from the requirement to wear motorcycle helmets under s 2A of the Motor-Cycle Crash Helmets (Religious Exemption) Act 1976.

[109] Fredman, *Comparative study of anti-discrimination and equality laws of the US, Canada, South Africa and India*, n 12 above, 78 and 80.

[110] ibid ('The concept of disparate impact was imported to the UK in the form of the concept of indirect discrimination. UK law in turn influenced EU law. In the framework of EU social law, the concept was adopted and developed by the Court of Justice in establishing that discrimination against

area, and there is no reason why foreign experiences cannot continue to serve as a source of inspiration or emulation for Europe. Certainly, that has been the case with regard to reasonable accommodation for persons with disability.

Such emulation is not to be rejected, but embraced:

> Law does not develop in a vacuum; it is shaped by the intellectual, cultural and linguistic backgrounds of those who create and administer it. In a world where legal systems increasingly interact, the enduring power of legal tradition necessitates a constant recalibration of theoretical and practical tools to deal with diversity.[111]

An important contrast can be noted between the Anglo-Saxon and the continental European approaches to work, accommodations and minorities. In the United States and in the UK the idea is that 'work is the best welfare' (Tony Blair) and people need to be included. This comes with a limited labour protection, low minimum wages and minor safety net, reflecting in more labour inclusion but also higher wage disparity and the creation of the 'working poor'.[112] Still in the ideology of inclusion, religion or belief needs to be accommodated. In contrast, in Continental Europe, labour protection is stronger but mainly protects 'insiders'. High protection is meant to avoid the problem of the kind of socially unacceptable wage disparity that exists in the US, but it pushes some groups into unemployment and exclusion (sometimes with, sometimes without safety net). 'Higher standards' in the workplace also justify stricter requirements when it comes to work, and overall fewer religious accommodations. Thus, there are pitfalls in either system. In the former, religious minorities are disadvantaged because of their socio-economic status, while in the latter their religion—seen as an obstacle to participation—is one reason for exclusion or under-participation. The ideal would be to combine the best of both worlds, to have an adequate general labour employment protection, generous religious accommodations to promote inclusion but also a decent safety net for those who inevitably will fall through at times. Such a solution would arguably be in line with the theory of justice[113] advocated by Iris Marion Young

---

part-time workers was a form of sex discrimination. Merging with the concept as developed in the context of free movement of workers, the concept of indirect discrimination received statutory formulation first in the former Directive on the burden of proof in sex discrimination cases, passed in 1997, and subsequently in the Racial Equality and Employment Equality Directives, passed in 2000. This concept is now central to the modern EU directives'.)

[111] See call for papers for *Cambridge Journal of International and Comparative Law* Conference, 'Legal Tradition in a Diverse World', Cambridge, 18 and 19 May 2013.

[112] See, generally, H Sarfati and G Bonoli (eds), *Labour market and social protection reforms in international perspective: parallel or converging tracks?* (Aldershot, Ashgate, 2002).

[113] Even if Young herself would object to the use of the term; see IM Young, *Justice and the politics of difference* (Princeton NJ, Princeton University Press, 1990) 3–4: 'Although I discuss and argue about justice, I do not construct a theory of justice. A theory of justice typically derives fundamental principles of justice that apply to all or most societies, whatever their concrete configuration and social relations, from a few general premises about the nature of human beings, the nature of societies, and the nature of reason … [and] fails in one of two ways … A theory of justice that claims universality, comprehensiveness, and necessity implicitly conflates moral reflection with scientific knowledge'. Young's discourse on justice, however, is based on listening to the specific claims made by social groups who see themselves as dominated or oppressed in society.

in her seminal *'Justice and the Politics of Difference'* (1990), which even today remains relevant as it is to our topic.[114] Young significantly grounded her arguments on justice on 'the fact of heterogeneity in society rather than on illusion of or hope for homogeneity'.[115]

For Young, justice consists of 'the social and institutional conditions necessary for achieving both nondomination and nonoppression, where the latter means the achievement of human flourishing, for all members of society'.[116] She thereby rejected the 'distributive paradigm' in political philosophical theories of justice including Rawls' which focuses on the allocation of material goods. Young did regard distribution as important, but argues to capture the whole perspective of justice one needs to regard non-distributive aspects as well, and people should not only be seen as 'possessors and consumers' but also as actors who have an interest in developing and exercising their capabilities). Instead, the discourse of justice needs to focus on non-domination and non-oppression.[117]

This is particularly relevant in the intersection of employment participation and unemployment benefits. Monetary benefits allow the unemployed to provide themselves and their families with the material goods they need and to have a relatively comfortable living standard, but this does not take away from their claim to be included and not marginalised in society. If anything, such claims are even more important, and are not about distribution; they are about justice. Young sought a situation where it is possible for people to be part of social groups and enjoy social differentiation, without having to suffer exclusions. In emphasising the role of social groups, she rejected the atomic individualism of liberalism but she also rejects a communautarism where the homogenised nation subsumes the individual. Instead, she conceives a situation of a community of communities. In

---

[114] ibid. The starting point of Young's inquiry was the various 'new left emancipatory social movements' in the 1960s and 1970s in the US (and elsewhere)—of which she lists feminism, Black liberation, American Indian movements, gay and lesbian liberation. She notes that these movements, which often adopt a 'politics of difference' find little affinity in modern political philosophy (of which the inquiry is focused on justice) and she pinpoints some of the reasons why. See p 40: 'My starting point is reflection on the conditions of the groups said by these movements to be oppressed: among others women, Blacks, Chicanos, Puerto Ricans and other Spanish-speaking Americans, American Indians, Jews, lesbians, gay men, Arabs, Asians, old people, working-class people, and the physically and mentally disabled ... Obviously the above-named groups are not oppressed to the same extent or in the same ways. In the most general sense, all oppressed people suffer some inhibition of their ability to develop and exercise their capacities and express their needs, thoughts, and feelings'. 'These movements all claim in varying ways that American society contains deep institutional injustices. But they find little kinship with contemporary philosophical theories of justice'. (p 7) The situation of Muslims and other religious minorities in the West was not within the purview of her book; had she written her book two decades later no doubt the fate of religious minorities would have figured much more prominently in her work. Despite this, the general teachings of the book are highly relevant and applicable to the topic at hand.

[115] Young, ibid, Foreword (D Allen).

[116] ibid, Foreword (D Allen).

[117] ibid, 12. Young shows oppression in its five faces: exploitation, marginalisation, powerlessness, cultural imperialism and violence. Young instead focuses on the contribution and effects on justice of three elements: decision-making processes, division of labour and culture.

the end, she wanted people—all people—to be able to flourish as social beings: 'where social group differences exist and some groups are privileged while others are oppressed, social justice requires explicitly acknowledging and attending to those group differences in order to undermine oppression'.[118] Young did not discuss the topic of reasonable accommodations for religion or belief[119] but in the case of affirmative action she wrote in support of these programmes 'not on grounds of compensation of past discrimination, but as important means for undermining oppression, especially oppression that results from unconscious versions and stereotyping and from the assertion that the point of view of the privileged is neutral'.[120]

To conclude this chapter, one can say there are good grounds for adopting an explicit duty of reasonable accommodation—complementing the current legal protections which need to be advanced simultaneously. This is not to be seen as 'icing on the cake'; reasonable accommodation stands for an approach to diversity that is urgently needed in Europe. However, this is not to say that reasonable accommodation, which has its own limits and shortcomings, is a panacea when it comes to the issue of diversity in employment.

[118] ibid, 3.

[119] She paid overall very little attention to religious groups as oppressed social groups, only mentioning this possibility in the abstract by including 'religious group' in a list a number of times eg at pp 43 and 40 in the particular examples of 'Jews' and 'Arabs'.

[120] IM Young, *Justice and the politics of difference*, n 114 above, 12.

Conclusion

'It is not our differences that divide us. It is our inability to recognize, accept, and celebrate those differences'.[121]

One aspect of modern societies, which presents continued political and legal challenges for all secular, liberal-democratic nations, is the diverse religious and philosophical affiliations of their constituents. In the European context, which is one of the few regions where the secularisation thesis holds true (at least with regard to the majority population), religion is approached predominantly as a *problem*. Perhaps this is because 'deeply held European assumptions'[122] are challenged by the demands of this diversity, and in particular the establishment and growth of the Muslim population.

At a time when the freedom of religion or belief, both its status as a fundamental right as well as its meaning and application in particular situations, is under pressure, cases and controversies involving the topic of religion and belief in the workplace have sparked attention in law and in society. Yet despite its emergence as a critical topic in a diverse European society, this has remained a largely underexplored area of inquiry.[123] This study aimed to address that gap by answering the following questions. To what extent and through which legal mechanisms are private sector employees' religious beliefs and practices protected in the workplace today in different European countries? And how do different countries compare when it comes to the treatment and protection of recurring issues such as the wearing of religiously distinct dress, conflicts between professional and religious time demands, and religiously motivated objections to particular job duties or work expectations?

Religion—and to a lesser extent belief—is present in a multitude of ways in today's European workplace; employees do not sign off their deeply-held beliefs, religious customs, obligations and commitments at the gate despite various pressures to adapt to accepted norms. The consequences, however, can be grave and employees have been dismissed or subjected to adverse employment actions, which together with severe limitations on employment opportunities, exclusion and marginalisation, is cause for collective concern. Notwithstanding the fact that religion or belief is a potent source of disadvantage, hostility and discrimination, religious or philosophical identity remains a source of empowerment, strength

---

[121] See Audre Lorde, *Our Dead Behind Us: Poems* (Norton, 1994).

[122] G Davie, 'Is Europe an exceptional case?' (Spring & Summer 2006) *The Hedgehog Review* 24, 32.

[123] See H Bielefeldt, *Interim report of the UN Special Rapporteur on the Freedom of religion or belief. Tackling religious intolerance and discrimination in the workplace*, no A/69/261 (United Nations, 2014) 7.

and pride for many individuals, who at times are strengthened in their faith by experiences of intolerance, exclusion and marginalisation.[124] Can we use law and policy to alleviate some of the disproportionate cost that is currently weighing on religious minorities in Europe, by guaranteeing a genuine enjoyment of the fundamental freedom of religion or belief and protection from exclusion and discrimination? Are we willing to (re)assure that all Europeans can take advantage of the rights and freedoms proclaimed in the Charter of Fundamental Rights of the European Union and the European Convention on Human Rights? And are we willing to accept that in some instances to achieve substantive equality, we will need to go beyond formally equal standards and need to confront social discomfort and bias? In the symbolic/political domain, formal equality amounts to non-recognition[125] and thus what is called for in light of the need for recognition is precisely a level of 'politics of difference'. As Modood argues:

> The challenge of creating equality between historically privileged and disadvantaged groups within a citizenry is unlikely to be achieved by acting as if group identities no longer exist. In relation to color-racism, such pretense is called the pursuit of colorblind policies ... full civic equality will require not just policies treating all citizens as individuals but additionally, policies, institutions, and discourses which 'recognize' (Taylor 1994) that certain group identities are victims of negative treatment ... So the best approach is a politics of respect which turns these negative identities into positively valued ones and to remake our sense of common citizenship and nationality to include them.[126]

As Iris Marion Young posited, the politics of difference does not merely involve distribution of goods but rather is a matter of justice.[127]

Employers, co-workers and customers do not act in a cultural vacuum but take cues from cultural and social norms which set the confines of the allowable and the appropriate. These norms are in part shaped by law, or at least by particular understandings of law and its operation. Therefore, looking at the law as an opportunity to reshape some of the more harmful effects or negative responses to this particular form of difference is fitting. Law should seek to (re)design rules to diminish rather than confirm or increase society's prejudices and intolerances.

Currently, when disputes involving religion or belief in the European workplace escalate into conflicts, and these are subsequently framed as *legal* conflicts in terms of rights due to *religion or belief*, the issue can be addressed under two legal frameworks: human rights and non-discrimination law. The first has been the purview of the European Convention on Human Rights and the Court in Strasbourg, while the EU has taken the lead in formulating non-discrimination standards under a series

---

[124] Connor, 'Contexts of immigrant receptivity and immigrant religious outcomes: the case of Muslims in Western Europe' (2010) 33 *Ethnic and Racial Studies* 376.
[125] L Beaman, 'Deep Equality: Moving Beyond Tolerance and Accommodation', n 93 above ('Similarity can and should shift, depending on the parties involved. If it doesn't, it can too easily lapse into sameness, or disrespect for difference').
[126] T Modood, 'Is There a Crisis of Secularism in Western Europe?', n 60 above, drawing from political theories on multiculturalism by Charles Taylor, Bhikhu Parekh, Marion Iris Young and Will Kymlicka.
[127] Young, *Justice and the politics of difference*, n 114 above, 3 et seq.

of Directives, in particular the Employment Equality Directive, which prohibits religion or belief discrimination in the area of employment. More than anything, the *Eweida* judgment shows that the law in this area is in flux and subject to change. This can be seen as a sign that European judges are also struggling with finding context-appropriate and time-sensitive answers to religious diversity challenges. In their endeavour, they adhere to an evolutive interpretation of a living instrument, to set *a minimum threshold* and to fulfil a compass function in Europe. The CJEU now has a momentous opportunity to tangibly improve the employment opportunities of religious minorities across the EU by adopting effective discrimination standards in the pending *Achbita* and *Bougnaoui* cases.[128] This story is to be continued.

Within the broader challenge of diversity management in modern secular societies, the topic of faith, identity and participation in the workplace is of utmost importance, as it goes to the very heart of the matter. Would our integration policy be advanced if accommodation were provided to employees and job-seekers with particular requests motivated by their convictions or religious practices? What do we stand to gain or lose when 'giving in' or when allowing 'special treatment' on the basis of religion or belief? I argue that an *explicit* right to reasonable accommodation for religion and belief in employment would have added value. Going beyond but building on the existing legal protections for religion or belief, an *EU-wide* right would level (up) the protection for European employees. It would additionally strengthen the free movement[129] of workers across the EU which is currently restricted because of divergent and conflicting national case law decisions.

Although it is important to not forget that, from an international perspective, individuals in Belgium, the Netherlands and the UK enjoy a comparatively enviable level of basic religious freedom and equality, employment discrimination is persistent and hinders the inclusion and participation of members of religious minorities in the European labour market. Addressing religious discrimination and liberty is crucial as a part of the larger struggle for equality and fairness, since religion or belief is but one of many layers of potential disadvantage. Indeed, a multi-ground approach towards the inclusion of ethno-religious minorities who suffer compound or intersectional discrimination is needed. Both freedom and equality are important considerations upon which a just European society is to be built and the suggestions advanced here are to be seen as a part of a more holistic law and policy approach.

Various case law examples illustrate how employees can struggle when trying to reconcile their religious beliefs and commitment while remaining gainfully employed. Legal claims—the tip of the iceberg—have been raised with respect to

---

[128] Case C-157/15, *Samira Achbita and Centrum voor gelijkheid van kansen en voor racismebestrijding v G4S Secure Solutions NV*; Case C-188/15, *Asma Bougnaoui and Association de défense des droits de l'homme (ADDH) v Micropole SA*. On 14 March 2017, the CJEU held that the prohibition on employees wearing any visible signs of their political, philosophical or religious beliefs in the workplace did not give rise to direct discrimination as long as certain conditions were met. These being the first CJEU judgments on religious discrimination under EU law, many questions remain (including the interaction with ECtHR cases) and will have to be worked out in the years to come. See Case C-157/15, *Achbita v G4S Secure Solutions NV*; Case C-188/15, *Bougnaoui v Micropole SA*.

[129] See recital 11 Employment Equality Directive.

religious dress, religious time, conscientious objections to work duties and a variety of other religion-work matters. Only some of these claims present potential clashes with other fundamental rights or values. Besides such 'hard cases', softer cases have also been subject to rejection despite the fact that accommodating these types of requests would harm no compelling interests and produce beneficial outcomes for the employee and perhaps other parties.

The headscarf worn by Muslim women in Europe remains the most recurring religious dress issue. Across the EU, different courts have adopted divergent decisions under similar legal frameworks. One striking example of conflicting judicial treatment relates to company 'neutrality policies' which typically ban any and all manifestations of religious, political and philosophical belief in the workplace and have sweeping effects on employment opportunities, and which have been judged differently. The Belgian labour court see the headscarf as the obstacle to successful participation and the proclaimed neutrality as the solution to inevitable tensions, while the Dutch and British courts regard such policies as direct discrimination or as disproportionate measures that fail to justify discriminatory effects on certain groups. The Belgian approach is reflective of a smoldering (dis)comfort with Islam and its visibility in the public space, which explains overly swift rejection of religious manifestations through religious dress and potentially justifiable practices such as a refusal to shake hands with members of the opposite sex. In such context the concept of neutrality and 'blind' formal equality standards are often articulated (but not necessarily applied as conscientiously) in seemingly unproblematic terms. However, the idea of neutrality as a religion-free space is far from impartial but rather a very normative position that produces winners and losers. Neutrality thus serves as shorthand for preserving and defending the status quo.

The 'conflict-avoiding' strategy of many employers takes cues from and contributes to the increasing European discomfort with the presence and visibility of minority religions, and Islam in particular, in the public space and in the public sector. Adopting a company 'neutrality' policy is the jewel in the crown in this strategy, rendering any attempted discussion or negotiation on accommodation illegitimate and out-of-place. The strategy and its judicial legitimation provides primacy to the freedom *from* religion, thus diluting the fundamental right to freedom of religion or belief. Though it may pay off in the short term, an avoidance strategy misdirects efforts and valuable resources. The personal and societal damage resulting from such exclusionary policies only adds to the stratification of society and places a mortgage on genuine debate on religion, minorities and equality. Employers, as distributive agents, must contribute to a more equal and fair society.

The idea behind reasonable accommodation is to give employees adequate— and reasonable—opportunities to reconcile their various identities and commitments while pursuing their professional ambitions. While true inclusiveness would reject all pressures to conform to the prevailing workplace standards, it cannot be maintained that reasonable accommodation would be able to make away with the need for any sort of adaptation to the workplace setting. Clearly employees will still have to adapt to the particular work and the many expectations that come from giving up a part of one's freedom when accepting any job, but this is very different from supporting assimilation as a requirement for employment participation.

For the added value of a right to reasonable accommodations *for reasons of religion or belief* in the European workplace one can point to both *tangible* as well as *intangible* benefits. The tangible benefits relate to the role of a reasonable accommodations framework in correcting legal-technical limitations and shortcomings in human rights and non-discrimination law in their application, which currently does not guarantee directly that requests receive due consideration and if possible are accommodated. In contrast to indirect discrimination claims, a claim based on the failure to provide reasonable accommodation requires neither showing of group *disadvantage* nor the comparison of the claimant with other employees. The focus is on the individual employee working for an individual employer in a concrete context.

The *intangible* benefits relate to this *positive language* and *mode of framing* (straightforward and direct) that reasonable accommodations embed potential conflict situations in: the framework offers employers, employees and society an alternative language to address tension between legitimate needs, without the need to resort to *discrimination* or *fundamental rights* rhetoric. While the discrimination discourse is powerful it is also pejorative—hence the preference in the Netherlands to use 'distinction' instead—and can be counter-productive if the aim is to maintain a working relationship. Certain features make a legal rule more effective in the sense that it will produce 'general effects'[130] and trigger the actual use of the rule by the addressees on the shop-floor level. It is submitted that a duty directed towards employers to provide an accommodation (with which they should be familiar from the disability context) and a right given to the employee is more communicative than the rule against indirect discrimination, which requires additional explanation and interpretation for people to even grasp the content. The question would simply be: can the religious beliefs or practices of a given employee be reasonably accommodated in a way that causes no disproportionate burden for the employer in question? For instance, the request to wear a headscarf or take time off for Yom Kippur are run of the mill and presumed to be reasonable,[131] so the question would turn on the potential disproportionate concrete burden on the employer. While in the end not all accommodations can, will and should be awarded, there is at least a guarantee that due consideration is given to a request and a genuine proportionality test is performed in cases of bona fide

---

[130] The idea of 'general effect' of a rule can be criticised; Moore notes 'universality [of application of law] is often a myth. Most rules of law, in fact, though theoretically universal in application, affect only a limited category of persons in a limited number of situations': SF Moore, 'Law and Social Change: The Semi-Autonomous Social Field as an Appropriate Subject of Study' (1973) 7 *Law & Society Review* 719.

[131] In the sense of effective, 'run of the mill' or not causing excessive difficulties or problems, for the various possible meanings, see Waddington, 'Chapter six: reasonable accommodation', n 25 above, 635.

requests for accommodations to reconcile or facilitate observing both professional and religious commitments. Reasonable accommodation thus provides vital procedural justice and recognition. Resourcefulness, flexibility and goodwill *in the shadow of the law* could take parties a long way. In the end, the process of accommodation is always a two-way street which builds on what can be already considerable adaptation, (self)accommodation and coping strategies by the employee.

Reasonable accommodations is not a free-standing right, it is embedded in a broad legal framework with, amongst other things, human rights, anti-discrimination law and labour law and it remains essential to simultaneously work to 'rehabilitate' existing tools. This can be done by advocating and developing techniques for a more 'maximal' approach to human rights[132] or a more 'dynamic' approach to indirect discrimination claims where that is not happening today. The risk of disappointment too exists if all hope is placed on the technique of reasonable accommodation. In general, the ability of law, as a blunt tool, to bring about transformative changes to the level of the shop-floor, meaning effective changes for actors on a daily basis, is not boundless. Reasonable accommodation will not be able to force productive relationships where those are fractured. But this does not take away from the merits of a—complementary—reasonable accommodation mandate. Under the best conditions, these various tools can contribute to a progressive realisation of the 'aspiration of civil rights—the aspiration that we be free to develop our human capabilities without the impediment of witless conformity'.[133]

'Voluntary' accommodations too can help employees reconcile professional and religious duties and in that sense are a good—even great—practice, but a system solely based on goodwill fails to recognise the existence of significant power imbalances in labour relations. Understood not as a limitless right to—potentially expensive—workplace adaptations, but as a *guiding shadow* under which negotiation in labour relations can take place, the framework may bolster good practices already growing on the ground in certain companies and give signals to less willing employers or less self-motivated segments of the labour market. This is a huge win in itself.

Finally, it merits stressing that accommodation must be complementary to more transformative and structural changes to the labour market and beyond. Reasonable accommodation should never become an excuse for ignoring opportunities to 'redesign' or equalise the rules of the game, to rid our law and policy from anachronism and double standards and to work towards what Beaman calls 'deep equality'. The example of reassessing the societal relevance and sustainability of majority-oriented holiday schedules is a good example and could alleviate

---

[132] E Brems, 'Human Rights: Minimum and Maximum Perspectives' (2009) 9 *Human Rights Law Review* 349; Alidadi and Foblets, 'Framing multicultural Challenges in Freedom of Religion Terms. Limitations of minimal human rights for managing religious diversity in Europe' (2012) 30 *Netherlands Quarterly of Human Rights* 388.

[133] K Yoshino, 'The Myth of the Mainstream' (2006) 52 *The Chronicle of Higher Education* B11.

employers from the oft-recurring religious time requests. Thus, the various tools discussed are to be seen as complementary rather than as crowding out each other. Indeed, the urgency of the matter may call for combining both short-term and long-term policy answers towards the same goal of participation, inclusion and human flourishing for all in a society where all can feel respected and can exercise and develop their talents and skills as productive members of society.

BIBLIOGRAPHY

Adam, I and Rea, A, *Culturele diversiteit op de werkvloer: praktijken van redelijke aanpassing in België* (Brussels, CEOOR, 2010).

Alidadi, K, 'Gevangene heeft recht op religieus aangepast gevangenisdieet', *De Juristenkrant*, 22 December 2010, 6–7.

—— 'Werkgever kan hoofddoek verbieden op basis van ongeschreven regels', *De Juristenkrant*. 26 May 2010, 1–2.

—— 'Studie over redelijke aanpassingen voor religie op Belgische werkvloer', *De Juristenkrant*, 12 January 2011, 6–7.

—— 'From Front-Office to Back-Office: Religious Dress Crossing the Public–Private Divide in the Workplace' in S Ferrari and S Pastorelli (eds), *Religion in Public Spaces* (Ashgate, 2012).

—— 'Muslim Women Made Redundant: Unintended Signals in Belgian and Dutch Case Law on Religious Dress in Private Sector Employment and Unemployment' in K Alidadi and others (eds), *A Test of Faith? Religious Diversity and Accommodation in the European Workplace* (Ashgate 2012).

—— 'Reasonable Accommodations for Religion and Belief: Adding Value to Article 9 ECHR and the European Union's Anti-Discrimination Approach to Employment?' (2012) 37 *European Law Review* 693.

—— 'Out of sight, out of mind? Implications of routing religiously dressed employees away from front-office positions in Europe' (2013) 1 *Quaderni di diritto e politica ecclesiastica* 87.

—— 'Redelijke aanpassingen voor religieuze praktijken op de Belgische werkvloer: van "goodwill" naar afdwingbaar recht?' in M-C Foblets and JP Schreiber (eds), *Les Assises de Interculturalité/De Rondetafels van de Interculturaliteit/The Round Tables on Interculturality* (Brussels, Larcier, 2013).

—— 'Approches comparatives du débat sur la "neutralité": la liberté de culte des enseignants des écoles publiques et des fonctionnaires à travers l'Europe de porter des vêtements religieux' in D Cabiaux et al (eds), *Neutralité et faits religieux Quelles interactions dans les services publics?* (Academia-L'Harmattan, 2014).

Alidadi, K and Foblets, M-C, 'Framing multicultural Challenges in Freedom of Religion Terms. Limitations of minimal human rights for managing religious diversity in Europe' (2012) 30 *Netherlands Quarterly of Human Rights* 388.

Allen, R, 'Article 13 EC, evolution and current contexts' in Meenan H (ed), *Equality law in an enlarged European Union: understanding the article 13 directives* (Cambridge University Press, 2007).

Alston, P and Heenan, J, 'Shrinking the International Labor Code: An Unintended Consequence of the 1998 ILO Declaration on Fundamental Principles and Rights at Work?' (2004) 36 *New York University Journal of International Law and Politics* 221.

Amnesty International, *Choice and Prejudice. Discrimination against Muslims in Europe* (Amnesty International, 2012).

Bader, V, *Secularism or democracy? Associational governance of religious diversity* (IMISCOE/Amsterdam University Press, 2007).

—— 'Constitutionalizing secularism, alternative secularisms or liberal-democratic constitutionalism? A critical reading of some Turkish, ECtHR and Indian Supreme Court cases on "secularism"' (2010) 6 *Utrecht Law Review* 8.

Baer S, 'A closer look at law: human rights as multi-level sites of struggles over multi-dimensional equality' (2010) 6 *Utrecht Law Review* 56.

Barnard, C and Hepple, B, 'Substantive Equality' (2000) 59 *Cambridge Law Journal* 562.

Barry B, *Culture and equality: an egalitarian critique of multiculturalism* (Cambridge MA, Harvard University Press, 2001).

BBC, '1969: Sikh busmen win turban fight', *BBC*, 9 April 1969.

BBC news, 'Muslim Pc refused to shake hands', *BBC news*, 21 January 2007.

Beaman, L, 'Deep Equality: Moving Beyond Tolerance and Accommodation', www.luthercollege.edu (undated).

—— 'Religion and Rights: The Illusion of Freedom and the Reality of Control' (2005) 6 *Culture and Religion* 17.

Bell, M, *Anti-discrimination law and the European Union* (Oxford University Press, 2002).

—— 'Chapter two: direct discrimination' in D Schiek et al (eds), *Cases, materials and text on national, supranational and international non-discrimination law* (Hart Publishing, 2007).

Bentley, P, 'Witch sacked for taking Halloween off work to attend Wiccan ceremony wins £15,000 after claiming religious discrimination', *Daily Mail*, 13 December 2013.

Berger, P, Davie, G and Fokas, E, *Religious America, Secular Europe? A Theme and Variations* (Ashgate, 2008).

Berry, JW, 'Integration and Multiculturalism: Ways towards Social Solidarity' (2011) 20 *Papers on Social Representations* pp 2.1–2.21.

Berry, JW et al (eds), *Cross-cultural psychology: research and applications*, 2nd edn (Cambridge University Press, 2002).

Bielefeldt H, 'Freedom of Religion or Belief-A Human Right under Pressure' (2012) 1 *Oxford Journal of Law and Religion* 1.

—— 'Misperceptions of Freedom of Religion or Belief' (2013) 35 *Human Rights Quarterly* 33.

—— *Interim report of the UN Special Rapporteur on the Freedom of religion or belief. Tackling religious intolerance and discrimination in the workplace*, no A/69/261 (United Nations, 2014).

Blanpain, R, *Principes de droit du travail* (La Charte, 1984).

Blom, JAH, *De effectiviteit van de Wet gelijke behandeling m/v: tweede deelonderzoek* (Vuga, 1995).

Bouchard, G and Taylor, C, *Building the Future. A Time for Reconciliation (report)* (Government of Quebec, 2008).

Brems, E, *Conflicts between fundamental rights* (Intersentia, 2008).

—— 'Human Rights: Minimum and Maximum Perspectives' (2009) 9 *Human Rights Law Review* 349.

Bribosia E, Chopin, I and Rorive, I, *Rapport de synthèse relatif aux signes d'appartenance religieuse dans quinze pays de l'Union européenne* (Migration Policy Group, 2004).

Bribosia, E, Ringelheim, J and Rorive, I, 'Aménager la diversité: le droit de l'égalité face à la pluralité religieuse' (2009) 78 *Revue trimestrielle des droits de l'homme* 319.

Bribosia, E and Rorive, I, *In search of a balance between the right to equality and other fundamental rights* (European Network of Legal Experts in the Non-discrimination Field, 2010).

Bruce, S, *God is Dead: Secularization in the West* (Wiley-Blackwell, 2002).

Brunelle, C, 'The Growing Impact of Human Rights on Canadian Labour Law' in C Fenwick and T Novitz (eds), *Human Rights at Work: Perspectives on Law and Regulation* (Hart Publishing, 2010).

Ceuppens, B, '"De mijne is van de Filippijne": Racisme en seksisme in het hoofddoekendebat' (2005) 12 *Samenleving en Politiek*.

Chopin, I and Uyen Do, T, *Developing Anti-Discrimination law in Europe. The 27 Member States, Croatia, Former Yugoslav Republic of Macedonia and Turkey compared* (European Commission, 2011).

Choudhry, S, 'Distribution vs. Recognition: The Case of Anti-Discrimination Laws' (2000) 9 *George Mason Law Review* 145.

—— 'Rights Adjudication in a Plurinational State: the Supreme Court of Canada, Freedom of Religion, and the Politics of Reasonable Accommodation' (2013) 50 *Osgoode Hall Law Journal* 589.

Coleridge, B, 'Religious expression in the public sphere', *EuropInfos #158*.

Commissie Blok, *Bruggen Bouwen (onderzoek Integratiebeleid)* (2004).

Communication from the European Commission to the European Parliament, the European Economic and Social Committee and the Committee of the Regions, *Non-discrimination and Equal Opportunities: a Renewed Commitment*. COM(2008) 420 final.

Connor, P, 'Contexts of immigrant receptivity and immigrant religious outcomes: The case of Muslims in Western Europe' (2010) 33 *Ethnic and Racial Studies* 376.

Cormack, J and Bell, M, *Developing Anti-Discrimination law in Europe: The 25 EU Member States Compared* (European Commission, September 2005).

Council of Europe, 'Overview of the Court's case law on freedom of religion' (2013) available at: www.echrcoeint/Documents/Research_report_religion_ENGpdf.

Crenshaw, K, 'Demarginalizing the Intersection of Race and Sex: A Black Feminist Critique of Antidiscrimination Doctrine, Feminist Theory and Antiracist Politics' (1989) 1 *University of Chicago Legal Forum* 139.

Cumper, P, 'The Accommodation of 'Uncontroversial' Religious Practices' in MLP Loenen and JE Goldschmidt (eds), *Religious Pluralism and Human Rights in Europe: Where to Draw the Line?* (Intersentia, 2007).

Cuypers, D, Meeusen, C and Kempen, M, 'Culturele minderheden in het sociaal recht' in J Velaers (ed), *Recht en verdraagzaamheid in de multiculturele samenleving* (Maklu, 1993).

Davie, G, *Europe: the Exceptional Case. Parameters of Faith in the Modern World* (Darton, Longman & Todd Ltd, 2002).

—— 'Is Europe an exceptional case?' (Spring & Summer 2006) *The Hedgehog Review* 24.

Davies, A, 'Workers' Human Rights in English Law' in C Fenwick and T Novitz (eds), *Human Rights at Work: Perspectives on Law and Regulation* (Hart Publishing, 2010).

Day, S and Brodsky, G, 'The Duty to Accommodate: Who Will Benefit?' (1996) 75 *La Revue du Barreau Canadien* 433.

De Blois, M, 'Two Cities in Conflict' in Loenen MLP and Goldschmidt JE (eds), *Religious Pluralism and Human Rights in Europe: Where to Draw the Line?* (Intersentia, 2007).

De Ceulaer, J and Pauli, W, 'Liesbeth Homans: "Jammer dat men te pas en te onpas over racise spreekt"', *Knackbe*, 21 May 2014.

De Schutter, O and Tulkens, F, 'Rights in Conflict: The European Court of Human rights as a Pragmatic Institution' in E Brems (ed), *Conflicts between fundamental rights* (Intersentia, 2008).

De Vos, M, 'Worden Europese arbeidsrelaties Amerikaans? Kritische rechtsvergelijkende perspectieven bij de discriminatieverboden in het arbeidsrecht' in D Cuypers (ed), *Gelijkheid in arbeidsrecht: gelijkheid zonder grenzen?* (Intersentia, 2003).

—— 'De bouwstenen van het discriminatierecht in de arbeidsverhoudingen' in De Vos M and Brems E (eds), *De Wet Bestrijding Discriminatie in de praktijk* (Intersentia, 2004).

—— *Beyond Formal Equality. Positive Action under Directives 2000/43/EC and 2000/78/EC* (European Network of Legal Experts in the Non-Discrimination Field, 2007).

Dernstädt, T, 'Religious Tradition or Political Symbol? Muslim headscarves Test the Limits of German Tolerance', *Spiegel Online*, 20 June 2008.

Donald, A, *Religion or belief, equality and human rights in England and Wales* (London, Equality and Human Rights Commission, 2012).

Durham, WC, Jr 'Against Free Exercise Reductionism', *Religious Freedom Discussion Series*: www.iclrs.org.

Durham, WC, Jr and Scharffs, BG, *Law and Religion: National, International, and Comparative Perspectives* (Wolters Kluwer, 2010).

Dworkin, R, *Taking Rights Seriously* (Harvard University Press, 1978).

Eck, D, *A New Religious America: How a "Christian Country" Has Become the World's Most Religiously Diverse Nation* (Harper SanFrancisco, 2001).

Eeckhout, B, 'Het besef rijpt dat integratie alleen kan werken als iedereen zijn eigen identiteit en cultuur mag ontwikkelen', *De Morgen*, 12 March 2014.

Eisgruber, CL and Sager LG, *Religious Freedom and the Constitution* (Harvard University Press, 2010).

El Guindi, F, *Veil: Modesty, Privacy And Resistance* (Berg, 1999).

European Commission, *Joint Report on the application of Council Directive 2000/43/EC of 29 June 2000 implementing the principle of equal treatment between persons irrespective of racial or ethnic origin ('Racial Equality Directive') and of Council Directive 2000/78/EC of 27 November 2000 establishing a general framework for equal treatment in employment and occupation ('Employment Equality Directive') from the Commission to the European Parliament and the Council*, Brussels, 17.1.2014, COM(2014) 2 final.

European Commission, *Green Paper on Equality and Non-discrimination in an Enlarged EU COM(2004) 379 final* (2004).

European Commission. Directorate-General Justice, *Special Eurobarometer 393 'Discrimination in the EU in 2012'* (November 2012).

European Network Against Racism, *Shadow Report 2012–2013 on Racism and Discrimination in Employment in Europe* (ENAR, March 2013).

—— *Reasonable Accommodations and Cultural Diversity in the Workplace. Report of the Third Equal@Work Meeting* (ENAR, 2012).

European Trade Union Confederation, *The Flexicurity debate and the challenges for the trade union movement* (ETUC, 2007).

European Union Agency for Fundamental Rights, *Access to Justice in Europe: An Overview of Challenges and Opportunities*, 2011).

Evans, C, *Freedom of religion under the European Convention on Human Rights* (Oxford University Press, 2001).

Evans, M, 'From Cartoons to Crucifixes: Current Controversies Concerning the Freedom of Religion and the Freedom of Expression before the European Court of Human Rights' (2011) 26 *Journal of Law and Religion* 345.

Evans, MD, *Religious liberty and international law in Europe* (Cambridge University Press, 1997).

Evans, SJ, 'M&S tells Muslim staff they CAN refuse to serve customers buying alcohol or pork', *Daily Mail*, 22 December 2013.

Ewing, K, 'foreword' in C Fenwick and T Novitz (eds), *Human Rights at Work: Perspectives on Law and Regulation* (Hart Publishing, 2010).

Feldblum, CR, 'Moral Conflict and Liberty. Gay Rights and Religion' (2006) 72 *Brooklyn Law Review* 61.

Fish, S, *There's no such thing as free speech: and it's a good thing, too* (Oxford UP, 1994).

—— 'Our Faith in Letting It All Hang Out (op-ed)', *New York Times*, 12 February 2006.

Foblets, M-C, 'Perspective 1: legal anthropology in Imperative Inheritance Law in the Late-Modern Society' in C Castelein et al (eds), *Imperative Inheritance Law in a Late-Modern Society: Five Perspectives* (Intersentia, 2009).

Foblets, M-C and Alidadi, K, 'The RELIGARE Report: religion in the context of the European Union: engaging the interplay between religious diversity and secular models' in Foblets M-C et al (eds), *Belief, Law and Politics What Future for a Secular Europe?* (Aldershot, Ashgate, 2014).

Foblets, M-C and Kulakowski, C, *Final report Roundtables of Interculturalism (Rondetafels van de Interculturaliteit)* (Brussels, 8 November 2010).

Foner, N and Alba, R, 'Immigrant Religion in the U.S. and Western Europe: Bridge or Barrier to Inclusion?' (2008) 42 *International Migration Review* 360.

Fransen, G, 'Klanten hoeven geen Marokkanen. Firma Feryn vindt geen valabele werknemers.', *De Standaard*, 28 April 2005.

Fredman, S, *Comparative study of anti-discrimination and equality laws of the US, Canada, South Africa and India* (2012).

Fregosi, F and Kosulu, D, *Secular Law, Religious Diversity and Public Space. Controversies, areas of tension and actors' contributions: the case of France (French sociological report RELIGARE project)* (RELIGARE, 2012).

Galanter, M, 'Justice in many rooms: courts, private orderings, and indigenous law' (1981) 19 *Journal of Legal Pluralism* 1.

Ghumman, S and Jackson, L, 'The downside of religious attire: the Muslim headscarf and expectations of obtaining employment' (2010) 31 *Journal of Organizational Behavior* 4.

Goffman, E, *Stigma: notes on the management of spoiled identity* (Touchstone, 1963).

Goldschmidt, J, '"Implementation of Equality Law. A Task for Specialists or for Human Rights Experts?" Experiences and Developments in the Supervision of Equality Law in the Netherlands' (2006) 13 *Maastricht Journal European & Comparative Law* 323.

Goswami, R, 'Human rights and the private sphere: a comparative analysis' (2008) *National University for Juridical Studies Law Review* 185.

Green, TK, 'Work culture and discrimination' (2005) 93 *California Law Review* 623.

Griffiths, J, 'The social working of anti-discrimination law' in Loenen MLP and Rodrigues PR (eds), *Non-Discrimination Law: Comparative Perspectives* (Kluwer, 1999).

Gunn, JT, 'The Complexity of Religion and the Definition of 'Religion' in International Law' (2003) 16 *Harvard Human Rights Journal* 189.

Habermas, J, 'Religion in the Public Sphere' (2006) 14 *European Journal of Philosophy* 1.

Heneghan,T, 'EU sees faith bias problem, but not sure of solution', *Reuters*, 7 December 2012.

Henrard, K, 'De Verhouding tussen de concepten redelijke aanpassing, indirect discriminatie en proportionaliteit' in C Bayart et al (eds), *Les Nouvelles Lois luttant contre la discrimination/De Nieuwe Federale Antidiscriminatiewetten* (Die Keure/La Charte, 2008).

—— 'A Critical Appraisal of the Margin of Appreciation Left to States Pertaining to "Church-State Relations" under the Jurisprudence of the European Court of Human Rights' in K Alidadi et al (eds), *A Test of Faith? Religious Diversity and Accommodation in the European Workplace* (Ashgate, 2012).

Hepple, B, *Equality: The New Legal Framework* (Hart Publishing, 2011).

Hirschman, A, *Exit, voice, and loyalty: responses to decline in firms, organizations, and states* (Harvard University Press, 1970).

Hitchcock J, 'The Enemies of Religious Liberty' (February 2004) *First Things: A Monthly Journal of Religion & Public Life* 26.

Hooks, B, *Feminism is for everybody: Passionate politics* (South End Press, 2000).

Hoque, A and Shah, P, *UK Report On Fieldwork (UK sociological report RELIGARE project)* (RELIGARE, 2012).

Huys, J, 'Het niet voorzien van redelijke aanpassingen voor de persoon met een handicap is een vorm van discriminatie' (2003) 91 *Tijdschrift voor Sociaal Recht* 391.

Jacobs, D, 'Waarom ik 'allochtoon' voorlopig blijf gebruiken', *De Morgen*, 22 September 2012.

Jolls, C, 'Antidiscrimination and Accommodation' (2001) 115 *Harvard Law Review* 642.

Jones, O, *Chavs. The demonization of the working class* (Verso, 2012).

Jonlet, S, 'Les discours des musulmans sur la place de leur religion au travail' in D Cabiaux et al (eds), *Neutralité et faits religieux Quelles interactions dans les services publics?* (Academia-L'Harmattan, 2014).

Joppke, C, *Veil: Mirror of Identity* (Polity, 2009).

—— 'Religion in the European Union: Comments on the RELIGARE Project' in Foblets M-C and others (eds), *Belief, Law and Politics What Future for a Secular Europe?* (Ashgate, 2014).

Kepel, G, *La Revanche de Dieu. Chrétiens, juifs et musulmans à la reconquête du monde* (Le Seuil, 1991).

Killian, C, 'The Other Side of the Veil: North African Women in France Respond to the Headscarf Affair' (2003) 17 *Gender & Society* 567.

Knights, S, 'Approaches to Diversity in the Domestic Courts: Article 9 of the European Convention on Human Rights' in R Grillo et al (eds), *Legal Practice and Cultural Diversity* (Ashgate, 2009).

Koppelman, A, 'The fluidity of neutrality' (2004) 66 *The Review of Politics* 633.

—— 'You can't hurry love: Why antidiscrimination protections for gay people should have religious exemptions' (2006) 72 *Brooklyn Law Review* 125.

Kunst, JR et al, 'Coping with Islamophobia: The effects of religious stigma on Muslim minorities' identity formation' (2012) 36 *International Journal of Intercultural Relations* 518.

Lamghari Y, *L'Islam en entreprise: La diversité culturelle en question* (Editions L'Harmattan, 2012).

—— 'La neutralité à la STIB' in D Cabiaux et al (eds), *Neutralité et faits religieux Quelles interactions dans les services publics?* (Academia-L'Harmattan, 2014).

Legrand, P, 'What 'Legal Transplants'?' in D Nelken and J Feest (eds) *Adapting Legal Cultures* (Hart Publishing, 2001).

Lenaerts. K and Van Nuffel. P, *Europees Recht* (Intersenti, 2011).

Lester, A and Uccellari, P, 'Extending The Equality Duty to Religion, Conscience, And Belief: Proceed With Caution' (2008) 5 *European Human Rights Law Review* 567.

Lindley, J, 'Race or Religion? The Impact of Religion on the Employment and Earnings of Britain's Ethnic Communities' (2002) 28 *Journal of Ethnic and Migration Studies* 427.

Locke, J, *A Letter concerning Toleration (1689)* (Merchant Books, 2011).

Loenen, MLP, 'Botsing tussen de vrijheid van godsdienst en gelijke behandeling ongeacht geslacht of seksuele oriëntatie' in Nieuwenhuis A and Zoethout C (eds), *Rechtsstaat en religie* (Wolf Legal Publishers, 2009).

—— 'Accommodation of Religion and Sex Equality in the Workplace under the EU Equality Directives: a Double Bind for the European Court of Justice' in K Alidadi et al (eds), *A Test of Faith? Religious Diversity and Accommodation in the European Workplace* (Ashgate, 2012).

Loenen, MLP and Goldschmidt, JE, 'Religious pluralism and human rights in Europe: reflections for future research' in MLP Loenen and JE Goldschmidt (eds), *Religious pluralism and human rights in Europe: where to draw the line?* (Intersentia, 2007).

Loobuyck, P, 'Critical remarks on the pro-religion apriority of the RELIGARE project' in M-C Foblets et al (eds), *Belief, Law and Politics What Future for a Secular Europe?* (Ashgate, 2014).

Łopatowska, J, 'Discrimination based on religion or belief in the EU legal framework' in *Derecho y Religión. Vol. IV: Religion in the European Law* (Delta Publicaciones, 2009).

Lorde, A, *Our Dead Behind Us: Poems* (Norton, 1994).

Ludlow, A, 'Book review of Engineering Equality: An Essay on European Anti-discrimination Law (A Somek)' (2012) 50 *Journal of Common Market Studies* 534.

Malik, M, *'From conflict to cohesion': competing interests in equality law and policy* (Equality and Diversity Forum, 2008).

—— *Religious Freedom in The 21st Century*, Westminster Faith Debates, 2012.

Marcus, E, *Making Gay History: The Half-Century Fight for Lesbian and Gay Equal Rights* (Harper Perennial, 2002).

McCann, D, 'Decent Working Hours as a Human Rights: Intersections in the Regulation of Working Time' in C Fenwick and T Novitz (eds), *Human Rights at Work: Perspectives on Law and Regulation* (Hart Publishing, 2010).

McCarron, E, 'Veiled racism: the manipulation of gender equality to oppress Muslim women', *enargywebzine*, 20 November 2102.

McColgan, A, 'Class wars? Religion and (in)equality in the workplace' (2009) 38 *Industrial Law Journal* 1.

McCrudden, C and Kountouros, H, 'Human Rights and European equality law' in H Meenan (ed) *Equality law in an enlarged European Union: understanding the article 13 directives* (Cambridge University Press, 2007).

McGoldrick, D, *Human Rights and Religion: the Islamic Headscarf Debate in Europe* (Hart Publishing, 2006).

Meenan, H, 'Introduction' in H Meenan (ed), *Equality law in an enlarged European Union: understanding the article 13 directives* (Cambridge University Press, 2007).

Meenan, H (ed), *Equality law in an enlarged European Union: understanding the article 13 directives* (Cambridge University Press, 2007).

Mertus, J, 'The Rejection of Human Rights Framings: The Case of LGBT Advocacy in the US' (2007) 29 *Human Rights Quarterly* 1036.

Modood, T, 'Muslims and the Politics of Difference' (2003) 74 *The Political Quarterly* 100.

—— 'Is There a Crisis of Secularism in Western Europe?' (2012) 73 *Sociology of Religion* 130.

—— 'Four modes of integration' in M-C Foblets and JP Schreiber (eds), *Les Assises de Interculturalité/De Rondetafels van de Interculturaliteit/The Round Tables on Interculturality* (Larcier, 2013).

Montgomery, J, 'Legislating for a Multi-faith Society: Some Problems of Special Treatment' in B Hepple and EM Szyszczak (eds), *Discrimination: the Limits of the Law* (Mansell, 1992).

Moore, SF, 'Law and Social Change: The Semi-Autonomous Social Field as an Appropriate Subject of Study' (1973) 7 *Law & Society Review* 719.

Morano-Foadi, S, and Vickers, L (eds), *Fundamental Rights in the EU. A Matter for Two Courts* (Hart Publishing, 2015).

Morsink, J, *the Universal Declaration of Human Rights: Origins, Drafting and Intent* (University of Pennsylvania Press, 1999).

Nelken, D, 'Towards a Sociology of Legal Adaptation' in D Nelken and J Feest (eds), *Adapting Legal Cultures* (Hart Publishing, 2001).

Noorlander, CW, 'Godsdienst, levensbeschouwing en politieke gezindheid' in C Forder (ed), *Gelijke behandeling: oordelen en commentaar 2011* (Wolf Legal Publishers, 2001).

Nuijten, M, 'Legal Responses to Cultural Diversity: Multi-Ethnicity, the State, and the Law in Latin America' in M-C Foblets et al (eds), *Cultural Diversity and the Law State Responses from Around the World* (Bruylant/Éditions Yvon Blais, 2010).

O'Brien, C, 'Equality's false summits: new varieties of disability discrimination, "excessive" equal treatment and economically constricted horizons' (2011) 36 *European Law Review* 26.

Oldenhuis, FT (ed), *Religie op de werkvloer* (Protestantse Pers, 2013).

Ouald Chaib, S, 'Religious Accommodation in the Workplace: Improving the Legal Reasoning of the European Court of Human Rights' in K Alidadi et al (eds), *A Test of Faith? Religious Diversity and Accommodation in the European Workplace* (Ashgate, 2012).

Parekh, B, 'Religion in Public life' in Modood T (ed), *Church, State and Religious Minorities* (Policy Studies Institute, 1997).

Parekh, B, *A Commitment to Cultural Pluralism* (UNESCO, 1998).

Peeters, B, 'Cohen heeft gelijk, hand schudden hoeft niet', *Elsevier*, 22 February 2008.

Pitt, G, 'Religion or belief: aiming at the right target?' in H Meenan (ed), *Equality law in an enlarged European Union: understanding the article 13 directives* (Cambridge University Press, 2007).

Polakiewicz, J, 'The EU's Accession to the European Convention on Human Rights—A Matter of Coherence and Consistency' in S Morano-Foadi and L Vickers (eds), *Fundamental Rights in the EU: A Matter of Two Courts* (Hart Publishing, 2015).

Poulter, S, 'The Limits of Legal, Cultural and Religious Pluralism' in B Hepple and EM Szyszczak (eds), *Discrimination: the Limits of the Law* (Mansell, 1992).

Rawls, J, *Political Liberalism* (New York, Columbia University Press, 1993).

Reese, W, 'Conflict of Law and the Restatement Second' (1963) 28 *Law and Contemporary Problems* 680.

Ringelheim, J, 'Athéisme et liberté de conscience en droit international des droits de l'homme' (2011) XIX *Quaderni di Diritto e Politica Ecclesiastica* 33.

Rorive, I, 'Religious Symbols in The Public Space: In search of a European Answer' (2009) 30 *Cordozo Law Review* 2669.

Salkeld, L, 'M&S faces boycott as it lets Muslim staff refuse to sell alcohol or pork', *DailyMail*, 23 December 2013.

Sandberg, R, 'The changing position of religious minorities in English law: the legacy of *Begum*' in R Grillo et al (eds), *Legal Practice and Cultural Diversity* (Ashgate, 2009).

—— 'Laws and Religion: Unravelling McFarlane v Relate Avon Limited' (2010) 12 *Ecclesiastic Law Journal* 361.

Sarfati, H and Bonoli, G (eds), *Labour market and social protection reforms in international perspective: parallel or converging tracks?* (Ashgate, 2002).

Sarkozy, N, 'Respecter ceux qui arrivent, respecter ceux qui accueillent [responding to the Swiss referendum to ban minarets]', *Le Monde*, 8 December 2009.

Schiek, D, 'A new framework on equal treatment of persons in EC law?' (2002) 8 *European Law Journal* 290.

—— 'Indirect discrimination (Chapter three)' in Schiek D and others (eds), *Cases, materials and text on national, supranational and international non-discrimination law* (Hart Publishing, 2007).

Seligman, A, 'Socio-Historical Perspectives on the Public and the Private Spheres' in Ferrari S and Pastorelli S (eds), *Religion in Public Spaces* (Ashgate, 2012).

Shachar, A, 'The Birthright Lottery: Response to Interlocutors' (2011) 9 *Issues in Legal Scholarship* 1.

Shaffer, G, 'Transnational Legal Process and State Change' (2012) 37 *Law & Social Inquiry* 229.

Sharlet, J, 'Inside the Iron Closet: What it's like to be Gay in Putin's Russia', *GQ magazine*: www.gq.com/news-politics/big-issues/201402/being-gay-in-russia.

Smith, SD, *Foreordained Failure: The Quest for a Constitutional Principle of Religious Freedom* (Oxford University Press, 1995).

Somek, A, *Engineering Equality. An Essay on European Anti-Discrimination Law* (Oxford University Press, 2011).

Spinner-halev, J, 'Liberalism and Religion: Against Congruence' (2008) 9 *Theoretical Inquiries in Law* 553.

Stahl, W, *Deep equality: does it go far enough?*: www.luthercollege.edu (undated).

Stakim, C and Johnston, I, 'Religious Discrimination and Muslim Employees' (December 2013) 25 *Employment Law Commentary*.

Stein, A, 'Reasonable accommodation for religion and belief: can it be accommodated in EU law without an express duty?' in M-C Foblets et al (eds), *Belief, Law and Politics What Future for a Secular Europe?* (Ashgate, 2014).

Stox, Y, *Discriminatie en Identiteit. Identiteitsgebonden Werkgevers in het Belgisch en Europees Arbeidsrecht* (Larcier, 2010).

—— 'Religious-Ethos Employers and Other Expressive Employers under European and Belgian Employment Law' in K Alidadi et al (eds), *A Test of Faith? Religious Diversity and Accommodation in the European Workplace* (Ashgate 2012).

Strhan, A, 'Spirituality, Inc.: religion in the American workplace' (2013) 11 *Journal of Management, Spirituality & Religion* 91.

Tanyeri-Erdemir, T, Erdem, M and Weitzhofer-Yurtışık, T, *Challenges of Religious Accommodation in Family-law, Labour-law and Legal Regulation of Public Space and Public Funding (Turkish Socio-Legal Research Report RELIGARE project)* (RELIGARE, 2012).

Taylor, C, 'The politics of recognition' in C Taylor and A Gutmann (eds), *Multiculturalism: Examining the Politics of Recognition* (Princeton University Press, 1994).

Taylor, PM, *Freedom of religion: UN and European human rights law and practice* (Cambridge University Press, 2005).

Tzadik, E, 'Jewish Women in the Belgian Workplace: An Anthropological Perspective' in K Alidadi et al (eds), *A Test of Faith? Religious Diversity and Accommodation in the European Workplace* (Ashgate, 2012).

Van den Boer, R, 'Een Open Doekje voor de Commissie Gelijke Behandeling?' in R Holtmaat (ed), *Gelijkheid en (andere) Grondrechten* (Kluwer, 2004).

van der Ven, JA, *Human rights or religious rules?* (Brill, 2010).

van Hoorn, A and Maseland, R, 'Does a Protestant work ethic exist? Evidence from the well-being effect of unemployment' (2013) 91 *Journal of Economic Behavior and Organization* 1.

Van Horenbeek, J, 'N-VA'er aangesteld bij Gelijkekansencentrum: "Discrimineren is een fundamentele vrijheid". Matthias Storme (N-VA): controleur of saboteur?', *De Morgen*, 25 October 2014.

van Ooijen, HMAE, *Religious symbols in public functions: unveiling state neutrality. A comparative analysis of Dutch, English and French justifications for limiting the freedom of public officials to display religious symbols* (Intersentia, 2012).

van Os, R, 'Negative effects of flexible employment' in WFC Monitor (ed), *The implications of the flexibilisation of work for workers and trade unions Experiences from various sectors* (FNV Company Monitor, March 2009).

Van Rossum, W, 'Introduction to Framing Multicultural Issues in terms of Human Rights: Solution or Problem?' (2012) 30 *Netherlands Quarterly of Human Rights* 382.

Vermeulen, B, 'Waarom de vrijheid van godsdienst in de Grondwet moet blijven' (2008) 65 *Socialisme en democratie: Maandblad van de Wiardi Beckman Stichting*.

Vermeulen, BP, '2006-220 Handenschudden op school?' in *Gelijke behandeling: oordelen en commentaar 2006* (Wolf Legal Publishers, 2007).

—— 'On Freedom, Equality and Citizenship. Changing Fundamentals of Dutch Minority Policy and Law (Immigration, Integration, Education and Religion)' in M-C Foblets et al (eds), *Cultural Diversity and the Law State Responses from Around the World* (Bruylant/Éditions Yvon Blais, 2010).

Vermeulen, BP and Overbeeke, AJ, 'Godsdienst, levensbeschouwing en politieke gezindheid' in C Forder (ed), *Gelijke behandeling: oordelen en commentaar 2010* (Wolf Legal Publishers, 2011).

Vermeulen, F, *Socio-legal research on accommodation of religious diversity in family and labour law, in public space and state funding of religions in the Netherlands (Dutch sociological report RELIGARE project)* (RELIGARE, 2012).

Vermeulen, F and El Morabet Belhaj, R, 'Accommodating religious claims in the Dutch workplace: Unacknowledged Sabbaths, objecting marriage registrars and pressured faith-based organizations' (2013) 13 *International Journal of Discrimination and the Law* 113.

Verschelden, W, 'Waarom wij, De Morgen, "allochtoon" niet meer gebruiken (opinion)', *De Morgen*, 22 September 2012.

Vertovec, S, 'Super-diversity and its implications' (2007) 30 *Ethnic and Racial Studies* 1024.

Vickers, L, *Religion and Belief Discrimination in Employment-the EU law* (European Network of Legal Experts in the Non-Discrimination Field, 2006).

—— *Religious freedom, religious discrimination, and the workplace* (Hart Publishing, 2008).

—— 'Indirect Discrimination and Individual Belief: Eweida v British Airways plc' (2009) 11 *Ecclesiastical Law Journal* 197.

—— 'The relationship between religious diversity and secular models: an equality-based perspective' in M-C Foblets et al (eds), *Belief, Law and Politics What Future for a Secular Europe?* (Ashgate, 2014).

—— 'Law, religion and the workplace' in Ferrari S (ed), *Routledge handbook of law and religion* (Routledge, 2015).

—— 'Freedom of Religion and Belief, Article 9 and the EU Equality Directive: living together in perfect harmony?' in F Dorssemont, K Lörcher and I Schömann (eds), *The European Convention and the Employment Relation* (Hart Publishing, 2013).

Vileyn D, 'Standpunt BDW: Verboden?', *Brussel nieuws*, 21 August 2013.

Waddington, L, *The Expanding Role of the Equality Principle in European Union Law* (European University Institute, Robert Schuman Centre for Advanced Studies, 2003).

—— 'Chapter six: reasonable accommodation' in D Schiek et al (eds), *Cases, materials and text on national, supranational and international non-discrimination law* (Hart Publishing, 2007).

—— 'Future prospects for EU equality law: lessons to be learnt from the proposed equal treatment directive' (2011) 36 *European Law Review* 163.

—— 'Reasonable Accommodation. Time to Extent the Duty to Accommodate Beyond Disability?' (2011) 36 *NTM/NJCM-Bulletin* 186.

Waddington, L and Bell, M, 'More equal than others: Distinguishing European Union equality directives' (2001) 38 *Common Market Law Review* 587.

Waddington, L and Hendriks, A, 'The Expanding Concept of Employment Discrimination in Europe: From Direct and Indirect Discrimination to Reasonable Accommodation Discrimination' (2003) 18 *International Journal of Comparative Labour Law and Industrial Relations* 403.

Wentholt, K, 'Formal and Substantive Equal Treatment: the Limitations and the Potential of the Legal concept of Equality' in MLP Loenen and Rodrigues PR (eds), *Non-Discrimination Law: Comparative Perspectives* (Kluwer, 1999).

Whelan, D, *Indivisible human rights. A history* (University of Pennsylvania Press, 2010).

Woldringh, C, 'Arbeidsorganisaties en gelijke-behandelingswetgeving' in IP Asscher-Vonk and CA Groenendijk (eds), *Gelijke behandeling: regels en realiteit* (The Hague, Sdu, 1999).

Woodhead, L, *'Religion or belief'*: *Identifying issues and priorities*, Equality and Human Rights Commission Research report 48 (2009).

X, 'Controversial Court Ruling: Muslim Shelf Stockers Can Refuse to Handle Alcohol', *Spiegel Online*, 25 February 2011.

X, 'MIVB zoekt paard en vindt varken in eigen sandwiches', *Brussel Nieuws*, 5 March 2013.

X, 'Geen job voor Ahmed door "vreemde naam"', *De Standaard*, 7 March 2014.

X, 'Elke Sleurs krijgt geen kus van Charles Michel', *De Morgen*, 11 October 2014.

X, 'Stad ontslaat bekeerde moslim die vrouwen geen hand geeft', *Brussel nieuws*, 13 May 2013.

X, 'Verdonk: Schaf Commissue Gelijke Behandeling af', *Elsevier*, 6 November 2006.

Yildirim, M, 'Conscientious Objection to Military Service: International Human Rights Law and the Case of Turkey' (2010) 5 *Religion & Human Rights* 65.

Yoshino, K, 'Covering' (2002) 111 *Yale Law Journal* 769.
—— 'The Myth of the Mainstream' (2006) 52 *The Chronicle of Higher Education* B11.
Young, IM, *Justice and the politics of difference* (Princeton University Press, 1990).
Zondag, WA, *Religie in de arbeidsverhouding. Over religieuze werkgevers en religieuze werknemers* (Uitgeverij Paris bv, 2011).
Zucca, L, 'Conflicts of Fundamental Rights as Constitutional Dilemmas' in E Brems (ed), *Conflicts between fundamental rights* (Intersentia, 2008).

INDEX